The Politics of Critique

The Politics of Critique

Dick Howard

University of Minnesota Press Minneapolis

Published by the University of Minnesota Press
2037 University Avenue Southeast, Minneapolis, MN 55414.

Published simultaneously in Canada
by Fitzhenry & Whiteside Limited, Markham.
Printed in the United States of America.

Library of Congress Cataloging-in-Publication Data

Howard, Dick, 1943-
The politics of critique / Dick Howard.
p. cm.
Bibliography: p.
Includes index.
ISBN 0-8166-1681-7
ISBN 0-8166-1682-5 (pbk.)
1. Political science—History. 2. Political science—Philosophy.
3. Kant, Immanuel, 1724-1804—Contributions in political science.
4. Marx, Karl, 1818-1883—Contributions in political science.
I. Title.
JA81.H647 1988
320'.01'1—dc19 88-15467
CIP

Contents

Preface

Kant wrote three "Critiques"; Marx wrote more. Marx never explained what he meant by "critique," nor did he write the methodological theory in which he promised to explain why and how his "dialectic" differed from its Hegelian predecessor. Kant sought constantly to explain the conditions of possibility of his own critique, which took finally the form of a system made explicit in the introduction to the *Critique of Judgement*. At that point, said Kant, philosophy can pass from critique to "doctrine." But Kant never explained what he meant by this doctrinal philosophy. I have tried to suggest that it points to the need for a political complement to critical philosophy.[1] Marx was concerned constantly with just this political complement, whose theoretical necessity he saw founded on the incomplete realization of the critical philosophy in Hegel's dialectical system. But Marx's failure to elaborate his own political dialectic made itself felt in the constantly present temptation toward an economistic reductionism from which he did not always escape.[2] *The Politics of Critique* is first of all my attempt to inherit the legacy of Kant and Marx.

The nineteenth-century heirs of Kant and Marx sought a synthesis which could salvage critical philosophy and politics. Two schools developed, known by their geographical centers in Marburg and Heidelberg. The Marburg neo-Kantians proposed a two-world theory, suggesting that causality reigns supreme in the phenomenal world, as in *The Critique of Pure Reason*, whereas the ethical imperatives of *The Critique of Practical Reason* determine moral demands whose application points toward politics. This "Kantianism" permitted its adherents to accept the economic theory of Marx's *Capital* while engaging in political activity under the banner of Social Democracy. The Heidelberg neo-Kantians sought their synthesis in the domains of culture and history to which neither Kant's first nor his second *Critique* was addressed. Their theory was not concerned so much to integrate Marxism and its politics as to go beyond their limits.[3] The result of the

Heidelberg rethinking of its heritage is a "hermeneutical" philosophy, which has been more fully developed in the twentieth century under the influence of Heidegger and Gadamer. The Marburg syncretism, on the other hand, was simply one of the minor casualties of the Great War.

The twentieth-century heirs of the quest for a Kant-Marx synthesis gathered in another geographically defined school: the Institute for Social Research located in Frankfurt. Under the direction of Max Horkheimer, the Frankfurt School sought to develop a "critical theory" in the pages of its *Zeitschrift für Sozialforschung*. Their inspiration was drawn from Lukacs's monumental integration of German Idealism into the framework of Marxism in *History and Class Consciousness*. Fascism drove the Frankfurters into exile; increased lucidity about developments in Russia induced doubt in their Marxist assumptions. The twin forms that Horkheimer called the "authoritarian state" dashed the optimism that animated the earlier critical theory. The progressive Marxist dialectic was replaced by Horkheimer and Adorno's "dialectic of enlightenment," for which modernity is the culmination of a world-historical process through which the critical force of Reason has been subverted by an "instrumental reason" capable only of determining means toward ends that it can accept only blindly and without critique. This world-historical pessimism rediscovers the insights of the hermeneutic philosophy in its condemnation of modernity. Yet the Marxist optimism, and combativeness, of the old critical theory remained present in thinkers like Marcuse and Adorno. The latter's assertion that philosophy remains actual precisely because "the moment of its realization was missed" and the former's insistence on "the permanence of the aesthetic" point to a crucial aspect of the Kantian critique which the Marxists had neglected: the distinct role of aesthetic judgement. The analysis of the problems of modernity could be approached from this new perspective.

The renewal of the Frankfurt critical theory has not followed the aesthetic track suggested in the last works of Marcuse and Adorno. Insofar as that source has been mined, the impetus has come from French "post-modernism" whose philosophical roots lie with the radicalized Heideggerian hermeneutics. The issues raised in that context go beyond my concern in this volume.[4] Jürgen Habermas has attempted to reconstruct a critical theory that is true to the intentions of the original Frankfurt School while avoiding the philosophical antinomies on which that theory came to grief. Habermas's first synthetic effort, *Knowledge and Human Interest* (1968), was rooted in the tradition of German Idealism from Kant to Marx. The new version of this critical theory, *The Theory of Communicative Action* (1981), makes possible a direct confrontation with the problems of modernity (and with the French), undertaken in *The Philosophical Discourse of Modernity* (1985). Disillusionment with modernity in the twentieth century had been based on the twin *political* experiences of fascism and Stalinism. Habermas takes a different tack, seeking a philosophical foundation for a socialist and democratic politics in the face of what he calls in another recent volume *The New Unintelligibility* (1985). However adequate for the analysis of the forms of modern *society*, Habermas's new theory does not address directly their properly political foundation.

The philosophical problem of a modern politics was not posed first in the twentieth century; its roots lie with the phenomenon of Revolution, which Kant and Marx confronted each with his own tools of critical thought. Kant's well-known sympathy with the French Revolution, even after his disciples and successors had turned away from its more radical phases, has posed a problem for interpreters. One key to his position is found in the influence of Rousseau on his thought. Read as Kant might have interpreted him, Rousseau provides a first approach to the question of modern revolution by posing philosophically the question of its *origin*. The French Revolution was, of course, not the result of Rousseau's theories; nor does the French Revolution incarnate once and for all the essence of modern revolution. In addition to reading critically the French Revolution, a contemporary "politics of critique" has to explore that other foundational revolution, the American "War of Independence" declared in 1776 and consummated by the creation of a constitutional structure which functions still today. If the proposed "politics of critique" is adequate, it will have to be able to explain both of these Revolutions, as they occurred and as they have continued to affect the contemporary history which we call modern.

I have explained more fully the title and internal logic of this volume in the introduction. The politics of critique has first to legitimize critique as a theoretical stance; it must then define what it means by politics; only then can the critic go to work. Critique is made legitimate by "Unmaking a Case" (Part I); politics is generated in "Making a Case" (Part II), it remains for "The Working Critic" to draw the implications (Part III). This progression is clear in the two chapters on Kant (Chapters 1 and 5) and the two chapters on Marx (Chapters 2 and 6), which are brought to a working synthesis by the question of modernity (Chapter 9). The privileged status of Kant's notion of reflective judgment in Parts I and II does not mean that the synthesis of critique and politics takes place in the realm of aesthetics, or that either term can be reduced to what Kant called reflective judgement. The specificity of politics must be preserved, as must the autonomy of critique. This demands a specific method, whose nature is presented from the side of critique (Chapter 3) and from the side of politics (Chapter 7). The transition from autonomous critique to the question of politics is made necessary by the contemporary "crisis" of critical theory which is illustrated by a return to the usual interpretations of the American Revolution (Chapter 4). The transition to the working critic is suggested by another "crisis," this time within political theory, which suggests another return, this time from Kant to Rousseau (Chapter 8). The question of the *origin* of political and critical theory in the concept of revolution suggests the concept of *the* political as the condition of the possibility of both critique and politics.

The political reader may yet be unsatisfied. I offer no definition of *the* politics of critique, no formulas to delimit its goals or strategies, no tactics for its realization. Two concepts which recur repeatedly may help to explain this self-limitation while concluding these prefatory remarks. The notion of origin, which grounds what I call in *From Marx to Kant* an ''originary philosophy,'' is introduced both negatively (Part I) and positively (Part II). Its effectiveness—in the dual sense of the German *Wirklichkeit*: actuality and activity—is illustrated in the example of the French Revolution (Chapter 10). The institutional political form assumed by the originary structure is that of the republic. The implications of ''originary politics'' as republican is illustrated by the rereading of the American Revolution (Chapter 11). This critical rereading of a political revolution underlines the activity of the originary politics *as democratic*.[5] This is not to say, however, that ''democracy'' defines the politics of critique. Democracy is neither a goal to be sought nor a method for its realization. Democracy is a practice which emerged in those very conditions which I have defined as originary. In *this* sense, the politics of critique is democratic *and* revolutionary. The addition of the qualification ''revolutionary'' cannot, however, imply a voluntarism any more than it can suggest a foundationalism or determinism. Critique ''has'' a politics, and politics ''is'' a critique, precisely and only insofar as the autonomy of each is preserved.

*** *** ***

Books, modern critics tell us, refer to other books. Although things are a bit more complex than that, the aphorism can serve to explain briefly the relation of this book to at least my own recent work. These essays were written within the context of a larger philosophical-political project. My attempt to understand and to reclaim *The Marxian Legacy*[6] concluded that Marx himself blocked the path to an adequate political theory. Marx assumed the primacy of capitalist civil society, of which, in the last resort, politics could be only an epiphenomenon. What Hegel had taken as a problem became for Marx the locus of its solution. Contemporary society—which hardly merits the appellation ''civil''—is neither the problem nor the solution; and that scant formula grounds the anachronistic proposal made in my *From Marx to Kant*.[7] Kant's philosophical politics turns around the challenge of the *creation* of civil society, as problem and as solution. But a philosophical politics must be accompanied by a political philosophy. Kant only points toward the outlines of such a theory. The second part of my larger project has been to provide the historical demonstration on which a political philosophy capable of creating civil society can be founded. Some of the steps in that direction are presented in the companion volume to this one, *Defining the Political*.[8] Their full elaboration will be presented in a comparative study of the birth of modern society in the Prussian, American, and French Revolutions.[9]

But this book could not have come into being without the critical help offered by others, friends, institutions, and the journals in which the first forms of these chapters were originally published.

Thanking friends is always the most difficult; they are many, often helping without knowing it; and one, alas, always remembers too late the help offered by one or another. Nonetheless, without them one would not write, or write as well, or as pertinently. Over the years I have received friendly criticism from Andrew Arato, Seyla Benhabib, Richard Bernstein, Cornelius Castoriadis, Jean Cohen, Val Dusek, Jean-Marc and Luc Ferry, Joe Flay, Jürgen Habermas, Gerhardt Horst, Karl Klare, Herman Lebovics, Claude Lefort, John Mason, Sigrid Meuschel, Olivier Mongin, Ulrich Rödel, Joel Roman, Burghardt Schmidt, Fred Siegel, and Paul Thibaud. I was helped also by several of the editors of the journals in which these articles appeared: David Rasmussen, Florindo Volpaccio, Jacques Julliard, and Stanley Diamond. Another editor, since returned to graduate study, Gerry O'Sulliven, first encouraged me to think about republishing some of my work. The philosophy department at Stony Brook supported the final preparations of this manuscript, for which James Clarke did the proofreading and constructed the index.

Most important, however, has been the generous help and the insights of Terry Cochran, my editor at the University of Minnesota Press. Terry read through a batch of things that I had written over the past decade and told me what it was that I had been asking without ever being able to ask it directly. I have learned enormously from talking with him in the process of preparing this volume, which would not have existed without him.

Institutional help over the years has come first of all from the Philosophy Department at the State University of New York at Stony Brook. In addition, I was supported for 15 months by a grant from the Humboldt Stiftung. Stimulation came also from my position at the Research Institute for International Change at Columbia University.

*** *** ***

The original versions of these essays were published as follows:

1. "Kant's Political Theory: The Virtue of his Vices," *Review of Metaphysics*. Vol. XXXIV, Nr. 2, December, 1980, pp. 325–350.

2. "On the Transformation of Critique into Dialectic: Marx's Dilemma," *Dialectical Anthropology*, Vol. 5 (1980), pp. 75–110.

3. "Hermeneutics and Critical Theory," originally presented at the Society for Phenomenology and Existential Philosophy, published in *Critical and Dialectical Phenomenology*, ed. Donn Welton and Hugh J. Silverman (Albany: State University of New York Press, 1987).

4. "Why Return to the American Revolution?" originally published as "Pourquoi revenir à la Révolution américaine," *Intervention*, Nr. 15, janvier-mars, 1986, pp. 88–96. English translation by James Clarke.

5. "Kant's System and (its) Politics," originally a lecture given at the University of Copenhagen, published in *Man and World*, Summer, 1985, pp. 1–20.

6. "Restoring Politics to Political Economy," originally published as "A Political Theory for Marxism: Restoring Politics to Political Economy," *New Political Science*, Winter, 1984, pp. 5–26.

7. "The Origins and Limits of Philosophical Politics," originally published as "Philosophy and Politics," Center for Humanistic Studies, University of Minnesota, Occasional Paper, Nr. 10, 1986.

8. "Rousseau and the Origin of Revolution," *Philosophy and Social Criticism*, Vol. 8, Nr. 4, 1979, pp. 349–370.

9. "The Politics of Modernism: From Marx to Kant," *Philosophy and Social Criticism*, Vol. 8, Nr. 4, 1981, pp. 361–386.

10. ''The Origins of Revolution,'' *Journal of the British Society for Phenomenology*, Vol. 14, Nr. 1, January, 1983, pp. 3–16.

11. ''Reading U.S. History as Revolutionary,'' originally a lecture at the Collège International de Philosophie, published in the *Revue Française de science politique*, février, 1988. My translation.

Introduction
The Politics of Critique

A. A Simple Intuition

All books begin with a simple intuition. The author then spends years tracking down its implications, sometimes losing sight of the originary intuition in the process, sometimes rediscovering it in unlikely places or forms. The intuition is not somehow true or false, immediately meaningful or fully present, an *arché* or a *telos*. The intuition need not be singular, a unified sense or univocal idea; nor must it be intentional, the product of a searching mind or a consciousness seeking fulfillment. The intuition is not the immediate product of practical experience, nor does it depend on theoretical engagement; the opposition theory/practice is not pertinent in this context, although habit usually reintroduces that categorial pair to give determinacy to the intuition, which is better described as originary or *symbolic*. The habitual categories of metaphysics can be reinvoked without destroying the uniqueness of the originary intuition so long as their logic is followed through to its paradoxical conclusion. That is why the first two parts of this volume can use metaphysical categories in the service of ''Unmaking a Case,'' as well as in ''Making a Case.'' Such apparently contradictory results lead to the rediscovery of the originary intuition. The return to the origin takes time; its results justify the republication of essays written over a decade in the form of a single work.[1]

The operative function of the simple intuition as ''originary'' articulates its symbolic status. Immediate stipulation is not sufficient; and conceptual specification can come only after the work of the intuition itself is described. My concerns are philosophy and politics; the intuition of their originary relation took the form of a game, played on an interminable Texas highway with another political philosopher: if the Being of truth is the Truth of being, what about the Breakfast of champions and the Champion of breakfasts? or the God of love and the Love of god? The Power of the word and the Word of power? This game can go on and on, with or without capital letters; in the present context, it might conclude with the formulation that "the Politics of critique is the Critique of politics." But what could that really mean? Autobiographically, my originary insight was founded on a social critique of representative political institutions; the New Left attempt to create a participatory democracy seemed to unite the imperatives of philosophy and politics. But the critique of mundane representative politics could become simply the *art* of critique-for-its-own-sake; the identification of critique and politics that results from such an attitude denies the autonomy of each.[2] In this sense, the originary intuition founds a *strategy of avoidance*. The relation of this "strategy" to the originary insight is not accidental; although its first two parts might have been grouped under the reciprocally interacting headings of the critique of politics and the politics of critique, this volume has only a single title. The "Working Critic" in Part III does not pretend to offer a "dialectical" synthesis.

Intuitions belong to the language of everyday experience before they become the stuff of and for philosophy. My simple intuition could be expressed as the distinction between criticism and critique. Criticism is carping or biting, one-sided or unjust, engaged and motivated; critique claims to be neutral, objective, espousing the lines of the object it presents. Criticism is *external* to its object, incapable of justifying its own standpoint and of explaining the applicability of its measures to the issues at hand; critique is immanent, developing the *self*-critique of its object, making explicit what could not be expressed directly. Criticism presupposes a dualism between subject and object, knowledge and judgment, theory and practice; critique attempts to mediate between these metaphysical poles by showing them to express an "identity-in-difference" founded on a shared essence. Whether criticism is empiricist or rationalist it is always one-sided, dogmatic, and anti-historical; critique is dialectical, open-ended, and immanently historical. But the simple option for critique suggested by ordinary language sits ill with the common-sense demands of everyday politics, which are closer to those of criticism. If critique "has" a politics, the political implication of the simple intuition will have to be reevaluated radically. Politics will not be defined as the *social* struggle among competing interests played in a political arena defined by pre-given rules and roles. Politics will be neither reduced to society nor separated form its actual structure.

The young Marx formulated the intuition that seeks to combine radical philosophy and radical politics. "To be radical," he wrote in 1843, "is to go to the root; and for man the root is man himself." This aphorism expresses only a variant of the traditional notion of philosophy as the attempt to get beneath appearances, to find their "really real" or essential foundation. The philosophical quest for the Being of beings is transposed to the practical, human level. Radical humanism can claim to be political insofar as it uncovers the Archimedian point from which the world can be not only understood but changed. This political turn of classical philosophy marks Marx's philosophical critique as *dialectical*. The philosophical question and the political response are *immanent* within a single mode of questioning. As a humanism, philosophy is necessarily radical because the agent of the uncovering and the essential reality it uncovers are both human: subject and object, theory and praxis at once. This simple intuition permitted Marx to develop the philosophical theory of alienation into the social theory of alienated labor and then into an all-encompassing political theory which could include the structural and historical logic of the critique of political economy. All domains of human existence, its relation to nature and its inscription in history, could be derived from this one simple intuition. Past and present could be understood; the shape of the future as their dialectical humanist overcoming was defined; subjects who had become objects could reconquer their originary subjectivity. This, no more and no less, was what was meant by *revolution*. Politics, in turn and without mediation, was identified with Revolution.

The appeal of Marx's originary intuition can be understood easily. Despite the ringing denunciation, two years later, of those philosophers who "had only understood the world," Marx's proposals for changing it develop actively the dialectical critique that the Hegelians had ontologized into a metaphysical law of World History. The "Theses on Feuerbach" condemn the metaphysical separation of subject from object which treats the latter as dumb matter whose inertia acquires form only from the external intervention of the philosopher's criticism. Marx's dialectical critique accentuates instead a material world which is active because human praxis is immanent within it. He insists on the central place of "revolutionary praxis," but this praxis is no more clearly defined than was the "lightning of thought" that was to activate proletarian practice in 1843. Despite this remnant of externality (or "idealism"), the intuitive identification of politics and revolution is satisfying; politics appears to descend from the heavens, its difference is reduced through its humanization. But the externality of what Marx called the feudal "democracy of unfreedom" is replaced by a dialectical image of society as a self-contained field of forces immanent to civil (or bourgeois: *bürgerliche*) society. The result is a "revolutionary" theory founded on a "Critique of *Political* Economy." The "political" nature of this economy cannot be explained by the dialectical critique which makes a virtue of its immanence within civil society. The radicality of the intuition is thus avoided by the "dialectical" unification of critique and politics.

The difficulty centers on the relation of political criticism and dialectical critique. Marx does not want to adopt the metaphysical identity philosophy canonized as Hegelianism. As opposed to the criticisms from the "German Ideology" preached by the "Holy Family," Marx refuses to identify "the politics of critique" with "the critique of politics." He does not play the game in which the "Truth of being" corresponds to the "Being of truth." Rather, already in 1843, he insists that the "weapon of the critique" must *replace* "the critique of the weapons." The dialectic that underlies this critique is historically specific. The humanism which founds the entire project as revolutionary is not ontological; the immanent critique formulated by Marx's praxical humanism is possible only under historically specific social and economic conditions. That is why Marx insists on the *proletariat* and not simply on "man" as the revolutionary subject; and that is why his critical theory claims to be the world's own *self*-critique, a reflexive project possible only when that world has arrived at a certain level of maturity. Critique and criticism come together in this concrete historical moment. The difficulty is that, however historically specific, the world's dialectical self-critique becomes a metaphysical identity philosophy; the Being uncovered by philosophy is treated on the same level of reality as the beings of which it is supposed to be the foundation. Formulated more concretely, *the critique's virtue of remaining immanent to civil society becomes a vice at the level of politics. "Revolutionary"* politics has to be defined more precisely if the immanent dialectical ontology is not to be replaced by the arbitrariness of external criticism cloaked in the dialectical materialist garment of Marxism.[3] This would be simply the inversion of the dialectical unification of critique and politics.

A different implication of Marx's originary insight is suggested by another passage from his early work. "We do not face the world in doctrinaire fashion, declaring, 'here is the truth, kneel here' . . . We do not tell the world, 'Cease your struggles, they are stupid; we want to give you the true watchword of the struggle.' We merely show the world why it actually struggles; and consciousness is something that the world *must* acquire even if it does not want to."[4] Marx clearly intends to oppose an immanent dialectical critique to the external criticism adopted by his erstwhile Young Hegelian friends. His philosophical argument can be generalized politically. One can distinguish between a *theory for* revolution, which seeks to give slogans, tactics, or 'weapons' to the political agency, and a *theory of* revolution, which develops dialectically the logic immanent to the human history which has reached the dynamic potential contained in capitalism. The difficulty that vitiated the immanent dialectical theory of revolution from within civil society is brought to a head in this formulation; the "revolutionary praxis" of the young Marx's humanism can become the historical economism of the mature Marx for whom praxis becomes a dependent function of an immanent historical logic whose motor is economic. Politics is replaced either by history or by economics—or by their confused unity. The result is that critique and criticism, philosophy and politics, have been once again identified; but this time, instead of subsuming critique under criticism the relation is inverted; critique is now simply identified as "revolutionary," and nothing more need be said.[5]

What Marx took to be solutions to "the riddle of history" are analyzed here as "strategies of avoidance." This concept puts into question both the idea that Marx had found solutions (in "Unmaking a Case") and the assumption that he knew what in fact the riddle asked (in "Making a Case"). Strategies of avoidance are formulated to ensure certainty, about the answers or at least about the questions. Criticism thinks it knows the answers; critique is certain of its questions. Marx seeks to unite them in an immanent dialectic. To succeed, he must provide a *mediation*, something in which both poles participate but with which neither is identical. The mediation may be provided by the practical humanism and accompanying theory of alienation; it may be suggested by a theory of historical progress which explains why problems arise as they do and when solutions can be proposed with the same necessity; or a structural logic of material production may be invoked to the same end. Each proposed mediation is based on an identical structure: criticism and critique are assumed to partake of a common identity which makes each possible. Economic crisis is interpreted as the inevitable product of a *structural* logic considered as a *natural* development which will produce its own healing process. Historical development obeys a linear logic which includes "free" individual choice in its calculations. Such dialectical mediation leaves no room for politics; critique is equated simply and univocally with revolution; there is no place for a *politics of critique*.[6]

This presentation of the strategies of avoidance suggested by Marx's originary insight underlines its difference from my own simple intuition. Of course, a "better case" can be made for Marx: he is brought closer to my own originary intuition by "unmaking" his dialectical theory on the basis of his own discovery of the distinction between the criticism and the critique of ideology (Chapter 2); while my intuition serves to "make" the place for a Marxist questioning of the political (Chapter 6). But the politics of critique cannot be formulated with the tools that constitute the Marxian legacy.[7] The strategies of avoidance analyzed in the first two parts of this volume were discovered in the attempt to inherit the legacy as such a politics. In "unmaking" the strategies by which political critique is defined, the implicitly presupposed concept of critique is made explicit; the result is not a new definition of politics but rather an awareness of the complications and complicity of the activity of critique and the object it intends and yet constantly, if unconsciously, schemes to avoid. On the other hand, when the case for critique is "made," the necessity of such evasive maneuvers on the part of the critique is presupposed in order to reconstruct the definition of a political space which makes possible an autonomous critical theory of the type which was "unmade" in the first part. The pattern that appears in these two parts is similar to the structure analyzed by Paul de Man as a necessary "blindness" which is the price of critical "insight." But that pattern is not itself the originary intuition; it does not govern the "working critic" who is politically active in Part III.[8] The simple intuition is not reducible to a single, univocal or universal ground or cause; the *originary* or *symbolic* structure that underlies the operative strategies of avoidance remains to be specified conceptually.

B. Its Conceptual Formulation

The simple intuition attempted to hold open the space between critique and politics by avoiding the "strategies" which transform critique into an immanent dialectics and politics into external criticism. The open space preserves the autonomy of critique and politics; at the same time, their presence in it prevents them from becoming indifferent to each another. This "space" of the originary intuition was defined as symbolic. The categories of theory and practice could be applied to this symbolic structure only as metaphysical determinations which must be constantly "unmade" by the anti-strategy that affirms the autonomy of critique. At the same time, the temptation to treat this symbolic space as if it were a *real* mediation that founds the immanent dialectical critique in which politics and criticism are identified and conflated has to be avoided. The symbolic space is "real" in the sense that it exists as actual; as a mediation, it is *wirklich*, active, known only in its effects, never in the plenitude of existence. The conceptual formulation of the simple intuition concerning the symbolic space that is the condition of possibility of both critique and politics must show how this *wirkliche* mediation works. This will also explain why the simple intuition was called *originary*. At the same time, this originary symbolic structure permits a clarification of the constant recurrence of the "strategies of avoidance" whose different forms are obedient to a simple but systematic logic that allows not only for "unmaking" the deformations Marx called ideology but also for "making" an originary method which "governs" the working critic.

The strategies of avoidance are defined by their denial of the autonomy of critique, their refusal to accept its act-character and to understand its peculiar status as mediation; instead, explanation replaces interrogation, the symbolic is treated as real, the origin as a cause. These strategies attempt to cope with the dilemmas of the "dialectic of enlightenment."[9] How can reason justify the critique of reason? If the justification is political, the problem of the externality of criticism re-emerges; if the justification lies within reason itself, the ensuing dialectic presents only the appearance of an autonomous politics. The critic is caught in a dilemma. Either the critique is its own self-foundation—in which case the critic is not necessary because the critique lies in the things themselves; or the critique is founded on something external to the criticized relations—in which case the critic cannot avoid the accusation of arbitariness since the critique depends on criteria to which it can appeal but which it can know only by falling into that immanence of self-foundation which makes the critic unnecessary. Kant called these twin errors "dogmatism" and "scepticism"; his critical philosophy showed the necessity of each pole, and the danger of its one-sided acceptance. Kant's notion of "critique" differs from the dialectical concept developed by Hegel and Marx. For him, critique tends to become identified with philosophy itself. This preserves the autonomy of critique, but it leaves open the question of the political space which defines the mediating and active character of the critique.[10]

The difficulty of maintaining philosophy as critique against the temptation to integrate it dialectically into a system is made apparant by the ambiguous genetive that defines Kant's *Critiques*. Who, or what, is criticizing whom, or what in the *Critique of Pure Reason?* Is reason the subject or the object of the critique? Under what warrent, according to what criteria, and from what motivations is this "critique" initiated? What is the standard according to which it is judged valid? The reader will recognize these questions as the "game" which introduced my simple intuition. From that perspective, it might be thought that Kant is criticizing negatively the claim of reason to be pure; but in that case he would not have written a *Critique of Practical Reason* to affirm pure reason's practical import. Similarly, if his goal were to analyze empirical knowledge in the critical reflection of pure and practical reason, he would not have accompanied each positive *Critique* with a "transcendental dialectic" to explain the necessity of the errors it criticizes. Kant is adding to the originary "game" an analysis of the strategies of avoidance. But Kant's own temptation to integrate the autonomous critique into the immanence of system becomes clear in the the third moment of his critical philosophy. The *Critique of Judgement* is explicitly reflexive[11]; its subject and its object are identical; judgment is the self-critique of reason as at once necessary and yet not motivated or justified by a dialectical immanence. The structure recalls, anachronistically, Marx's theory of the revolutionary proletariat. It suggests why the systematic elaboration of my originary intuition adopted the title *From Marx to Kant*. The "'Kant" to whom critique returns to discover its own political implications has to be reconstructed in terms of the originary intuition.

The temptation is to develop the simple intuition by equating critique with the faculty of judgment and suggesting that its politics is defined by the specific form of judgment introduced in the third *Critique*. As Kant explains, the judgment of beauty is backed by no scientific or moral universals; its validity depends on the communication among humans by which they learn to think, disinterestedly, in the place of the other. This reflective judgment could be called "political" because it is not defined by pre-existent scientific or moral universals. The difficulty is that, instead of preserving that autonomy of critique and of politics through which the presence of each makes necessary that of the other, this proposal conflates the two in a mediation whose dialectic is the inverse identical to that proposed by Marx. The *Critique of Judgement* can serve to define negatively the necessity of a properly political domain (Chapter 1) by demonstrating the strategies of avoidance through which critique denies its own autonomy. It cannot define positively the structure of that autonomous political domain within which the critique can assert itself. That further move comes when Kant turns his attention from history to its political preconditions (Chapter 5).[12] The temptation to equate politics with history in terms of their common origin cannot be grounded by a dialectical system of critique. The unification is achieved at the cost of the distinctive domains it pretends to unify.

Critique at once depends on an autonomous political domain and yet preserves its own autonomy by "unmaking" the strategies by which the independence of the political is denied. This relation of dependence and independence between critique and politics can be called *originary*. The originary relation is not real; the originary function is not causal; the originary intuition is not univocal. The strategies of avoidance seek to destroy the originary tension, to fixate its instability, to define its meaning. Formally, the strategies are simple; one pole can be said to integrate, dominate, determine, or even to "overdetermine" the other; the poles may be separated, treated as really autonomous, or formally independent from each other; or they may be analyzed as if they were identical to one another, simple dependent appearances of a common essence. Materially, the difficulty arises from the peculiar relation of *reversibility* that exists between the poles of the originary structure. The poles of the originary structure can be designated as respectively *genetic* and *normative*—so long as care is taken not to confuse these categories, which refer to the symbolic domain, with real causal or constitutional categories. The autonomy of critique which is affirmed by "unmaking a case" can be said to generate the kind of political domain which then "makes a case" that legitimates precisely that critical autonomy on which its sense depends. But the relation can be inverted; the political institutions can also function to generate a kind of autonomous critical sense which serves to legitimate in turn the political institutions which generated it.[13] This reversibility makes the originary structure appear to be simply another illustration of the "game" that served to introduce the simple intuition. In fact, the reversibility serves to hold open the space that unites, while rendering autonomous, politics and critique.

The space that holds together and assures the autonomy of politics and critique has a conceptual structure which unites, in a relation of reversibility, genesis and normativity. This structure integrates as strategies of avoidance the metaphysical categories of theory and practice, which fail to express the simple intuition, with the Marxist unification of a theory *of* and a theory *for* revolution. For example, Marx's theory of ideology, as analyzed in Chapter 2, grasps this originary relation, but then it mistakes its symbolic status by attempting to unite the reversible poles in the really existing proletariat.[14] Critique becomes dialectic, and the autonomy of the political is lost in the process. The attempt to "make" a better case in Chapter 6 is only partially successful because its account of Marx's debt to Hegel remains within the dialectic of essence and appearance as presented within civil society. The originary relation of genesis and normativity that is still identified with the proletariat—defined now as a question—can only point toward the absent place of the political. Marx can take the argument no further. Avoiding a critique of politics, he returns to the theory (and to the critique) of historical reality. The relation of critique and politics cannot be comprehended in such a dialectic; a *method* adequate to the originary structure is necessary.[15]

The preservation of the originary space cannot be assured simply by ambushing the multiple stategies of avoidance that attempt consciously and unconsciously to subvert it. The politics and the critique whose autonomy is preserved are not maintained in splendid isolation, as an end in themselves. They interact with each other, and they do so in a world which is not simply and consistently defined by the originary structure. Yet it is only within such a structure that the coordinate and autonomous action of politics and critique can take place. The "practical" task of method is to assure the advent and the preservation of such a symbolic structure.[16] Two independent but interdependent moments define the method. As politics, method defines those *particulars* whose very particularity must be preserved by means of the reflective judgment whose place was demarcated by Kant. Not every particular, after all, can be said to be beautiful; nor does every particular have the autonomy that preserves it from subsumption under and reduction to a universal law. On the other hand, as critique, method is concerned with the *receptivity* of the historical world to the particular judgments of politics. Not every autonomous particular for which a political universal can be formulated can be received by the world at any and every historical moment; not every evil can be righted, nor every good realized. If critique is not to separate itself from politics, becoming an external criticism or unrealizable utopia; and if politics is not to separate itself from critique, becoming the immanent dialectic of scientific development or the replacement of individual moral freedom—these two moments must be maintained in their autonomy and their interdependence, as the moments of what I am calling method.

The need for an autonomous methodological moment within the originary structure can be explained negatively, by "unmaking a case" in which its absence blocks the critique through a strategy of avoidance; or it can be explained positively, by "making a case" through the reconstruction of that political space which makes possible autonomous critique. This method for the introduction of method is not developed in Kant and Marx. It can be demonstrated from the side of philosophy or from that of politics. For example, the opposition between the Frankfurt School's critical theory and the hermeneutics of Gadamer (Chapter 3) appears to pose the alternative between an external politics and an immanent dialectics; in fact the positions stand as two methodological moments within a larger framework which provides their horizon of sense. From the other side, the originary structure of the American Revolution (Chapter 4) makes it possible to identify the particular "crisis" that calls for historical action as the result of the break-down of the originary tension, while the receptivity of society to that particularity depends upon the generalized authority of the Whig critique which takes on the status of an ideology.[17] The case for methodology can be "made" positively by showing that the strategies of avoidance recognized by the critique do not imply that philosophy is condemned to the choice between imposing its own universals or limiting its reach to councils of prudence (Chapter 7). The place "made" by this refusal of self-limitation can be justified by restoring to radical politics its autonomy as originary, and thereby preserving the autonomous place of critique (Chapter 8) Although these illustrations serve only to place the chapters that follow, they suffice to pose a final question that leads forward to the attempt to define the politics of critique as practiced by "the working critic."

The method by which the originary relation between the autonomous moments of critique and politics is maintained insists in its turn on the necessary co-presence of the two moments defining the instance of particularity and the institutions of receptivity. Method presents a sort of mediation, but the originary structure that is repeated within the two interdependent moments of method prevent that mediation from taking an ideological form or pretending to incarnate a real unification of the autonomous moments which it nonetheless binds together. The two parts through which I elaborate the "case" for the simple intuition seem to correspond to the two moments of method. "Unmaking a case" by uncovering the strategies of avoidance that destroy the autonomy of the critique establishes conditions of receptivity; ''making a case'' by reconstructing the autonomy of the political space presupposed by the independent critique determines those particulars without which politics is arbitrary or abstractly universal. But the parallel is not perfect; a final determination is missing. The ''working critic'' cannot simply juxtapose or apply arbitrarily the originary implications of the simple intuition. Marx's turn to real history proved to be a strategic avoidance of the political question posed by his own critique. But such strategies are not simply wrong paths, errors or worse; the working critic too has to turn to history, aided this time by the originary method.

C. The Simple Intuition as Modern

The originary structure explains not only the conditions of the possibility of the space which preserves paradoxically the interdependence and the independence of critique and politics; it explains also the necessity of this instable originary relation. This necessity, and that of the strategies seeking to evade it, is founded by the *immanent* relation of the autonomous poles that articulates their interdependence. This immanent interdependence is not to be confused with the real immanence by which critique becomes dialectic and loses its relation to politics. The originary immanence is symbolic; it can never be entirely realized, and must constantly be sought anew. This structure founds Rousseau's recognition that the state of nature is ''in fact'' born with the social contract of which it is only apparently the real presupposition (Chapter 8). It provides a transition to the ''working critic'' in the same way that the attempt to ''unmake'' the evasions which denied the 'revolutionary' nature of the American Revolution (Chapter 4) provided a transition from the first formulation of the simple intuition as ''unmaking'' the certitudes through which the critique hides from itself its own presuppositions. The originary tension is broken constantly, and it is just as repeatedly renewed even as each evasion purports to destroy it by opting for one or the other pole, or by the claim to have solved the ''riddle'' of their mediation. This second type of avoidance will be seen in a moment to be central to the definition of the ''*politics* of critique''; for the moment, it suffices to recall the more frequent option for the priority of one or the other of the poles which recalls the structure of the Kantian ''dialectic'' that was essential to the preservation of the *critique* as such.

The immanence which can never be realized entirely because of its symbolic character explains why the originary structure is *modern*. Modernity is not the product or result of a linear historical progress[18]; it is a structure which expresses the sense of human activity at particular moments. As a process of secularization, modernity seeks constantly to eliminate all forms of external legitimation, whether natural or supernatural. This project cannot be completely realized; human reality cannot be reduced to sheer brute givenness from which all sense, and all society, is absent. Secularization replaces the reality of external justification by the originary relation between genetic and normative moments. In whatever domain, this originary structure means that modernity is self-legitimating *in principle*; in reality, however, modernity is a goal that is constantly sought and never achievable, because its symbolic structure is treated as if it were real. The "working critic" finds this dilemma explicitly thematized in modern art and politics (Chapter 9). The critic must work through each of the positions, as they seek to "make" a case which is quickly "unmade" by the ideological structure and self-destructive forms of modern capitalism. The critic adopts the strategy of the revolutionary critique which seems to be most vividly defended in the practice of the artistic avant-garde only to find that it becomes immediately the revolutionary politics of a vanguard that loses its self in a History which it takes as real. The critic, seeking to remain a critic, returns to Marx's discovery of capitalism-as-ideology. But, like Marx, the critic cannot trust the immateriality of this intuition, and turns out again to history, this time in the archetypical form of the French Revolution. The confusion of the symbolic with the real that vitiated the discovery of ideology reappears in the action and self-conception of the revolution itself. This calls for another return to the roots of the critique, this time to Kant, whom Marx had mocked as the "philosopher of the French Revolution." At this point, the working critic has brought together the twin concerns of critique and politics, repeating in one movement of thought the process prepared in the first two parts of this volume. The question of Revolution, and of its politics, can now be put on the agenda; the simple intuition is put into practice.

The French Revolution is usually analyzed retrospectively as the entry into political modernity. It also serves, if inconsistently, as the model of a modern revolution; its phases, slippages, inventions, and masks provide the categories through which revolutionary politics seeks to define itself (Chapter 10). The French Revolution can be defined as modern insofar as it was the action of society seizing its destiny and overthrowing the separated political state of the Ancien Régime. Although this appears to have been the self-conception of its actors, Marx saw the need for a further critique of "the political illusion" to bring it to its completion. This revolutionary immanence explains the historians' difficulty in understanding the individual events which marked its real course. The French Revolution was originary; it can be explained neither by the conditions and institutions that existed before it, nor is it realized in the social or economic effects that it produced. "The" revolution does not exist, any more than "revolution" can be taken simply as the definition of a political project, as the simple intuition seemed for a moment to imply. Revolution as originary cannot be a goal that a subject seeks to achieve in reality. A mediation by a specifically originary method is necessary. This method appears to be "conservative" in its goals: the originary relation must be preserved against the slippages constantly proposed by the strategies of avoidance that are built into its very structure. But such intentional labels are not applicable to a politics founded on an originary intuition: the point is not to "make" the revolution, but to make it possible and necessary.

The redefinition of the revolution as originary is not simply a methodological proposal; it has practical consequences. The genetic corollary to the normative political moment institutionalized in the republican state is democracy. The American Revolution must stand alongside the French as the modern political model (Chapter 11). Two historically new achievements of the American Revolution make clear its uniqueness; at the same time, they suggest the relevance of the originary method. On the side of particularity, the Americans were the first to recognize the legitimacy of political parties. Although they fought to achieve a republic, they came to understand that it was possible to be united by a 'public thing' and yet divided among themselves. On the side of receptivity, the Americans came to recognize the supremacy of the constitution over the momentary decisions of their representatives. The acceptance of judicial review by a nonelected branch of government is the methodological correlative to the particularism of the political parties. Neither of these developments was predicted nor sought; their contemporaries spoke of a "Revolution of 1800" that completed the liberation from the English colonial system. That concept should surprise only the 'realist,' whose imagination is fraught with "revolutionary" scenes from a history whose wealth blinds him or her to the symbolic effectiveness of the originary. The originary tension between the genetic and normative moments means that the democratic republic internalizes revolution in the immanent, modern *sense* of that term. This is why the three phases through which the American Revolution passed between 1763 and 1787 can be described by the same concept that is applied to the events following 1789 in France. At this, the common sense of the revolutionary realist revolts: how can democratic electoral politics be claimed to be "revolutionary"?

The relation of democratic and revolutionary politics within the historical framework defined by modernity is neither one of identity nor simple polarity. The experience of *totalitarianism* complicates the task of the critique and the definition of its politics. The issue is thematized specifically here only at the outset of Chapter 7. Totalitarianism is a constant threat within an originary political structure; indeed, as opposed to the classical forms of tyranny, totalitarianism is a specifically modern phenomenon.[19] The specificity of totalitarianism lies first of all in the fact that it is a strategy of avoidance which is, at least partially, self-conscious. It recognizes the danger of the slippage toward one or the other pole in the originary structure; it is constantly vigilant against the dangers that this entails for the practice of democracy. But totalitarianism does not stop with this (external) critical function; it proposes to replace the unstable formal democracy which is constantly threatened *because it exists only symbolically* with a "real democracy" which will *realize* the dialectical mediation between the genetic and normative poles, between society and state, nature and man, man and men, even men and women. Totalitarianism represents the *political* form of the tendency to transform critique into an immanent dialectical system to which there is no outside and against which there is no politics. This immanence of totalitarianism within the originary structure of democracy makes it a constant threat to modern societies. But anti-totalitarianism alone does not constitute a politics, let alone a "politics of critique."

The unmasking of strategies of avoidance can become itself another illustration of the systematic flight from the politics of critique. That is why the first two sections of this volume treated the making as well as the unmaking of the originary case and its method. The "politics of critique" has not been defined here, and *is not defined in this volume*—despite its title—because the structure of immanence which defines the originary as modern *excludes the separation or distinction of a properly political domain*. The originary structure which founds the simple insight remains too closely tied to Marx and Kant, for both of whom *civil society* was the key to modern politics. Kant saw the creation of this civil society as a problem, Marx took it as a solution. Marx's solution in fact makes clear the nature of the problem. The feudal "democracy of unfreedom" was supposedly replaced after 1789 by a bourgeois state form which represents still only the "illusion of politics"; it is in turn to be overthrown by society's own agent, the proletariat. But between feudalism and capitalism, which are economic forms of social relations, there arose a new phenomenon: the absolute state, wholly sovereign in its particular domain, and incarnating symbolically the principles of right or law. *This* state, in its dual principle of particularity (among other states) and universality (as the *Rechtsstaat* responsible only to itself) has a structure that is originary. It represents the missing form of the political which makes possible a "politics of critique."

The univocal title under which the pursuit of the simple intuition is presented here suggests that none of these modes of critical activity itself exhausts the task of a critique which *seeks to be political*. This does not mean that the forms are somehow erroneous, or that they represent deadends, reproduced here simply as warnings to the unwary. On the contrary, each in its own way represents one moment within the broader framework of the politics of critique. But that politics is not the sum of these, or indefinitely many other, parts. *The* politics of critique which emerges from this attempt to rethink the simple originary intuition goes beyond and differs from any of its parts. Just as capitalist civil society is the product of a *political* revolution that created the conditions in which this new economic form could become dominant, so too are these partial critiques made possible by a more encompassing *political* critique. The politics of critique is made possible by that broader framework which defines that modern state within which critique and politics define a space which is originary.[20] Although democracy defines the originary structure of a modern *society*, my repeated insistence on the republican form is explained by this primacy of the political *question* in defining "the politics of critique."

There is no moral with which to conclude this Introduction; no lesson to be drawn, no set of guidelines to help the reader find the correct way through the labyrinth. There is a negative conclusion, however: Critique cannot "seek to be political," as was suggested a moment ago; the political is not some existent thing or structure to which the critique seeks to become adequate or whose realization it wants to bring about. Critique *is* political—so long as it succeeds in maintaining its interdependent/independent relation to the political, and so long as it avoids those strategies of avoidance defined here as criticism and dialectic. For this reason, I can do no better than to conclude as I did in the preface to *Defining the Political*: ''This Preface carries no conclusion, just as this book makes no claim to have defined the political. The simple intuition is presented; the mediations for its realization are sketched. It remains to acknowledge my debts, and to begin again.''

I
Unmaking a Case

1

Kant's Political Theory: The Virtue of His Vices

A. Historical Misunderstandings

When Marx called Kant the "philosopher of the French Revolution," he did not have in mind the "jacobin" Kant who continued his enthusiastic support of the Revolution long after his freedom-loving younger contemporaries such as Schiller and Goethe had become disillusioned with its course.[1] Marx's image of Kant is that of the "philosopher of the bourgeoisie" in its struggle for freedom from the constraints of the feudal order. The substitution of a socio-economic class for a political revolution in these two phrases entails a dangerous reduction of politics to economics which typifies a caricatural Marxism.[2] What is more, such a reduction distorts the object of analysis, be it the Kantian philosophy, the French (or bourgeois) Revolution, or our own contemporary socio-political context. Treating Kant within the context of his historical reception, and the contemporary problems to which it points, suggests a different reading—of Kant, of Marx, and of our times.

Toward the end of the nineteenth century, when Marxism had become the accepted philosophical stance of a growing Social Democratic Party in a now-unified and apparently bourgeois Germany, it was confronted with a renewed Kantian philosophical movement which put the debate between "Marx" and "Kant" back onto the intellectual and political agenda. The confrontation was sometimes polemical and determined by immediate political matters; sometimes comradely and open toward a broader strategic perspective; and at times more abstractly formulated as a scientific and methodological inquiry. The debate was carried on through the pages of the Social Democratic press as well as those of the scholarly world. The arguments could be quite simplistic and dull, as when Karl Kautsky, the "pope" of Social Democracy, set up historical parallels to explain the rebirth of Kantianism through the rise of a vulgar materialism analogous to the utilitarian empiricism of the Enlightenment that so upset Kant. Or they could be quite subtle and theoretical, as when the methodologically inclined Marburg neo-Kantians such as Hermann Cohen, or the brilliant Austro-Marxist Max Adler, tried to show that Marx's contributions could be brought into theoretical harmony with those of Kant. Or, they could combine theory and politics, as when Karl Vorländer joins Kant and Marx to take the side of Marxian orthodoxy in the ''Revisionist'' debates in order to show that Bernstein's famous stress on the ''movement'' as opposed to the ''goal'' leads to disaster on all planes.

Rereading some of these debates today, one is struck first of all by their syncretic nature. All agree (''ideology-critically'') that Kant could not have formulated the economic arguments of Marx because his time was not yet ripe. Further, these Marxist economic-historical analyses are taken as valid by all the participants. On this point, the neo-Kantians' argument is only that there is no methodological reason to assume that Kant would disagree; nor, for that matter, is there any moral or biographical grounds for objection (as is then shown by numerous quotes detailing Kant's stance toward feudality, education, exploitation, etc., etc.). Marx's method, as it is laid out for example in the 1859 ''Introduction to the Critique of Political Economy,'' with its move from the abstract to the concrete, is read in a Kantian manner as the formulation of the ''conditions of the possibility'' of a given experience and of our knowledge of it. Methodologically, Marx and Kant agree that the realm of appearances must be governed by a law-like causal order. When this approach is applied to the phenomena of history, Kant finds a lawfulness in apparently random, individualistic, and willful actions (such as the number of marriages, migrations, commerce, etc.); and on this basis he suggests a politics (which, he says, a ''race of devils'' could formulate, ''if only it were intelligent''). What Kant adds to Marx in this context is said to be the ethical factor, which Marx did not sufficiently stress (although Vorländer busily points to the many ''value overtones'' that pervade Marx's writings.) The contribution of Kant, therefore, is found in the ethical domain, which a naive materialism ignores at its own peril.

Whether I read these debates as a ''Kantian,'' or as a ''Marxist,'' they seem to me extraordinarily unfruitful! Changing the material conditions to which the Kantian ''method'' is applied adds nothing to my understanding of what Kant is doing as a philosopher. It does not help me to understand why his ''Copernican Revolution'' still engages our questioning today. Indeed, the Marxian framework seems to exclude a number of important Kantian insights, to which I shall be returning. Does it help, for example, to show that Kant's discussion of the negative impact of the maintenance of standing armies implies precisely the Social Democrats' demand for militia?[3] Or, to mention another example, is the objection to Kant's formalistic ethics eliminated when one shows how his theoretical position as well as his lectures on pedagogy fit with the Social Democrats' demand for the *Einheitsschule?* From the side of Marx, the problem is that the neo-Kantians are too apologetic, giving away too much in always trying to show that Marx ''could'' have developed the Kantian ethical stance had he only taken the time away from his practical work to do so. Or, if the Kantians do offer criticism of Marx—as when Cohen tries to show the importance of the *Idea* of God, those of Right and of the State, and that those of the *Volk* or nationality are methodologically essential—it is too easy for Marxists such as Mehring to show, however rhetorically, that these are but excess baggage which do not help the movement, although they are no more dangerous to it than the Bible and the Mass Book were to the healthy struggle of Wallenstein.[4]

The debate is the more disappointing if, as I have tried to show elsewhere, one finds Marx "methodologically" (to use the neo-Kantian's term) incapable of formulating a political theory adequate to our own—or even his—times.[5] It is not the ethical dimension that is lacking in Marx, nor the economic that would somehow complete the Kantian perspective. It is the political dimension that is crucial.

B. Marxist Misreadings

Kant opposed revolution and supported the French Revolution. He apparently could not *think* this leap, and yet recognized it as an instance of the very causality of freedom on which his ethics (and ultimately his entire system) had to rest. His problem comes out clearly in a passage from the First Appendix to "Perpetual Peace," entitled "On the Disagreement of Morals and Politics in Relation to Perpetual Peace":

> Thus political prudence, with things as they are at present, will make it a duty to carry out reforms appropriate to the ideal of public right. But where revolutions are brought about by nature alone, it will not use them as a good excuse for even greater oppression, but will treat them as a call of nature to create a lawful constitution based on the principles of freedom, for a thorough reform of this kind is the only one that will last.[6]

Putting the responsibility on "nature" will hardly do here—and we shall be seeing that Kant's tendency repeatedly to do just that is a crucial problem that he cannot quite resolve. Nor, however, can he go the route suggested in one of the *Lose Blätter*:

> In order to institute a Republic from a *pactum sociale* there must already be present a Republic. Hence, the Republic cannot be instituted save by *violence* (*Gewalt*), *not* through *agreement*.[7]

Kant's problem is *who* would exercise such violence, and how could it be justified morally? Kant has no place in his system for the external law-giver invoked classically by political theory; at best he can have faith in the Enlightened Despot, and this only insofar as his construction of world history shows the necessity of the Despot's instituting a Republican constitution that would lead to perpetual peace. But even in this case, Kant's ethics of freedom deny the possibility that his historical construction seems to show, for example, when he asserts in *Religion within the Limits of Reason Alone*:

> I admit that I cannot agree with the expression used even by quite intelligent men: that a certain people . . . is not ripe for freedom. . . . Because from such a presupposition freedom will never emerge; for man cannot ripen to freedom before he is placed in free conditions; one must be free in order to use one's forces in a goal-oriented manner.[8]

Well and good, we may say; but this hardly gets us further as concerns the transformation of present conditions. Indeed, one could oppose to this citation a structurally identical one from the first Introduction to the *Critique of Judgement* where Kant asks himself why we wish for things which we cannot have, and replies that it is *nature's* wisdom which so arranges things, for by these wishes we gradually grow and learn to go beyond our apparent limits.[9] There is an apparent inconsistency between an option for nature or for freedom in Kant's position on this matter, which might lead one to conclude, as does Leonard Krieger, that it is typical of the weaknesses of German liberalism's failures ''in the revolutions of 1848 and 1918'' as well.[10] The problem, is more than simply theoretical.

The Marxified Kant of the neo-Kantians solves the problem of revolution paradoxically: by eliminating it. Kant's account of the lawless lawfulness of historical development is invoked; the necessity of lawful state forms, increased education and freedoms, etc., are shown to lie in the interest of the modern state itself; and one concludes, with Kant in the *Conflict of the Faculties*, that revolution is merely the ''*evolution* of a constitution governed by *natural right*.''[11] There are numerous grounds for this reading of Kant. For example, in ''Theory and Practice'' he puts it in a quite general manner:

> . . . it will rather depend upon what human *nature* may do in and through us to *compel* us to follow a course we would not readily adopt by choice. We must look to nature alone, or rather to *providence* (since it requires the highest wisdom to fulfill this purpose), for a successful outcome which will first affect the whole and then the individual parts. The schemes of men, on the other hand, begin with the parts and frequently get no further than them. For the whole is too great for men to encompass; while they can reach it with their ideas, they cannot actively influence it, especially since their schemes conflict with one another to such an extent that they could hardly reach agreement of their own free volition.[12]

An invisible hand is thus invoked; providence or a mysteriously rational nature enters and is rendered responsible for revolution. The result is that revolution disappears, change is lawful, and the new becomes just a manifestation of what was already present in the old. Granted, an almost identical passage to the above appears in the second introduction to the *Critique of Judgement*, suggesting that Kant's assertion here is intended as a reflexive, teleological judgment and not as the predicative assertion of factual matters.[13] That only points to what the Marxification neglects, as we shall see. What is more, however, that Marxification is not a misrepresentation of Kant. In the just-mentioned *Conflict*, Kant had posed the question of the way in which the human race will become aware of its general interest in peace. He replied with the Humean image of two fighters in a china shop who learn from the damages they do the cost of their quarrel. He went on to suggest that the "present war" with the French implied that the turn is "already in sight." What would take place, he described as follows:

> The profit which will accrue to the human race as it works its way forward will not be an ever increasing quantity of *morality* in its attitudes. Instead, the *legality* of its attitudes will produce an ever increasing number of actions governed by duty, whatever the particular motive behind these actions may be. . . . Such developments do not mean, however, that the basic moral capacity of mankind will increase in the slightest, for this would require a kind of new creation or supernatural influence.[14]

In short, what is lost here is the basis of the entire Kantian morality, not to speak of what Marx praised him for, that philosophy of freedom and individuality. With it is lost the problematic of the causality of freedom which would permit one to think of a revolution as something not merely necessitated by the phenomenal order of world development. All that remains is the barren shadow of a *Rechtsstaat*, whose formal emptiness the Marxist can then criticize, or fill in with socioeconomic data derived elsewhere.

In the following pages, I shall try to follow Kant's groping, often apparently contradictory attempts to formulate a theory of politics. I could apologize in advance for him, by pointing to the fact that politics, as we conceive of the term since the French Revolution, as well as revolution itself, were phenomena that were newly appearing on the horizon of his time. But precisely the rigor of Kant's own developments, as well as the apparent disappearance of the properly political from our own society, make such apologies unnecessary. Kant's insistance on the Republic as the only valid state form because it preserves the properly political space might well be repeated today, when political choice is ever-more reduced to economic or technical necessity. Kant's theory of history, which is intimately bound to his politics, avoids the monistic idealisms of a Hegel or a Marx, and maintains history as a problem, not as a solution. Reflection on these political and historical phenomena is not incidental to the Kantian philosophy as a whole, as we shall see in a moment. Their centrality points, I think, to a rereading of Kant which may suggest that the neo-Kantians' slogan—Zurück zu Kant!—is once again on the agenda for political theory.

C. The Systematic Place of the Political

Concern with the political was both systemically and personally necessary to Kant. At the more anecdotal level, one might recall the famous passage where he expresses his debt to Rousseau:

> There was a time when I believed that this [i.e., the thirst for knowledge] is what confers real dignity upon human life, and I despised the common people who know nothing. Rousseau has set me right. This imagined advantage vanishes. I learn to honor men, and should regard myself as of much less use than the common laborer if I did not believe that my philosophy will restore to all men the common rights of humanity.[15]

Or, one might follow Hans Saner's demonstration that the very method of Kant's writings, from the early scientific concerns through to the end, are determined by the striving toward "perpetual peace."[16] Historically, one might refer to Kant's Pietist background, recalling that Spener's Halle experiments were a reply not only to the frozen emptiness of doctrinaire Lutheranism, but too were intended to have, and did in fact have, practical political influence. Or, biographically, one might recall passages such as: "One can use whatever artifices one likes, but one cannot force nature to follow other laws; either one works oneself, *or others work for one*; and this work will rob these others of just as much of their happiness as one gains thereby."[17] Or, leading now to the systematic concerns, one might add that the frail hypochondriac did not hesitate to interrupt the work of completing his formal system to write the two historical essays, "What is Enlightenment?" and "Idea for a Universal History from a Cosmopolitan Point of View," in the year 1784—before revising the first, and publishing the second and third *Critiques*.

Turning to the work itself with this political question in mind, one notes of course the expression of contemporary concern already in the preface to the first *Critique*. One might read the "Copernican Revolution" as the theoretical justification of a new social individualism based on human self-activity; while the Transcendental Dialectic could be seen as a sustained attempt to preserve that individuality and self-activity. To cite but one example:

> In the absence of this critique reason is, as it were, in the state of nature, and can establish and secure its assertions and claims only through *war*. The critique, on the other hand, arriving at all its decisions in the light of fundamental principles of its own institution, the authority of which no one can question, secures to us the peace of a legal order, in which our disputes have to be conducted solely by the recognised methods of *legal action*. . . . The endless disputes of a merely dogmatic reason thus finally constrain us to seek relief in some critique of reason itself, and in a legislation based upon such criticism. As Hobbes maintains, the state of nature is a state of injustice and violence, and we have no option save to abandon it and submit ourselves to the constraint of law. . . .
>
> This freedom [under law] will carry with it the right to submit openly for discussion the thoughts and bouts with which we find ourselves unable to deal, and to do so without being decried as troublesome and dangerous citizens. This is one of the original rights of human reason, which recognises no other judge than that universal human reason in which everyone

> has his say. And since all improvement of which our state is capable must be obtained from this source, such a right is sacred and must not be curtailed.[18]

This example is the more interesting since, as we shall see, it anticipates many of Kant's guiding political ideas. But it is important, first, to note that the price paid for the "peace" which the first *Critique* is to establish is considerable: the dualism accepted at the outset and transformed into the phenomenon/noumenon distinction at once costs us Nature while holding out Freedom either as an inexplicably given fact or as an Idea for continual striving. Thus, Beck observes that the *Metaphysik der Sitten* which Kant hoped would follow the first *Critique* had to be put off for over fifteen years; and the *Grundlegung's* account of the "fact" of freedom had to be supplemented first by the *Critique of Practical Reason* and then by the *Critique of Judgement* where according to Beck one still finds the "most profound treatment of freedom . . . in Kant's works."[19] I would add to this last remark, however—and this is the point of the present argument—that the reflections on history and on politics were in fact the necessary preliminaries.

Kant's ethical writings attempt to resolve the dualism with which the first *Critique* had left him. The solution offered to the Third Antinomy had not satisfactorily accounted for the problem of the causality of freedom; it was a truce, not a Republican Peace. Kant's new attempt focused on duty and the good will as the only thing of which we can say that it is good in itself and universally. But he buys his solution only through the explicit rejection of Nature (in the form of a hedonist or utilitarian ethics). The unhappy result echoes through in some of his most famous lines where he asserts that even if "the niggardly provision of a step-motherly nature" did not permit morality to achieve its ends in the world, nonetheless "like a jewel, it would still shine by its own light. . . . " What is more, not only cannot Kant be sure of freedom's effects in the world, he cannot even explain the source of that freedom or morality. His admirer, Beck, thus has to admit that "the manner in which moral concern comes into experience is never satisfactorily examined."[20]

The failure of the ethical writings is the explicit occasion for the turn to the *Critique of Judgement*, whose place within the system is explained in the second Introduction:

> The understanding legislates *a priori* for nature as an object of sense—giving a theoretical knowledge of it in a possible experience. Reason legislates *a priori* for freedom and its peculiar causality which, as the supersensible in the subject, gives unconditioned practical knowledge. The realm of the concept of nature under one legislation and that of the concept of freedom under the other are entirely removed from all reciprocal influence which they might have on one another (each according to its fundamental laws) by the great gulf that separates the supersensible from the phenomena. The concept of freedom determines nothing in respect of the theoretical cognition of nature, and the concept of nature determines noth-

> ing in respect of the practical laws of freedom. It is therefore not possible to throw a bridge from the one realm to the other.

But the limitations on knowledge do not apply strictly to the world of practice. Kant continues his argument from this second standpoint. The difficulty he confronts is evident in the linguistic maneuvers he has to propose.

> But although the determining grounds of causality according to the concept of freedom (and the practical rules which it contains) are not resident in nature, and the sensible cannot determine the supersensible in the subject, yet the inverse is possible (not, to be sure, in respect of the cognition of nature, but as regards the effects of the supersensible upon the sensible), and it is in fact involved in the concept of a causality through freedom, the *effect* of which is to take place in the world according to its formal laws. The word *cause* (Ursache), of course, when used for the supersensible, only signifies the *ground* which determines the causality (Causalität) of natural things to an effect in accordance with the laws of nature proper to them, although harmoniously with the formal principle of the laws of reason.[21]

Kant covers over "dialectically" the terminological difficulty by adding immediately that although we cannot understand the possibility of this causality, it is simple to refute those who would call its assertion a contradiction. Perhaps. But thus far Kant is still on the grounds of the Dialectic of the first *Critique*, save perhaps that the problem is more explicitly posed. Indeed, the general ontological *solutions* offered in the third *Critique*, however intriguing, are not satisfactory. On the one hand, there is the notion of Genius, the exceptional happy solution to the doctrinal dualism. Since the individual case is no theoretical resolution, there is also the suggestion of teleological causality—but there too Kant's premises drive him to assert that the rational structure and order of nature is but a "lucky accident." But unless the accident can be shown to be precisely the causality of freedom, the causally structured natural world of the first *Critique* remains. Kant's proposal needs further detail.

The experience of the beautiful is a disinterested experience characterized by the feeling of purposeless purposefulness. To claim the universality of true judgment, it must be law-like. But this law cannot be phenomenal, for there is no room in nature for purpose; it is "lawfulness without law." As a judgment, the aesthetic experience is the relation of a subject and object; but the object is not the sensuous thing out there and the judgment is not predicative; rather, it is the feeling gained from the object, a reflexive judgment. The subject, on the other hand, is not untouched or unchanged; especially in the experience of sublimity, it recognizes in the object that gives it this pleasure something for which it can hope but never reach; its own ideas of greatness, force, completeness are manifested there in a way to which it will never attain. The correlative of the feeling of sublimity, then, is a feeling of incompleteness, of respect for the object and dissatisfaction with self. The result is thus a new awareness of the Ethical Task; an awareness of the humanity in my own person. The heroic individualism of the "bourgeois" Kant thus remains, strengthened. But the suggestion of a transformation of the subject is not taken up. One aspect of this will appear insofar as the notion of taste is a subjective judgment claiming universality—thus communicability and reciprocity. Here, with Hannah Arendt, one might talk about a notion of political judgment—but that gets us well ahead of our story.[22]

The systematic counterpart to the aesthetic judgment is the teleological structure of organic nature. An organism is a system which is self-organized such that it appears to set the goals which its organization carries out. All of its parts function together in terms of the whole, relate to one another not for some external reason but owing to a goal apparently posited by the organism itself. Whereas in the case of the aesthetic experience we were concerned with our representation of a thing, here we are talking about the thing itself. But such an organism seems to counter the law-like causality of the phenomenal world, where causality implies the succession of cause and effect and supposes the difference of the two. In the organism the same thing is both cause and effect; its goal is to remain itself, and it generates actions to that end, actions which it itself carries out. In trying to understand this peculiar phenomenon, we realize that we ourselves act in this manner: our goals are teleological causes of our action. But we are subjects; nature is not. We posit goals, then act; nature does not separate goals and their accomplishment. This leads Kant to suggest that we can talk about the Idea of a totality of Nature, a Nature which is organically, teleologically organized. He must immediately grant that such an assumption cannot be proven; but nonetheless he suggests that it may prove useful in the quest for law-like relations in nature which might otherwise have not appeared to us. Further, Kant indicates that such teleological causality differs from natural causality in that natural causality subsumes a particular under a universal law while in the case of teleology the movement is on the reflexive path from the particular to the universal. With this final specification of teleology, we can return to politics, philosophy, and history—since it will be recalled that the general passage I cited a moment ago to support the Marxified Kant argued precisely from this teleology and from the "schemes of men" which "begin with the parts" and cannot get to the whole.

D. Enlightenment Politics

Kant's brief essay, "What is Enlightenment?" was published in 1784 in the context of a quarrel over the limits and the possible abuses of enlightenment debunking.[23] He begins aggressively, defining enlightenment in his first sentence as "man's release from his self-incurred tutelage." The Marxist would, of course, tax this as "idealistic," but he or she would have to agree with the critique of alienation in the next assertion:

> If I have a book which understands for me, a pastor who has a con-

> science for me, a physican who decides my diet, and so forth, I need not trouble myself. I need not think, if only I can pay—others will readily undertake the irksome work for me.

Although one might still say that Kant's concern is only with individual moral reform, one recalls that already in the preface to the first *Critique* Kant had defined his as an ''Age of Critique'' (Axiii). Kant insists there that it is ''the freedom to make public use of one's reason at every point'' which is crucial. Be that as it may, it is true that Kant typically stresses here the striving and not the achieving, the will toward and not the content of the goal. But again, one can't just write off the argument, which has as its critical implication the fact that:

> . . . a contract, made to shut off all further enlightenment from the human race, is absolutely null and void even if confirmed by the supreme power, by parliaments, and by the most ceremonious of peace treaties. . . . That would be a crime against human nature, the proper destination of which lies precisely in this progress.

The source of Kant's argument is obviously Rousseau, who is also responsible for the further assertion that ''the touchstone of everything that can be concluded as a law for a people lies in the question whether the people could have imposed such a law on itself.'' These arguments will later be reformulated in Republican terms.[24]

The problem with the notion of Enlightenment-as-process is that it is empty. This is the cost of avoiding utilitarianism; and it has left Kant open to attack ever since, most recently by Leonard Krieger, as we have seen, and also by Max Horkheimer and the Frankfurt School of Marxism who argue that, as empty, this conscience has no central axis on which to base any revolt, and thus can be easily manipulated. An enlightened individual on this definition is one who has overcome heteronomy, has become self-determining and self-motivating. No content is offered; nature remains outside, accidental. Moreover, it is not clear how this enlightened consciousness could grow, learn, or change. Kant was not unaware of the problem, having formulated his theory in opposition to the empty rationalism of the Leibniz-Wolff school as well as the fatuousness of the *Popularphilosophen's* utilitarianism. One can see two possible interpretations between which Kant is torn: the enlightened moral individual takes duty as the guide to action, rejecting the heteronomous goals entailed in material happiness in order to become worthy of happiness; or, from the experience of the aesthetic, the sublimity of purposeless purposefulness, there comes about the sense of a lack in oneself and the greatness entailed in the ethical task. Formally, the structures of consciousness are the same here; but the latter makes possible a historical account of growth (as Schiller suggests in the *Letters on Aesthetic Education*) while at the same time—because the aesthetic judgment is social or communicative and not monological—it points toward a social analysis different from that of atomistic liberalism.

Kant spells out his notion of history in the "Idea of History from a Cosmopolitan Point of View" in the same year, 1784—as if he felt the need to concretize the "thin" enlightenment consciousness. Although he had not yet written the *Critique of Judgement*, he begins with a teleological argument in order to overcome the reduction of history to mechanical causal relations. The individual acts freely; and yet the new sciences of statistics and demography show that:

> Each, according to his own inclination, follows his own purpose, often in opposition to others; yet each individual and people, as if following some guiding thread, go toward a natural but to each of them unknown goal; all work toward furthering it, even if they would set little store by it if they did know it.

But when he comes to ask for the source of this "guiding thread," Kant introduces "nature" and "natural purpose" in a manner which we have already seen to be problematic. Thus, nature is invoked as having "willed" that we, by ourselves, produce that which makes our lives more than animal; and that our happiness be produced not by instinct but only by reason. This of course fits with Kant's view of morality as worthiness to be happy, however rationalist a stance it imputes to nature. What is more, Kant introduces here the notion of our "unsocial sociability" which balances us between selfish urges and social obligation. Because of this unsocial sociability there arises the necessity of social rules which permit human development which changes "a society of men driven together by their natural feelings into a moral whole." Rather than live in concord and mutual affection, or happy isolation like Rousseau's "animal stupide et borné," our unsocial sociability (whose real manifestations Kant spells out here and elsewhere in very concrete social-historical terms) leads us to progress. Hence, concludes Kant, Nature knows better than man: "Man wishes concord; but Nature knows better what is good for the race; she wills discord."

There are numerous problems that we might address here were there time, particularly the relation to Rousseau and the problem of the growth of needs. But it is most important to stress that the attribution of rational purpose to nature might be legitimate if Kant were not holding to his dualistic postulates; if he had not made this particular move precisely in order to "thicken" his "thin" enlightenment consciousness. What is more, he wants to talk at once about the birth of reason (from the situation of unsocial sociability) and at the same time to insist that what makes man different from the animals is the innateness of reason (or what Rousseau called the "capacity" for reason). The problem lies in the teleological judgment which is taken here as predicative. The result is an unclear blending of two types of account, when Kant's goal was precisely to show how from their incompatibility the growth of freedom was possible. But this is not Kant's last word on the matter.

The fifth and sixth theses on "Cosmopolitan History" suggest that the greatest problem for humankind, and the most difficult and last to be solved, is the formation of a universal civil society administered by law.[25] Again, nature's mysteriously rational ways are invoked in a famous passage:

> It is just the same with trees in a forest: each needs the others since each in seeking to take the air and sunlight from others must strive upward, and thereby each realizes a beautiful, straight stature, while those that live in isolated freedom put out branches at random and grow stunted, crooked and twisted.

But human intervention returns in the sixth thesis, which asserts, against Herder's anarchism, that "Man is an animal which, if it lives among others of its kind, requires a master." Whence the master? It can only be another human, who in turn needs a master. The solution, of course, would be self-mastery. Here, nature is of no help; and human nature, clearly, is a hindrance. "This task," concludes Kant, "is . . . the hardest of all; indeed, its complete solution is impossible, for from such crooked wood as man is made of, nothing perfectly straight can be built." At this point, however, the problematic nature of history returns, and politics becomes more than the action of providential Nature. Indeed, as if replying to himself, Kant was to write later in the "Conflict" (1798):

> One must take men as they are, they tell us, and not as the world's uniformed pedants or good-natured dreamers fancy they ought to be. But 'as they are' ought to read 'as we have *made* them by unjust coercion, by treacherous designs which the government is in a good position to carry out.' For that is why they are intransigent and inclined to rebellion, and why regrettable consequences ensue if discipline is relaxed in the slightest.[26]

But Kant does not follow this path yet. Rather, he suggests that the solution begins by the establishment of "a lawful external relation among states." He argues theoretically for the possibility of this League of Nations coming about just as he had done for unsociably social men, but then moves on, in his eighth and ninth theses, to a more practical resolution. First, he asserts that "the history of mankind can be seen, in the large, as the realization of Nature's secret plan. . . ." To his own query, whether this is utopian, nay, millenarian, he gives three answers. First, "the Idea can help, though only from afar. . . ." Second, nature does, to however small a degree, reveal progress and, with Rousseau, Kant insists that we cannot remain indifferent to the possibility of helping here. Finally, concretely, Kant sees that it is in the interest of the state to develop the capacities of its citizens, citing the example of the beneficial effects of commerce.[27] Thus the state—or as we shall see, a specific form of state—will have an interest in the progress of enlightenment.

But the problem of the individual, and of enlightenment, remains; it is in effect the problem of revolution from which we began. The goal of the state is the development of an enlightened citizenry from whose enlightenment *then* follows the promise of material happiness; but to achieve this goal the state must itself be enlightened, and that presupposes the existence of those very enlightened citizens that it was to produce. The ninth and final thesis therefore places the philosopher on the stage of history: ''A philosophical attempt to work out a universal history according to a natural plan directed to achieving the civic union of the human race must be regarded as possible and, indeed, as contributing to this end of Nature.'' This position is rather different from the pre-critical stance of the *Lectures on Ethics*, where to the same question Kant could only plead for support of the Basedow institutions and their educational reform. It is also different from the position then in the air, for example in the leader of the Illuminist Masons, Weishaupt, whose *Geschichte der Vervollkommnung des menschlichen Geschlechts* (1788) stressed the role of philosophy as well. Kant is able to play on the dual nature of Nature insofar as the praxis he seeks is embedded in a natural development of which the theory is the expression. This is a position isomorphic to Marx's 1843 turn to the proletariat as the subject-object of history.[28] Philosophy can be seen as ''contributing to this end of Nature'' insofar as it renders explicit what was only implicit in Nature and permits individuals to become self-conscious, i.e., enlightened. But the ambiguity of the notion of Nature invoked throughout, as well as the problems with Marx's isomorphic solution, stand to warn us that—as Kant himself stresses in the corresponding section of the *Anthropologie*[29]—this is not a constitutive or predicative judgment but only a regulative argument. If it is taken along the lines of Marxism—i.e., that real natural developments justify the theory which, in turn, as their expression, is to bring about what is prophesied—then Kant's uniqueness is lost.

E. Reconstructing Republican Theory

The pre-1789, or pre-third *Critique* Kant could have described the philosopher's task along with Marx; could have understood historical necessity along with Marx; and could have reduced the specificity of the political sphere as Marx was to do. Curiously, Kant's reaction to 1789 and the following years went in just the opposite direction—although he by no means explicitly or implicitly gave up on the ''pre-Marxist'' stance just described . . . or on Kantianism! There were of course problems. To begin with, there were the historical facts. The radical Jacobin Constitution of 1793 declared in its first Article, that the task of the revolution was to achieve happiness. This was Robespierre's theme as well, although he is of course better known for the Terror. There was too the fact that when the people assumed the war-making power they promptly utilized it . . . for war, indeed for the development of a historically new kind of war. Yet, in 1798, in the ''*Conflict*,'' Kant remained with the revolution, adducing the old arguments and adding a ''sympathy which borders almost on enthusiasm,'' whose effect he explains as follows:

> All this, along with the *passion* or *enthusiasm* with which men embrace the cause of goodness (although the former cannot be entirely applauded,

> since all passion as such is blameworthy), gives historical support for the following assertion, which is of considerable anthropological significance: true enthusiasm is always directed towards the *ideal*, particularly towards that which is purely moral (such as the concept of right), and it cannot be coupled with selfish interests.[30]

This relation of enthusiasm and the ideal as giving rise to the moral sense was present in the *Critique of Judgement* as a specific aspect of the more general notion that the beautiful is a symbol of the moral.[31] What is more, we saw that the result of the experience of the sublime is precisely an *active* enlightenment, a feeling of lack which drives me to go beyond my own limits. But Kant does not develop the possibilities of this position in any active communicatory practice, as one might think possible; it is enough for him that the revolution can be justified, in some sense confirming his own theoretical position. Beyond that, his parenthetical remark that "all passion as such is blameworthy" recalls his fundamental ethical position, which he has not abandoned.

What does Kant's ethics hold out with respect to the new situation? The "Introduction to the Theory of Law," in the *Metaphysik der Sitten* (1795), is built on the ethical position. Kant asserts, "If it is not our intention to teach virtue [which of course cannot be taught, for it is not empirical], but only to state what is *right*, then we may not and should not ourselves represent this law of right as a possible motive for actions."[32] But this was the problem of the relation of theory to practice that Kant had debated two years earlier against the *Popularphilosoph* Garve, the translator of Adam Smith and his teacher Adam Ferguson.[33] Agreeing with Garve that we need an incentive to set us into action, Kant suggested:

> The incentive also can obviously be none other than the law itself through the esteem it inspires (irrespective of what ends one may have and seek to attain through obedience to the law).[34]

Leaving aside the technical, but perhaps significant question as to whether it is the law that inspires us, or—as in the *Grundlegung*, the Representation of the Good that does so—the point is that duty has a causality.[35] It has no particular end, insists Kant, "but rather itself *occasions* a new end for the human will, that of striving with all one's power for the highest good possible on earth. . . . " Again, we hear echoes of the aesthetically enlightened active subject. But Kant continues to define this "highest good possible on earth" as "the law, as the formal aspect of the will," such that the social goal gets further definition, namely: a society governed by law.[36] While this goal was already laid out in the "Idea of a Cosmopolitan History," its present context suggests that it takes on the role of the "causality of freedom" which had been reserved to the noumenal ethical will. It begins to appear, in other words, that politics—or at least political forms—come to solve the systematic problem that haunted Kant since the first *Critique*. But not just any politics is at issue, as we see when we look at Kant's first proposition—the "race of devils"—which is perfectly compatible with the pre-1789 stance (as well as with Marxism).

Kant is aware, and far more aware than his successors and epigones, that morality and politics can neither be conflated nor divorced. But he does flirt, so to speak, with both temptations. At times it appears that one could translate the categorial imperative through the universalizability principle into a civil code; or that one could formulate concretely the version of that imperative that insists that others be treated always as ends, never as means. In that vein lie Kant's continual stress on publicity, the necessity of a free press, and the criterion that law must be such as a people could have given itself in full consciousness. Or, from the side of "politics first," one recalls Kant's frequent invocation of nature's causality or purposes, the image of people and nations learning their true interests like Hume's fighters in a china shop, and so on. The two possibilities are not of course unique to Kant, but run through the entire natural law tradition, even from its Roman origins. Kant's contribution is that he offers a political reconstruction of the problem.

Kant addresses the problem of politics in the first supplement to Perpetual Peace, called "On the Guarantee for Perpetual Peace." He recalls Rousseau's remark that only a race of angels is fit to live in a Republic, and replies:

> But precisely with these inclinations nature comes to the aid of the general will established on reason, which is revered even though impotent in practice. Thus it is only a question of a good organization of the state (which does lie in man's power), whereby the powers of each selfish inclination are so arranged in opposition that one moderates or destroys the ruinous effect of the other. The consequence for reason is the same as if none of them had existed, and man is forced to be a good citizen even if not a morally good person.
>
> The problem of organizing a state, however hard it may seem, can be solved even for a race of devils, if only they are intelligent. The problem is: Given a multitude of rational beings requiring universal laws for their preservation, but each of whom is secretely inclined to exempt himself from them, to establish a constitution in such a way that, although their private intentions conflict, they check each other, with the result that their public conduct is the same as if they had no such intentions.
>
> A problem like this must be capable of solution; it does not require that we know how to attain the moral improvement of man but only that we should know the mechanism of nature in order to use it on men, organizing the conflict of the hostile intentions present in a people in such a way that they must compel themselves to submit to coercive laws.[37]

There is much that one could say to this extraordinary passage where interest, which Kant rejects in ethics, becomes the basis of a politics which apparently abandons the goal of progressive enlightenment in favor of a formal peace. One could compare it with the arguments adduced recently by A. Hirschman's *The Passions and the Interests*, in an attempt to explain the success of legitimating capitalist expansion, because the passion which is most rational is that of the means-ends logic of the entrepreneur. One could see in it, with Sheldon Wolin, a precursor of bureaucratic administration sublimating politics, comparing it with Fourier's series of 810 passions or Lenin's ''post-office'' discipline. Or with Patrick Riley, one could say that this frees us from the temptation of the senses and at least makes morality more probable, if not a certainty.[38] For our purposes, however, the assertion is striking since it contradicts so much of Kant's own reasoning, including the first appendix to Perpetual Peace, which addresses the relation of morality and politics. Kant asserts there that politics ''is the art of using this mechanism for ruling men, while morality serves it as a limit condition.'' He continues:

> This implies only that political maxims must not be derived from the welfare or happiness which a single state expects from obedience to them, and thus not from the end which one of them proposes for itself. That is, they must not be deduced from volition as the supreme yet empirical principle of political wisdom, but rather from the pure concept of the duty of right, from the *ought* whose principle is given a priori by pure reason, regardless of what the physical consequences may be.[39]

One mighty try to bring these two assertions together through two types of explicitly Kantian arguments (or through a third, suggested by H. Lübbe, that the moral ought be understood decision-theoretically as a steering mechanism).[40] The first would invoke the critical implications of the regulative idea in order to unite the ethical and the political, as when Kant writes that we have an

> *idea* of reason, which nonetheless has undoubted practical reality: for it can oblige every legislator to frame his laws in such a way that they could have been produced by the united will of a whole nation, and to regard each subject, so far as he can claim citizenship, as if he had consented within the general will.[41]

Or, we could follow the second appendix to Perpetual Peace, which treats ''the Harmony which the Transcendental Concept of Public Right establishes between Morality and Politics.'' There Kant extends his argument to assert that

> All maxims which stand in need of publicity in order not to fail their end agree with politics and right combined.[42]

In this manner the original stance from ''What is Enlightenment?'' would be retained, and its political extension indicated.

Kant argues that the Republic is the *only* political form that is capable of instancing the harmony of morality and politics. In it are guaranteed the freedom of the members of society (as men), the dependence of all on a single common legislation (as subjects), and their equality (as citizens). Kant admits to problems as to the details of the republican form, for example in discussing the nature and rights of active and passive citizenship (which the French Revolution had maintained), concluding that "it is somewhat difficult to define the qualifications which entitle anyone to claim the status of being his own master."[43] But where the Marxicizing neo-Kantians took umbrage, and the Marxists pointed out that Kant's liberalism showed through in his replacement of the French *fraternité* with the idea of *Selbständigkeit*, and where our contemporaries are blinded by words and ignorant of history in writing off Kant for his rejection of democracy, we need to be more careful. The strength of the republican form, Kant insists, is that "*law* is the sole ruler, independent of all particular persons; it is the ultimate end of all public right, and the only condition in which each individual can be given his due *peremptorily*."[44] What is at issue in Kant's republicanism is the form of sovereignty, not the form of rule (which could be democratic, or Kant insists, monarchic, as when Friedrich the Great said that he was only the "first servant" of the state). The danger of democracy, avoided by the republic, is the collapsing of the law and its execution or—in the terms of the third *Critique*—the conflation of reflexive and predicative or constitutive judgment, to which we have already referred as a danger in the theory of history. The separation of the law, and by implication of the political, from the sphere of social freedom implies—as Rousseau had already known—the universality of the law which cannot, therefore, be distorted by being put to use for individual gain; and at the same time it implies the limitation of the sphere of the law as well. In this manner, Kant's demand that it be duty or virtue and not happiness or utility which governs lawmaking is justified. For the consequence of legal utilitarianism, as Kant and the tradition since Hobbes knew, is either that the ruler who tries to create happiness becomes a despot, or that the people, invoking the demand for happiness, become rebels—and in both cases, progress in enlightenment is shut off.

Is this republic of law simply the empty, formal *Rechtsstaat* of the liberals? The rejection of any utilitarianism leads to this appearance.[45] Kant's rejection of the right to revolt could lead to a similar conclusion. He asserts in "Theory and Practice," for example, that this "error"

> arises in part from the usual fallacy of allowing the principles of happiness to influence the judgement, wherever the principle of right is involved; and partly because these writers have assumed that the idea of an original contract (a basic postulate of reason) is something which must have taken place *in reality*. . . . Such writers thus believe that the people retains the right to abrogate the original contract at its own discretion if, in the opinion of the people, the contract has been severely violated.[46]

The former segment of the argument is familiar to us; the latter is more interesting since it plays implicitly on the third *Critique's* notion of reflexive as opposed to predicative judgment. A further passage from the same essay plays on another aspect of that third *Critique*:

> A *patriotic* attitude is one where everyone in the state, not excepting its head, regards the commonwealth as a maternal womb or the land as the paternal ground from which he himself sprang and which he must leave to his descendants as a treasured pledge. Each regards himself as authorized to protect the rights of the commonwealth by laws of the general will, but not to submit it to his personal use at his own absolute pleasure. This right of freedom belongs to each member of the commonwealth as a human being, insofar as each is a being capable of possessing rights.[47]

One might suggest that a passage such as this fits Kant into the tendency of German Idealism that verged toward a romantic politics; or that it frees him from the attack on a vague ''cosmopolitanism'' suggested by Meinecke, fitting him in fact into Meinecke's positively valued trend of historicism. More important is Vorländer's remark that ''patriotic'' was a code word at the time for support for the French Reovlution.[48] Following that hint, we note Kant's discussion, in paragraph 65 of the third *Critique*, on ''Things as natural goals are organized Beings,'' where he asserts in a footnote:

> Thus one has quite correctly used the term Organization in the case of a recently undertaken total transformation (*Umbildung*) of a great people to a state in order to describe the structure of the magistrates etc. and in fact the entire body of the state. For each member in such a whole must of course not be a mere means but also an end and insofar as it works together toward the possibility of the whole, it is in turn determined in its position and function by the idea of the whole.[49]

It is, in short, the categories of the third *Critique* which must be applied to understand Kant's argument—and it is here that the neo-Kantian defense and the Marxist counterattack miss the boat. And it is for this reason that Kant cannot be accused of being unable to reconcile his ethics and his politics.

F. The Problem of the Political

The return to Kant is motivated by the need to rethink and to rehabilitate that specificity of the political sphere, which today has been reduced either to the social (or economic) or to that of technical necessity. This entails on the one hand a modification of our notion of philosophy in the direction indicated by the third *Critique*; and on the other hand, it implies a return of the historical as that problematic junction of freedom and necessity. One might point to contemporary illustrations which put these questions back on the agenda, although that is not my task here. My argument is simply that Kant's ''vices''—the generality of his political framework, the unresolved duality of moral freedom and political necessity, and the self-imposed limits of the critical philosophy—turn out on analysis to be ''virtues'' today.

It is possible to read the succession of *Critiques* as driven by the attempt to overcome the originally postulated dualisim such that the writings on history would be a "fourth" *Critique* that finally offers a solution. I hope to have shown that unless such an argument integrates the reflections on politics, it will be inadequate. In his last published text, the "Conflict of the Faculties," Kant returned to his question, "How is history a priori possible?" and replied that "The answer is that it is possible if the prophet himself occasions and produces the events he predicts."[50] But the prophet is not the philosopher who knows the "true" direction of history or the will of Providence. On what basis, then, is action possible? Kant takes up this problem at the conclusion to the *Metaphysics of Morals*:

> If a person cannot prove that a thing exists, he may attempt to prove that it does not exist. If neither approach succeeds (as often happens), he may still ask whether it is *in his interest to assume* one or the other possibility as an hypothesis, either from theoretical or practical considerations. In other words, he may wish on the one hand simply to explain a certain phenomenon (as the astronomer, for example, may wish to explain the sporadic movements of the planets), or on the other, to achieve a certain end which may itself be either *pragmatic* (purely technical) or *moral* (i.e. an end which it is our duty to take as a maxim). It is, of course, self-evident that no one is duty bound to make an *assumption* that the end in question can be realized, since this would involve a purely theoretical and indeed problematic judgement; for no one can be obliged to accept a given belief. But we have a duty to act in accordance with the idea of such an end, even if there is not the slightest theoretical probability of its realization, provided that there is no means of demonstrating that it cannot be realized either.[51]

Such an end in which we have an interest, and which can be shown to be a practical duty, is the achievement of the Republic. The judgment that is involved here is reflexive, not constitutive; and thus, as Jaspers notes,[52] although we can conceive of war as helping to bring it about, we cannot *know* that war, or *this* war, will do so. The end does not justify the means any more than History will absolve us. Rather, the communicative nature of the judgment, which is a particular and public expression asking for confirmation and discussion, becomes central. And in this context, the insistence on formal lawfulness in the Republic can be understood as asserting the conditions of the possibility of such communication as being that of a reciprocity of positions and viewpoints, and thus more than the empty *Rechtsstaat*.

It is not the case, however, that on this view everything becomes political. Such an assertion would do violence to the careful analytical work of Kant. The distinction between the Republican and democratic forms is important in this context, for it sets limits to the domain of politics. The political sphere is that which permits enlightenment and its growth, but it is not, itself, the bearer of that enlightenment. This is why the replacement of the French Revolution's *fraternité* with Kant's *Selbständigkeit* is not simply the sign of a ''bourgeois'' prejudice. What is to be criticized, or at least elaborated today, is the nature of that *Selbständigkeit* in a contemporary context. To do so, however, entails political and not simply moral or sociological thinking. This is where Kant returns.

2

On the Transformation of Critique into Dialectic: Marx's Dilemma

It is well known that Marx titled or subtitled nearly everything he wrote with the label ''critique.'' His early evolution consisted in large part in differentiating and articulating the specificity of this critique from the impotence of mere ''criticism.'' His later development moved further, from critique to ''dialectic.'' This internal development of Marx's theorizing suggests an orientation for an understanding of the specificity and the limits of his contribution. Criticism is nay-saying; it stands *outside* of what it criticizes, asserting the validity of norms against facts (or of purportedly 'real' facts against pseudo-norms). Criticism appeals for reasonable action against unreasonable conditions, but it can offer no material base, no immanent analysis of why people would in fact act to change their conditions. The externality of the critic to the object criticized is the result of a presupposed dualism separating subject and object, theory and practice, and condemning criticism to remain impotent. Recognition of this difficulty drives Marx toward a dialectical account of the immanence of revolutionary possibility in a specific complex of material conditions. This dialectical account is rooted in the idea of a *real* proletariat as the object and product of past history and as the potential subject of a new history. But this *idea* of a real proletariat is in a position structurally isomorphic to the outside stance of the critic whom Marx rejected in developing his notion of ''critique'' before moving on to the fully developed dialectic. Attention must be concentrated on this middle stage of his development if one seeks to save his originality in the face of the two symmetrically one-sided interpretations defined by criticism and dialectics.

Critique can be interpreted at first as a political position. Criticism and dialectic have evident political corollaries in reformism and revolutionism. Criticism privileges genesis while dialectic articulates normative validity. Criticism introduces norms only from outside while dialectic admits material genesis as an external determinant. Neither is properly historical. Criticism is an indefinite process which can never end in a synthesis which would overcome its presupposed dualism; dialectic is the elimination of contradiction in one fell swoop putting an end to the history which only apparently engendered this possibility of political intervention. As politics, then, criticism tends to be reductionist while dialectics tends to be totalitarian. Critique, and the very specific conception of ideology which is its corollary, is democratic. The apparent paradox to which this oversimplified sketch (which will be fleshed out later) leads is that in capitalist society it is democracy, not revolution, that is revolutionary. Where revolution, like capitalism, pretends to offer solutions democracy poses problems. Democracy accepts the challenge of immanent historicality which, as Marx came to realize, capitalism introduces only to occlude it by its own immanent functioning—or by producing the reformist or revolutionary options as its inverse identical. When he fell back to criticism as a theory *for* revolution, as when he leaped forward to dialectics as a theory *of* revolution, Marx closed to himself the political dimension which only the critique theory could open up. At the same time, and for the same theoretical reason, he misunderstood the *political* question carried by democratic modern societies.

Marx's formulation of a critique theory came at the close of the internal theoretical development of German Idealism, after Hegel. Historians of philosophy, conveniently ignoring history, usually suggest that the legacy of Hegel's synthesis was divided among "left" and "right" followers whose inheritance was quickly spent as they fell back into practical insignificance. Debunking such unhistorical history is less difficult than understanding its immanent illogic. German Idealism could be integrated into the social and political history of Germany itself, along the lines suggested by the conservative Prussian Meinecke. The strands of philosophical reflection could be traced as they pass from the professional philosophers to historians of the temper of a Droysen or Ranke. In the sphere of administrative and political reform, the efforts of the German Liberals which flowered before 1848 and withered after its failure make an extraordinary tale. Among the philosophers themselves, the labels "left" and "right" conceal as much as they reveal. F. J. Stahl, the archtheorist of reaction, campaigned just as vigorously against Hegel as he did against Hegel's historicist opponents, von Haller and Savigny. The "right" Hegelians were far more progressive (and effective) in their reformist political practice, using Hegel's defense of such civil freedoms as the press, and developing a theory of the functioning of political parties that might avoid the archaic recourse to pre-modern "corporations" in Hegel's otherwise exceptionally modern understanding of civil society and its relation to the political sphere. In short, the labels tend to blur rather than to focus.[1] The Marxian critique theory has to be understood as theory, not as a simple political device.

The philosophical distinction between the two groupings of Hegelians in the early 1840s proves useful in one specific instance. It is paradoxical at first glance that the "left" Hegelians concentrated their fire on the philosophy of religion, where the "right" Hegelians defended religious orthodoxy while intervening in a progressive reformist manner in the sphere of politics. (It is this distinction of the objects of criticism that permits one to put Kierkegaard among the group of "left" Hegelians with Marx, however different their further developments.) The attack by the left began in 1836, with the publication of D. F. Strauss's historical-philological demonstration that the historical Jesus could not in fact have existed. Hegel's theory had required the existence of this historical Jesus not only to demonstrate the veracity of the Christian-Protestant religion, but more important as a keystone to the demonstration of the historical actuality of his objective idealist system as a whole. Jesus' life is the foremost concrete demonstration of the reality of the Idea as the unity of the universal and the particular. If the real Jesus is only a myth, as Strauss suggested, might not the entire Hegelian System be of the same imaginary fabric? The critique of religion by the left-Hegelians was thus an attack on the basis of Hegelianism's claim to have united particularity and universality, genesis and validity, in a theory which proved the rationality of the real and the reality of the rational. This critique was philosophically more radical than the criticisms and adjustments which the dialectical "right" Hegelians were proposing in the political domain. The left-Hegelians put into question the (dialectical) premise of the system as such, whereas the right sought only to reform by patching up errors and filling lacunae. Further, the left's critique pointed to social consequences, since the strength and endurance of the "myth" of Jesus' existence posed the question of the kind of society that could generate and preserve such a myth-making capacity. (Here, of course, Kierkegaard appears to be the exception among the left-Hegelians; but the context of their criticism suggests why Kierkegaard's religiosity and existential leap necessarily entailed for their elaboration a social criticism as well.) The critique of philosophy led the left-Hegelians to society, whereas the dialectical criticism of politics from the right-Hegelians remained caught in its own systemic presuppositions.

Marx was an active participant in the left-Hegelian movement in the years when he was writing his doctoral dissertation. It appears that he even (anonymously) co-authored with Bruno Bauer a satirical broadside against the Hegelian philosophy of religion. More important, however, he came to understand and define his philosophical task in the terms of a critique. The concept had not been thematized as such by the left-Hegelians. Marx himself came only gradually, and never explicitly, to recognize its central role. He spoke of the need "to make philosophy worldly and to make the world philosophical," and grappled with this task in his doctoral dissertation and in the preparatory notes for it. There was nothing particularly original in this general project. The poet Heinrich Heine had suggested something similar a decade previously when he pointed out that Hegel's identification of the rational and the actual could be taken as the statement of an imperative to be accomplished rather than, as is usually done, as the benediction of the established order. In the late 1830s, before Marx's own formulation, the independent Polish Hegelian (usually associated with the "right" group), August Cieszkowski, had formulated the same program more systematically in his *Prolegomena zur Historiosophie*. The "Socialist" Moses Hess had proposed the same task in his *Die europäische Triarchie*. The uniqueness of Marx's achievement could be credited to the rigor with which he held to the demands of critique while engaged in practical journalism for the *Rheinische Zeitung* after the reactionary policies of Friedrich William IV had made his hopes for a teaching career impossible. When his friends reacted to the new monarchical reaction by upping the ideal ante, increasing the vigor of their normative criticism, Marx took to blue-penciling their contributions and demanding factual documentation for their contentions. By the time of his move to Paris, Marx had broken with the friends of his past in order to remain true to what had been their common project.[2]

The left-Hegelian critique of religion led to social analysis by the mediation of the concept of ideology. Today, ideology has come to be somewhat of a commonplace or conceptual sponge. Marx's own usage was not always consistent either. For example, the two books he and Engels wrote in 1845 and 1846 in order to break with their philosophical past (*The Holy Family* and *The German Ideology* tend to offer a rather straightforward notion of ideology as simply the misguided belief in the independence of and power of ideas. This definition defines also the form adapted by the criticism of ideology. Criticism of ideology consists simply in showing the material origin of these ideas, and consequently their normative impotence and deceptiveness when they are taken in isolation from their material genesis. Ideology, in this sense, can be defined as the separation of genesis from validity (or vice-versa) and the absolutization of the claim of one or the other side. A second use of the concept lies in the same vein, although it is a bit more subtle. This is the recursive use of the criticism of ideology which is operative in the 1843 "Introduction to a Critique of Hegel's *Philosophy of Right*" where the proletariat is discovered for the first time on the basis of a triple or recursive criticism of ideology. First, Marx accepts a criticism of religion that shows its social basis; this, he says, is the "premise of all critique."[3] From this first reduction to material foundations, a second criticism, or "irreligious critique," is proposed; its premise is that "man makes religion, religion does not make man." The criticism must be applied once again, since separation is still present because Marx recognizes that "man" is not some abstract being "squatting outside the world," but is a social agent and product. Hence, this third criticism opens up the analysis of the material social world, where the potential unity of subject and object, genesis and validity, is discovered in the proletariat.

Whether it is applied simply or recursively, the reductive criticism of ideology is not sufficient. It is a necessary first step, but only a first step. If it is absolutized as a universal method, the result is a relativism which preserves and fixes the gap between genesis and validity as unbridgeable, since every claim to normative validity can be shown to have its genesis in specific social conditions, which can then, recursively, be criticized as illegitimately claiming to have absolute value. This kind of ideology criticism is an unending quest. The other possible form of criticism is its identical opposite. It suggests that there will come a time when the ideal and the real will coincide, when Hegel-like, the real will be the rational and the rational will be the real. Marx's proletarian revolution moves toward this latter solution, which represents the transformation of criticism into a dialectic. This transformation leaves out the intermediary step, the theory of critique itself as a specific mode of philosophical or political analysis that satisfies the Marxian desire to avoid the contemplative idealism of "bourgeois" theory while being capable of understanding the possibility of radically changing society by political intervention. The key to such a project lies first in the possibilities inherent in the notion of ideology itself, and then in the application of these possibilities by Marx to the problems of the State, History and Revolution.

A. Ideology: The Reductionist View

The Feuerbachian criticism of ideology was merely a further development of pre-Kantian Enlightenment philosophies applied to the context dominated by Hegelianism. That religion has a material foundation in the social world was no theoretical novelty. One need only think of Voltaire, Diderot, D'Alembert, or even the British Empiricists. The pre-1789 criticism of religion was cloaked in the names of Science and Humanity. (In this sense, it was a "bourgeois" criticism, for reasons that will be explained in the next section.) Religion had to be explained *away* so that unity could be restored, division eliminated. Its prejudices were said to prevent the development of the scientific rationality and domination of nature which would free mankind and order its relations rationally. The goal was to eliminate the mysterious Beyond which clouded people's vision, preventing them from seeing clearly what was before their eyes. The world was matter, to be ordered and manipulated according to human rational purpose and not blindly following some divine plan which escaped human comprehension. Religion was to be combatted because it brought into the social world a transcedent and external principle of order which hid from men and women their actual social conditions. By stressing otherworldly virtue at the expense of present utility, religion was seen to be a conservative force against human betterment. Religion had to be replaced by the domination of the Rational over a world which it created and understood. In a more naively cynical and social-critical version, this criticism went further to argue that religion was foisted off on the basically good people by those who wanted to rule over them. In the first case, the criticism of religion provided alternative explanations in scientific form for the phenomena religion purported to explain; in the second case, the criticism of religion as the ideology of a ruling class demonstrated the material interests that stood to profit from religion's function as a mechanism of social control.

Marx of course wanted to go beyond the Enlightenment materialist criticism of religion. The 1843 essay, "On the Jewish Question," argues that it is not sufficient to achieve religious, or even mere "political," emancipation: such freedom leaves untouched the root material causes of the religious projection. Marx criticizes Feuerbach's neglect of the social-political dimension, and his naive psychological belief that once we recognize that it is we who created God, not he who creates us, we will take back those creative powers which we have alienated in the religious projection. The fourth of the "Theses on Feuerbach" (1845) suggests that once we have recognized that the secular family is the secret of the Holy Family, we have still the need to destroy the secular family as well. A similar argument is made concerning the state, and could be extended and generalized for all cultural and institutional structures. Logically, the argument claims that the condition of particularity in which each individual lives generates the projection of a universal or community which then functions to give normative meaning and unity to the life of the particular individual. This can be done either by taking genesis as normative, e.g., by absolutizing the familial relations so that God is the paternal authority; or an outside norm can be invoked and accepted as giving meaning e.g., to familial relations that are unsatisfactory. The criticism points out that this giving of meaning is a mystification, since in fact nothing other than the psychological consciousness of the individual is changed. The practical proposal is to change the cultural and institutional setting itself. But this practice is not yet grounded in anything but an ideal Appeal to Reason. More than criticism of ideology is necessary for the formulation of a politics.

This form of ideology criticism paradoxically does too little and too much. It argues that the religious and ideological norms are necessarily generated from the material conditions. If that were strictly speaking, i.e., causally the case, however, it would not be possible to change the material conditions: either all of us are caught up in the mystification, and in that case we could not even know that it is a mystification; or, some of us are mystified in one way, some in another, depending on our specific material conditions; but in this latter case, there is still no sense in calling for change since whatever we do is already inscribed in the material conditions, to which all the forms are relative. Further, the mystification is said to cover over the very reality which generated it. The reality itself is assumed to be an irrational or "false" one insofar as its divided structure leads people to project their imaginations and creative powers onto an inexistent Thing whose norms turn against them, standing between them in their relations to others and to the world, and imposing values and morals on them. This completes the paradox: the mystifying normative projections are generated necessarily and are the expression of a given reality; in turn, however, they are said to cover over that reality, to falsify our perception of it; and, finally, the generative reality itself is said to be an irrational one. Further specification is clearly necessary.

One way of avoiding the paradox is suggested by the *base/superstructure model of explanation*. This is ultimately a reductionist proposal, grounded on a materialism which suggests that ideas or norms can be reduced to, and explained by, the material conditions which generated them. In the first part of *The German Ideology*, Marx and Engels suggest that philosophical problems must be reduced to empirical facts. The reason for this is that:

> As individuals externalize their lives, so are they. What they are thus falls together with their production, both with *what* they produce as well as with *how* they produce. Therefore, what individuals are depends on the material conditions of their production.

This assertion is not simply reductivist, as in the caricatural Marxism of "diamat." The productive *base* of society includes everything from the raw materials available to it, the machines it has invented, the products it produces, *as well as* the social relation among the producing people themselves (The "as well as" implies the rejection of a simple productivist materialism.) This productive base determines the *superstructure*, which consists of the ideas, institutions, politics, art, religion, and all other intersubjective forms of social relations. Insofar as the superstructure depends on the base, it is a dependent variable; its history is not its own but depends on the evolution of the base for its own development. The difficulty in applying the model will emerge from the fact that "social relations" are described as part of the complex productive base as well as being forms of the dependent superstructures.

Again, this attempted materialist explanation by reduction to the material base is not original to Marx. Not only were there philosophical precedents; the position had also been anticipated by bourgeois historians. One of the most influential of them, Guizot, had written in his *Essais sur l'histoire de France* (1821) that "the first question for the historian is . . . the *mode of life of men*," and that therefore "it would be wiser, *first* to study *the society itself*, in order then to know and to understand its political institutions."[4] Guizot, who was later to expel Marx from France in his capacity as a minister, was certainly not the first or most radical proponent of the role of material conditions on social life. And his most important direct successor was not Marx but Tocqueville, who followed out Guizot's stress on the ambiguous political role of the new middle classes. As for the source of the reduction in Marx, one might recall that Hegel had cited Aristotle in the introduction to his *Science of Logic* to the effect that philosophical reflection can only emerge on the basis of a pre-given economic development. Economic determinism cannot be taken as Marx's fundamental theoretical innovation. If his theory lends itself to a determinist reading, this possibility must also be explained by an attempt to reconstruct Marx's specific project.

Marx attempts to ground this materialist explanation-by-reduction in the theory of critique. The result is at first a more impoverished, reductionist antitheory. The criticism which searches continually for a genetic mediation of the normative or superstructural institutions recursively pushes the theory further back, beneath the appearances toward their ultimate ground. This ground is finally the production and reproduction of the means of human social existence. Roman society may appear to be regulated by its highly evolved legal system; the Middle Ages in Western Europe may appear dominated by the Universal Church—in fact, however, neither laws nor religion can be eaten! Production of the means of physical existence appears to be the ultimate basis (or real genetic cause) of all the other social institutions. In this sense, the base determines the superstructure, which is generated by the unresolved division of social relations whose unity it normatively hypostatizes.

This reductionist explanation flies in the face of Marx's earlier definition of the base as including ''as well'' the relations of production. Production is not simply the activity of a single individual, using a tool, in the process of changing nature. That picture is based on a representation built from the model of an abstract, monological subject working on an inert, passive nature eternally foreign to it. Production as human, however, entails the institutional dimension of social interaction as well. This means that the productive base must itself be analyzed in its complexity. Marx notes in volume three of *Capital* that ''on the same economic base . . . innumerable different empirical conditions—natural conditions, racial relations, external historical influences, etc.—can produce an infinite number of variations and gradations in the form of appearance, which can only be understood by the analysis of these given empirical conditions.'' Reacting to the simple economic reductionism of many Marxists after Marx's death, Engels's well-known letters to Bloch, Schmidt, and Starkenburg[5] recognized the need to modify the strict determinist thesis; Engels insisted, rather, that the economic base is determinant only ''in the last instance.'' Engels's modification, however, will be seen to be only cosmetic. The difficulty must be grasped at the theoretical, not simply the empirical, level.

Before turning to the *dialectical* critique of superstructural phenomena, it should be noted that the reductionist usage of the base/superstructure relation did become dominant within the official tradition of Marxism. In the Second International, under the influence of nineteenth-century progress in science and technology, this doctrine received a biological and physico-chemical complement which was supposed to anchor the scientific necessity of socialism in the materialist sense. For example, the orthodox Marxist Plekhanov, called the ''philosopher'' of the Second International, attempted to show that Marx's theory could be understood on the basis of a neo-Lamarkian version of evolution theory, based on ''matter itself having a soul.'' While such speculations which can be multiplied can hardly be grounded in Marx, they do find some legitimation in chapters of Engels's *Anti-Dühring* (which Marx had read and approved) as well as in Engels's posthumous *Dialectics of Nature*. Statistics from the lending libraries set up by the nineteenth-century German Social Democrats show that this kind of scientific literature was extremely popular with the working classes.[6]

The reductionist criticism has become a common device of political rhetoric today. One analyzes the ideas of one's opponent, shows their compatability or functionality with a specific material base, points out that the material structure of production serves one group against another, and then, on the base of the justice or morality of one's own cause, condemns the ideas as ideological. For example, the Bolshevik leader Bukharin's *The Economic Theory of the Leisure Class* shows the parallels between the material life-situation of the owning class and the economic theory of marginalism: they are consumers but not producers, individualist because of their independence from production, ahistorical and fearing the future because they are satisfied with the status quo, turned inward to their own psychic problems owing to their excess of leisure time, etc. From this follow the psychologistic theses of marginalist economics. While the parallels are suggestive, one can hardly be satisfied with this "Marxian" criticism. In *Capital*, Marx did not refute the theories of Smith, Ricardo, and the classical economists by demonstrating their inherent capitalist bias and then *opting* for the proletariat. *Capital* is a critique theory; it analyzes other theories with regard to the reality they attempt to describe, not as simple "superstructures" to be thought away or to become the object of polemic. Functionalist reductionism cannot provide the basis for a political theory that would surpass the existing contradictions from which it nonetheless arises. The reasons for its attractiveness must be explained before an alternative approach can be proposed.

The base/superstructure reduction is based on an implicit assumption whose theoretical and political consequences make praxis impossible. It supposes the existence of an absolute standpoint removed from and outside of the social conditions which are judged. To call something ideological, or to reduce it to its material or functional preconditions, I must stand outside the process. More: I must know the process in its totality past, present, and future. The reduction supposes a kind of god's eye view of a static world. From that transcendent position, I see a series of interacting points which I can then chart on a graph, scientifically. The Hegelian dialectic was developed precisely as a rejection of such a position as is clear, for example, in the introduction to the *Phenomenology*, where the question of the standpoint of the philosopher, and his critical "measure," is explained. There is no standpoint outside the world; and to think that I could step outside supposes that social life is but soulless atoms in random movement. Moreoever, the belief that such a standpoint exists is dangerous insofar as one group—scientists, technocrats, the Party—thinks that it possesses the truth about the others. This provides a justification for what is nothing other than a totalitarian dictatorship! This illusion of mastery, which preserves the apparent autonomy of the judging subject, is deeply rooted in the Western tradition at least since Descartes's insistence on the subject or "master and possessor" of nature.

The base/superstructure reduction has a tempting aura of common sense about it; it fits well with the scientific mentality. Despite their awareness of its problems, Marx and Engels often fall back on it. For example, the passage cited a moment ago from volume 3 of *Capital* as a demonstration of Marx's flexibility is preceded by the following assertion:

> *It is always the immediate relation of the owner of the conditions of production to the immediate producers*—a relation whose specific form always corresponds naturally *to a specific stage of development of the mode and manner of labor and to the social productive forces—in which we find the deepest secret, the hidden basis of the entire social construc-*

> *tion*, and thus also of the political form of the relations of sovereignty and subservience, in short, the specific form of the state.

In the case of Engels, even when he modifies his strict determinism or determinism "in the last instance," he still suggests that *on the average*, in terms of statistical correlations, the priority of the economic can be established. Such an argument, however, operates from the standpoint of inductive science, not at all as a dialectical critique. What must be explained is why even Marx could think that the base/superstructure reduction provided an adequate explanatory schema. The concern to explain "the specific form of the state" as opposed to the attempt to look at the "empirical" variability of the relations of production may be the locus of the difficulty. Marx's problem is the translation of his "anatomy of civil society" into a political theory.

B. Ideology and Critique

The third "Thesis of Feuerbach" indicates explicitly what Marx sees as the revolutionary thrust of his theory, and its difference from his Enlightenment predecessors; it also points to a more refined theory of superstructures.

> The materialist doctrine of the modifying influence of the change in conditions and education forgets that the conditions are changed by men, and that the educator himself must be educated. It is thus forced to divide society into two parts, one of which rises above the society. The coincidence of the changing of conditions and of human activity or self-transformation can only be conceived and understood rationally as *revolutionary practice*.

The external or transcendent observer is rejected; there is no "truth" about society which is absolutely separate from its object, no norm separated from the genetic base. If the educator or critic claims to tell people that, and why, they have been blind to their own life-conditions, this simply perpetuates the division of society (consecrated in the division of manual and mental labor). If the knowledge which the "ignorant" must acquire depends on the educator/critics, then it itself is ideological in a specific sense that has not yet been defined. Separated from society, possessed by the educator/critics, this truth becomes false because no longer involved in the actual life conditions of society. "The educator must himself be educated." If that education is generated by material conditions, then the educators have simply the best vision of those caught in the cave. If their norms come from elsewhere, from their teachers, where did the teachers acquire their wisdom? The point is that either the ideas of the educator/critics are so far abstracted from reality as to be false and ideological; or, if derived from reality, these ideas must be more than a simple mimetic reflection of it. Marx suggests that it is "revolutionary practice," a learning that arises from an *activity* which both changes the world and the person acting on the world, that accounts for the knowledge of the world.

The notion of "revolutionary practice" is a theoretical concept with immediate political importance. In *The German Ideology*, for example, Marx and Engels write:

> Both for the production on a mass scale of this communist consciousness, and for the success of the cause itself, the alteration of men on a mass scale is necessary, and alteration which can only take place in a practical movement, a *revolution*. This revolution is necessary, therefore, not only because the *ruling* class cannot be overthrown in any other way, but also because the class *overthrowing* it can only succeed in ridding itself of all the muck of ages and become fitted to found society anew in a revolution.

Revolution is necessary to change *people*, not just power relations or institutions. The revolutionary class is not *immediately*, by virtue of its relation to the means of production, by its total alienation, or by any other *actual* property, able to make the revolution. *It is in acting that it learns*, becomes capable of "founding society anew" because it has thrown off the "muck of ages." This implies that the reductionist base/superstructure model is not adequate either to explain the given social ideology or to account for the process of social change. The proletariat is not outside of, or transcendent to, the historical present. The knowledge which makes it a revolutionary class is not the technical, instrumental knowledge produced in and by the labor process; it is an institutional or communicative knowledge, critical and self-critical, genetic and normative, at once.

Praxis is often misunderstood as an instrumental action of a subject on an object, just as knowledge is conceived in terms of this dualistic paradigm. Hegel's Kant-critique, and Marx's theory of a material synthesis by labor (as presented by Habermas[7]) argue against this apparent common-sense view. The subject is never free of involvement with and determination by the material world; and that world, in turn, affects the subject only because human labor has transformed it and rendered it meaningful. The upshot of such an analysis is that *ideology can be defined as that historical procedure by which the dualism of subject and object, of genesis and validity, is introduced and uncritically made the principle of a unifying analysis*. An ideological perspective makes the epistemological presupposition that there is a truth "out there," possessed or possessible by a subject separate from it and unaffected by the process by which it is known; material reality is treated as a self-subsistent object, a static thing which can be known in and for itself. Empiricism would be an extreme example of such an ideological position. A subject is supposed to receive immediate impressions from the world out there, combining them to reconstruct an accurate picture or reflection of what really is there. This ignores not only the interaction between subject and object, which affects both; it supposes that there is such a thing as a "fact," a discrete thing which can be known. But all "facts" are contextual, and derive their sense only within the totality in which they exist. The green pieces of paper (not to speak of the tinny alloys) that we exchange for commodities are not "in themselves" and immediately money; they have a value only in a specific context. A machine is simply a machine; only in certain social conditions does it become a means for the production of profit. The two sides of the reductionist ideology must be put back into a total context. Both the position which separates ideas from their material base, and the view that there is a direct and immediate correspondence between base and superstructure, operate in terms of the dualism—the one privileges the subjective while the other opts for the objective side. Neither suffices.

This epistemological definition of ideology was already contained in Hegel, although the term itself was not used. In the *Phenomenology*, Hegel attempted to reconstruct the path of knowledge. Starting from knowledge of what seems to be most full, rich, and immediate—the thing now before me—he demonstrates that it is in fact the poorest, most impoverished, and least determinate thing: what is immediately before me is a "this," which has as its properties only a "here" and a "now"; it is nothing but an empty universal (since anything and everything is a "here" and a "now"), or a senseless pointing. It only becomes more determined when I take it in its context, develop and critique its sources; and when I myself grow beyond the status of a mere abstract perceiving subject. In this sense, Karl Korsch's formulation of the notion of ideology in *Marxism and Philosophy* is adequate to the meaning of both Marx and, by implication, Hegel: *ideological thought takes the part for the whole*. It thereby rules out any change, and is fundamentally ahistorical. Further, it is an *inverted* consciousness insofar as it absolutizes and treats as independent that which can only be understood within the context of the total social perspective. At the same time, it makes the subject into a transcendent *spectator*, gazing at a process which it can at best reflect but never change. The world becomes a spectacle of discrete acts. *This powerlessness of the subject is the further mark of an ideology*. When applied to the example of marginalist economic theory already referred to, the implication is that its error is the separation of one aspect of social behavior, particular to one class perhaps, from the total social process, and then the claim that this one aspect explains the unity of the whole. In the same sense, *Capital* can claim to break with the ideological attitude of the bourgeois economists insofar as it is not the theory of a partial aspect of social relations—the economic—but is a social theory which takes into account the impact of *all* aspects of social production and reproduction in a unity which remains unstable because it is based on an unbridgeable division. In this way, *Capital* avoids the objectivist ideology of the powerless subject *and* the inverse identical form which postulates an all-powerful subject whose task or function is to ensure the social unity. This redefinition implies, as we shall see in more detail, that it is not the fact of a split between subject and object alone that constitutes an ideology. The crucial point is that ideology consecrates that division while at the same time privileging one or the other pole as guaranteeing the social unity. It is here that Hegel becomes an ideologue in spite of himself, hypostatizing a unity whose impossibility is demonstrated by his own categories. And it is here that the "end-of-ideology" shows itself to be yet another ideology, for it too hypostatizes a unity.[8]

Although the formal, epistemological grounds for a discovery and critique of ideology were present in Hegel, it is only with Marx that the notion of ideology—and more generally, the theory of superstructures—emerges as a central thematic. Hegel's theoretical concern was that of a logical or categorical reconstruction of the world. He could reflect on the past, and the way the past was integrated into the present; he could reflect on the active role of the subject, the functioning of institutions, and the structure of history; what he could *not* do, however, was to account for the *constitution* of the New. The Hegelian system is round, white, and glistening like a perfect sphere, too good to be true. By contrast, Marx's is rough, shadowy, and open to its horizon: it is a theory of creation. This means that for Marx *the present is a problem*, in Lukacs's pregnant phrase, Marxism is a theory of "the present as History." Theory's concern is not the traditional contemplative transcendental stance which assumes that I know and then asks how in fact I go about knowing; the world itself becomes a problem, nothing can be taken for granted, questions not answers further the investigation. "Revolutionary practice" is not science, not a subject with a plan acting on an object out there; it begins when the boundaries of the taken-for-granted world are shaken, and the subject takes on the responsibility for constituting its world. But it does not end with the individual or "class" subject.

That Marx *discovered* the problematic of ideology is doubly significant. The difference of appearance and reality is a leitmotif through the history of philosophy. If this were the grounds of Marx's theory of ideology, then his contribution would at best have been the argument for the economic reductionist base/superstructure model. In one sense, of course, this is precisely what he did do; and it is in this sense that his theory remains still within the bounds of philosophy as classically conceived. But classical philosophy was shaken by Kant—particularly by the emergence of the Historical and the Political as problematic—and the classical world is not that of capitalism. The uniqueness of capitalist civil society is that it conflates the conditions of genesis and validity, creating a new conception of individuality freed from the bonds of tradition. It does this by institutionalizing change, and through the institution of the social division of labor as justified *immanently* by its ability to deliver the goods, instead of the more familiar legitimation from a transcendent norm, as in traditional societies. This *historically new* stage of human history makes possible for the first time the problematic of ideology. Capitalism is an immanent unity-in-difference whose institutional unity is generated by its economic difference. Ideology is not simply located in the subject(s), who may err in their perception of reality because of their social situation, their past training, their religious beliefs, etc. Ideology, rather, *is inscribed in the structure of the capitalist world*. Marx's discovery of its problematic is not the formulation of simply another critical category which helps in the quest to pierce the veil that conceals the structures of the ''really real'' in order then to change them; it is ideology itself which *is* the structure of capitalism.

The specificity of ideology to the capitalist phase of human history explains why religion is *not* the model to be used in explaining its structure. Religion is the general form by which a community assures itself of its identity or unity by positing a *transcendent* force or norm which serves to guarantee the cohesion of the members and the consistency of their world views. Religion functions as a way of avoiding (or controlling) the risk of change, eliminating the historical character of society, absolving the individual of personal responsiblity by prescribing rites, forms of interpersonal relations, and the relation to nature. Ethnographic data illustrate this functioning: religion *creates from outside* the world in which the religious community then lives. Capitalism, however, is characterized by precisely the opposite structure; it is, and knows itself as, a changing, historical society in which individual responsibility is continually engaged. In capitalism Nature is not fixed and charged with symbolic significance; it is ''objective'' matter, to be scientifically understood and technologically changed according to individual plan. Capitalism is a peculiar *form*; it is progress, production, consumption; an endless process in which the ''emancipated'' but empty and abstract individual is caught. In this sense, the functional nature of religion within the pre-capitalist community, where it served as a principle of order and meaning, is dissolved in capitalism. Religion is replaced by ideology, whose structure is radically different: internal legitimation replaces the reference to a transcendent origin.

Ideology's specificity to capitalism also serves to explain *partially* why the base/superstructure model of reductionist explanation tempted Marx. Pre-capitalist (not to speak of primitive) societies were articulated into a functioning, hierarchical whole in which all activities in all life-spheres received their meaning from the transcendent force. There was no difference between the sphere of the economic and that of religion, politics, or culture; planting and chanting, pottery and art, the social division of labor and the plan for production took the constancy that Mauss called a ''total social fact.'' That we can look backward and analyze the ''economic'' form, or the ''political'' structures of a pre-capitalist society does not mean that they were *lived* separately by the people themselves. Capitalism at once separates these life-spheres and suffuses them with a common, internal meaning. Each is separate, different; yet each shares the historical form and immanent meaning; and each tries to account for the unity of the whole. A first form of ideology arises here insofar as these different spheres think of themselves as independent, separate from the total context. The lawyer thinks of the law, as the philosopher thinks of ideas, as if the separation were really water-tight. The particular life-sphere is treated as if it were universal, with the result that the whole that is the unity of all of these spheres appears accidental and crises cannot be accounted for save as accidents. From this observation, the critique methodology suggests the search for that structuring force which ties together the apparently discrete parts *from within*. From within, because capitalism's uniqueness is that it does away with the transcendent viewpoint. As a social form divided into seemingly independent spheres of activity, capitalism's inner bond and determining force can only be the material production and reproduction of its physical existence. The economic or capitalist civil society is dominant because there is no transcendent sense or meaning for the whole; everything human and everything natural are but grist for the system which generates its own lawful forms and norms. The economic is dominant; not simply physically but as the only available unitary meaning of life!

The critique of ideology thus permits a critical reappropriation of the reductionist base/superstructure model. Because of the coincidence of the productive and the symbolic or normative dimension of social life in capitalist civil society, the mode of production does exercise a dominant role. However, it would be ideological—taking the part for the whole—*to generalize this model to the past or the future*. The danger—into which Marx himself, as well as most of his successors fell—is to neglect or reduce the role of the symbolic or normative dimension; in other words, to forget the educative, constitutive role of "revolutionary praxis." The tendency toward a productivist determinism, to which we have already pointed, and to which we will be forced to return, results from this neglect. This *partial* explanation of the dominance of the reductionist base/superstructural model explains why Marx thought that *Capital*, subtitled a "Critique of Political Economy," could be a theory of revolution.

On the most immediate level, ideology appears in the categories of capitalist political economy insofar as the particular appearance is taken for the reality. The method of criticism opens up and defetishizes its objects. *Capital* begins with a highly abstract analysis of the structure of the commodity, whose "fetishism" it denounces. The first error of the political economists is to start from an abstract conception of human nature and its needs. The contribution of the Marxian critique was to show that humans are both social and historical beings. Notions of "human nature" as essentially acquisitive, or having an "instinct to truck and barter" (Smith), neglect the changing social and historical context in which a society and individuals exist and reproduce themselves. Not only does such an approach project what exists in the present onto the past and into the future; it falsifies what is central to capitalist social relations, their dynamic and historically changing character. The result is ideological in a double sense. The system of values and motivations developed for the first time under capitalism is made universal, serving as a model and a justification of the present system. Thus, Robinson Crusoe, shipwrecked on his island, functions and flourishes like a typical English small shopkeeper, keeping account books, treating his time as if it were money, as if there were one and only one way of living, alone or in society. On a second level, the immediacy of political economic categories is ideological in that it prevents a correct understanding of capitalism itself! If the treatment of humans as abstract individuals with fixed drives and motivations is the image which capitalist society has of itself, capitalist reality denies its own self-image.

Changed need structures, the declining role of religion and of the family, new conceptions of law, crime and punishment as well as schools and education, the rise of nationalism and ethnic ties as well as changing relations among primary and secondary socialization processes—the list of changes that have occurred makes it impossible to cling to a fixed notion of human nature. "All that is solid melts into air," proclaims *The Communist Manifesto*.

The the place of ideology in theories of capitalist economics is explained by the structure of capitalism which we have discussed. It is not sufficient simply to historicize the economic categories. Because rent on property preceded industrial capitalist profits, it is not therefore a more central category today. The order of genesis does not determine that of validity. Rent on land was essential to capitalism at its origins; but in the fully constituted capitalist system, its role is comparatively minor, and Marx treats it only late in the systematic theory of *Capital*. A theory of economics must explain the structure of the totality of capitalist relations. But the paradox which makes ideology inherent in any descriptive theory of capitalism is that, since capitalism is essentially a historical system based on continually expanding production, no such total perspective is possible. To repeat, this is why Marx's *Capital* is a *critique* of political economy.[9]

Capitalist social relations *create* the individual as an isolated particular. Taking account of this, what Marx calls "vulgar economics" attempts to elaborate a theory of capitalist social relations from the standpoint of this individual. Its model, as noted, is the mentality of the English small shopkeeper. Profit, for example, appears to be the result of buying cheaply and selling dearly. Crises are the result of bad judgments by individual capitalists, who let their stocks grow too high, or who produce more than the market will bear, or who pay their laborers too dearly. The decisions of the customer are the "law" which determines the distribution of products and profits. However detailed its attempts, vulgar economics is doomed to failure precisely because of its particularist capitalist starting point. The social totality becomes simply the more or less accidental sum of individual actions whose connection cannot be elaborated. This is the "anarchy" of capitalist production as a whole, which contrasts so sharply with the calculations of the individual capitalist who runs the firm with the greatest of rationalizing efforts. Because capitalism is a peculiar kind of social whole in which each individual looks out for her own interests, and makes economic decisions from the standpoint of these particular concerns, its "laws" can only have the ad hoc status of a theory vainly chasing its tail. Since its nature is continual expansion, capitalism is *not* a smoothly functioning fixed totality. Failure to recognize this leads vulgar economics to postulate its particularistic and ultimately ad hoc knowledge in the form of universal laws. This, of course, is nothing but the false universalization of a given social stance that constitutes an ideology.

Capitalism's peculiarity is rooted in the objective division of labor; each social sphere, each sector, each profession strives to account for the totality. But each is locked into the laws and methodology which generates its particularity, and which it universalizes in its explanations. Yet the totality is not the sum of the separated parts, such that a self-critical particularism could come to grasp it or an outside observer sum it up. Indeed, as I have stressed because of capitalism's historical nature, the *totality does not in fact exist!* From this structural feature, we can define the fundamental forms of capitalist ideology, which in each case are based on the abusive universalization of a particular phenomenon.

In its most general form, capitalist ideology functions in terms of what Lukács analyzes in *History and Class Consciousness* as ''second nature.''[10] Insofar as ideology *is* the reality of capitalist society, it is ''logical'' to operate on the assumptions, for example, of vulgar economics. Since everyone else acts in this way, we know for example, that if we buy cheaply and sell dearly we will make a profit; we know that each person we encounter is trying to make a profit, has a personality structured according to the capitalist model, and thinks more or less as we do. As a result of our each and all making this assumption, a self-fulfilling prophecy is achieved. Even though it is not ''human nature'' to act in a capitalist manner, within capitalist society acting in that way becomes our ''second nature.'' In this sense, bourgeois social science can be said to have a certain truth—the truth of ''second nature.'' The goal of the Marxian critique is the defetishization of this second nature. In addition, Marx's positive theory attempts to account not only for the origins of second nature, but also for those contradictions—be they economic, social, or political—which suddenly cause a crisis which shows the holes in the fabric of second nature. The danger which Marx does not always avoid is the assumption that there remains a ''first nature'' or really real infrastructure which, somehow, suddenly manifests itself in these moments of crisis.

One form of capitalist ideology which appears to go against our general definition of ideology as the universalization of the particular needs to be noted. The cult of the ''facts,'' of trial and error, and the attempt to demystify ''speculative'' thought is typical of contemporary pragmatic and positivist theorizing. A seemingly critical attitude against those who ignore the necessities and complexities of nature and of social relations sometimes accompanies the conservative formulations of this tendency—as in de Maistre's famous insistence that he had met many individual and diverse men but had never encountered the ''men'' so dear to the reformers' theory. If we examine this approach more closely, however, it reveals the traits of ideological thought. By insisting on the concrete, the complex, the scientific, and the pragmatic, it ignores the historical structure of the capitalist social system, treating as eternal and natural what is social in origin. It accepts only a one-tiered universe, that of the factual immediate. It opts for a world of pure objectivity seen from a standpoint of a non-embodied, purely receptive consciousness. In its reduction of the world to a ''one-dimensionality,'' it takes second nature for the first and only nature. It does not explicitly universalize the particular, since it is a world constituted only of details, combined and permuted in an infinite variety of equally one-tiered structures. But precisely this reduction of the world to one level has the effect of universalizing the merely detailed: the denial of the universal is itself a form of universalization!

To critique the ideological structure of capitalism does not imply the rejection of ideology in favor of "science." Science itself, when rendered absolute, is ideological; this was the point of Habermas's critical reconstruction of Marx's "material synthesis." But paradoxically, in the very act of universalizing its particulars, capitalism as well as ideology point beyond the bare present in the direction of normativity. Mediating the immediate, a domain of possibility—what Ernst Bloch called the ontology of the "non-yet"—is opened because the normative is no longer absorbed into the genetic. Marx's criticism of the ideology contained in the French Revolution's *Declaration of the Rights of Man and of the Citizen* shows how the universality of the grand ideals of the revolutionaries served to cloak the specific social relations in a formal but abstract account which ultimately left free room for the laws of competitive bourgeois economics. At the same time, however, the ideals of Liberty, Equality, and Fraternity portray a universal-to-be-realized. Marx's insistence in *The 18th Brumaire* that "the social revolution . . . cannot draw its poetry from the past but only from the future" is based on the assumption that the present-as-history points beyond itself, as we shall see in our analysis of Marx's actual writing of history.

But the positive political function which ideology also indicates cannot be absolutized in its turn; the norms cannot be separated and rendered absolute. Engels's suggestion that Marxism is to function as a force answering the felt needs of the masses analogous to the beliefs of the early Christians falls short of the achievement of Marx's critique theory of ideology. Gramsci's assertion that because the masses are not ready to listen to the abstract discourses of science, Marxism must have a psychological dimension appealing to the emotions may be tactically important, but it subordinates the concept of "revolutionary praxis" (which Gramsci's own earlier journalism in fact adopts). If Marxism is a science, it cannot be taken, as its earlier supporter Dietzgen had it, as "the religion of science." Nor, inversely, can it be treated as a "myth" in the sense of Sorel's actionism.[11] None of these suggestions for the practical translation of the critique of ideology remains on the level of the particular historicity of capitalism and its logic of immanent, if paradoxical, self-legitimation.

In order to talk about the political function of the critique of ideology, one must have a better understanding of the position of politics in capitalist civil society. Marx's political analysis of the capitalist state is, as Miliband correctly notes in the title of his book, *a theory of the state in capitalist society*.[12] Consequently, the critique of ideology will also be applicable to the analysis of politics; and the tendency toward reductionism, as well as the application of critique, will also be present. The other part of the explanation for the widespread acceptance of the reductionist base/superstructure theory lies in the difficulty of formulating a Marxian theory of the political.

C. The Capitalist State as Ideology

It should be amply clear at this juncture that the modern state cannot be simply treated as a dependent superstructure whose nature and role can be explained (away) by reduction to the economic infrastructure. It is true that Marx's criticism of the Hegelian theory of the state lends itself to such a reductionist attitude. But Marx did not stop with criticism of the state's dependence on civil society; he turned then to the analysis of civil society itself and the forms of alienation encountered there. The theoretical form of his critique of capitalist civil society shows the repressive and exploitative content of *all* forms of social relations that are structured by the separation between the universal and the particular, whether the separation is maintained by an independent political sphere on which individual or group action has no effect, or whether it is the result of capitalist civil society's separation of manual and mental labor, command and execution, ownership of the means of production and actual productive labor. The critique of the capitalist mode of production denounces the false closure of the whole, whether it be in the form of an economic universalization from within of the "system of atomism" of civil society, or whether it takes the form of an attempted closure or universalization from without by the state.

Capitalist civil society cannot provide its own internal closure because it is based on continually expanding social reproduction. Its self-maintenance depends on the ideological structure that makes personal relations of domination appear as objective laws of the market, laws of "second nature." As long as this second nature is now thrown into question by crisis, capitalist social relations can be maintained without direct political state intervention. "Crisis," however, is a vague term which tends to be applied only post hoc. When capitalist development was at its beginning, the state tended to serve only as "nightwatchman," creating the frameworks for capitalist development and insuring it against internal or external threats.[13] The "crisis" which threatened capitalism (as Hegel had already generalized from England) was the creation of a pauperized proletariat (*Pöbel*) driven from its rural roots and left with no new forms of social solidarity. The individual capitalists could not be expected to provide security for this new stratum whose presence helped them by holding down wages; and the old corporations and guilds to which Hegel's theory (among other conservative approaches) pointed had been nearly destroyed by the new conditions. The state was apparently the last recourse. In Marx's Prussia, all attention turned to the new monarch, Frederick Wilhelm IV. When the new king did not take the vigorous measures for which they had hoped, the liberals blamed the monarch. Marx went further, to the structural reasons for this failure, in a remarkable short article, "The King of Prussia and Social Reform" (1845). The normative role prescribed to the state intervention cannot be realized because the state must continually react to the problems generated by a divided civil society. This division prevents any adequation of genesis and validity. Either the state blames social problems on civil society, insisting that its own universal and normative function prohibits it from intervening to aid particular individuals; or, if it admits to its responsibilities, it places the blame for its failure on one or another kind of administrative error which is said to be responsible for the misinformation that misguided its intervention into the problems involved. In either case, it tips the social balance away from the self-regulation that was supposed to characterize capitalist civil society. Either way, the state is condemned to being an external Third unable to intervene successfully in a divided civil society which cannot immanently legitimate itself in a crisis situation which destroys its ideological facade.

The state is "ideological" in the sense that this term has been defined previously. Its function is to conjure away the social division and immanent historicality of the capitalist form of expanding social reproduction. Its action is condemned from the outset, since it is only called upon when civil society is in a "crisis" which reveals its inability to stabilize itself. When the state does intervene, its task is so defined that success would in fact be failure: if it did guarantee a harmony and stability of civil society, it would do so by making it into a closed and static—and therefore non-capitalist—unity. The state is supposed to know and to activate through its normative demands the totality of the particular actions of individuals in a divided society; and at the same time, it must not destroy the freedom of the individuals to generate their own forms of social reproduction. The state is ideological because it can neither play the normative role alone, nor can it simply give normative legitimation to the forces of social genesis. It is caught between the two poles. For this reason, Marx tended to ignore the State in most of his theoretical analyses, treating it at best as a dependent variable. But "the" empirical state cannot be equated immediately with the political form through which a society relates to itself, interprets itself, and changes itself. To reduce the political to the capitalist state *in* civil society would be to fall prey to the ideological universalization of particularity, creating a one-dimensional world.

The immediate temptation is to apply the base/superstructure model whose reductionist analysis has the apparent advantage of at least permitting an understanding of the actual choices the state makes. The state would then be the "executive committee of the ruling class," and its actions would be analyzed as contributing to the maintenance of that class in power and to the preservation of the capitalist civil society. If it is pointed out that contradictory interests and competition among capitalist sectors prevents such a unification and lead to anarchy, the reply is either that this "committee" serves as a private meeting-ground for these interests to thrash out their problems, by force or compromise; or one suggests that a balance of power among capitalist interests may occur at specific times, such that the state can act independently, bringing together various sources of information and generalizing from their sum. In both cases, it will be noted, this state institution is seen as functioning in terms of an instrumentalist logic, determined by the goals of expanded social reproduction. From this one might draw the political conclusion that since the state must always act for the preservation of capitalism, one ought to take Marx's reduction of the political state to the primacy of civil society as the justification of a revolutionary politics oriented around social-economic change to the exclusion of the institutional sphere. Trade union activity would be the primary source of political activity; gradual reform—or the General Strike—its goal.

Or, one might interpret the state's role in terms of a *productivist optimism* such as the following suggestion in Engels's *Socialism Utopian and Scientific*, which indicates another possible reading from the reductionist standpoint:

> In this or that manner, with or without the trusts, the official representative of capitalist society, the state, must finally take over the direction of production. . . . All social functions of the capitalists will now be taken care of by salaried employees. And again, the modern state is only the organization which civil society gives itself in order to maintain the general external conditions of the capitalist mode of production against the attacks both of the workers and of the individual capitalists. The more productive forces it takes into its possession, the more it actually functions as Total Capitalist, and the more citizens it exploits. The workers remain wage laborers, proletarians. The capitalist relation is not eliminated; rather, it is driven to the extreme.

Engels, then, *does not take state ownership of the means of production as the equivalent of socialism*. That catastrophic misunderstanding was left to his "heirs." His suggestion is that the increasing role of the state is the necessary result of the contradictions of a constantly expanding mode of production for which stability, i.e., non-expansion, is death. The contradictions of this mode of production manifest themselves in the mounting number of tasks which the state must assume. The central contradiction, however, remains that of wage-labor and capital. Indeed, with state-ownership, Engels thinks that this contradiction becomes blatant, so that the polarization is ripe for explosion. But even in our own ever-more statist societies, let alone in the Soviet bloc, the explosion has not come—suggesting that revolution is not the direct and immediate result of contradictions within a productivist logic or the end of all contradictions once and for all.

In terms of the logic of capitalism itself, the state is caught in an impossible—an ideological—situation: It is both *in* the capitalist society and yet has to claim to be *above* it—"above" not simply as the theoretical universal acting for the good of all, but also, as the real Total Capitalist, it has to be able to function as an external third which can see, judge, and act on the divided totality so as to insure its harmony. If the state is simply *in* society, it is that meeting ground where the struggles among the several capitalist interests take place; it is a kind of second or higher level marketplace where decisions are made in terms of the supply and demand of social-economic power; and in this case it serves simply to mask the reality of power in the cloak of formal electoral democracy. If the state functions (or tries to function) as Total Capitalist outside and independent of the society, it must change the fundamental nature of capitalist existence: the free market for goods and for wage laborers is eliminated, the objective division of labor is replaced by a Plan, and the "free" social individual disappears. In this case, the state is no longer *in* capitalist society, for the specificity of capitalism as a social form has been eliminated. If the state as superstructure remains dependent on the capitalist base, if it functions as Total Capitalist in this context, then it is condemned to impotence; for to act in terms of the totality of capitalist contradictions, it must eliminate them—or else choose to represent one or another partial position. In either case,it must penetrate the society at all levels, take initiatives previously reserved to the private sphere—from infrastructural investment to the building of schools and hospitals, from direct and indirect subventions of business to day-care and minimum wage requirements. This, however, supposes an independence of state action which the reductionist model does not permit.

Another problem of the base/superstructure analysis also serves to explain its limits. The discussion of ideology showed that insofar as civil society is factually dominant, the reduction makes some sense when explicitly worked out, for example, through a theory of "second nature." Its limit is that it neglects the institutional logic of social interaction, treating all relations as instrumentally functional. Here, as with ideology, one must recognize the positive role played by the pretended universality of the state. To function, any social system needs a dimension of *legitimation*, institutional norms in terms of which its members understand their place within the system. In pre-capitalist societies, this legitimation came from the transcendent meaning-system provided by the community, its religion or social mores; it was not explicitly political. With capitalism's destruction of such legitimation, civil society must bring these normative considerations into the immanent functioning of institutions; the state's function is laissez-faire. But capitalism's growth implies the accentuation of its contradictions, such as that between the power of the monopolies and the powerlessness of the consumer. The coincidence between production and legitimation, genesis and validity, can no longer be taken as self-evident. The political role of even the laissez-faire state becomes explicit. Capitalism demystifies its own ideology. Its political state *does* play a crucial role, independent from the forces and relations of production at its base.

In this context, the role of the authoritarian or totalitarian state, in fascism and so-called socialism, can be understood. (In general terms, the difference of the two forms is that the authoritarian state justifies itself by an appeal to Nature, while the totalitarian state appeals to Reason.) The economic base is no longer able to provide the normative legitimation needed by the social system. The role of the state expands. But since the state cannot be a Total Capitalist, it has to modify the capitalist civil society. The result is "politics in command." Daily life is politicized; all individual action acquires a universal sense, an explicit meaning with regard to the preservation of the social totality. The introduction of a planned society attempts to conjure away the essential historicity and the threat of change by englobing all responses in its network. The Party is used as a constant incarnation of the political, the total and universal, within the sphere of daily life, giving every activity a meaning beyond itself. Social particularity is eliminated insofar as everything particular is related to the goal of social universality. Where capitalism was a basically individualistic social form, totalitarianism—which is made possible by problems capitalism is unable to solve—is based on the total organization of *everything*, from the economic plan to daily life. The legitimation of totalitarian society is *success*. If its organizing works, its claim is that it has found the solution. But a new paradox emerges. The solution it finds is said to be at once "natural" or "rational" and therefore necessary, while on the other hand, to maintain its control, the totalitarian state must take the credit for the change it introduces. If its success is due to its having found the "natural" or "rational" order of things, then its own total power should not be necessary: the closure and meaning that the state gives to society in its particularity could exist without it. If, on the other hand, its success is due to its own activity, then it loses its claim to naturality and rationality, for it is only one group imposing itself on a society basically different from it. With the loss of legitimacy through universality, the only recourse is legitimacy through terror!

Capitalist civil society entails the depoliticization of daily life, a break with the hierarchical status constraints of feudalism; its totalitarian successor is, paradoxically, the repoliticization of daily life *and* at the same time the loss of the Political as a separate institutional sphere. As the ideological structure of the state forces it to intervene in civil society to attempt to achieve a harmonious closed totality, its dual nature is increasingly opened to criticism. At this point, the "politicization of daily life" takes on a sense transcending the indefinite back-and-forth characteristic of ideology. The positive sense and constitutive function of ideology becomes apparent as the state's claim to universality takes the form of the demand for community from within an atomized society. This would be an "institutional optimism" quite different from Engels's productivism. In order to understand this development, we need to follow through first on Marx's attempt to at once theorize and concretely describe the capitalist form of history, confronting the inadequacy of his theorizing with the rich fruits of his practice as a historian. Only then will the distinct place of the political become clear.

D. Theorizing History

Marx's *theory* of History is at once the most comprehensible and theoretically least adequate aspect of his work. He tends toward a linear view of historical development, which could also be designated by the terms: rationalist, scientist, evolutionist, or determinist. The critique of ideology collapses into reductionism. History is seen as a continual process, a developing line resulting from the successive interplay of harmonious and conflicting forces. These forces are reduced to a common denominator and thus rendered compatible so that they can be imagined as if on an engineering diagram where a series of force vectors is exercised on a point (the present) and resolved by a movement which is ultimately determined by the modifications that the weaker forces exercise on the direction of the central one. The image suggests that history is ultimately a rational process which we could understand and eventually control. It is rational either as a play of material forces or, when the element of praxis is introduced, as plural human praxis which is intelligible to other human beings who themselves are praxical.[14] The element of determinism enters—if only "in the last instance"—because in principle all the forces are measurable and the result of their clash predictable. Even human praxis, building on the experience of the past and operating within the physical constraints of the present, is assumed to be rationally understandable and calculable for a sufficiently subtle hermeneutic reason. The evolutionist component appears insofar as the "fittest" forces survive the clash, and insofar as each temporary stage of history is the result of the past plus the new, and hence is "higher" than the stages that preceded it. On these grounds, Marx and Engels concretize Marx's 1844 equation of natural and social science in *The German Ideology*: "There will be only one science, the science of history." The past is understood in terms of the present, and the present-as-history is the result of the past and the future possibilities it opens. Ambiguity is reduced insofar as the theorist stands outside the actual historical process, analyzing its sense and direction rigorously.[15]

The two best illustrations of Marx's linearization of history are *The Communist Manifesto* and the *Preface* to the 1859 *A Contribution to the Critique of Political Economy*. The story of History presented in the *Manifesto* is a teleological theory, in many ways the mirror image—or inversion, standing on its head—of the worst of the Hegelian theory. Thus, Landshut and Mayer suggest in their introduction to the first publication of the 1844 *Manuscripts* that the statement that "all history is the history of class struggles" would well read: "all history is the history of alienation." The telos of history, the proletarian revolution and the end of exploitation, is taken to be inscribed with necessity in the very first stage of History. Each succeeding stage is the development of the contradictions, building on the preceding; *no stage can be skipped* in the progression that leads to the abolition of the contradiction.[16] The same basic antagonism is present in each of the stages (excepting perhaps that of "primitive communism"); only its form changes, until the final opposition of proletariat and bougeoisie is reached. Then, with logical necessity, the negation is negated: the revolution occurs. But this seemingly concrete description of each of the linearly progressing stages is in fact nothing but a cloak for an essentialist structural logic whose presence guides the unraveling of the successive stages.

In the *Manifesto*, the theory of universal history is ideological: *it eliminates History*. The central contradiction is, for all practical purposes, present from the outset, as is the structure which its solution must take; novelty is eliminated, replaced by the various combinations of elements in differing kaleidoscopic figures. The stages of history are pre-ordained; the class struggle, which realizes the move from one stage to another, simply consecrates what was already necessary. There are no historical events or actions, since these are interpreted simply as manifestations of an underlying necessity built into the original contradiction. If the oppressed class does not achieve its goal, either the situation was unripe, or the failure is explained away as simply a stage in the necessary subjective and objective ripening of the preconditions for change. Discontinuity, chance, and the non-rational are eliminated. Whatever fails to fit the unfolding logic is an "accident," or an illusion, like law in Rome or religion in the Middle Ages. We will see later how this supposition affects Marx's account of the proletariat as the subject of revolution. For the moment, its plausibility, and its problems, demand further analysis.

The *Preface* to *A Contribution to the Critique of Political Economy* permits a clarification of the methodological problems that underlie Marx's linear theory. Its place in Marx's theoretical development also permits one to avoid the reproach that the *Manifesto*, after all, was only a propaganda piece, not "real" theory. Marx rejects explicitly, for autobiographical reasons, the Hegelianism of his youthful theory of alienation in favor of a theory rooted squarely in political economy. In fact, the anti-Hegelianism is only apparent as the crucial passages of his argument show. Marx begins with a basic statement of the base/superstructure model:

> In the social production of their existence, men enter into determined relations which are necessary and independent of their will. These relations of production correspond to a given degree of development of the material forces of production.

The reductionist theory is here generalized for all human history. Marx immediately explains what he means by the base and its functions:

> The totality of these relations forms the economic structure of society, the real foundation on which a juridical and political edifice is built, and to which correspond determinant forms of social consciousness. The mode of production of material life generally dominates the development of social, political and intellectual life. It is not the consciousness of men that determines their existence; on the contrary, it is their social existence that determines their consciousness.

As the totality of the relations of production, the base is not only composed of machines, the physical environment, inter alia; the personal relations among the producers themselves are also a productive factor. We can neglect for the moment the problems posed by the flat assertion that social existence determines consciousness, as well as the reductive notion that personal relations among people are only relations of production. More important is that this passage counters a typical misinterpretation, canonized in the Bolshevik Bukharin's *The Theory of Historical Materialism: A Common Sense Textbook of Marxist Sociology* (1922).[17] Bukharin suggests the need to replace the mystifying dialectic with "the language of modern mechanics." To this end, he argues that the infrastructure consists of the tools and technology of a given epoch, which in turn determined the division of labor and consciousness of the workers. The problem, as the Menshevik Martynov objected at the time, is that Marx did not usually speak, for example, of hand mills, wind mills, and steam mills, but rather of handwork, cooperative labor, manufacturing and modern industrial labor. Moreover, as Gramsci's critique of Bukharin points out, this ''primitive infantilism'' cannot account for errors by the ruling class or splits within it. Further, it supposes that somehow the base can be captured by a sort of still photo, whereas in fact its capitalist nature means that it must constantly change. This ''positivistic Aristotelianism,'' continues Gramsci, ''reduces a world view to a *mechanical formula* which gives the impression that one has the entirety of history in his pocket.'' The dangers of a politics based on such a mechanical view of history viewed from a standpoint outside the process itself have been mentioned, and will be stressed again. In the history of ''socialism'' the results of this separation of validity from genesis have been disastrous.[18]

Marx continues his argument by turning to the question of social change; the forces and the relations of production are now distinguished—as if Bukharin's reading were in fact credible.

> At a certain degree of their development, the material forces of production of society enter into collision with the existing relations of production, or with the property relations within which they had hitherto moved and which are their juridical expression. Only yesterday a form of development of the productive forces, these conditions change into heavy weights. Then begins the era of social revolution.

By definition, a clash between the base and superstructure must be resolved in favor of the base, since it determines the form of the superstructure. The superstructure functions to accommodate a given level of productive forces—for example, feudal relations of dependence; it becomes a hindrance when the productive base demands new conditions—for example, the free laborer who can sell his or her labor-power on the market, or the expansion of production beyond the limits imposed by the guild contracts. Marx clearly has in mind an image of the transition from Feudalism to Capitalism. The problem is whether the same model—if it is even adequate—can be used for the proletarian revolution (not to speak of problems involved in the application of this model to the transition from the Antique to the Feudal mode of production). Theoretically, the proletariat is a revolutioniary class because it is the negation of the *entire* existing order; it does not represent a new mode of production as did the rising bourgeoisie. Institutional change through ''revolutionary practice,'' not a new mode of production, is crucial to the proletarian revolution.

Marx qualifies his analysis immediately, as if he saw the difficulty:

> The change in the economic foundations is accompanied by a more or less rapid upheaval in all of that enormous edifice. When one considers these upheavals, one must always distinguish two orders of things. There is the material upheaval of the conditions of economic production. It must be

> studied in the rigorous spirit of the natural sciences. But there are also the juridical, political, religious, artistic and philosophical—in a word, the ideological forms—in which men become aware of this conflict and press it to the end.

Reductionism is apparently rejected, for the consciousness people have of a situation is sharply distinguished from the scientific analysis of the causes of that situation. Indeed, the forms of consciousness seem to be given an independent, active role in the course of action. Yet, Marx continues:

> One does not judge an individual in terms of the idea that he has of himself. One does not judge a revolutionary epoch according to the consciousness it has of itself. That consciousness, rather, will be explained by the contradictions of material life, by the conflict which opposes the social productive forces and the relations of production.

This abrupt intrusion of the reductionist view swings back to a more determinist position, although it should be noted that Marx talks of a conflict of "social productive forces" and "relations of production," both of which contain a human, intersubjective, and practical relation that could be said to differ from the strict material determinism which is to be studied "in the rigorous spirit of the natural sciences." Marx's intent comes out clearly in the continuation:

> A society never disappears before all the productive forces that it can obtain have been developed. Superior relations of production are never developed before the material conditions of their existence have arisen in the very womb of the old society. That is why humanity never gives itself any tasks but those it can accomplish: if we look carefully at things, we see that the task always arises where the material conditions of its realization have already formed or are in the process of creating themselves. Reduced to their general lines, the Asiatic, Antique, Feudal and modern bourgeois modes of production appear as the progressive epochs in the economic formation of society.

This is grotesquely Hegelian: freedom is the recognition of necessity, in the most rigid sense of that aphorism. Certainly, when we look back, it appears that old societies develop to the full before expiring. But that is a tautology: since they disappear in favor of the new, we never in fact know what they could have been. Humanity may give itself only tasks that it can accomplish; but that again is either an ex post facto truism or the result of a deterministic accounting for consciousness by material conditions. This assertion is no slip of the pen. Marx had expressed the same thought twenty-five years previously in the *Deutsch-Französische Jahrbücher*, writing that "mankind does not begin any new work, but only completes its old work consciously." At the time,he was under the influence of the Enlightenment view of the necessary progress of humanity guided by the light of science and reason. In the same place, he wrote, in a Left Hegelian phrase, that ''reason has always existed but not always in a rational form,'' suggesting that the task at hand was to bring into existence the rational form of social life. Plausible, acceptable at first glance, these statements imply an implicit reduction that rules out the creation of the New. The linear theory and the more (Hegelian) dialectical approach are not so inconsistent as it might seem.

Before citing Marx's conclusion, we should look for a moment at the implications of the linear theory, whose rationalist, evolutionist, scientistic, and determinist forms have emerged here. The implication is passivity; the abolition of history as the creation of the New; the rejection of discontinuity. Genesis determines validity. Human suffering and hope fall into the ''trash can of history.'' Munzer was overcome by Luther, the Girondins by the Montagnards, the Commune of 1871 by the reaction: might makes right . . . and the theory of linear history consecrates might.[19] Revolution becomes a part of natural history or a ''Cunning of Reason,'' while what made the proletarian revolution specific—that the proletariat was the *conscious* negation of society—falls away. The linear theory becomes a ''science of legitimation,'' as Oskar Negt has put it.[20] The ''revolutionary praxis'' is eliminated in favor of the praxis of the Party or rather, of the Party-State. The critical theory has been transformed into a dialectical philosophy.

This lengthy paragraph that we have been following concludes with a prognosis whose implication, that economic contradiction is only central to certain types of social relations, apparently runs counter to the linear view.

> The bourgeois relations of production are the last antagonistic form of the social process of production. It is not a question here of an individual antagonism. We understand it rather as the product of the social conditions of existence of individuals. At the same time, the productive forces that develop in the womb of capitalism create the material conditions necessary to resolve that antagonism. With this social system, the prehistory of human society comes to an end.

Communism will require a new type of history, adapted to the new forms of social relations institutionalized in a society which has conquered material scarcity. Granted, the productivist logic that we have seen throughout this methodological paragraph dominates still, for example when the ''productive forces'' growing in the womb of capitalism are said to permit a resolution of the social antagonism. But the recognition that another logic of social relations is possible after the revolution questions the projection of the linear rationalism throughout history. That projection is an ideological absolutization of a particular moment. It points to the *ideological* element in Marx's theory, an element which also appears when we recall that the glorification of production and of labor appears historically only with capitalist civil society.

The problem is that if the reductionist approach is rejected, theory appears to lapse into an indeterminacy which renders it useless. Indeed, one of the major reasons for Marx's unsatisfactory linearization of History seems to be his constant concern that theory be a weapon *for* praxis and not "just" a theory *of* its tendential movement. The tension between genesis and validity or particularity and universality appears to rule out both science and calculating pragmatic reason by making a grasp of the totality of capitalist civil society an impossible ideal. Some have tried to make a virtue out of this necessity. Since we are historical beings, both products of the Past and producers of the New, we can never *have* the whole, like a thing, in our possession. To have it would mean to be outside of it, different from it, which is obviously not possible for a historical being. What is more, this impossible knowledge from outside would prohibit praxis or intervention, since the "thing" or system has its own laws which we can, at best, only understand, not change. The quest for an understanding of History would then be the opening for praxis, would be itself praxical, and in this sense one could agree with Marx and Engels's statement that History is "the only human science." This, in turn, would permit a non-reductionist reinterpretation of previously cited assertions that immediate self-consciousness is not an accurate reflection of the actual reality lived by a person. Such assertions would be an ideology-critique whose intent is to show the multivalence of "reality," and to indicate that the possibilities on which an individual choses to act are not fixed or univocal determinations of Being. This interpretation retains the "vagueness" and trans-historicality whose irksome presence Marx's revolutionary imperative continually drives him to subsume. It is hard to imagine that Marx himself could have accepted it.

To understand Marx's approach, we need to recall why he thought that his *theory* could claim to be revolutionary. The key was the proletariat, the subject-object of history created by capitalism. Marx came upon the proletariat after rejecting the possibility of change coming from outside, from ideas or from the state. If the source of change is external, one can have only a theory *for* revolution, an instrument to be applied to the real. Because of its dual nature, which accounts for the genesis of capitalism and at the same time puts into question the validity of capitalist exploitation, the proletariat is the immanent self-criticism of capitalism. A theory which expresses the being of the proletariat, a theory *of* the proletariat, is therefore at the same time a theory *of* revolution. The theory of revolution does not bring norms from outside, nor offer tools to be applied to reality; it is generated by the capitalist civil society of which it is the immanent self-critique. The linear, mechanical interpretation of history loses this specificity, transforming the theory *of* into a theory *for* revolution, making a social interaction into a technology. The key to Marx's critique theory, which could be called a theory *of* revolution insofar as it does not claim to impart normative truths from without, is the proletariat. Its being and its history are the being and history of the revolution, which is not an ideal or ethical Ought but a concrete, real group existence. While it is of course possible for the proletarian struggle to make use of any and all knowledge—as a theory for revolution—a strictly proletarian theory *of* revolution must be like the proletariat itself—neither normative, nor genetic alone, the articulation of the tension which I have called critique theory.

The role of the proletariat is determined by, and helps in turn to explain, the structure of capitalism-as-ideology.[21] The specificity of the proletariat can be seen on three levels: its *social* existence as labor-power; its existence as part of the *production* process; and its existence as a *political* class.

(1) Where small independent producers relate to others through the mediation of commodities, they still know themselves to be different from commodities, to be individuals. The proletarian tends to be nothing but a commodity, labor-power to be bought on the market place. But the proletarian is a commodity only because the revolution that introduced capitalism freed the individual from the social bonds of personal servitude, creating at least formal liberty for the individual. Hence the proletarian lives the contradiction of formal freedom and real social servitude. This contradiction is brought clearly to consciousness in that the determination of the value of that peculiar commodity, labor-power, is not fixed by the amount of past labor needed to produce it, or by any natural laws or fixed human needs. The value of labor-power, wages, is fixed in the course of a struggle between capitalists and proletarians. Hence, the proletarian discovers the arbitrariness of the wage-labor relation, sees it as a relation of force, and recognizes that its determination depends on social relations. (That this poses problems for the economic crisis theory of *Capital* is a problem we need not address here. If wages depend on the class struggle, then the "law" of the tendency of the rate of profit to fall cannot be valid as Marx presents it.

(2) The proletarian enters the production process as an individual. But the production process of capitalism is socialized; the individual worker functions as part of a collectivity with others. Yet, at the end of the working day, the collectivity dissolves; all return home, to their own concerns, to their individual particularity and formal freedom. There is thus an oscillation between individuality as atomization and its integration into a collective production unit. (a) Already with the form of cooperative labor, and explicitly with modern industrial production, the veils that hide the sources of social life are lifted. The social nature of production becomes explicit. Even if the single individual is prevented from knowing the entirety of activity in the factory or society, what he/she does know is that individual labor is part of and depends on a social totality. (b) Moreover, the scientific form of modern industrial production, its reified nature and the use of the techniques of industrial sociology, mean that the proletariat is continually forced to adapt to new work situations as the mode of production changes, at the same time that the reified job structure permits each worker to labor in the entire gamut of jobs, giving him or her a universality of knowledge of production impossible in previous, more stable productive relations. The continual adaptation of capitalist production to new forms of rationalization means that the proletarian is not a stranger to this form of rationality, even though the individual worker is not its independent subject. (c) Insofar as the proletariat is not tied to a specific branch of production, or even to one enterprise, and insofar as it is not forced to subordinate its use of rationalized production techniques to the imper-

ative of profit-making and maintenance of class domination, it can take advantage of what it learns from the capitalist production process without any of its disadvantages.

(3) In the political process, the proletariat has a further advantage. Its struggle is not simply defensive; it seeks explicitly to take political power in order to reshape society. Because of the ideological structure of capitalism, the bourgeoisie necessarily hides from itself its real reasons for opposing the proletariat; it has to clothe its particular class interests in the garment of the universal interest. This means that the proletariat has a superiority precisely insofar as it must concern itself with the whole, must be honest with itself, whereas the point of view of the bourgeoisie is always partial, in both senses of the term.

It is important to recognize that Marx's claim is not that because of its position in the productive process, the proletariat *has* the knowledge of the totality—the point is only that this ambiguous ideological position makes it *possible* to have such knowledge through a continual process of practical struggle which implies critique and self-critique. Because the proletariat is still a part and product of bourgeois society, even while being its theoretical negation, it is limited by the same limits as those imposed on other members of bourgeois society. The actual knowledge of the totality can only be achieved in the praxical process of surpassing bourgeois society. In this context, Georg Lukács combines Weber and Marx to introduce the notion of "ascribed class consciousness" as indicating the consciousness which the class *could* have under the prevailing socio-economic conditions. Ascribed class consciousness indicates the limitation by, and participation in, the historical process whose central actor is the proletarian class.

This presentation of the notion of ascribed class consciousness appears to be faithful to Marx's theory; and yet its practical implications point to a problem inherent in the theory which has had disastrous practical effects. The ascribed consciousness is not the actual consciousness of the members of the class. The ascription is determined by factors which are independent of actual class activity, even though these factors are the result of past activity by the class. Ascribed class consciousness is a normative concept whose contours are open to continual modification as conditions change. But precisely its separation from actual activity, and its normative structure, become the open door through which the linear view and the instrumental theory *for* revolution reenter. If we cannot judge the class by its present actions, and if the class is by definition revolutionary, then it seems logical to turn to those infrastructural forces which constitute the revolutionary nature of the class. The productive base thus reacquires its independence, and revolution is explained in terms of a genetic economic crisis theory that complements and completes the normative theory of ascribed class consciousness. For the same reasons, if the class is quiescent and unaware of its ascribed possibilities, the Party, which claims to know theoretically that material conditions are revolutionary, will claim to be the carrier of true class consciousness. *The Party tends to replace the class as revolutionary subject.* The Party thus makes the genetic conditions normative, eliminating the active role of what Marx called "revolutionary praxis." Both of these consequences were drawn by Lukács in *History and Class Consciousness*. We will see that they are consistent with at least one reading of Marx.

The degeneration of Marx's theory of History that we have been following can in part be accounted for by its own ideological tendency which eliminates history—historical *events*. The notion of ascribed class consciousness generalizes the genetic logic of production at the expense of the normative logic of social interaction or "praxis." Marx's critique of ideology could have enabled him to avoid this danger. The structure of capitalism as ideology demonstrates that the bourgeois view which sees only subject and object neglects the symbolically mediated structures of social interaction, reducing their polyvalence to a single meaning. After all, it was not Marx's *theory* which debunked the bourgeois rhetoric of liberty-equality-fraternity and showed the economic sphere as central to capitalist existence. That debunking was the result of capitalism itself; and Marx's theory *of* capitalist society can be revolutionary only in showing how this debunking points to the need of revolutionary rupture and not just cosmetic reform. Of course, Marx's rhetoric includes the demonstration and denunciation of the economic relations of capitalism. But his actual practice as a historian of the event goes further.

E. Writing History

The most important aspect of Marx's historical interpretations is that they are just that : *interpretations*. They are open-ended, future-oriented accounts of events which attempt to see forms of the possible future in the practice of the present. Whether in the discussion of the Silesian Weavers' Revolt (in "The King of Prussia and Social Reform"), or in the analysis of Louis Bonaparte's seizure of power, what strikes the reader is Marx's ability to see in often minor symbolic gestures and acts the potential for instituting new forms of struggle, creative human praxis and class behavior. Understanding history is, in Bloch's phrase, an "exact phantasy." History is more than the surface of facts, more than the conscious intentions of the actors, and certainly more than action pre-defined by the logic of production. It is at once *memory and hope, past and future* shooting through an open present. Such metaphors as these of course demand concretization.

Marx the historian is a historian for us; for his contemporaries he was a pamphleteer, writing what Lukács called *the present as history*. In an ideological capitalist present, events are always potentially more than they appear, accidents are necessary, as we saw. Marx was of course influenced by his general theoretical construction of History's path, and by his specific analyses of capitalist social relations. But his accounts were not simply examples of how the theory worked, practical illustrations of a conceptual structure. The dimension of praxis is not reduced to its infrastructural determinations. As a *class* struggle, revolution entails the dimension of social interaction. The proletariat does not maneuver in a free field. There is a continual give and take, feint and parry, where the opponents affect each others' choice of tactics. *The past plays an active role as its sense lives on*, and is reinterpreted, in the present. The present-as-history is thus a theory of constitution where the genetic account of how things have become entails as well a specific assertion of normativity or validity. Thus, the economic analysis cannot tell the proletariat what it would, could, or should do. It elaborates some of the genetic constraints on class action, playing only a limiting, or structuring role. More important—and paradoxical—is the positive stance of normativity from which the class itself is constituted as historical actor.

Marx's understanding of the present-as-history pervades even the journalism through which he earned his living. It is often alleged that these journalistic articles are to be taken with a grain of salt insofar as Marx (or Engels, who often wrote in Marx's place) produced them for bourgeois papers and did so merely to survive. In fact, however, Marx wrote articles on similar subjects for leftist political papers as well. Indeed, his greatest literary success (in terms of sales) during his lifetime was his vitriolic polemic against Lord Palmerston, which purported to demonstrate, on the basis of documents dug up in the library of the British Museum, that British foreign policy had fallen into the hands of the Anglo-Russian Trading Company, and that Palmerston had sold out British interest to the half-Asiatic Russian Czardom. Behind this penny journalism was Marx's belief that the revolutionary party should take an active part in public life, educating the proletariat; and (interestingly for the linear theory) that it was in the interest of the proletariat to end the reactionary allegiance of England and Russia so as to permit the more rapid spread of capitalism's corroding and revolution-preparing influence. In the case of Marx's articles on the U. S. Civil War, and Engels's articles on Ireland, the motivation was a "moral" one: to show the proletariat that as long as some were enslaved because of color or national and religious origin, none could be free. The articles on India and China, in addition to providing a fascinating application of the theory of history which we have already discussed, aim to demonstrate how the events shaking and making the British Empire while preparing colonial wars can only be understood in the complexity that arises from the interpenetration of two civilizations, and, further, that this complexity is organized by the dominance of capitalism and the superposition of its proper contradictions onto the older culture.

In all of this journalism, a double and sometimes self-contradictory motif is operative. On the one hand, Marx is writing *for* a proletarian political movement which has begun to arise, and which needs reinforcement; Marx's analyses of events in distant lands, in remote times, must therefore be connected to the situation of the here-and-now movement. This can sometimes lead to forced conclusions, leaps in the line of reasoning; and often the tactical considerations are thought through in terms of a linear model of history, along the lines of the *Manifesto's* suggestion of capitalism increasingly dividing the world into two classes which must then confront each other in a struggle to the death; or along the lines of the "religious" use of socialist ideology. In this sense, Marx's historiography is similar to the Enlightenment's discovery of the historical weapon which paints foreign conditions so that people can react critically to their own, or which uses the device of the foreign observer, like Montesquieu's *Lettres persanes*, to show the artificiality of what has been taken for granted. On the other hand, Marx is continually applying and developing the nuances of his theory of history. This is particularly true in the analyses of India, China, and Russia, where the notion of "Asiatic Despotism" takes the first steps toward concretization. The crucial issue—then and today—is the way in which the penetration of capitalism into pre-capitalist communities affects the social relationships among people, and whether a stage of capitalism is necessary—as the linear theory would assume—before arriving at socialism. In the case of Russia, which by the 1870s had begun to develop a revolutionary movement and had (before any other country) translated Marx's *Capital*, the question was of burning political importance. Indeed, Marx delayed the writing of the final versions of the last volume of *Capital* while he learned Russian and began to digest a heavy diet of statistical and historical material on the Russian peasantry. While Marx's own results were inconclusive, the very notion of a "mode of production" called Asiatic Despotism points to the fact that Marx realized that the economic is *not* always dominant, even in societies where socio-economically and politically contextualized scarcity still reigns. Asiatic Despotism is a political, institutionally determined social formation, whose economy is not the central determinant. Marx did not, however, draw the consequences from these studies; he did not attempt to conceptualize the political overdetermination of the capitalist society.

Turning to Marx as historian of the capitalist present, it is striking that even when he explicitly attempts to account for events by reference to their economic underpinning, he avoids overly simplified reductionism. If the economic is "determinant in the last instance," the questions are: Why are events always so blurred, why do they seem accidental, why and how does the symbolic mediation take place? Moreover, the economic theory uses the model of a two-class system. That simplification may be legitimate for the purposes of a general theory; for understanding events in the present-as-history, it cannot be immediately or schematically applied. The existence and functioning of other classes which blur the precise opposition of bourgeoisie and proletariat, remnants of the past or new forms spun off by capitalism in its continual creation of the new, must be brought into the analysis. The historical *event*—economic, political, social—is situated at the juncture of a manifold of spheres; it is conjunctural, appears almost accidental, contingent. But its *accidental appearance* is in fact *necessary*. The analysis of capitalism as ideology has shown that each sphere tends to shut itself off into itself, to separate from the others and universalize its own particularity. The result is that their interpenetration, the historical event which crystallizes the totality, *appears* accidental, can never be asserted with certainty from any single perspective. All that can be claimed is that accidents, surprises, conjunctural events are part and parcel of the structure of capitalism as historical, however much state intervention attempts to regularize the process. This accounts for another frequent device in Marx's historical writing: the use of history as metaphor. The positivity and apparent self-evidence of an event is dissolved through its metaphorical assimilation to other events, in the past, in other societies, from other parts of the globe. Granted, the device can be misused, as with the Stalinist tendency to label opponents in order to discredit them. But in Marx's work—although the labeling tactic is also used—the device functions mainly in the context of the critique of capitalist ideology.

Perhaps the best illustration of Marx's understanding of the Historical is his *The 18th Brumaire*.[22] The failed June Revolution of 1848 had taken initiative from the defeated proletariat. There emerged a stalemate between the factions of the bourgeoisie on the one hand, and the peasantry and defeated proletariat on the other. In these circumstances, the nephew of Napoleon I, Louis Bonaparte, was dramatically elected to the Presidency and then, in 1851, fearing electoral defeat, seized power in a bloodless coup which established the Third Empire.[23] The event astounded everyone, coming so closely on the heels of the democratic Revolutions that had swept Europe in 1848–49, and since the central actor was a character to whom Victor Hugo's mocking pamphlet referred as "Napoléon le Petit." Marx's account shows how the integration of the economic into the symbolically mediated social relations made possible this anomaly. Classes do not act in the same way as purely rational, abstractly profit-maximizing capitalists whose behavior forms the basis of the reductionist economic theory.

The bourgeoisie of the time was divided into two factions, the Legitimists and the Orleanists. The Legitimists represented older wealth, whose base was the remnant of feudal agricultural forms, while the Orleanists were the "new" bourgeoisie which arose after the Restoration of 1815, when France took the road of industrialization. The two were unable to see their common interest, and consequently acted to block each other—opening the road to the intervention of a third party, Louis Napoleon. The balance of power within the bourgeoisie had led it to support parliamentary democracy, a system which permitted it to exercise power without confronting the sources of its internal division. The bourgeoisie was thus "democratic." It opposed Napoleon III not because of its immediate economic interests, but simply because in the democratic game of influence its own divisions and limits were reflected and cancelled each other out; any other system would clearly reveal the inabilities of the economically dominant class to in fact rule—which is precisely what Napoleon III's seizure of power and installation of a new stratum of state bureaucrats was to show. The further irony exposed in this theater of impotence that was the politics of the French bourgeoisie was that, in fact, there was no longer any actual social or economic infrastructural reason for the two factions to oppose each other! In the half-century since the Revolution and its regicide, the Legitimist bourgeoisie had become as much involved in the world of affairs as the parvenus of the Orleanist faction had entered the world of pseudo-feudality in their search for titles and legitimacy by buying land, becoming notables in the villages, etc. Marx's point is that, in fact, *economics explains very little*: both factions were haunted by an imaginary image of the past which prevented them from realizing their own unity. Fighting among themselves, they were incapable of understanding their place within the society as a whole.

Marx's description of the petite-bourgeoisie follows in the same vein. This stratum of society, once part of or close to the rulers, is "objectively" doomed to be ruled, to be proletarianized. But it cannot admit its fate, cannot side with the proletariat—which it hates, and must hate as an Other which it might, but refuses to become. The petite-bourgeoisie is that social stratum which shows most typically the role of the symbolic ideological mediation in determining the behavior of a class. A squeeze is exercised on all those who once, whether in the feudal or even early bourgeois past, possessed something, were members of the dominant group, but whose claim to membership is not backed up with sufficient cash or a sufficiently strong economic position within the changing mode of production—shopkeepers, small artisans, the whole strata of middlemen who live by selling to the wealthy. Either they can admit that the capitalist system, with its ruthless drive toward concentration, does not work to their advantage—and can thus join with the politics of the proletariat; or they can let their behavior be governed by that passionate but false pride which holds on to the last remnants of the illusion of power—spending the last sous for a party or dress for their daughters, one good suit for church on Sunday, and the like. This class lives on illusion, but is constantly reminded of the reality of its situation by the immediate pressure of the economy. It is an untrustworthy ally which may fall now on the side of the proletariat, now on the side of the reaction whose stress on authority and the honors of the past appear to resolve its dilemma and make whole its doubtful world.

The immediate and strongest base of Napoleon III's power was the peasantry. This class has always posed a problem for the orthodox Marxian analysis. In sheer capitalist economic terms, the traditional peasantry has no *raison d'être*; it is doomed to be replaced by a mechanized, industrialized agriculture. Yet it is artifically kept alive—then as now—by governments who need its support. The classical peasantry is a class which is not a class: its members each live in the same situation—small plot, the whole family working, the same rhythm of work, same problems—yet they are divided from one another. Each peasant household is identical with the others, yet they are unable to come together, to form an image of themselves as a unity, to develop a collective will. They can have no ideology in the specifically capitalist sense. They cannot see themselves as ruling the nation, as incarnating the norms of what the nation ought to be; they can make no claim to being a "universal class," all the more so as capitalism roots itself within society. As a result, they project their unity—and that of the nation—onto a military force. This unitary force is not just any unifier; it must be able to identify itself with the past, with the glories that were. In the case of the French peasantry, the great unifier was Napoleon I. It was he who created and cemented *their* nation, taking over the centralizing functions of the state whose origins began in feudalism, and turning them to the favor of the small peasant, freeing their small parcel of land from feudal control and, through his Empire, giving them a mission and a sense of honor as the major support of the conquering and liberating revolutionary army. All of this, brought on by the revolution which defeated feudalism, was of course accompanied by the rise of capitalism. The result was that, within a short time, the peasant was no longer the free individual proprietor but once again indebted—no longer to the feudal lord, but to the village usurer, who was also the political notable of the town. The peasant was quickly reduced to the economic status of a rural wage laborer. But the myth of Napoleon, the government which had represented and glorified the peasant, remained. The peasant could not side with the proletarian of the city, despite their common economic interest; the myth was too strong. And this myth not only was used by that usurper, Napoleon III; the same myth created him, gave his Third Empire its sense, and covered over its real economic significance. But Marx does not linger over this "real" economic base of the new Empire. He remains at the level of the symbolic constitution of the new political power.

The army played a symbolic role of the first order. It had been, under the first Napoleon and the liberating Revolution, the point of honor of the peasantry, their defense against the past but also a source of patriotism and a sense even for dying. Certainly, there was an economic ground for this: the nation which they were defending was the nation which had freed them from the feudal yoke, given them land, and hope for the future. Yet, the army retained its significance for the descendants of the peasantry; they did not support it because they had something to gain from it, but because they were obsessed by the memory of the past significance of military service. The peasantry was not the most patriotic element of France because it stood to profit from the successes of the nation, but because its imagination was dominated by the past symbolic function of the army. Finally, the state, which had been centralized before the Revolution, was taken over and used by the revolution; its function was to break down all local particularisms, to integrate the society into one harmonious whole. But the form of integration which this state achieves appears as precisely the dream of the peasantry, that class/non-class: a society of particulars, each identical to the other, and each finding its completion in a state separate from it onto which it can project its unity. Thus, Marx can claim an amazing coincidence: the state achieved by Napoleon III is precisely that state of which the peasantry dreamed; and at the same time, Napoleon III can base his rule on the fact that what his state achieves is a society broken down, atomized, homogenized, and differentiated in terms of that very same peasant form of existence. Napoleon could thus base his rule on popular plebiscite.

The accidental conjuncture of the imaginations of each of the classes and strata in question resulted in a leap forward in French capitalism; it produced a state which, in retrospect, seemed necessary to the development of capitalism. But this new state form was not consciously willed, and certainly not willed by the dominant bourgeois class. It was a conjunctural accident, but a necessary accident. It need not have happened as it did; but something like it was necessary for capitalism to grow. A state which rules as the projection of the unity of an atomized civil society, and which in its turn does everything it can to maintain both the projections and the atomization, fits perfectly with the ideological structure of capitalism. It cannot be predicted; but once it is there, it can be understood—not by reduction, but only insofar as the historical past is part of the lived, symbolic present. In this manner, the notion of the state as ideology is confirmed in practice. This view of the state, however, is still embedded in the logic of capitalism. A theory of revolution demands a political analysis that is not reductive.

The question that immediately arises is "What happened to the proletariat which was supposed to be the driving force of History?" In the events Marx has analyzed, its activity is passive; it is the latent threat to economic and political power. Its presence is that of a myth, present as absent. Marx was writing about a defeated revolution, begun in February 1848. In the first lines of his book we find the famous assertion about historical events, that "the first time as tragedy, the second as farce." The intention is to show not only the farcical character of Louis Napoleon, but also that of the revolution of 1848, which looked reactively to the past for its forms instead of drawing its poetry "from the future." Bourgeois revolutions of the eighteenth century are said to "storm swiftly from success to success; their dramatic effects outdo each other; men and things seem set in sparkling brilliants; ecstasy is the everyday spirit." As opposed to this:

> proletarian revolutions . . . criticize themselves constantly, interrupt themselves continually in their own course, come back to the apparently accomplished in order to begin it afresh . . . recoil ever and anon from the indefinite prodigiousness of their own aims, until a situation has been created which makes all turning back impossible, and the conditions themselves cry out: *Hic Rhodus, hic salta!*

The implication is that Bonaparte's *coup* is simply an event within a larger process, the revolutionary necessity digging away like that "old mole" Marx liked to summon up. And, from this point of view, the events that followed some twenty years later, when Napoleon's power had been thrown into question and he had been forced—like his model and uncle, Napoleon I—to engage in military adventure in order to maintain the myth of the Empire, would confirm Marx's suggestion. The Paris Commune was turned not to the reactionary past but toward new possibilities that remained to be created.

Even if we are willing to call the Commune a proletarian revolution, and even if we neglect the absence of followers of Marx among its actors, Marx's depiction of the course of proletarian revolution burrowing through History poses problems. The mocking imagery of the bourgeoisie's inability to understand its own role which leads it to deck itself in archaic garb, playing at installing the Republic of Virtue, implies that there is a sort of quasi-Hegelian, economically determined, Cunning of Reason operating in History. The ideological structure of capitalism would account for the inability of the bourgeoisie to understand the social totality and its place in it. The proletariat, however, is supposed to be privileged. And yet, its advance is described as coming in spite of itself, after a hesitant process, when, finally, turning back becomes impossible. The proletariat's "*Hic Rhodus, hic salta*" is forced upon it by an external necessity. The implication is that the *struggles* in which the proletariat finds itself are constitutive for its class nature. It is a blind, elemental force, for which theory emerges from experience. In this ambiguity we find again a Hegelian remnant—or confusion!—when we recall those World Historical Individuals who are at once conscious actors and yet unconscious tools of Hegelian History. This is of course perfectly consistent with the understanding of Marxism as a theory of revolution and even with the idea of education as "revolutionary praxis." But it does pose problems for the status of Marx's theory of History, at least insofar as that *theory* is supposed to have a practical effect. Marx's invocation of the phrase *Hic Rhodus, hic salta* recalls Hegel's citation of it in his resigned preface to the *Philosophy of Right*, where he makes the famous assertions about the rationality of the real and the impotence of theory's "grey on grey." Indeed, in our context, their meaning could be identical: that theory comes only after the fact, that its task is to understand what has *already* taken place! But that interpretation would reduce human intervention into History to just another natural and non-conscious force among other natural forces. The imperative of the revolutionary, then, would be to develop a theory *for* the use of practice. This clashes with the avowed goal of the critique theory: to formulate a theory *of* revolution.

F. The Problem of Revolution

What is most striking in all of Marx's activity as a revolutionary is the *lack* of a consistently developed theory of "what is to be done." He recognized the need for the proletarian cause to be represented by a party, and to be organized into an International; and he was active in these efforts, attempting to make the proletarian presence a political force that could help individuals to achieve self-clarity and join in action *as* a class. Within the organization, Marx's role often appeared to be sectarian: doctrinal defenses, polemics against those whose economic theories (e.g., Proudhon) he opposed, or whose practice he considered incorrect and damaging (e.g., Bakunin, Lassalle). Indeed, in the struggle with the Bakuninists for control of the First International, Marx used his majority to transfer the seat of the International to the U. S., so that it could peacefully die there rather than fall into the wrong hands. This intense activity seems to imply that Marx saw the leadership of those with the right ideas, the right theory *for* revolution, as crucial to the movement. But there is another side to his practice as well. For example, in a debate with Schweitzer in 1868 concerning the statutes of the German Workers' Organization, Marx defends the practical task: "to teach [the workers] to *function independently*."[24] Or, in reply to the accusation that the International was the agent behind the Paris Commune, he insisted that its sole function was material and moral support of spontaneous and independent movements of workers throughout the world. Indeed, in the same year, in the course of his struggle with the Bakuninists, perhaps only as a tactic, he introduced a resolution in the

International forbidding the formation of secret organizations on the grounds that such groups "rather than educating the workers, subject them to authoritarian and mystical laws that hinder their independence and direct their consciousness in the wrong direction."[25] In short, there are two sides to Marx's politics as well as to his theory.

Marx's discussions of the revolution are shot full with womb and birth metaphors: revolutionary midwives ease labor pains while the theorist-doctor tries to explain the length and source of the pregnancy. The imagery is suggestive, but problematic. Such a revolution is based on natural necessity; the seed has been sown, and now the only question is its ripening and bearing fruit. The harvest can be slowed, incomplete, or inadequate, either because of external factors beyond the cultivator's control or because of indecisiveness or lack of theoretical foreknowledge on his part. This argument was succinctly and pathetically put by Trotsky in exile:

> If an artillery man misses the goal, he does not in the least put into question ballistics, i.e., the algebra of artillery. If the army of the proletariat suffers a defeat, or if its party degenerates, this does not disprove Marxism, which is the algebra of revolution.[26]

The linear, reductionist, and rationalist side of Marxism here reduces the "revolutionary praxis" of which Marx spoke in the *Theses on Feuerbach* to a dialectical notion of freedom-as-the-recognition-of-necessity. It suggests that, after all, one cannot break the laws of nature: what makes us free and human is that we can discover these laws and make use of them consciously. The result is the kind of dictatorship of the bureaucratic Party that we have come to know in the Soviet Union and elsewhere.

The basis of this side of Marx's position is spelled out clearly in the *Communist Manifesto's* sweeping characterization of capitalism. In a crucial passage, Marx traces the interaction between industrial development and the creation of the proletariat, which has already been described.

> But with the development of industry not only does the size of the proletariat increase; it is in larger masses *forced together*, its strength grows and it becomes more aware of it. The interests, the mode of life of the proletarians become more and more equal because the machinery more and more erases the differences of work and wages, sinking them nearly everywhere to an equally low level. . . . The workers then begin to form coalitions against the bourgeoisie; they come together to fight for their wages. They themselves form enduring associations in order to prepare themselves for the eventual revolt. . . . From time to time the workers are victorious, but only temporarily. The actual *result of their struggles* is not immediate success but the ever greater *unification* of the workers.

The proletarian class is thus formed by the activity of capital, as its by-product. It is a specific kind of object, a product to whose production it itself contributes every day. From objective necessity at first, in order to insure its own living conditions, it comes together to fight what are at first defensive battles against capitalism. In this defensive struggle, it forms its organization—the Party; and then, when it recognizes its longer term interests and its community with others, the International. Through its organization it gradually realizes the possibility of acting in a conscious and coordinated manner, as a class subject and no longer simply as an object defending its mere physical existence. In short, Marx offers "objective" reasons for the development of proletarian subjectivity and revolutionary praxis. At the same time, however, the "actual *result*" is defined by its effect on the proletariat, *not* in terms of one or another objective economic gain. But again, this is only one side of the story. The objective logic that makes possible subjective autonomy can take on an (ideological) life of its own.

The danger of an objective and linear account of the formation of a class conscious proletariat is evident in a further passage from the *Manifesto*, where Marx discusses the tasks of the organized and conscious elements of the proletarian class: the Communists. This passage, among many others, was the basis of Lukács's theory of ascribed class consciousness.

> The Communists are different from the rest of the proletarian parties only insofar as, on the one hand, in the different national struggles of the proletarians they stress the *interests of the entire proletariat* independently of the nationality, and on the other hand, in that in the different stages of development through which the struggle between bourgeoisie and proletariat passes, they continuously represent the interests of the entire movement.
>
> Thus the Communists are practically the *most decisive and broadly directed part of the working class parties of all countries*; they have the theoretical advantage over the rest of the proletariat of an insight into the conditions, the path and the general results of the proletarian movement.

Theory and practice are united insofar as the theory understands the *totality* of the historical conditions of the class struggle, *including its necessary result*. But how is this possible, given the analyses which the Marx of the "critique" had offered? The Communists would seem to arrogate to themselves a stance outside of History, an objective gaze into its necessary results. The political consequences of this can be seen in Marx's comments on two actual revolutionary failures. In *Class Struggles in France*, he asserts that the Revolution could not possibly have been socialist because "the state of economic development on the continent at that time was not ripe enough for the elimination of capitalist production." Similarly, in the *Neue Rheinische Zeitung*, after the failures of 1848, he had expressed the general political warning that one should beware of "moving ahead of the revolutionary process of development, pushing it artificially to a crisis, pulling a revolution out of one's pocket without making the conditions for that revolution.'' In short, the Party and its theory alone are capable of judging the objective conditions; and it is these conditions, and not human social praxis, which make for revolution. Luther was right against Münzer!

The passage from the *Manifesto* need not lead to these objectivistic conclusions. Mention of the ''actual result'' of the process could be read as suggesting that it is *in* its actual struggles that the proletariat becomes aware of its own subjective interests and capacities. The conclusion, that it is not the objective results of struggle but the communitarian gains in the form of increased organization and unification of the workers which are important, points in the same direction. This interpretation finds support in an oft-cited passage from *The Poverty of Philosophy*: ''The economic relations first of all change the mass of people into workers. The domination of capital has created for this mass a common situation, common interests. That this mass is already a class over against capital, but not yet for itself.'' The idea of a class ''for itself'' expresses in a more Hegelian and dialectical language the problem that emerged when Marx discovered in 1843 the role of the proletariat in the revolutionary process: whence comes that ''lightning of thought'' (as he put it then) which can transform possibility into actuality, objective conditions into the praxis of a subject? This is the perennial problem of the origin of class consciousness.

We saw that Marx's theory of revolution is the paradoxical attempt to combine a genetic theory of actual revolutionary practice with a normative theory *for* the use of the class. At its best, it recognizes that a theory *for* revolution is inadequate because it is based on a separation of the goals from the actual movement and therefore doomed either to utopianism or technocracy. The separation of genesis and validity leads either to reformism or to the imposition of revolution from without. Thus, Marx insists in *The German Ideology* that ''Communism for us is not a *state* (*Zustand*) which must be established, an *ideal* according to which reality must be formed. We call communism the *actual* movement which eliminates the present state of affairs.'' Yet, while this actual movement is that of the working class, it has been shown not to depend on the subjective knowledge or will of that class alone. The working class itself is described as a product of capitalism. It is the very movement of capitalism, including the subjective action of the class, which forms the class. The initiatives of the capitalists—depressing wages to a minimum, maintaining a reserve army of labor ready to take the jobs of their fellows, creating economic crises or wars—force the class *from the outside* to unify itself and elaborate its goals consciously. This is the justification for the objectivistic theory that is to be formulated ''in the rigorous spirit of the natural sciences''; it is the theory of capitalism's internal contradictions and crises. This is the reason that, in his correspondence and his journalism, every economic crisis, threat of war, even minor shifts in the market or economy, play a central role in Marx's predictions and calculations of the coming revolution.

The linear or reductionist view of history thus makes a subtle re-entry into the practice of revolution. The subjective activity of the class depends on the objective and (in principle) predictable developments in the economy. Even when the proletarian initiative expresses itself in the creation of new institutional forms, the linear view affects the way in which the revolutionary understands them. Discussing the Paris Commune, Marx writes: "The working class has no fixed and pregiven utopias to introduce through popular referendum. . . . It has no ideals to realize; it has only to free the elements that have already developed in the womb of the collapsing bourgeois society." Genetic factors are made to dominate here (despite Marx's recognition in the same text of the radical novelty of the Communal institutions as political); the proletariat is receptive, reactive, dependent. Worse, since the revolutionary theorist is said to know the future direction of the totality, the revolutionary's presuppositions may prevent the recognition of what is truly new in revolutionary action, looking instead for the "elements that have already developed in the womb" of capitalism. Armed with an all-powerful theory, the revolutionary may well miss the revolution—or worse, transform or destroy its originality!

Marx's revolutionary proletariat is said to be the "solution to the riddle of history" because it is the unity of genetic production with normative validity incarnate in a *real* subject. This "riddle," however, is the riddle of capitalism—not that of all human history. It is capitalism that sets up the task of unifying genesis and validity in one real structure. It is capitalism that produces the proletariat as the subject-object of history. If the proletariat is a product of capitalism, then its self-realization through revolution, which makes it "for itself" what it was "in itself," is only the realization of the immanent, ideologically dialectical logic of capitalism itself. This is not revolution as the creation of something New, as capitalism was radically New and not deducible from the logic of feudalism. Marx's assertion that the revolution brings about the end of that "pre-history" where, in conditions of scarcity, humans did not consciously control their own destiny is an expression of the optimism of the Enlightenment belief in scientific progress and quest for the domination of nature. History properly speaking is constituted by the tension between genesis and validity which does not exist in pre-capitalist social formations. If genesis and validity are brought together in the proletarian revolution, then the end of ("pre") history is in fact that totalitarian closure which was discussed above in the analysis of the totalitarian state. History is born with capitalism, yet capitalism—like a certain theory *for* revolution—seeks to put an end to history. Critique must overcome this ideological veil.

Marx's solution of the "riddle of history" is too powerful, and too Hegelian. He destroys the thrust of his own critique of ideology by dissolving or reducing the ideological tension into a real unity just as, from its own point of view, capitalism dissolves and reduces ideology in its own rationalist materialism. The "Hegelian" aspect of Marx's dialectical solution is its obedience to the demand that theory be self-grounding, self-justifying; like the Hegelian Spirit which is present at the outset "in itself" and becomes "for itself" at the conclusion, Marx's proletariat is the always present motor of history. As with Hegel, the apparently accidental character and singularity of the event is dissolved into the manifestation of an inherent necessity. In Marx's left-Hegelian reading, however, the rationality of the real is promised for the future. But, as in the case of "ascribed class consciousness," this justification by a future which is only present "in itself" turns out to be a rationalization of the role of the all-knowing Party both before and after the revolution. By incarnating history in a real subject, Marx has solved its riddle by eliminating it. The absence which poses a question is replaced by a real presence which announces the solution. The "myth" of the proletariat that was described in *The 18th Brumaire* is taken as a reality. There is no place in Marx's argument for autonomous political action.

The fact that Marx did not work out a consistent theory of revolution, is not accidental. In one sense, it stands as a condemnation of Marx's theory; in another view, it is a testimony to his critical self-awareness. We saw that capitalism's tendency is to eliminate the sphere of politics by reducing it to just another aspect of civil society. Insofar as Marx claims only to present a critique of that capitalist civil society, he is constrained by his object. Marx has, and can have, no theory of politics—save of course in the tactical sense of competition for power within civil society. A theory which gave politics its independence would not be an adequate description of the structure of capitalism. It might, however, be the point from which a theory of revolution could begin. We saw how the *18th Brumaire* in fact does move toward a theory of the specificity of the political event. Marx began that essay with the famous passage: "Men make their own history, but they do not make it as they please; they do not make it under circumstances chosen by themselves, but under circumstances directly encountered, given and transmitted from the past." And, he continued, "The tradition of all the dead generations weighs like a nightmare on the brain of the living." An emergent, creative conception of both the political sphere and of the historical is suggested by the denial of its reduction to the manifestation of the presence of a real subject, be it the proletariat or the economic infrastructure. Revolution is not reduced; the riddle is not solved. Capitalism offers material solutions; revolution continues to pose critical problems. The dialectic is Hegelian and immanent to capitalism; critique makes possible the opening to the New. Perhaps there is a different opposition to be developed between a theory *for* revolution and a theory *of* the political?

3

Hermeneutics and Critical Theory: Enlightenment as Political

A. The Problem: Founding Politics

In a letter printed as an appendix to Richard Bernstein's *Beyond Objectivism and Relativism*, Gadamer describes the central difference between himself and Habermas as political. Obviously, ''political'' here does not refer simply to *Weltanschauungen* or party politics; more important, it refers to different conceptions of the practical role of philosophy. As Gadamer describes it, Bernstein and Habermas deny that truly modern societies share the *Ethos* or community of normative consciousness which founded Aristotle's transition from the *Ethics* to the *Politics*. Modern conditions demand instead the move from practical philosophy to social science. Gadamer rejects the ''*hubris*'' of this claim; he insists that social solidarities do exist, and that we are not living in a society ''constituted only by social engineers or tyrants.''[1] ''Plato,'' he continues, ''saw this very well: there is no city so corrupted that it does not realize something of the true city.'' This ''something'' shared by the community founds that *phronesis* which is, for Gadamer, the philosophically adequate form of practice.[2] The question is how to found the demonstration of its presence or absence.

Bernstein's book is a remarkable effort to draw together the disparate threads of contemporary philosophy around the structure of a modernity which he epitomizes as the ''Cartesian Anxiety.'' The reader familiar with the ''Critical Theory'' elaborated by the first generation of the Frankfurt School will recognize in Bernstein's study the attempt to ground *immanently* the distinction between Critical and Traditional Theory which Max Horkheimer brought to a head in his 1937 article of the same title. Although Horkheimer's method differs from Bernstein's, their ''political'' goals are the same: in Bernstein's words, without sharing ''Marx's theoretical certainty or revolutionary self-confidence,''nonetheless to ''dedicate ourselves to the practical task of furthering the type of solidarity, participation and mutual recognition'' which will *in fact* ''move us beyond objectivism and relativism.''[3] Unfortunately, neither Horkheimer nor Bernstein succeeds in founding this political imperative *as philosophical*.

It would be wrong to oppose critical to hermeneutic theory as if the former were resolutely ''modern'' while the latter's appeal to authority or ''prejudice'' is a dogmatic, external, and ultimately traditional foundation. Gadamer's reply to such criticism refers explicitly to Horkheimer and Adorno's *Dialectic of Enlightenment* as well as to Lukâc's *History and Class Consciousness*.[4] He attempts to show the specifically historical character of a philosophically founded hermeneutics that goes beyond the naivetiés of nineteenth-century historicism. ''Truly historical thinking must think simultaneously its own historicity. . . . The true historical object is no object; it is . . . a relation in which the actuality of history as well as the actuality of historical understanding are co-present. An adequate hermeneutics would have to demonstrate the actuality of history in understanding itself.''[5] This immanence of historical understanding and the historically given object refuses to appeal to external norms to explain either the genesis or the validity of hermeneutic knowledge. This leaves the philosopher confronted with the need to found his arguments.[6] The refutation of the claim that hermeneutics is premodern makes explicit a theoretical dilemma which the definition of hermeneutics as ''ontology'' tends to obscure. Gadamer's hermeneutics, like the politics of Critical Theory, must be founded philosophically.

From the point of view of political theory, Gadamer's description of an ''adequate (*sachgemessene*) hermeneutics'' recalls Hegel's insistence that true history can only be the history of states.[7] Critical theory and hermeneutics share an origin in German Idealism. Kant's critical theory was built on an ambiguous premise, expressed in the very title of the *Critique of Pure Reason*. Kant never explained the ambiguous genitive: is it reason criticizing, but under what warrant? Is reason being criticized, but by whom or what? Or is it the claim to purity that is at issue? But why then admit practical reason? Kant's *Critique* can claim either to show the conditions of the possibility of experience or the conditions of the possibility of knowledge—or, as Hegel noted, it can do both, becoming an ontology. But then, asks Hegel in the *Logic*, with what must philosophy begin? This implies that the question of foundations and the question of beginnings imply each other. The result apparently excludes political practice.[8] At the end of the *Philosophy of Right*, Hegel's state is dissolved into the flow of History, which is ''the Court of the Last Judgment.'' Exit Hegel—enter Marx.

The Critical Theory of the 1930s was simply a code name for Marxism. Horkheimer's Inaugural Lecture as director of the Frankfurt Institut für Sozialforschung in 1931, ''The Present Situation of Social Philosophy and the Tasks of an Institute for Social Research,'' explains the birth of social philosophy from German Idealism without mentioning Marx. Yet, his definition of the ''tasks'' of social research is perfectly orthodox.[9] Marx did not worry about beginnings or foundations. His doctoral dissertation accepted the Hegelian realization of philosophy as philosophy; the next task was to ''make worldly'' that realized philosophy. Two years later Marx found the locus or beginning of realized philosophy in civil society, in the essay "On the Jewish Question," and then its agent and foundation in the proletariat in "Toward a Critique of Hegel's *Philosophy of Right.*" Nearly a century later fascism's seizure of power and the Russian experience made it difficult to accept either the locus or the agent postulated by Marx. Without Marxism's foundational guarantee—whether as a proletarian praxis or a logic of historical or economic necessity articulated in civil society—Critical Theory is in the same position as modern hermeneutics. It retains from Marxism a theory of the immanence of crisis in capitalist society, but its political choices cannot be justified either by material or by theoretical necessity. The result is the tendency to conflate empirical research with metaphysical claims in the vain effort to conjure forth a new "revolutionary subject" in the guise of a new working class, a rainbow coalition of the oppressed, or perhaps the Third World or the Periphery. Each of these efforts must fail, and this, for theoretical reasons. The crisis is in theory "always-already" there, but the practical political solution is nowhere guaranteed. Critical Theory is no better off than Gadamer's assumed *phronesis*, based on an undemonstrable but taken-for-granted communal solidarity.

B. The Politics of Theory

In their foundational essays of the 1930s,[10] Horkheimer and Marcuse seek to explain not only the "conditions of the possibility" of their critical theory, but also the conditions of its necessity. This philosophical demand for objective foundation as well as subjective beginning means that the "hermeneutic" quest for understanding is incorporated along with the "revolutionary" concern that "the point is not to understand . . . but the change" the world. This double imperative makes explicit the sense in which, philosophically, Marx goes beyond the ontological tradition of transcendental philosophy's *quid juris*. Although Horkheimer is aware of this philosophical demand, he is unable to satisfy it. For example, his second contribution moves toward an almost pathetic conclusion: "But when its concepts which are rooted in social movements today seem vain because nothing stands behind them but their enemies in pursuit, the truth will nevertheless emerge—for the goal of a rational society, which today appears to exist only in the imagination, is of necessity in every human."[11] The only ground given for this faith in the human power to resist is sociological. At best, Horkheimer speaks of an "existential judgment" based on the difference between stable feudalism's categorical judgments and modernizing capitalism's hypothetical or disjunctive judgments. The difficulty is compounded by the fact that this attempt to found necessity in external material conditions is one of the often stressed criteria that define a theory as "traditional." It is correlative to the other major criterion of traditional theory, its "Cartesian" subjectivism.[12] A better case for Critical Theory can be made . . . hermeneutically!

Whereas Horkheimer spoke of social theory, Marcuse begins his argument from the imbrication of philosophy with the very definition of humanity. "Philosophy wanted to discover the ultimate and most general grounds of Being. Under the name of reason it conceived the idea of an authentic Being in which all significant antitheses (of subject and object, essence and appearance, thought and being) were reconciled. Connected with this idea was the conviction that what exists is not immediately and already rational but must rather be brought to reason. Reason must represent the highest potentiality of man and of existence. Both go together."[13] While this "idealism" designates philosophy's inherently critical nature, it does not make philosophy itself into social, let alone political theory. The realization of Reason is not supposed to be left to philosophy itself. Marxism expected the proletariat to perform that task which would eliminate (or *aufheben*) philosophy. When this expectation was falsified historically, the nature of philosophy as critical is reaffirmed ; philosophy acquires a social role for the philosopher. This grounds the subjective possibility of philosophical critique; its objective necessity remains to be demonstrated.

Critical philosophy without the proletariat must develop a specific technique which combines demystifying criticism with positive critique. Marcuse wrote "The Concept of Essence" because "so much of men's real struggles and desires went into the metaphysical quest for an ultimate unity, truth and universality of Being" that analysis of such concepts reveals concretely the "phantasy" and "desire" for "material happiness" that animate mankind. Thus, for example, Marcuse asks why Descartes accompanies his mechanistic philosophy, analytic geometry, and treatise on machines with a philosophy based on the *ego cogito*. Marcuse does not interpret this as the "original sin" of modern philosophy's abstract subjectivism and dualism that lead to the "anxiety" diagnosed by Bernstein. He sees rather Descartes as seeking to preserve a domain of human freedom and autonomy in the face of the new mechanical-rational external world. The famous admonition to conquer one's self rather than fortune is not interpreted as the abandonment of freedom, but, rather, as the paradoxical attempt to preserve it. Similarly, what Marcuse analyzes elsewhere as the "affirmative character of culture" is not just an escape from hard reality. Culture contains also that Stendhalian "*promesse de bonheur*" which preserves the real-dream and existential phantasy of freedom even when material conditions do not allow its realization. The aim of Marcuse's critical philosophy is thus to provide a "hermeneutic" demonstration of Horkheimer's phantasy and "existential judgment" by showing how philosophy's imbrication in the human world makes it a material force.

The difficulty with this solution is that, like the proletariat or Hegel's Spirit, it remains within the confines of a "philosophy of the subject." There is no demonstration of the necessary *receptivity* of the external world to the deliverance of the "existential judgment" and phantasy, just as Kant can be accused of incompleteness in the Transcendental Deduction of the first *Critique* because he does not show why the sensible manifold should be *in fact* receptive to the imposition of the categories of the Understanding.[14] Hegel's assumption of the rationality of the actual at least recognized this imperative. Marx's *Capital*, or the logic of "alienation," provided the concrete demonstration of what Hegel and Kant could only postulate. The next move was suggested by Lukács's 1923 *History and Class Consciousness*. The logic of alienation, or the commodity logic with which Marx introduces the "fetish" character of capitalism, explain what Lukács described as "second nature." But Lukács could still appeal to the class-conscious proletariat. Historically wiser, Critical Theory tries to transform Marx's "Critique of Political Economy" into a "Critique of Instrumental Reason." "False consciousness" expresses the structure of the modern world within which the apparently autonomous and affirmative subject becomes either the analytic *Verstand*, which Sartre describes as a "passive activity" whose social relations are those of powerless "seriality,"[15] or the passive receptive subject hiding its dependence in the illusory affirmative culture which substitutes dreams for happiness. The analysis of the modern world as shaped by instrumental reason claims to overcome the dualism that vitiates a philosophy of the subject; because philosophy and social reality have the same structure, critical theory claims both subjective and objective necessity.

C. The Missing Theory of the Political

The Critique of Instrumental Reason is based on a significant paradox. As philosophy, Critical Theory was able to explain the conditions of its own possibility. It was unable, however, to demonstrate its necessity. The attempt to resolve this difficulty by showing the receptivity of the world to the deliverances of theory demanded the transition to critical theory as social theory, followed by the analysis of modern society as dominated by the principle of instrumental reason. Leaving aside the immanent difficulties in this proposal,[16] it fails for the symmetrically inverse reason: it is unable to explain the conditions of the possibility of that Critical Philosophy from which the entire quest began! The practical consequences of this circle of paradoxes emerged starkly in Herbert Marcuse's *One Dimensional Man*: Marcuse was left with recourse to notions like a qualitative physics, the revolt of the outsider, or the Great Refusal. The move to the critique of instrumental reason was too powerful; it destroyed the question from which it emerged.

Marcuse's radical posture was the result of his violation of one of the cardinal premises of Critical Theory. If one-dimensional society were the *totality*, there would be no place from which that totality could be criticized, and no fulcrum from which it could be moved. As with Adorno's aphorism "the whole is the untrue," this assumes the validity of the theory of instrumental reason; its difficulties suggest problems for that theory. The quest for an Archimedean point makes an illicit assumption. It introduces an externality, something or somewhere freed from the spell of instrumental or one-dimensional reason. This reintroduces the philosophy of the subject. It neglects the concept of totality which founded Lukács's attempt to transcend the theoretical and practical consequences of reification. Lukács's Hegelian Marxism, however, assumed that the proletariat as the subject-object of history represents the modern totality. Critical Theory could not accept this presupposition.

Marcuse recognizes that the standpoint of totality has to be reintroduced. The analysis of instrumental reason describes an atomism of abstract individuals striving to maintain their mere existence. The result is an increasingly incoherent, crisis-ridden process of social reproduction. As the whole grows more irrational, rationality is flung to the outside and to the outsiders who refuse to submit. But if the totality is truly total, these outsiders are insiders, needed to keep the system functioning through what Paul Piccone calls a "dialectics of negativity."[17] Either the instrumental reification is total, in which case critique is at best immanent and ultimately affirmative despite its own expressed intentions, or the critique is external to the totality it criticizes, in which case there is no guarantee that the results of the critique will be received by the intended addressees. In the one case, the possibility of critical theory excludes its intended political results; in the other, the intended political results cannot be grounded theoretically.

The source of the dilemma is the overly narrow conception of civil society which Critical Theory inherited from Marx. Hegel knew that the structures of modern civil society *pose a problem* which has to be resolved at the level of the political state. Marx took this problem to be *a solution*. By equating modern civil society with capitalist society, Marx developed a theory of political economy which showed why and how capitalist society creates the subjective and objective conditions of the possibility of its own overcoming. Marx could not, however, demonstrate the necessity that this possibility be realized. The theoretical consequence is drawn in the first sentence of Adorno's *Negative Dialectics*: "Philosophy which once seemed obsolete, lives on because the moment to realize it was missed."[18] The political consequence need not, however, be the pessimism of Horkheimer and Adorno's *Dialectic of Enlightenment*.

A conception of modern civil society which does not equate it with the capitalist economy permits the reintroduction of the standpoint of totality. Horkheimer and Adorno treat the Enlightenment from the point of view of a philosophy of the subject. Conceptualization of the Enlightenment as political was suggested already by Kant, for whom the creation of a lawful civil society was *the problem* of modernity.[19] Kant's solution turned around what historians, conscious of the paradox, call "Enlightened Despotism." The circle is familiar, but it is not hermeneutic; it is political. The equation of modern societies with capitalist (or socialist) *economic* formations is erroneous. The classical question of the Good Life in the City has not disappeared. On the contrary, modernity has made it more acute by robbing society of its traditional political institutions. The turn to economics, to subjective reason or to objective instrumental reason, obscures this fundamental fact.[20]

D. Hermeneutics and Critical Theory as Methodology

The necessity of both a subjective and an objective foundation for a modern philosophy results in a paradoxical "dialectic" in which either one or the other, but not both, demands can be met. Without a demonstration of the conditions of the possibility of philosophy, the adventure loses its rational seal. Modernity introduces self-doubt into philosophy, thrusting it toward the subjective pole. When the doubt becomes anxiety, philosophy seeks an objective anchor in the positive world. With this, it sacrifices it's self in order to maintain itself. The other option is the ontological "identity philosophy" which subsumes the particularity of the world under the lawfulness of philosophical reason. The resulting monism veers toward solipsism when it avoids schizophrenia. This paradoxical structure is the result of a philosophy of subjectivity which cannot ground itself without losing the world, or ground the world without losing itself.

If modern society is conceived as political, the dispute between Bernstein's critical theory and Gadamer's hermeneutic can be resolved by showing each to be correct—but for the wrong reasons. The immanence of the political *as a question* to modern society means that Gadamer's insistence on the possibility of political judgment and practical *phronesis* is justified. The difficulty, however, is to show *when* and *how* this *phronesis* functions. That demands a theory of those *particulars* which make necessary political reflection; and it demands a theory of judgment which avoids the subsumption by which "identity philosophy" reduces otherness to mere appearance. This is where Critical Theory enters, following the model suggested by the relation between Adorno's *Negative Dialectics* and his aesthetic theory. The "existential judgment," "mimesis," and "phantasy" are grounded in the immanence of the political question within the modern. This is, however, only the first step. The goals Bernstein and Horkheimer postulate as *telos*, or totality, guiding the critical theory could not be grounded because of the Marxian tendency to equate civil society with the capitalist economic form, neglecting the political question of the theoretical and institutional foundation of the being-together of society. This question emerges when particular events or institutions release practical energies whose repression constitutes social injustice. The result is that possibility is completed by necessity, and particularity is completed by totality, without their conflation or their irreparable separation.

Hermeneutics explains the conditions of receptivity that ground the necessity of the particular assertions whose possibilty is designated by Critical Theory. Critical Theory stands as the political pole whose task is the articulation of particularity; hermeneutics provides the philosophical complement whose universality assures that this politics is grounded. Their relation is thus one of inclusion; excluded is only the economistic Marxism—accepted by the first generation of Critical Theory—which denies the immanence of the political question to civil society. But inclusion is not identity. Each approach has its legitimate place and domain. This limitation transforms the nature of both hermeneutics and Critical Theory. Neither can make the totalizing claims which their philosophical formulation suggests. Each, rather, becomes a *methodological* moment within a theory of modernity that transforms both. In this context Bernstein's political critique of Gadamer is perfectly correct. Gadamer is a political naïf, . . . but there is no need to treat him as a political philosopher. The political philosophy of a non-economistic Critical Theory shows hermeneutics its proper limits and place, just as hermeneutics shows Critical Theory its own. Whether this reconstruction of a contemporary Critical Theory is compatible with the variant proposed by the second generations' *summum*, Habermas's *Theorie des kommunikativen Handelns*, is a topic which will no doubt return in our discussion.[21]

4

Why Return to the American Revolution?

I propose nothing particularly radical in asserting that we are experiencing a crisis of the political imagination. Witness the rise in "neos"—neo-liberalism, neo-conservativism—and the exhaustion of political combinations such as "social democrat" or "welfare state." At the same time, the era of the "post" dominates in the cultural domain. What is happening today is at best social, at worst psychological; and both are distinct from the political in their affirmed individualism and their tolerance of a pluralism which quickly risks becoming relativism, even nihilism.[1] This distinction of the social from the political is not introduced in order to disqualify the social or to deny that which is implicit in what are commonly called "new social movements." Rather, this distinction helps to formulate a question which cannot be posed if one accepts a definition of the social that affirms individualism as its basis and its principle. Are we witnessing the end of the autonomy of the political? Perhaps the political never really was autonomous? At any rate, we can ask whether it should be and whether it should remain so.

1. Contemporary Apolitical Politics

Suppose for a moment that the prevalent cynical attitude which nearly instinctively reduces the political to its social basis only expresses a partial truth; suppose that the infamous "dialectic of enlightenment," which seems to come to an end in the critique of all pretensions to found an autonomous truth, does not culminate in the abandonment of the search for a meaning which explains and justifies our social being-together.[2] One could then try to transform a fault into a virtue by affirming that the political success of our forefathers left us the heritage of a successful republican government within which social differences can be reconciled. This was the common attitude in the United States in the 1950s, when sociologists were celebrating the "end of ideology" and when historians were explaining the "liberal consensus" and celebrating "American exceptionalism." It may be also what founds the attitude of those who believe that the principal merit of the successful power shift in France in May 1981 was the elimination of the major differences between parties which, despite their labels, represent in fact liberals of the right and of the left. According to this argument, those who speak of a "crisis" are trouble-makers influenced by ideas and ideologies foreign to the republican community. If their arguments made any sense, this is due to the fact that their models are applied to societies which have not yet known the 'salvation' that the realization of the republican revolution brings. Once this revolution is accomplished, it seems that the autonomy of the political no longer has any meaning; and those who speak of "crisis" come finally to understand that their discourse has neither object nor coherence.

This implies that those who speak of the "crisis" of political thought are those who don't accept the realization of the political in the modern republic. But this way of avoiding real problems, which was typical in the U.S. during the '50s, does not succeed in masking the conflicts which quickly passed into the political arena. The civil rights movement is an example, as is the emergence of a counterculture which—though driven to excess in the anti-Vietnam War movement—cannot be reduced to that movement or, for that matter, be blamed for its failure. That new culture was and remains highly ambiguous. Without going into detail, one can assert that its evaluation depends in the last instance on the relation between its particular forms and the universalizing moment that is the political. For the new culture was not only a social fact; it was founded on a universalizing demand whose expression exceeds the particular interests it expressed by its demand for justice and right. The (perhaps provisional) failure of this new culture is explained by the fact that its purely social self-understanding prohibited the explicit passage to that universal which was nevertheless the motor and the source of its expression.

Another way out of the "crisis" of political imagination that affirms the priority of the social without putting into question its foundational principle is proposed by those philosophers and literary theorists who call themselves "deconstructionists." Just as the forgetting of Being, according to Heidegger, explains the planetary domination of technology and its superficial logic, the crisis originating from the domination of the political seems to have totalized itself to the point where its functioning is so habitual that we find ourselves without ideas to oppose its infernal machinery.[3] It follows logically that the crisis is only "ontic" (concerning only the empirical forms of politics) and that the weakening of our imaginations is rather a good sign; vice becomes virtue, political production is replaced by a sort of social '*Gelassenheit*' (or a liberal 'laissez-faire'). The universalization of the social thus furnishes a measure by which to judge the relative value of different social movements: those which seek to go beyond their own individualism toward any sort of universal are condemned: egalitarian socialism is rejected as much as is the conservative return to bygone values: consumate individualist anarchy is of no more value than the return to classical natural law advocated by Leo Strauss. But this universalization of the social, which has the advantage of accepting the necessity of a foundation for our social being-together, falls immediately into its opposite; everything is particular, nothing has an independent value—we have come to the end of History and of Knowledge.

As if it recognized the difficulty of giving positive form to its criticism, this latter attempt to escape the "crisis" sought to change itself into a historical and political Reason by an alliance of its Heideggerian or Derridean foundation with a critique of totalitarianism. That critique become common currency in France toward the mid-'70s, when the "new philosophy" came into fashion. Disregarding the "philosophic" character of the latter, it is new only because of its lack of historical memory. The critique of totalitarianism led, however, to reposing the question of democracy. The relation between these two forms—political and social—is hardly obvious. The most profound analysis of their relation can be found in the work of Claude Lefort, who has reflected on this question since his essay on "La contradiction de Trotski," published in *Les Temps Modernes* in 1948. This is not the place to review the path pursued by Lefort; I should say, however, that I am greatly indebted to him.[4] Instead, I will start from another analysis, which is also inspired by the reflection on totalitarianism, and which is preoccupied by the ambiguities of democratic thought—namely, Hannah Arendt's essay "On Revolution."

B. Two Revolutions and Two Traditions

Hannah Arendt's thesis is at first approach entirely unproblematic. The American Revolution was above all a political revolution, whereas the French Revolution quickly became a social revolution. Political revolution ignores and leaves aside private life; the '*res publica*,' the public thing, is its foundation, its justification, and its goal. This "public thing" is by definition universal, shared by all; since private interests exist only through the maintenance of political bonds, this pursuit of the common good can be said not to harm those interests. It follows that American republican politics did not result from the relative material equality that characterized the thirteen rebellious colonies; their struggle was not the political reflection of a social cause. Arendt insists that the American Revolution was a political *creation*; for her, revolution is nothing other than this creation. The argument is impressive; however, an analysis of the French Revolution puts it in question. At an empirical level it is evident that the French had to take social inequalities more seriously than the Americans did. But the revolutionaries of 1789 were looking to found a constitutional republic; their successors, the Girondins, were following the same course. As for the Jacobins, was it their fault if the political revolution was abandoned to social individualism? That would be to attribute to them retrospectively Lenin's famous definition according to which a Bolshevik is "a Jacobin indissoluably bound to the proletariat." Moreover, the recent French critique of totalitarianism has devoted itself largely to refuting the

Jacobin pretension to speak in the name of a political universal which is to be imposed on an inert society. The difference between the two Revolutions must be situated elsewhere.

Jürgen Habermas proposes a comparison of the two Revolutions on the basis of a distinction between two schools of natural law.[5] The Anglo-Saxon school of natural law is optimistic: that which is natural is good. But natural society can be deformed or corrupted by an external intervention; the task of the political is to restore society to its natural freedom—a freedom which society alone is capable of administering. Good government is small government; it is 'laissez-faire' government. In a word, the political is negative; it teaches the legislator to abstain from external intervention. The American Revolution thus justified itself as a reaction against the ''political'' meddling of the English in the internal affairs of the colonies. As for the republican government that the revolution produced, Habermas treats it as secondary; one could imagine other superstructures which would permit the free unfolding of society according to its natural motion. In contrast, Continental natural law begin from a corrupted society, which it criticizes in the name of a State to be created (or recreated). It recognizes the reality of power, its capacity to influence in a positive or corrective manner. When it takes power, Continental natural law applies itself to the positive transformation of society; it is ready, as the saying goes, to force men to be free. Before the French Revolution, this type of natural law was expressed by that contradictory form of government called ''enlightened despotism.'' Its logic is explained by the fact that Continental natural law is rationalist; its Reason does not hesitate to construct a State capable of imposing itself upon society. One sees here a Jacobin interpretation of Rousseau. Revolution is the rational transformation of society by the State. As for the form of this State, it calls itself republican because the State acts in the name of the *res publica*; however, the *raison d'être* of this republican government is not political but social. Thus the failure of the French Revolution can be explained by the fact that, in making explicit the priority of the social without acknowledging its particularity, the political found itself caught in the pincers of contradictory social demands.

Neither Habermas nor Arendt thematize the relation between the Republic and democracy—perhaps because they remain tributaries of Marx's denunciation of politics as illusory. As such, the free play and egalitarianism of society expressed in republican politics appears to be only the ideological form which legitimates in fact the domination of private interests. In order that a society be democratized, its political structure must also be democratized. That, apparently, can happen only when society itself—incarnated, according to Marx, in the proletariat—takes political power. But the paradox is that this taking of political power by society results in the disappearance of the distinction between the social and the political—either in the form of the total domination of the political (which calls itself ''democratic,'' of course, even if it takes the form of a Soviet-style ''real democracy''), or in the form of the domination of the constraints imposed by actual society on the freedom of the political. The demand for democracy can be confused with a demand for transparency (from the social to the political, or from the political to the social) which results in the totalitarian phantasy (*l'imaginaire totalitaire*). This totalitarian tendency inherent in the logic of democracy brings us back to our point of departure—the "crisis" in political imagination. Paralysis not only comes from the manifest failures of the Socialist State, as well as of the Welfare State; it is founded also on a certain lucidity with regard to the political ambiguities of democracy. If democracy is defined as social activity and if the Republic is understood as the political form which preserves the public space where this social activity is carried out, then the realization of complete social democracy would destroy the republican public space. The danger is that this recognition of the "dialectic of democracy" can be directed against democratic politics.[6] This is why it is useful to re-examine the American Revolution, which started from a conception of political freedom and produced a unique integration of the political with the social.

C. Two Republican Concepts of Freedom in America

When the Seven Years War—which the colonists called the "French and Indian War"—ended in 1763, the thirteen English colonies of North America found themselves freed from external danger, whereas the mother-country found itself not only in debt but suddenly the master of a new empire. In order to deal with its debt, it had to reorganize its imperial relations. Economic exchanges between the colonies and England were structured in terms of a mercantilist politics. By definition, these relations had to work against the colonists' interest even before England found itself saddled with a new debt burden. But the colonists' reaction to this economic exploitation had to articulate itself and legitimate itself in political terms. Moreover, the colonists felt closer to the English than they felt the ties between themselves. This bond with England was maintained politically by the 'Whig' ideology of freedom. Without the constraints that had been imposed by the presence of the French, the dialectic between material reality and its theoretical reflection was able to play freely . . . until it produced a double reversal.

Whig thought had been installed through a violent revolution which beheaded a king in 1649, and through a peaceful revolution in 1688 which called itself "Glorious." In its most general form, Whig thought represents a world where power and freedom continually confront one another, the former seeking always to expand at the expense of the latter. Although it is power that plays the role of the aggressor, Whig ideology conceives of History as the long march toward freedom and its conquest of power. It draws sustenance from the constant increase of parliamentary power through successive confrontations with the monarchy which seems to supply the demonstration of the validity of its thesis. But Whig *ideology* must be distinguished from Whig *theory*. The latter furnishes a hermeneutic permitting the actors to uncover the hidden ends of historical and contemporary actors, whereas the former justifies the hope that motivates these actors when they pass into action. Whig ideology can easily be thought together with the classical idea of the Republic. Republican government, in this case, would be the incarnation of triumphant freedom. But it is here that the ambiguity of Whig ideology is revealed. To conceive of England according to the republican model, it was necessary to indicate how each person's private activity converges in the common good. In order to do that, the concept of "mixed government" was applied. This political theory suggests that each *social* estate (i.e., Monarchy, Lords, and Commons) is represented at the political level by an institution that incarnates its interests. Therefore, contemporaries said of England not only that it had a constitution, but that it *was* a constitution. This image of a Whig *social* Republic was able to serve as justification for the established order that took root in 1689 and was consolidated by Walpole. Some critics nevertheless saw that its reality could only be fictitious. A revival of Whig theory followed from this recognition; the new attitude took the name 'Old Whig.' The Old Whig critique reactivated the contrast and the competition between freedom and power; its denunciation of the abuses of power was often supplemented by an invocation of the idea of a Republic carrying out the common good (a "commonwealth")—whence the other designation of this current of thought, the "Commonwealthmen." The Old Whigs reactivated the political element that the social establishment of Walpole's Whigs tended to veil.

Given the geographical position of the colonies, Whig ideology in its formulation of the mixed social republic could not define the colonists' position within the new emppire. On the other hand, the Old Whig critique served them well as a hermeneutic, given that the English were beginning to impose new constraints on their commerce and new taxes on their affairs. This is not the place to retrace once again the pamphlet-strewn road leading to the Declaration of Independence. It is important to stress that each step was the outcome of a reflection in the Old Whig style that sought to uncover and to denounce the appetite for power beneath the British measures—even when those measures were anodyne and often justifiable from the point of view of the well-being of the empire to which the colonies did, after all, belong. As proof of the influence of Old Whig thought, one has only to reread the Declaration of Independence, in which the few general principles that preface the statement are followed by many pages illustrating English misdeeds and their intention of stifling colonial liberty. The debate over the "Lockian" character of the doctrine of natural law invoked by the premises of the Declaration of Independence is less important than the recognition of the deep hold of this Old Whig hermeneutic on the political thought of the future revolutionaries.[7] If our contemporaries reduce the political to the economic, our ancestors were past masters of the inverse tactic.

Another aspect of the application of Old Whig thought to the experience of the colonies explains the passage from revolt to revolution and also the republican hope of the new Americans. The colonies were very different from one another; animated by a jealous localism and often by an exclusionist religiosity, as well as by real differences of interest (for example, concerning the virgin land to the west), the creation of unity between 1763 and 1776 must be explained. The principal explanation is the experience of a common struggle; the colonists all shared an active concern for a freedom menaced by English power. This common *struggle* raises another important point. The first anti-English actions were led by those whose material interests were likely to suffer, the merchant elite, who were opposed also to a local political elite whose power was consecrated by England and its King. This merchant elite mobilized the crowd—which was more than willing to comply. The experience of the two sides appeared promising to both. The elite were learning not to fear popular participation, which showed itself to be controllable; the popular masses were learning about political action for the first time, and about their own power. Across the thirteen colonies a common experience of critical demystification and of political action was leading toward the unity that was the revolution. The Declaration of Independence was nearly anti-climatic from this point of view.

The conquest of independence did not consecrate the end of the political evolution of the new United States. Once declared, independence had to be given a political form. At first there were the thirteen state constitutions. Some were populist and participationalist (like Pennsylvania), whereas others preferred to copy the English model (like Maryland); the majority were unique creations (of which Massachusetts was typical). The government of this Confederation of thirteen states, which in theory directed the war and was responsible for the repayment of foreign loans, had no constitutional existence at all. It was only after eighteen months of independence and of war that a Constitution was proposed to the States, and it was not until 1781 that it was legally implemented. That same year, the War of Independence came to an end; in 1783 the treaty of Paris that ratified the victory was signed. The economic inflation during the war was followed by a deflation; freed of the Empire's mercantilist constraints, the economy was not able to find its own direction. Each state did what seemed best in its own eyes, but all were exhibiting the same difficulty: the people, finally in power, were showing themselves to be fickle, the self-interested victims of their passions, an easy prey for demagogy. It was as if all the warnings of political thought that since Antiquity had forecast the degeneration of democracy into anarchy, followed by the arrival of tyranny, were proving themselves to be true.

Of course, this image of a degenerating democracy was produced by a dominant class having much to lose if the situation did not improve. But more important is the political theory on which such an image depends for its verisimilitude. If the people, at last in power, apply to themselves the principle of doubt at the base of the Old Whig hermeneutic, what will be its result? How can one comprehend the idea that freedom could oppress itself? The fault must be sought in the particular republican political form that American social democracy gave to itself. It attempted to follow the English Whig model that balanced political institutions on the basis of a corporative relation of social estates in a socially mixed government. However, social estates no more existed in the now independent United States than did an external power against which freedom had to defend itself. Thus the Old Whig hermeneutic maxim was no more adequate than was its

Whig counterpart—and from its application came only the vision of a self-destructive democracy. In place of the Old Whig model that had dominated the pre-revolutionary struggle, it was necessary now to imagine a positive principle in order to give an institutional form to the sovereign freedom which had conquered independence by 1783. The constitutions of the confederated states, and that of the Confederation, were not sufficient for the realization of freedom because they were based upon an Old Whig principle and on an idea of the republic that the revolution had made useless and anachronistic.

The new Constitution produced at Philadelphia in 1787 was of course the result of a compromise between the material interests of individuals and of States. But it was founded also on the need to take into account a radical change of perspective. The mixed republican constitution was replaced by a system of checks and balances among the three branches of government. The governmental branches no longer represent social interests; now they were to incarnate *political* functions; and each branch would represent, in its own manner, popular sovereignty in its entire freedom. This representative political structure in which each branch totally represents popular will, implies at the same time that *no branch* can claim to embody actually and fully that freedom which founds political action and makes it possible. This means that freedom is identical to the *res publica*, which implies in turn that no single group can ever claim to possess its true meaning, any more than any political program can claim to be the full expression of a social order that is passive and homogeneous.

This is not the place to analyze further this Constitution still in force today;[8] nor need one harp on the flaws that have appeared in the course of its implementation. Obviously, for example, the bi-partisan political system wasn't predicted by the Constitution; and the practice of judicial review exercised by the Supreme Court is often criticized by one or the other of the political parties (depending upon whether the Court inclines toward a progressive or a conservative reading). More important is the result of the theoretical overthrow of the republican version of the Old Whig logic which guaranteed that the place of power and freedom must remain empty. The Constitution as supreme law is itself subordinated to this sovereign but empty freedom. But how does this freedom which is *everywhere and nowhere* express itself? Negatively, the function of this empty place is to articulate the moments of the political and to prevent the predominance of freedom over the State (i.e., anarchy) or of the State over freedom (i.e., despotism). Positively, the expression of freedom must permit the articulation of the relation of the political and of the social. This is where the history of the American Revolution meets our current "crisis."

D. The American Revolution and the Current "Crisis"

The "crisis" of the contemporary political imagination is expressed in the fact that the political is either reduced to an expression or an appearance of the social or is replaced directly by the social. What is troubling in this structure is the absence of criteria for differentiating what is positive from what is ambiguous or simply negative in the plurality of the social. Everything that moves is not *ipso facto* to be applauded; every social movement that draws public attention is not *eo ipso* a political movement. The simplest solution would be to treat the Republic as merely the political framework that permits and that legitimates the action of the social upon itself. The republican government of the United States differs from that which the French Revolution sought to bring about because the latter attempted to give real and immediate substance to the *res publica*, whereas for the Americans the application of Old Whig thought to their political behavior during the Confederation period demonstrated the impossibility of such a realization. Even so, this American Republic tends to replace the practical concept of democracy—i.e., the regulated and legal action of society on itself—by the metaphor of a generalized "democratization" (extended to family relations, school relations, etc. etc.). In this context the rereading of the transformations of the American Revolution leads to a rethinking of the relation between *social* democracy and its *political* form.

The caricatural picture of the American Revolution depicts it according to Whig ideology. Since the advent of freedom is supposed to be necessary, this approach tends to ignore the conflicts, contradictions, and incoherence of the politics which accomplish it. Whig ideology also ignores the false consciousness of the actors who quite probably aim for ends other than those which they attain. The equation of freedom and democracy throughout the American Revolution was in no way necessary; it was neither sought by the majority of 1776 nor by that of 1787. One is tempted therefore to explain democracy in America as Tocqueville suggested when analyzing its social foundation and establishment. Tocqueville's analysis appeals all the more to our contemporaries because he demonstrates the misdeeds of a social democracy which tendentiously takes the form we call "totalitarianism." But *this* totalitarianism is apolitical; it results from the absorption of the political in and by the social.[9] This raises the question: can one avoid the slide toward totalitarianism simply by the transformation or reorganization of the *social?* This difficulty in turn brings us back to the French Revolution which sought to impose Reason on society from the outside. But are we condemned to this choice between two models, the one giving priority to society but incapable of explaining the motor of its change, the other insisting on the necessity of political intervention without being able to explain its social foundation?

Truly political change must be certain of the 'receptivity' of the social to its decrees if it is not to become an enlightened *despotism*. On the other hand, change whose roots are purely social is not able to explain precisely what *particulars* are capable of bringing about this political transformation; it therefore risks supporting a "social movement" whose tendency is harmful to freedom.[10] These reciprocal limitations lead to a paradox: the action of society upon itself that we define as democracy poses a problem whose resolution can only be *political*, whereas the republican structure that the American revolutionaries identified classically as the political defines in fact the social form of a democratic society whose immediate reflections are political laws. This paradox returns us to our analysis of the American Revolution on the basis of two questions: that of the institutional articulation of freedom by a sovereign people, and that of the relation between the social and the political.

No one was seeking either independence or revolution in 1763; and those who were forced to declare themselves independent in 1776 resisted this step until the last minute. That resistence and those hesitations should be emphasized; they testify to the resistance of the social to political change. From the start, American society conceived of itself according to the English Whig-republican idea of a mixed constitution. The Declaration of Independence of that society involved putting into question its political self-conception. Once it was freed, society fell back on itself; the sovereign people in power provided itself with laws which depended only upon its will. The resulting instability can be conceptualized in Old Whig terms; society understood itself on the basis of an analysis founded on the politicization of all *social* relations. Suspicion with regard to the aims of power, which fueled the Anti-Federalist opposition to the 1787 Constitution, was shared also by the "nationalists" who supported that Constitution, and yet for just that reason they were seeking to go beyond the anarchy that they claimed dominated the life of the Confederation. Thus the centralization that the Constitution introduced was accepted only after bitter debate. But the opposition to the Constitution had to give in to the argument previously underlined: the Constitution is articulated such that the place of power cannot be occupied. Such a constitution can function only within a society where private interests set the wheels in motion. That is the famous lesson of the tenth 'Federalist' paper by James Madison, he whom the historian Charles Beard called the "Marx of the ruling class."

The stages of the Revolution can be reconstructed according to the logic of particularity and of receptivity that I have suggested. The Old Whig analysis is a *political* analysis that designates the *social* particulars which call for *political* action; the latter in turn prepares the social terrain to accept the measures which follow. Each reapplication or iteration of Old Whig analysis revives the social, another of whose particular aspects will subsequently be put in question. From this point of view, it is the political that determines the action of the social. But one can also invert the analysis. One could begin the analysis of colonial society by asking whether the English political measures could have succeeded; one would then study the political response that those measures roused, and their incapacity to express the social demand which is supposedly still only latent in the social. This type of study was briefly alluded to when we stressed the question about the political unification of the thirteen colonies and the republican form which their constitutions adopted.[11] After independence, one can study the manner in which the articulation of social interests hinders political reflection from procuring the requisite autonomy for preserving the freedom which guarantees the originary distinction of the social from the political. This obstruction, which lasted until there was a Federal Constitution, must be stressed, for it shows the danger in not permitting the autonomous existence of a political moment. From this point of view the creation of a strongly national federal government by the Constitution of 1787 must not be identified with a French Style Jacobin centralization. We saw that the structure of the federal government makes impossible such an aim.

This reconstruction may sound abstract to the ears of those accustomed to hearing the synecdoche that attributes all evil and all good to "Washington." That objection brings us back to the "crisis" in contemporary political thought. What "Washington" manages to do in this or that situation can be understood to result above all from the separation between the social and the political which makes possible that autonomous action. It may be replied that the weight of society explains that in fact "Washington" is not always able to do what it wants. Perhaps it would be better to abandon the dichotomy altogether, even while insisting on the autonomy of the two domains which necessarily refer to each other. That would imply that freedom can be reduced neither to its social nor to its political form. Does the same hold for the interests whose particularity suggests that they must be conceptualized as belonging to the social? But particularity, as we have seen, can only be determined from the standpoint of the political. This implies that the definition of democracy as society acting on itself does not suffice. Without the political reference society, strictly speaking, does not exist—although the citizens may be quite unaware of this, save in specific instances of "crisis" which result in what can rightly be called a "revolution."

Does this imply then, that the solution to our "crisis" is found in a revolution? The comparison of the French and American Revolutions should caution us against the abuse of this concept. The essence of the American Revolution was not the seizure of political power with the aim of transforming society—and yet we still accord it the title of "revolution." If our goal is not arbitrarily to remove this label from it, the concept must be redefined. It could be argued that a "revolution" occurs when the dimension of the political, or that of the social, which was kept hidden or repressed by the established order, regains its autonomy. Further, the success of this revolution depends on its capacity for preserving together those two elements. This suggests, finally, that the "crisis" we are currently experiencing is not to be surpassed but rather to be thematized both with regard to its necessity and with regard to its specific logical structure. That, however, is a task of another kind. For the moment, the return to the American Revolution, like the theory of the Old Whigs, makes necessary a political analysis of the social relations of power which are occluded by the liberal-Whig or socialist-Marxist evasions of the implications of the autonomy of the political.

II
Making a Case

5

Kant's System and (Its) Politics

A. Critique and Doctrine

The preface to the *Critique of Judgement* announces the conclusion of Kant's"critical business." As much as his "advancing age" would permit, Kant planned to turn to the "doctrinal" aspect of philosophy. The *Metaphysics of Morals* which appeared in 1797 does not explain the distinction of doctrine from critique. Although Kant does not stress these terms, their implications are useful for an interpretation of his work as a whole. The crucial text is the third *Critique*. Kant distinguishes a predicative judgment which subsumes the particular under a universal law from a reflective judgment which begins from the particular in order to seek the universal adequate to it. Critique is the method which asks for the conditions of the possibility of a given lawful relation. But these conditions of possibility do not explain why the empirical manifold is receptive to the a priori categories of the understanding or to the exercise of the free-rational will. Doctrine thus adds systematic completeness to the merely possible deliverances of critique. Doctrine determines *which* particulars are in fact susceptible to incorporation within the lawful philosophical universe. Critique and doctrine are mutually necessary if a theoretical position is to claim to be both complete and rational. Critique alone cannot be assured that the object whose conditions of possibility it deterimes is not simply accidental. Doctrine alone cannot be certain that the rational particularity whose necessity it demonstrates can in fact be realized in the empirical world. Critique shows the possibility of a lawfully universal realm at the risk of losing particularity. Doctrine preserves particularity within the context of the universal whose necessity can only be demonstrated by a critique.[1]

The innovations of the *Critique of Judgement* have implications for a theory of politics. Kant's account of teleological judgment avoids the kinds of errors that vitiated his 1784 essay on "The Idea of World History from a Cosmopolitan Point of View." The distinction between politics and history emerges clearly from the new perspective. The earlier position tended to integrate politics into a historical development of which it became the expression.[2] The reflective teleological judgment avoids this conflation. The concept of an aesthetic judgment avoids another difficulty, present in Kant's other political essay of 1784, "What is Enlightenment?" The formally free but empty and monological enlightened consciousness is now able to learn, grow, and interact with other persons and with nature. The addition of the analysis of the sublime to the account of beauty suggests that politics cannot ignore the resistance of the external world in its concentration on the forms of "lawfulness without law." Finally, the distinction between reflective and predicative judgment implies that politics is concerned with particularity in search of universal laws which themselves are constantly open to rational debate and change because particularity is preserved by their presence. Politics is not the task of an executive bureaucracy or government which subsumes particulars under formally universal laws. This distinction explains Kant's often repeated statement that "A contract made to shut off future enlightenment is null and void."

The systematic relation of Kant's philosophy and politics is fully elaborated only in one text: "Perpetual Peace." On the surface, this "philosophical project" is haunted by the old ingredients and problems. Kant invokes Nature as the guarantor of his system just as he did in 1784. The relation of morality and politics quickly becomes the one-sided affirmation of the priority of the moral. The concept of a "permissive law" which apparently could avoid subsuming the particular under a pre-given universal is not pursued. When he avoids the appeal to "rational" Nature, Kant explains the creation of a lawful civil society as he did in 1784 by recourse to the level of international politics. Although the account is more concrete than the earlier proposal, the flight to a new level of analysis is no more satisfactory. Of the six Preliminary Articles to his international Project, three are to be introduced immediately while the others are to be only gradually set into force. Kant does not explain this distinction. He does not explain why all six are presented under the same rubric. Nor does he explain why they are presented in no explicit order—the first, fifth, and sixth being absolute, the others relative. When Kant later tells the reader that politics is so simple that "a race of devils"could produce a good constitution "if only it were intelligent," syncretism seems the only adequate definition of approach.[3] Despite these difficulties, the formal structure of the text points to its systematic orientation. Preliminary Articles lead to Definitive Articles which are then justified by two supplements (*Zusätze*) and two appendices (*Anhänge*). These latter materials reproduce each systematic stage of the critical process. This systematic structure suggests an account of the place of the political within the Kantian system.

B. The Preliminary Articles: Common Sense and Constitution

The difference between the immediately applicable and the gradually introduced Preliminary Articles appears merely pragmatic. The relative Articles deal with matters about which diplomats could negotiate. Kant insists that "No Independent [States], Large or Small, Shall Come Under the Dominion of Another State by Inheritance, Exchange, Purchase or Donation." Pre-modern European history illustrates this concern. Gradualism is wise, since states acquired in this manner may have accustomed themselves to their new relations. A similar gradualism justifies the demand that "Standing Armies (*miles perpetuus*) Shall in Time Be Totally Abolished." Diplomats could negotiate gradual reductions toward this end. The same logic dictates that "National Debts Shall not be Contracted with a View to the External Friction of States." Caution is necessary because the state may already have such debts, which first must be repaid. But the common sense of these proposals is put into question by another side of Kant's pragmatism. Kant is aware of *Realpolitik*. He does not simply condemn the national debt, this "ingenius invention of a commercial [English] people." He admits its domestic usefulness for the stimulation of trade and industry. He does not rule out "periodic and voluntary military exercises" that permit a people to "secure themselves and their country." Nor does he exclude (although it is relegated to a footnote) a ruler inheriting the right to rule a new country, noting only that then "the state acquires a ruler" not the ruler a state. More than pragmatism must justify Kant's proposals.

A moral imperative can be seen beneath the pragmatic Preliminary Articles. Kant points out that the state is a moral person. Because it is not a thing, its incorporation into another "contradicts the idea of the original contract without which no right over a people can be conceived." The categorical imperative which forbids treating men as means or tools explains the need to abolish the army. Paying men to be killed or to kill is "hardly compatible with the rights of mankind in our own person." The moral basis for the abolition of the national debt is less apparent. Kant says that it adds the means to make war to "the inclination to do so on the part of rulers." This justifies an alliance against the offending state. The inevitable result of the debt is bankruptcy, which will involve costs to other states. Kant concludes from this chain of reasoning that the debt is "inflicting upon them a public injury."[4] Their aggressive action is the result of the immoral action of the first state. Kant's moral and pragmatic concerns are thus not mutually exclusive. The proposed gradualism is not justified by a merely pragmatic account.

The immediately applicable Preliminary Articles seem to warn against a facile pragmatism which forgets the moral basis of politics. Kant asserts that "No Treaty of Peace Shall Be Held Valid in Which There is Tacitly Reserved Matter for a Future War." A tacit reservation transforms the treaty into a truce to be broken once the combatants regain their energies. A similar logic guides the assertion that "No State Shall by Force Interfere with the Constitution or Government of Another State.'' When this article is brought into relation with the second, its immediate applicability is obvious. Finally, Kant forbids a warring state ''Such Acts of Hostility which would make Mutual Confidence in the Subsequent Peace impossible.'' These include the use of assassins, poisoners, incitation to treason, breach of agreement, and the like. As with the first Article, there must be no grounds for the outbreak of hostilities once the peace is concluded. In these Articles, perpetual peace is *both* the end sought and the means by which it is achieved. As means, the treaty must not contradict its end. But these moral reflections do not exclude considerations of *Realpolitik*. The first Article comments ironically that ''if, in consequence of enlightened concepts of statecraft, the glory of the state is placed in its continual aggrandizement by whatever means,'' these remarks remain academic.[5] The fifth Article points out that a civil war is a state of anarchy which permits other states legitimately to enter the fray. The rejection of dishonorable means admits that war is ''only the sad resource in the state of nature (where there is no tribunal which could judge with the force of law).'' The results of war are not just or injust by a ''so-called judgment of God.'' Kant's moralism has not blinded him to political reality.

Isomorphic to the moral aspect of the relative Articles, the immediately moral Preliminary Articles are also justified pragmatically. Justifications for future wars ''perhaps unknown to the contracting parties'' are rendered invalid ''even if they should be dug out of dusty documents by acute sleuthing'' which discovers the ''secret reservation.'' Another practical pretext for war-making and treaty-breaking is ruled out by the warning against the pretended obligation to rid the world of a bad example. The strict injunctions of the sixth Article apply in the state of nature brought by war. They are necessary to avoid ''a war of extermination, in which both parties and right itself might all be simultaneously annihilated'' creating ''perpetual peace only on the vast graveyard of the human race.'' The moral imperative is also a pragmatic necessity. The six Preliminary Articles thus cannot be explained by reference to the critical system or to the difference of morality and politics. The order and the difference in applicability of these Articles remains to be explained.

The moral imperative present in each Article directs attention to the first Appendix, ''On the Opposition between Morality and Politics with respect to Perpetual Peace.'' Kant's approach is at first familiar, and contradictory. Morality can show the defects of a constitution. It can demand that they be repaired. Repair must come ''as soon as possible'' since ''it would be absurd to demand that every defect be immediately and impetuously changed'' before conditions have matured. Reform can come only within a Republican framework, which Kant admits does not exist. The only possiblity seems to be a revolution, which Kant cannot justify. Yet, although he insists that revolutionaries are liable to punishment, Kant admits also that there is no ground for a return to the old regime once revolution has occurred. He adds here a footnote concerning ''permissive laws of reason'' which explain why morality need not intervene immediately.

The note concludes with a justification of revolution which points back to the question of pragmatism and morality.

> Thus political prudence, with things as they are at present, will make it a duty to carry out reforms appropriate to the ideal of public right. But where revolutions are brought about *by nature alone*, it will not use them as a good excuse for even greater oppression, but will treat them as a *call of nature* to create a lawful constitution based on the principles of freedom, for a thorough reform of this kind is the only one which will last. (My stress).

The "thorough reform of this kind" will be a political act like the perpetual peace which is both the end sought and the means for its achievement. The "permissive law" avoids the recourse to "despotic moralists" who act contrary to political prudence. It is a two-faced law. A future mode of action is declared invalid at the same time that one which preceded the law is accepted. Such laws are found "in the transition from the state of nature to a civil state." Kant clearly is seeking a tactic to justify his prudent pragmatism. The permissive law poses the question whether a law can include exceptions not as an afterthought but from principle. The critical answer is of course that the law must be universal, like mathematics. Kant concludes that unless we can find a principle of law that functions like mathematical principles, our laws will be valid only in general, not universally. The implications of this nuance are not spelled out. The Appendix does not clarify the Preliminary Articles.

The transition to the Definite Articles might be assumed to contain the explanation of the confusion in the Preliminary Articles. Kant does not make use of the permissive law. He does not appeal to the moral a priori. He stresses instead that the state of peace is not given with the state of nature. Politics has its place. Peace, he says in italics, must be *formally instituted*. A footnote then explains "the postulate on which all the following articles are based." For Kant, "all men who can at all influence one another must adhere to some kind of civil constitution." No justification is offered for this postulate, whose roots may be in Kant's reading of Rousseau. No deduction elaborates the transition. The only possible source of explanation is the Definitive Articles which themselves must explain the Preliminary Articles, and their transitional role. This means that the demonstration of their validity will in turn be contained in the supplementary materials that validate the projected pact insuring Perpetual Peace. Since the Preliminary Articles do not explain the Definitive ones, the systematic structure has to be demonstrated from the supplementary materials.

C. The Supplementary Justifications: System and the Place of Politics

The beginning of the first Supplement repeats briefly the development through the three Kantian *Critiques* before it strikes out on its own. This self-referentiality is remarkable. Kant begins from the invocation of ''that great artist, nature.'' He immediately refers to its ''mechanical course.'' Nature produces harmony for humans ''against their will'' by means of the kind of ''unsocial sociability'' that Kant had already described in 1784. To avoid the older position, Kant's footnote insists that he is talking here about ends or goals. He distinguishes the sense in which one can talk of ''providence,'' and suggests that although physical—mechanical causes explain how trees are carried north by the gulf stream to barren lands, ''we must not overlook the teleological cause.'' The teleological cause is not the deity. ''Providence'' must do systematically what the Postulates of Practical Reason did in the second *Critique*: ''compensate for our own lack of justice, provided our intention was genuine'' so that we will ''not relent in our endeavor after the good.'' After this allusion to the second *Critique*, Kant's discussion follows the third. The plan of ''providence'' is seen ''in questions of the relation of the forms of things to ends in general.'' This move from the particular forms of things demands that ''we can and must supply [the ends in general] from our own minds.'' The ''analogy to action of human art'' means that there is no predicative theoretical guarantee for these assertions. The limits of human reason mean that the guarantee cannot be causal. Yet, continues Kant, there is a guarantee which ''does possess dogmatic validity and has a very real foundation in *practice* . . . which makes it our duty to promote it by using the natural mechanism described above.'' The natural rationality of the first *Critique* is thus combined with the moral imperative of the second by means of categories from the third. This systematic structure suggests that Kant will be proposing a new strategy in these supplementary materials.

The remainder of the first Supplement develops a model of progressive human history that is only apparently similar to that of 1784. The difference is signaled by the fact that no attempt to mediate laws of nature with those of freedom is offered. Nature acts on men ''even against their inclination and without this *ought* being based on a concept of duty to which they were bound by a moral law.'' Nature acts ''to lead the human race, considered as a class of animals, to her own end.'' Her laws are mechanical, not organic. Man is simply an animal, not a rational or moral essence. Kant's formulations are deliberate. He asks ''how has she guaranteed (by compulsion but without prejudice to his freedom) that he shall do that which he ought to do under the laws of freedom?'' The subordination of the moral is clear in the question, ''What has nature done with regard to this end which man's own reason makes his duty?'' Lest he be misunderstood, Kant continues that ''I do not mean that she imposes a duty on us to do it, for this can be done only by free practical reason; rather, I mean that she herself does it, whether we will or not.'' These passages ring surprisingly un-Kantian.[6] The primacy of natural necessity over moral duty needs explanation.

The justification for Kant's appeal to mechanical nature reintroduces the active subject without direct reference to the moral law. Kant suggests that ''nature comes to the aid of the general will established on reason, which is revered even though impotent in practice.'' The manner in which Nature now intervenes shifts. The achievement of the Republic is said to be "only a question of a good organization of the state . . . whereby the powers of each selfish inclination are so arranged in opposition that one moderates or destroys the ruinous effects of the other." Kant's appeal to this familiar eighteenth-century *topos* is surprising only because he is Kant. The implication is that "the problem of organizing a state, however hard it may seem, can be solved even for a race of devils, if only they are intelligent." This assertion leaves the Kantian perplexed. Kant's political conclusion rejects morality altogether. "A problem like this must be capable of solution; it does not require that we know how to attain the moral improvement of men but only that we should know the mechanism of nature in order to use it on men." Kant's goal is the creation of institutions such that "man is forced to be a good citizen even if not a morally good person." The position of this "Machiavellian" ammoralism in Kant's argument suggests that the systematic context he is constructing will explain its sense. Kant's projected Perpetual Peace is based on a specific conception of political action that can be understood only as a whole. The sphere of politics will be defined by a specific kind of "critique."

The final remarks to the first Supplement reverse the implication that politics and morality are to be separated. Kant has shown how "nature guarantees perpetual peace by the mechanism of human passions." He is not satisfied that this demonstration gives "sufficient certainty that we can predict theoretically" on its basis. But it is, he says, adequate from the practical point of view. It implies that it is "our duty to work toward this end, which is not just a chimerical one." This claim might be read as a teleological argument in the sense of the third *Critique*. Kant does not make that suggestion. The conceptual place for his argument is the Regulative Idea. Just as the first *Critique* had to destroy reason to make room for faith, the stress on natural necessity here opens the practical moral domain. The first Supplement is thus the first stage in a systematic critical unity. It demonstrates the need for a moral critique which does not contradict the lawful necessities of nature. Kant is proposing to repeat the systematic development of the critical theory. The result of the repetition will demonstrate the "doctrinal" place for politics. The politics of the "race of devils" is not Kant's final word.

The politics proposed in the first Supplement is only apparently independent from morality. And it it only apparently political. Kant's insistence on "a state of peace . . . in which laws have force" is first a moral demand. Moral injunctions are valid only if they are realizable. Kant must demonstrate that moral freedom can be realized in political actuality. Moral commands that cannot be realized are meaningless and invalid by definition. The first Supplement provided the material element of such a demonstration. The second Supplement and first Appendix bring a complement from the side of morality. Little new is offered in the first Appendix. We cannot say that "honesty is the best policy," says Kant, since practice at times refutes that observation. What must be said is that honesty is better than any policy. It is the moral presupposition of politics. The empirical opportunism of the "political moralist" is doomed to failure. Only the "moral politician" acting from duty can be accepted. The arguments are familiar, although more polemical than usual. Kant lambasts those who "make a great show of understanding men . . . without understanding *man* and what can be made of him." He denounces the three "principles" on which the politician acts—do, then seek excuses; if you act, blame the other; divide and conquer—and finally cries: "Let us put an end to this sophism, if not to the injustices it protects." This cry is followed by Kant's acceptance of revolution as a "call of nature." The Appendix then concludes with the straightforward affirmation that "true politics can never take a step without rendering homage to morality. Although politics by its self is a difficult art, its unity with morality is no art at all for this union cuts the knot which politics could not untie when they were in conflict." This short circuit which reduces politics to morality is not adequate. Kant implicitly admits the difficulty when he adds a further discussion in the second edition of "Perpetual Peace." The new material provides a confirmation of his systematic intention."

Kant could have moved to a discussion of politics on the basis of a suggestion at the beginning of the moral argument of the first Appendix. He had noted there that "reason is not yet sufficiently enlightened to survey the entire series of predetermining causes . . . to be able to foresee with certainty the happy or unhappy effects which follow human actions by the mechanism of nature." He did not follow this argument, which could develop suggestions from the third *Critique*. The same systematic reasons explain the curious second Supplement added to the second edition. The role of the philosopher in this so-called Secret Article is not meant to be an ironic criticism of the government which had recently censored him. The "Secret Article" should have followed the first Appendix.[7] The analysis of morality in the first Appendix has the same structure and function as the critical grounding of morality in the *Foundations of the Metaphysics of Morals*. Morality is taken as a given whose conditions of possibility are to be analyzed. The systematic contribution added to Kant's ethics by the *Critique of Practical Reason* is the "Postulates of Practical Reason." These Postulates guarantee that the moral imperative is in fact realizable. The moral imperative whose conditions of possibility are analyzed makes sense—i.e., is realizable—only when these conditions are met. The "Secret Article" and the role of the philosopher provide a similar guarantee. Once they have been introduced, Kant can turn finally to the approach suggested in the third *Critique*. The final Appendix makes explicit this systematic structure in its title, "On the Harmony which the Transcendental Concept of Public Right establishes between Morality and Politics." Its content justifies the assertion that the systematic structure of Kant's work is articulated by the systematic interrelation of "critique" and "doctrine."

The two facets of the second Appendix correspond to the approaches designated as critique and doctrine. Kant presents first a "transcendental formula of public law." The justification of this formula is a constant in Kant's critical thinking.[8] "All actions relating to the right of other men are unjust if their maxim is not consistent with publicity." The explicit qualification of this argument as "transcendental" is new. Kant illustrates the application of this principle. From the sphere of civil law he chooses the issue of rebellion. His expected rejection is justified by the need of its leaders to keep their plans secret. Such a rebellion is not politics in the sense Kant is trying to define. Another illustration is taken from international relations. The transcendental principle forbids a state from breaking its promise to give aid, or from striking pre-emptively at a threatening neighbor. To say publicly what it intended to do would permit the other party to counter its intention. Politics is once again violated. Kant leaves the third domain, that of world citizenship, with the remark that "its analogy with international law makes it a very simple matter to state and evaluate its maxims."[9] The implications of the "transcendental" status of the political become clear in the next stage of Kant's demonstration. He provides what can be called a Transcendental Dialectic to accompany the Analytic formula first proposed. "We cannot infer conversely that the maxims which bear publicity are therefore just, since no one who has decidedly superior power needs to conceal his plans." This "dialectic" avoids the formalist conclusion that rulers who do not hide their aims are therefore not unjust. From the standpoint of system, it suggests that this first part of the argument is a "critique" explaining the conditions of the *possibility* of a just political structure. The expectation is that the second phase of the Appendix will show the political form of its *necessity*.

The doctrinal or positive phase of the argument has two parts. It begins from an "affirmative and transcendental principle of public law." The addition of the qualification "affirmative" to the definition suggests a new approach. Unfortunately, Kant does not illustrate the way this proposed principle will work. "All maxims which *stand in need* of publicity in order not to fail their end," he asserts, "agree with politics and right combined." The additional phrase indicating agreement with "politics" as well as with "right" provides a hint at its application. The first "transcendental formula" dealt with conditions of right. It did not explain how these conditions come into being, nor how they are preserved. It did not permit a solution to the problem of revolution which Kant accepted after the fact but could not justify. Kant's second transcendental condition clarifies the difficulty. "The condition of the possibility of international law in general is this: a juridical condition must first exist." This assertion apparently returns the argument to a familiar dilemma. The concept of a "permissive law" presented the same problem without carrying it through to the end. Kant had approached the issue in the first Appendix from the standpoint of critique. His conclusion was that law must be universal, like mathematics. When the issue returns here, in the context of the "affirmative and transcendental principle" that calls for a doctrinal completion, a different implication can be drawn. Measures which "stand in need of publicity in order not to fail their end" concern not only the possible receptivity of the world. Such measures are particulars whose success depends on finding an adequate universal formulation. This approach to the permissive law in terms of a reflective and not a predicative judgment points toward the place of politics in the Kantian system.

D. The Definitive Articles: Republican Institutions as Representative

The three Definitive Articles are disconcertingly general and vague. Kant first insists that the civil (*bürgerliche*) Constitution in every state must be Republican. He then claims that the law of nations (*Völkerrecht*) is to be grounded in a Federation of Free States. Finally, he defines a law of world citizenship that is structured by conditions of universal hospitality (*Hospitalität*) The first temptation is to see these articles as merely classificatory. They describe the situation of the individual within a single state, among states, and within the most general structure of human being as such. Another reading might propose a parallel to the final section of Hegel's *Philosophy of Right*. The difference is that Hegel's third moment is World History as the "court of the Last Judgement." Another approach could interpret the articles as the result of the type of contractual diplomatic negotiations suggested by the Preliminary Articles. The interdictions of the immediately applicable articles—forbidding tacit reservations, interference by force, or the use of illicit methods—are the presupposition of any contract. The permissive articles—concerning continuation of older, non-contractual traditions such as inheritance, exchange or donation; the attempt to equate the partners by forbidding either to grow at the expense of another; or the denial of the right to enlarge oneself by borrowing from a third party—are elements to be weighed in the contractual negotiations. The difficulty is the familiar one: that a contractual relation is only binding if there already exist legal structures that make is possible. The interpretation cannot presuppose what it wants to prove. An alternative might be to follow the pattern from the 1784 essay on "Cosmopolitan History" which invokes international relations among states to explain the institution of republican civil society. This proposal is refutated by the use of natural mechanical causality and the categories of moral obligation in the supplementary discussions. The path to a solution depends, finally, on the ability of the systematic framework to interpret the "universal hospitality" of the third Definitive Article.

The assertion that the Republic is the only normatively valid state form is given a more political definition in the present discussion. Much of Kant's argument is familiar. The Republic derives from the idea of the original contract which is the basis of all legislation. It is a universal form excluding all manifestations of privilege save that "to lend obedience to no external laws except those to which I could have given consent." This means that there can be no hereditary titles; a nobleman is not necessarily a noble man.[10] Hierarchy is permitted if it ranks only offices, not the present holder of office. Kant's explicitly political proposals begin from the assertion that "no one can lawfully bind another without at the same time subjecting himself to the law by which he also can be bound." This recalls Rousseau's insistence that because laws are by their nature universal, the law protects the particular person from injustice. It also recalls the problems of making a Rousseauian politics functional.[11] Kant avoids the difficulty by comparing the Republic to what he calls "democracy." Republican institutions provide formal guarantees of our freedom as men, our dependence on common legislation as subjects, and our equality as citizens. The Republic is an institutional administrative structure. It is not concerned with the question of sovereignty. It describes the exercise of power, not its constitution. The form of government, Kant insists, can be either republican or despotic. The specificity of the Republic is that it divides the executive from the legislative; democracy unites them in one hand. This is why democracy must be necessarily despotic. The identity of legislative and representative leaves no space for political action—although Kant does not define political action in his text. His implication has to be drawn from the systematic framework guiding the account.

The crucial aspect of Kant's Republican institutions is their representative character. The sovereign legislator and the governmental executor of the popular will cannot be the same. The result is that the locus of political action is in the executive. This assertion is paradoxical (or "reactionary") only to non-reflective modern ears. In the structure Kant is illustrating, the paradox disappears. The General Will legislates. It institutes univesal laws. An executive which only subsumed particular cases under these general laws would be a (quite Weberian) bureaucracy. As a subsumptive, the executive would be merely the agent of the legislative. It would be no different from it. If it is independent, as it must be in the Republic, the executive will be concerned with the political task defined by the reflective judgment. It proposes actions which correlate reflectively to the particular facts. The executive must formulate those particular issues and reflective universals on which the legislative acts. The legislature and the executive thus act in a complementary manner. Each needs the contribution of the other. This is why Kant asserts that the "smaller the personnel of the government . . . the greater is their representation and the more nearly the constitution approaches the possibility of republicanism." This does not entail a limit on the exercise of sovereignty. Kant has not yet attempted even to define that concept or give it content. He insists that "the mode of government . . . is incomparably more important to the people than the form of sovereignty." The mode of government must be representative. Its goal is not efficient execution for its own sake. Pope's "what's best administered is best" is philosophically naïve and practically wrong as well. Kant supports his position by citing cases from Roman history where a well-administering emperor is succeeded by a tyrant. A constitution guaranteeing the representative function would protect against such abuse which results from reducing the executive to a subsumptive bureaucrat. The ability of the executive to define those particulars with which legislation must deal protects against stagnation or oppression.

Kant has not explained the origin of his sovereign Republic nor *what* its politics is to represent. The representative Republic is to make possible "gradual reform," whereas the unification of executive and legislative permits change only through violent revolution. Kant's citation of Frederick the Great for having "at least *said*" that he was the first servant of the state is clearly ironical. He is not paying obeisance to the Enlightened Despot, any more than he is seeking a theory for revolution. The error of both positions is that they take the goal of political action to be the *constitution* of something empirically real—either a real happiness and utility for the subjects or a real original contract. The "Copernican Revolution" at the base of Kant's critical program has as its goal the elimination of such illusions. The "doctrine" which is implied by the third *Critique* proceeds differently. The task is not to argue from an empirical thing or goal *to* a model or a reproduction of that thing. The political relation of representation and the represented does not function to judge whether political action *really* expresses or stands in the place of the empirical thing or goal. Kant rejects such a notion of representation as the "democratic" confusion of the two levels. Politics would be redundant if it were the immediate representation of society. Useless at best, it would become in fact a hindrance to progress. The particular which must be represented is itself produced in the political process which represents it. This is Kant's originary insight.

Kant's only illustration of the process of representation takes place at the level of international relations dealt with by the second Definitive Article. The discussion began in the context of the Republic. Kant proposed that popular sovereignty would lead to an end to wars. The King can make war without sacrificing "the pleasures of his table, the hunt, his country houses, his court functions, and the like." He can "leave the justification which decency demands to the diplomatic corps who are ever ready to provide it." But the wars inaugurated by the French Republic (prior to the Jacobin seizure of power) refute this analysis based on domestic politics alone. This is why Kant begins his account of the founding of international law from the parallels between interstate and interpersonal relations. Both may demand the creation of a common civil constitution on the grounds that without it, the other may harm them. The difference is that since the state is independent and self-legislating, it cannot accept a master. That would mean giving up the independence that defines it. The foundation of international law can only be a Federation of Free States, not a unified Empire.[12] Kant's further arguments suggest that this is more than just a common-sense logic. He notes the paradox that theorists like Grotius, Pufendorf, and Vattel talk about a law among nations which they in fact use to justify war. Why not treat the law as preventing war? Granted, no law can coerce a nation. That would contradict its independence and the federal relation. Yet, the "homage which each state pays (at least in words) to the concept of law" appears to imply, counterfactually, that the others have a similar disposition. But nations do not plead their case before a common court. They war. War does not prove right. The treaty ending a war is by nature temporary since each state is judge in its own case. This means that the analogy of the transition from the state of nature must be rejected. I cannot force the state, as I force the individual, to enter a lawful constitution. The Federation of Free States can only be a "league." It is neither a treaty of peace nor the formation of a world state. The result is that despite the homage they pay to the concept of law, there is no means of making their relations lawful. Kant can talk only of a "negative surrogate" which might avert tendencies to war. When he asks himself whether this Federation can work, his reply is disappointing. "If fortune" permits a powerful and enlightened people—the French—to become a Republic! The second Article thus gets Kant no further in his fundamental problems.

The third Definitive Article is open to several levels of interpretation. Applicable to humans as world citizens, it has apparently the same formal and abstract status as philosophical assertions about "man" in general. Kant stresses that he is not arguing from philanthropy but in terms of the concept of right. The content of the Article is painted in details that would please the staunchest anti-colonialist. The discussion concludes that "universal hospitality" is "a supplement to the unwritten code of the civil and international law, indispensable for the maintenance of the public human rights and hence also of perpetual peace." This is the first mention of an "unwritten code," which is not the same concept of right with which Kant began the explanation. The details of Kant's criticisms of colonialist depredation suggest an interpretation. He attacks the Barbary pirates and Bedouins for violating a natural law that guarantees communication among peoples. This condemnation is followed by a curious erudite footnote concerning the intercourse of China and Europe *via* Tibet. It is this concern with communication among peoples that is Kant's premise. Its implication is that the "unwritten code" is the right and duty to further public communication among the nations of the earth. The code is to apply in civil and international law. Its international legal result is the condemnation of colonialist exploitation. The civil law implications remain to be clarified.

The unresolved problem of representation suggests that three Definite Articles are interrelated. The constitutional structures of the formal Republic apparently took no account of the material social existence of the citizens. Republican politics as representative could be defended against the results of the conflation of legislative and executive power that Kant calls "democracy." But democracy could reply that it can at least deal with real if "only" empirical content. The states whose federal relations are described by the second Article differ from one another because of just this material content. This particularity was what prevented them from being fused into a world empire. The material nature of this particularity which Kant recognizes only implicitly is a first step to defining the republican content. It is not sufficient by itself. It could lead to a political isolationism in which the content becomes fixed—"a contract made to shut off further enlightenment." This is where the third Article enters to provide a principle of action. The law of hospitality demands that the particular states interact. They communicate, exchange, learn "to think in the place of the other." The *possibility* of political action owing to the presence of the Republic in international relations is thus shown to be *necessary*. The kind of political action is indicated first at the international level. It will be action aimed at increasing the *material* equality among the particulars. The condemnation of colonialism was not just formal or moral. Kant's argument stressed the negative material effects of exploitation.

It implicitly urged what Kant would call a legal contractual exchange. Such an exchange was just what the realization of the Preliminary Articles demanded. When they were treated in isolation, they could not justify the exchange. The Federation of Free States constitutes the legal framework that is necessary. The apparent formality of the third Article makes it possible to give content to the political action among states. It avoids the difficulty that appeared when the second Article was read in isolation. This approach has consequences for international politics which are apparent today although they were not available to Kant.

E. The Implications of Systematic Politics

The systematic reading of Kant's text suggests a politics defined by "executive" action separate from the universal law-giving of the legislator. Kant's conception of representation gives content to the apparently formal Republican institutions. The illustration from international relations provides an explanation of the origin of the sovereignty that constitutes the particular independent state. This does not reduce sovereignty to an effect of relations among states, any more than representative Republican politics seeks directly to represent actual social forces. The systematic context suggests that international politics is the "critical" moment that accounts for the conditions of receptivity permitting successful political action. The political action within the republic is the "doctrine" that articulates the conditions of particularity. The equality demanded within the Republic by the "unwritten code" is a material goal that is not empirical, unlike the happiness sought by the rebel, the despot, or Garve. It is not a pre-existent material thing within the lawful phenomenal world. Nor is it the formal moral equality of citizens before the law. The changing critical panorama defined by the space of international politics means that the nature of the equality sought will continually change. It is the "non-real thing" that politics seeks to represent. It is constituted in the same process by which it is articulated. Perpetual peace must be both an internal and an international politics. The "positive transcendental principle" that guarantees its success is applied inside the Republic and by its politics. It is the public process in which those particulars which "*stand in need* of publicity in order not to fail their end" are articulated. Kant's Preliminary Articles attempt the concrete elaboration of such a process.[13] The conclusiveness of these particular implications is less important than the systematic unity of the argument as a whole.

Kant's theory of politics has theoretical, practical, and historical implications. Politics in this specific sense is not always possible. The copresence of an international structure and an internal institutional arrangement is its first premise. When one or the other institution lacks, politics consists in the attempt to reintroduce the balance through either international or internal measures. The politics that the Kantian structure describes has to avoid a double danger. The overstress on the critical orientation to actual equality can be present in internal politics. Particular content then becomes the central concern. This transforms the representative relation that structures the space of political action. "Further enlightenment" is foreclosed by the attempt to make politics adequate to reality's demands. The symmetric error overstresses the doctrinal insistence on the formal republican institutions necessary to preserve particular freedom. This lack of attention to the material critical aspect unbalances the political space in the opposite direction. This explains why Kant is able to avoid the dissolution of politics into history that typifies Hegel, Marx, and Kant's own liberal successors. He has no conception of a material "civil society" as that which is to be represented in politics. His successors were confronted with an apparently successful capitalist civil society dominated by its economy. The tendency to stress the formal doctrinal aspect is typified by liberalism's legitimation of the established order. The critical orientation is presented by Marxian productivist orientations. The crisis of capitalist civil society, and therefore of these proposed political orientations, makes Kant's suggestions more relevant today.

The justification of this systematic politics within the Kantian *oeuvre* suggests, finally, an interpretation of the relation of politics and philosophy for Kant. The first hint is the supplementary material to "Perpetual Peace." If Kant were a modern artist, this self-referentiality would be due great weight in the interpretation. Demonstration of Kant's modernity is the task for another paper.[14] The hint can be developed differently here. The manner in which the "unwritten code" actually functions as a necessary and not merely as a possible account has not been shown. The code stresses the place of public interaction similarly to the "doctrinal" "positive transcendental principle" of the second Appendix. Legitimate actions are those which must be public if they are to achieve their goals. The code thus performs two specific functions in the political edifice. It serves as a mediator by bringing together materials of apparently different types—the formal and the material senses of equality. Its second crucial role portrays it as *what* is to be represented in the republican form of government. These two functions recall an unresolved dilemma from Kant's first *Critique*. Two assumptions are necessary to Kant's theory: the "schematism" which makes the Transcendental Deduction both possible and necessary; and the concept of the Noumenon without which the edifice collapses. The temptation is to suggest that the "unwritten code" plays first a schematic, then a noumenal function within the systematic political structure. The political quest for equality, in the dual sense that the term has taken here, replaces both the "art hidden in the depths of the human soul" and the unknowable noumenal realm. However adequate this suggestion might be to the texts, it certainly corresponds to what we know about the man, Kant.

6

Restoring Politics to Political Economy

The happier days when Marxists could invoke economic categories (or realities) to debunk assertions passed off as "political science" have come to an end. Marxists are now confronting directly and in theory the issues posed by the (perhaps relative) autonomy of the state. Some, including myself, have been quick to criticize Marx's inability to elaborate a theory of politics. They claim that the very methodological foundations of Marx's theory prohibit such a venture. The result is said to have affected the "legacy" of Marx, in practice as in theory. No amount of empirical fudging seems able to repair this methodological weakness in Marx's premises.

Before confronting practical and contemporary issues, a theoretical reconstruction is necessary. This reconstruction involves Marx's debt, or relation, to Hegel, which has been discussed frequently. However it is interpreted, the least that can be said is that understanding Marx demands that one be conversant with Hegel—Marx, after all, fulfilled that requirement! But conversation is not enough. Neither history nor theory has stood still. Marxian practice and capitalist development pose new questions. Marx and Hegel can help to interpret this novelty which, of course, influences the way we today can now read them.

Marx subtitled *Captial* a "Critique of Political Economy." He explained the revolutionary implications of his theory in a laconic phrase in a letter to Lassalle (February 22, 1858).[1] His work in progress was to be "A presentation of the system and through the presentation a critique of that system." Marx's suggestion seems to be that a true or scientific presentation of an unjust or self-contradictory social system reveals the immanent self-condemnation that the revolution then brings necesssarily to fruition. The *object* analyzed is supposed to determine the revolutionary implication of its analysis. This does not, however, explain the *method* that permits Marx to reveal the object in its naked self-contradiction. To call that method "science" is too general; the usual alternative, "dialectic," is too disputed. Suffice it for the moment that there must be some method adequate to the self-contradictory object if the Marxian critique is to have revolutionary implications.

The concept of a "political economics" apparently resolves this epistemological dilemma. The capitalist system is a kind of "object" which is deeply political even though its economic form and ideological self-understanding deny that fundamental reality. Because Marx's "method" or orientation is political—or "revolutionary"—it can present the capitalist system in a manner that reveals its immanent self-contradiction. The difficulty is that Marx (and Marxists after him) have to decide whether it is the political "method" that reveals the revolutionary content, or whether the capitalist "object" determines the kind of political method appropriate to the given real conditions. This dilemma is both practical and theoretical, as will be seen in a moment.

A different reconstruction is possible. Marx's epistemological dilemma can be posed in more philosophical terms. The notion that the object determines the method implies that the given reality serves as a *norm* that determines the method by which the object can be known validly. Alternatively, the notion that the method reveals the truth of the object implies that the *genesis* of what is to be understood explains the validity of the knowledge we have of the system under investigation. These two possible philosophical orientations correspond to the structure of knowledge presented by Husserl and his phenomenological successors. Husserl distinguishes the act of knowing (the "noesis," called here the *genetic*) from that which is known (the "noema," called here the *normative*). The task of phenomenology is to analyze the correlation of the genetic and the normative within the experiencing consciousness. For Husserl, that analysis continues indefinitely; his successors—like those of Marx, as will be seen—attempted to "solve" the problem by opting for one or the other side. Only Merleau-Ponty, in his incomplete last work, *The Visible and the Invisible*, rediscovered the dilemma and reformulated it *as a question*. It is perhaps no accident that Merleau-Ponty was the phenomenologist most involved with Marxism and politics. Politics, I will argue, is precisely the *question* posed by the copresence, the independence, and the interdependence of the genetic and the normative moments.

A. Practical Illustrations from Marxism

Criticism is not what Marx meant by "critique." Criticism of the established disorder is nothing new. The cynic might even suggest that the institutionalization of the chance to vent criticism is necessary for the maintenance of capitalism. Criticism is a safety valve as well as a hint of potential trouble spots to which the rulers must turn their attention before they overheat and explode violently. Criticism is threatening only to a totalitarian order whose aim is the elimination of history, of progress, and of the growth of individuation. Capitalism is not a totalitarianism. It needs individuation, if only to encourage the work or consumer ethic; it needs progress and growth because it is built on competition and expansion; and it created history when it inaugurated the project of the transformation of nature for expanded profitability. Criticism, then, is not revolutionary.

Marx offered more than a sustained and powerful denunciation of the inhumanity and irrationality of capitalism; he presented an *immanent critique*—the self critique—of capitalism. Critique is not the same as criticism. Criticism appeals to values external to its object. This externality means that criticism cannot question these values, or be certain of their relation to society. Critique, on the other hand, is a theoretical stance with an immanent relation to practice. Criticism can only appeal for action; critique shows the necessity of that action. Criticism separates subject from object because it does not maintain the *immanence* that permits the critique to show the necessity of the action for which it calls. Thus, to cite two famous passages from *The German Ideology*, which was written to denounce the impotence of mere external criticism: "It doesn't matter what this or that proletarian thinks or does; what matters is what the class *is* and must do." Or, more aphoristically, "consciousness is conscious-being." (*Bewusstsein ist bewusst-sein*).[2] Marx's point here suggests that correct theory *is* practice. True consciousness or theory is immediate knowledge of the real; individual reflective consciousness or ideas tend to deform experience of the truly real class relations.

This notion of critique as wholly immanent covers over a crucial problem. Marx is, after all, talking about a revolution, which is more than just a reflex or reflection of the current state of affairs. If critique theory is revolutionary, this is because the conditions in which it is formulated are *potentially* revolutionary. The theory is *not* the crystallization or rational and normative expression of what in fact is the case—for then revolution would *actually* be occurring and theory would be superfluous. Critique theory is the description of a tension or gap that exists and poses a *question* to which the theory tries to give a normative reply. The revolution is radical only if it entails a break with the existing conditions. The realization or rationalization of what is potentially present is not sufficient. That would be, so to speak, Hegel, not Marx. Revolution would be more concretely, the replacement of competitive capital by a party functioning as the "executive committee of the ruling class." That was hardly Marx's intent. The theoretical problem of course has practical consequences for the analysis of so-called socialism. The notion of revolution itself must be reconsidered.

Critique theory combines what can be called a normative and a genetic approach. (For stylistic reasons, the term "normative" will often be replaced by "validity," with which it is identical.) The theory is normative in relating to existent conditions as their Ought, as the answer to a question of the norm for which they must strive. It is the standard in terms of which the actual is to be known, judged, and transformed. At the same time, the theory depends on what really and materially exists, on what it criticizes, for its genesis. Because it is not the application from outside of some sort of universal or ideal rational norms, the critique's immanent validity claim depends on its genesis. Critique theory is thus the paradoxical formulation of a norm which seeks to negate the genetic conditions of its own possibility. Not all social conditions generate and validate a theorizing which criticizes what is from the stance of a normative Ought. Only a specific social formation, with a specific historical set of social relations—that of capitalism—makes possible this combination of genesis and validity in a critique theory.

The theoretical temptation is to stress either the genetic or the normative orientation in order to resolve the uncertainty posed by their co-presence. Theory has practical consequences; the choices between the genetic and the normative poles illustrate the theoretical difficulty. The debate between the reformist and the revolutionary orientations represented by Bernstein and Lenin shows in turn the practical relevance of theory. Bernstein's *Evolutionary Socialism* can be summed up in his famous remark that "the movement is everything, the final goal is nothing." This attitude typifies a *genetic* approach to politics. Lenin's *What is to be Done?* illustrates the *normative* orientation. Because everyday trade-union activity does not create the political class consciousness necessary for revolutionary action, Lenin gives the party a determining role. The valid knowledge needed, for revolutionary practice is brought to the workers through the mediation of the political party which is aware of the totality of conditions within which the struggle is taking place. That these two extremes do not exclude one another can be seen in the approach of Rosa Luxemburg, where both are juxtaposed in a manner that is tempting but ultimately syncretic. Her refutation of Bernstein in *Social Reform or Revolution?* insists on the normative practical role of theory. She writes that "the final goal of socialism is the only decisive factor distinguishing the Social Democratic movement from bourgeois democracy and bourgeois radicalism, the only factor transforming the entire labor movement from a vain attempt to repair the capitalist order into a class struggle *against* this order." On the other hand, the genetic theory becomes crucial for her practice, for example when she insists in the *Mass Strike* pamphlet that "the element of spontaneity plays such a prominent role in the mass strikes in Russia not because the Russian proletariat is 'unschooled' but because revolutions allow no one to play schoolmaster to them." Luxemburg never unified these two orientations, precisely because she was above all else a *political* theorist. In her polemic with reformism, and in her critique of Lenin, she repeated her *political* solution in the form of a *question*: she spoke of "two reefs" constantly confronted, "abandonment of the mass character or abandonment of the final goal; the fall back to sectarianism or the fall into bourgeois reformism; anarchism or opportunism."[3] This political insight, which runs throughout Luxemburg's life, needs theoretical elaboration.

The normative theory stands outside the genetic conditions it wants to transform; the genetic theory is unable to introduce the normative arguments that would permit the radical intervention and directedness necessary to avoid the contingency of opportunism. Obviously, then, one wants to combine the two approaches. A juxtaposition which preserves the independence of each is not sufficient. Such a syncretism implies that revolution comes about when, somehow, the conditions of objective development of the capitalist economy (i.e., genesis) coincide with the conditions whereby the individual workers come to recognize their membership in an exploited and alienated class as well as the necessity of transforming the basic conditions of their social existence (i.e., normativity). Leninism is "idealist," suggesting that this political class consciousness can only be brought from the outside, by the party; reformism is "empiricist," suggesting that the objective developments will bring about that subjective awareness without forceful intervention from external forces. Actual developments over the past sixty years tend to confirm Lenin's critique of trade unionism's empirical limitations, while simultaneously refuting his own theory of the Party as bringing political consciousness from without. The theoretical ground of both failures lies in the split between normative and genetic approaches, and the impossibility of their being juxtaposed syncretically. This separation has had the same practical result: the preservation of the Party replaces revolutionary social transformation, whether as "Social Democracy" or as a "Socialism" that has crushed all velleities of democracy. This should not surprise; reformist and revolutionary can justly appeal to Marx for the grounds of their practice.

There are many misleading assertions in Marx as to the relation of theory to its object. Besides the already cited equation of consciousness and conscious-being in *The German Ideology*, perhaps the most famous and most typical is the insistence in *Capital* that if the essence and the appearance coincided there would be no need for theory at all. What Marx had in mind was that "what is" is the phenomenal appearance, a distorted self-presentation of an underlying essential reality. The task of theory becomes the demystification of the appearances, permitting the discovery of what is essentially and really the case. Theory makes use here of a method called laconically "Science." Once that critical demystification is accomplished, effective practical action is supposed to be possible; illusory ideas and ideals no longer can distort the good works once the Archimedian point has been found in reality. This is hardly a methodological innovation! Its presuppositions go back to the Greeks. It was institutionalized with the scientific revolution that introduces modernity. In politics, it is the stance of the Enlightenment. In each case, the result is only a modification of the genetic stance; it says that the roots of genesis are not found in appearances but in the "really real," which is now defined as essence. This, however, has the paradoxical implication that the apparent empiricism of science is founded on a belief in the existence of deeper or "essential" realities which generate the appearance as empirical phenomena. This paradox suggests that Marx's statement is only misleading to the reader who is unaware of the importance of the methodological question posed by the notion of critique and presented in the duality of the genetic and the normative orientations.

Marx's debt to Hegel explains how the difference of essence and appearance permits critique theory to combine genesis and validity in the analysis of capitalist social relations. Hegel's *Logic* explains that an essence is a relational, and so a dynamic structure. The essence of an essence is to appear; the appearance is the appearance of the essence. Appearances are not nothing. There are no essences which do not appear; and there are no appearances without an essence. Marx uses the Hegelian category of essence in analyzing capitalism. *Capital* analyzes a historically specific set of social relations. "Capital" is not a thing; it is not money, raw materials, factories, and the like. If the grammatical distortion is permitted, "capital" *is* the plural social relations among producers and owners which, through the division of labor, permits individual appropriation of socially produced wealth. Capitalist dynamics has its motor in the asymmetric relation of capital and labor, each of whose actions calls forth necessarily a reaction on the part of the other. If labor wins an increase of wages or improvement of conditions, capital must respond with technological innovation, increasing what Marx called "relative surplus-value" or having recourse to sheer force in the attempt to push down real wages. In Marx's Hegelian formulation, labor is the essence and capital the appearance whose transformation is forced on it by the action of labor. Labor's action in the phenomenal world is at the same time its self-transformation since it changes the relation of the essence to its appearance. The end of this process would be the identity of the appearance and the essence—in this case a society of, by, and for the workers. In this way, *Capital* is a dialectical critique theory combining genesis (i.e., the social-historical interplay of essence and appearance, and the transformations of each in their essential relation) and validity (i.e., normative critique from the stance of the essence "labor" which is advancing toward an appearance adequate to it). The relations among the articulations that compose the three volumes, as well as the preparatory study, the *Grundrisse*, can be presented in this framework.[4]

Marx of course intended to "stand Hegel on his head." Hegel's *Logic* reconciled the dynamics of essence in the unity of the Concept, where the actual is the relational and the rational is the actual. Marx replaced the Concept with the autonomous proletariat, which would *make* the actual rational and the rational actual. Marx set out this task in his 1843 "Introduction to a Critique of Hegel's Philosophy of Right," where he introduced the *concept* of the proletariat as both the subject or active force of history, and as a new object produced "artificially" by a specific historical social formation, capitalism. His stress on the artificial production of the proletariat pointed forward. In the first of the *1844 Manuscripts*, Marx concretized the necessary constitution of this "artificial" proletariat by means of long citations from the classical political economists. Although his later studies developed a different economics, the basic outline of his critique theory was established at this point. As subjective, the proletariat makes normative claims; as objective, these normative claims are genetically explained and justified. The result is that the dialectical critique theory is incarnate in the proletariat. Marxism therefore can claim to be the theory *of* proletarian revolution—an immanent critique and not just a criticism of capitalism; indeed, capitalism's own self-critique. The practical difficulty, however, was also present in these texts. The 1843 "Introduction" could not explain the origin of the class consciousness—called there the "lightning of thought"—that would actualize this potential. The 1844 concept of alienation did not get much further. Without a successful account, the revolution that Marx wanted to theorize risks the reproach that—like Hegel—this theory stands at the end of History. The revolution that only realizes what is already essentially present does not entail a rupture that creates a new history. The New that the revolution realizes must be conceived substantively if revolution is not—in Marx's words—to reproduce *die gleiche alte Scheisse*.

B. Revolution, History and the New

The term "revolution" has become today one of those "sponge" concepts that C. Wright Mills mocked as it sweeps together and liquidates indifferently whatever crosses its path. A concept so broad as to be applicable to the scientific, religious, social, aesthetic, political, and personal dimensions of human existence is too general to be helpful or meaningful. Peasant and scientific "revolution" may be legitimate usages, but their referents are as different from one another as religion from philosophy. Revolution in its modern sense presupposed the wrenching linearization of heavenly cycles that occurred when no new corollaries or adjustments could save the Ptolemaic world view. When earthly nature was no longer the divine center and *arché*, the origin and judge of all, then and only then, was transformation possible. Only after Copernicus' revolution was Kant's "Copernican Revolution" able to insert human agency at the origin; only then could there be "something new under the sun." Or, to use the terms of critique theory to describe these changes: revolution is possible only when genesis and validity are separated. Their separation poses a problem, which therefore unites them in a question. Revolution is, from this point of view, the *posing* of a question, *not* its purported answer. The difference is crucial to any radical conception of the political dimension of modern life.

The political concept of revolution is possible only when history becomes a problem. There are no Greek revolutions properly speaking. The Sophists could be read retrospectively as a revolutionary threat, just as Hegel saw Socrates as a "principle of individuality" menacing the organic unity of the polis. This reads back a modern notion of history into the Greek world view; it imposes a politics on the polis. The resulting amalgam is as useless as is the desire to recreate that polis in capitalist societies. The revolutionary individual who "succeeded" was, of course, Jesus—with the militant aid of Paul's transformation of the faith *of* Jesus into the faith *in* Jesus.[5] Jesus' success can be explained variously; most significantly from the present point of view, however, is that he can be conceived as the unity of genesis and validity. The "Son of God" is also the "Son of Man." But the temporality of traditional society transformed the Christian Revolution.

If Paul's achievement is conceived by analogy to that of Lenin, Paul's "Marx"—if the anachronism be permitted here—was Augustine. The *City of*

God constituted a dualistic history out of the decaying Empire. The result was that revolution became revelation and the New was eliminated. The secular city, and later the Thomistic *ordo*, received their validity and norms from an unquestionable Source or origin outside of them. The genetic aspect of Christianity was left implicit until the Protestant Revolution, in its varying guises, reintroduced this component. The avatars of this rejuvenated Christianity can be traced by those more competent or more concerned. The present illustration is introduced only to hint at the dimensions of History that pose the problem of the substantively New, whose capitalization here is thereby justified. The New is new; it is not a potential which is actualized, an acorn becoming an oak or a permutation and recombination of what was previously present and accepted. The New does not emerge gradually or violently from a temporal continuum. It breaks with temporality and institutes its own order. Such was monotheism, the invention of democracy and philosophy by the Greeks, or the Copernican and Kantian revolutions. (Such, too, was the advent of capitalism. The difficulty of indicating its temporal starting point poses a conceptual problem. But for now, because of its results, we can legitimately speak of it here as a revolution.) A well-known illustration is used by Engels to explain Marx's work. Its implications are significant. The ''discovery'' of oxygen by Priestly and Lavoisier was nothing new from the stance of the old phlogistic physics; yet, in fact, it inaugurated the new chemistry. Once it exists as *valid*, the New can explain its own *genesis*. The new chemistry can explain phlogistics and its apparatus; it can explain the legitimacy of its own emergence. But neither its genesis alone, nor its validity alone, suffice to institute the New. Neither the paradoxes of phlogistics nor the success of modern chemistry explains its emergence as the new ''paradigm.'' The paradox is that *the New does not emerge from* the womb of history; *it creates* History once it is instituted.

From this point of view, the oft-cited example of the bourgeois or capitalist character of the French Revolution takes on its full, non-ideological sense. The Revolution was not made possible *because* capitalism already existed as an actual potency constrained by the old feudal or absolutist order. The French Revolution was the New that instituted the specific history or temporality that *in turn* made possible what became French capitalism. The advent of capitalism elsewhere took different paths, less dramatic and more difficult to pinpoint. Included in them, always, was the significance of the French events whose vivid rupture gave significance to an otherwise gradual process. In each case, the New explains—and thus banalizes—the rupture that made it possible. The rupture appears to explain its genesis. yet, without the creation of the New, the conditions of the rupture—which had existed previously—were not perceivable. Genesis thus explains validity; but, *vice-versa*, the genetic depends on the normative validity for its own appearance.

Marx's theory suggests that capitalism creates a history ''pregnant'' with revolution. Two interpretations of his position can be offered at this point. Either the proletariat, as subject-object of history, is the agent of a total transformation which will end all opposition (including that of genesis and validity), and so put an end to history as it has existed up to now. Or, Marx can be understood, more subtly, to argue that the specific temporality of capitalism institutionalizes invention, transformation, and novelty because it destroys all attachment to nature and to traditional origins in its continual quest for accumulation in which anything and everything is grist for its all-encompassing mill. In this sense, *capitalism* (not communism) is the end of history as it has been lived previously; the New which it places on the agenda is that there is nothing any longer that can be qualitatively new; and the proletariat is revolutionary because it is the "nothing" and total negation of this self-reproducing and self-devouring system. There is much in Marx and in the contemporary experience of consumer society and "Mass culture" which argues for this latter reading. Capitalism is the great leveler or philosopher's stone which transmutes all difference into equal (quantitative) measures and renders the world a stage "full of sound and fury, signifying nothing." This, of course, makes problematic the position of the proletariat as subject-object of revolution *if the proletariat is conceived as a real sociological agent*. This difficulty explains the great variety of "revolutionary subjects" or coalitions that run today from "the" third world to women and minorities *via* new classes and the like down, finally, the full expression of the negation in Marcuse's espousal of a "Great Refusal" in *One-Dimensional Man*.[7]

If revolution institutes the New, which in turn institutes its own form of historical temporality, then a *theory* of revolution is a paradoxical venture which is not possible arbitrarily anywhere or at any time. Marx's theory is based upon the actual existence of a real *agent* of revolution. The proletariat is an actual, active class subject which incarnates the critique's unity of genesis and validity. As such, it is not the answer but a living *question*. It is not the New, but the agent which will make possible the New because it is the self-questioning, self-doubt and crisis of the old. Proletarian revolution does not inaugurate the rule of the proletariat; it abolishes the proletariat. The paradox is expressed in an oft-repeated phrase which Marx uses for the first time with his discovery of the proletariat in 1843: "its victory is at the same time its own defeat." The successful answer to a question eliminates the question, which no longer surprises, unsettles, or intrigues. Thus Marx insists repeatedly that the proletariat is "the riddle of history solved." This phrase must be read carefully: the proletariat is both the riddle of history *and* its solution. To unpack the image, the genesis of the proletariat must be understood and the validity of its claim laid out in further detail. In this way, these general assertions about Revolution, History, and the New will be clarified. The discussions will have to be abstract at first, before the generalities can be translated into sociological considerations of the relation of the state to economic society.

C. The Political and the Social

The revolt of the rebel can be distinguished from the struggle of the revolutionary (class). This formulation implies that the rebel is doomed. Against its invocation of the rights of genesis, those who control the social norms will beat down this manifestation of individuality. Against its invocation of the validity of norms, the weight of the real triumphs over its rebellious appeal. Neither factuality alone nor ideality alone is sufficient. Social change must be politically validated if it is not to wither in isolation; and political success is hollow without social substance. Social genesis needs political normativity, and *vice-versa*. The dream of building the new society in the pores of the old is as vain as the wait for the mythical lawgiver who will institute the just legislation. Conceptually, even the rebel would not doubt the need for mediation between the polar alternatives. The revolutionary mediation which unites the social and immediate genesis with the political and universal structure of normativity is, alas, easier conceived than produced.

Successful rebellion is impossible. The rebel must either go under or create anew precisely those conditions that the rebellion sought to destroy. The situation can be described logically. Rebellion is the assertion of the principle of One (individual or group) against the Many. The One, or individual, is only one *individual* because of its relation to the Many, who, in turn, are Many only as *many* individuals. I am this individual only because I am different from many others; therefore, my individuality is not something pregiven and wholly mine; my individuality depends on the others' too. Their social relations must be structured to permit my individuality; if they are unstructured, in the random state of a "war of all against all," then my individuality is unstable and threatened. Consequently, consistent individualism demands an ordered social whole, a politics, as the condition of its possibility. Since the condition of possibility is (logically or ontologically) prior to the individual it makes possible, stress has to be placed on the whole as normative. On the other hand, the Many only exist as many individuals, since without individuation they would be only an indifferent mass—they would be, in effect, One. The source of the individuation of the Many is the individual One on whom they depend. The One thus becomes the (logical or ontological) condition generating the possibility of the Many, whom it orders as individuals related socially to one another. Logically consistent rebellion thus recreates the unified structure against which it asserted its individuality.

Posed less abstractly, but still without historical specificity, rebellion can be defined as the affirmation of the social against the political. It is a reaction to a given set of conditions which it either seeks to maintain or which it wants to institute in place of present conditions. This explains the "right to resistance" that can be read into *social* contract theory. The conditions which call forth the rebellion are not political. The *social* contract is, after all, social; it is prepolitical logically and sociologically. The political comes about in reaction to social conditions; more specifically, the political presupposes social *divisions*. Social divisions are not necessarily those which contemporary Western eyes perceive. The division of labor, for example, may or may not be an actual opposition; similarly the relation of man/woman, parent/child, teacher/student, and so on, may or may not be actual social divisions that make possible political action. Historical specification is necessary. The problem, however, is that Marx, Freud, and Nietzsche have shown sufficiently that what people think motivates their action may be illusory, the ideological covering-over of what really is at issue. Thus, if the rebellion fails, one concludes that the social divisions from which it sprang were illusory. The successful rebellion, of course, would be rooted in "real" social divisions; it would then be that revolution whose genesis lies in the social and whose validity is its political translation. The sociological problem, then, is *which* are the real social divisions. Before treating this issue, further conceptual clarification will avoid the mistake of falsely concretizing the general categories of method.

The implication of social rebellion becoming political revolution is that social conflict leads to political action whose aim is to eliminate these very same conflicts. What is one to say of a politics whose aim is the elimination of the conditions which make it possible? With Sheldon Wolin,[8] one might point out that the idea is an old one, going back to Plato's Guardians who are to be "selfless servants" putting into dictatorial practice what is inscribed in the heaven of the Ideas. This makes politics an apparantly conservative venture. Plato's solution was the last gasp of a static society threatened by the emergence of individual subjectivity. Following this hint, and leaping merrily over the epochs, it appears that politics does in fact come to the fore at times of threat and disorganization. Its aim is not to restore the social but to eliminate it—and itself—as a threat. Looking more concretely at the history of political thought, the results of political success appear to create a series of further stratifications in the divided society as a way of preserving its stability. The result, however, at the same time introduces a New. The pattern can be stated abstractly. First subjectivity and social life are separated in Greece. Then a sphere of separate legal relations emerges in Rome. This is followed by the personalized domain of religious conscience, which is transformed as the sphere of interest-following economic affairs, until the modern, secularized, and relativistic sociality is created. Each of these stratifications was a Revolution in the sense that the term was defined above. Each was able, once it had achieved normative legitimacy, to explain the conditions that made necessary its genesis, although none could have deduced the new norm from its pre-condition until the revolution had occurred actually. The "agency" of revolution differed in each case owing to the specificity of the social divisions in which it existed. The revolution was not a punctual event in time as the messianic religious tradition would have it. In each case, a New emerged, structuring a specific temporality of history, and validating politically the new social divisions that made it possible.

The revolutionary unity of genesis and validity in a single agent can come about only when the stratification of the social has come so far that the political is itself the salient *social* division. As long as society was divided among *its* elements, and the political task was their unification or harmonious structuration, rebellion was condemned to failure. The dialectic of the One and the Many held sway. When the social division is itself political (instead of calling forth the political) the dialectic of the One and the Many in which the rebel was caught breaks down because the poles are no longer distinct and mutually self-defining. That traditional dialectic is replaced by the dynamics of essence, as Marx described capitalist relations. This is why Marx never felt the need to elaborate a political theory once he had completed his "Critique of Hegel's Philosophy of the State."

D. State and Civil Society

Hegel is usually considered the first philosopher to insist systmatically on the principled difference of civil society from the life of the family (*oikos*) on the one hand and the tasks of the state (polis) on the other. Civil society is based on the principle of atomism; its coherence is created by the interdependence of personal need which, through a kind of invisible hand, unites the differences while maintaining their difference. There is no need to insist here on the specifics of Hegel's account; he is describing an ideal of classical capitalist society on the basis of his reading of the British political economists. But Hegel is a political thinker. He refuses utilitarian optimism. He portrays graphically the problems inherent in the atomistic egoism on which civil society is based. Under the rubric "The Police and the Corporations," he describes the necessity of measures akin to those which a (corporate) welfare state would offer today, from street lights and taxation to health care and required school attendance. Hegel insists on civil society's responsibility to its members. When he confronts the social relations that impose the increasing impoverishment of workers, he insists on the danger that the creation of a rabble (*Pöbel*) entails for the stability of civil society in a manner recalling Adam Smith's fear that England would become "a nation of Helots." Hegel recognizes the threat of permanent social division resulting from economic inequality, sees how this leads to colonial expansion as one type of solution (although he thinks the colonies would serve the motherland better if they were freed), and suggests measures for insuring the economic protection of the individual within the civil framework. At another level, he recognizes also the threat to individuality that emerges with the alienating mechanization of labor as the worker becomes a mere appendage to the machine. To this social-psychological danger he opposes the corporation, a kind of craft union or guild which he also describes as a "second family." But neither the economic police nor the social-psychological corporations bring together civil society into an organic unity, since by definition civil society is the "system of social atomism" whose principle is particularity. Hegel's (corporative) welfare state is intended to serve only to protect this particularity.

Hegel's theory of the state proper—which is distinguished from the (corporative) welfare state described in the account of civil society—attempted to explain the nature and function of the political sphere within modern social conditions. Its three constitutive moments, the monarch, the administration, and the legislative, represent the moments of individuality, particularity, and universality, which are to be brought together in an encompassing unity which permits the independence of the constitutive parts. The debates about Hegel's alleged Prussian statism, his liberal or reactionary orientation, need not concern us here.[9] More important is Marx's critique—not for its theoretical details (whose polemical purposes at times misunderstand Hegel's theoretical stance), but for its practical effect and implications. Marx tries to demystify the unity which Hegel's state is to provide, reducing Hegel's political synthesis to the elements of civil society which it was supposed to legitimate and preserve. Marx's point is that insofar as the social relations described by Hegel have a normative unity, their genesis in civil society accounts for it. This genetic source can then be shown to be contradictory and unstable. Marx proceeds from this insight to offer a resounding critique of political alienation as a mystification which hides the real sources of human misery. His next step is to lay bare the social contradictions of civil society, where the proletariat and its revolutionary possibility are finally discovered, as was seen. Revolution is thus accounted for genetically by a demystification of the normative pretensions of Hegel's objective idealism.

At the level of description, the similarities between Marx and Hegel are greater than their differences. Both analyze civil society as a capitalist economy. Both show how this economy generates inequalities, social differences, and forms of alienation which make impossible the continued reproduction of the "system of atomism" on an expanded scale. The difference between the two is that Marx recognizes and thematizes the novelty of the capitalist economy and its proper historicity, whereas Hegel integrates it into his trans-historical conceptual machinery. One might attribute this distinction to the influence of real economic development on Marx, who after all was living at the time of capitalist penetration whereas Hegel's Germany was still a largely traditional society. But explanation of theory by historical circumstance is often the disguise for conceptual laziness.[10] As a theorist, Hegel saw the dangers of civil society's system of (economic) atomism sweeping over all human relations, and tried—however inadequately—to oppose the reduction of politics to sociology that this entailed. Hegel is thus a political liberal, anticipating Tocqueville, fearing the closure which would make constant social change the immanent principle of all life and thereby eliminate meaningful change, human freedom, history, and the New.

Marx's description of the economic domination of civil society is closer to contemporary experience than is Hegel's attempt to preserve the difference between the social and the political. What the political had accomplished previously—the normative validation of social relations—becomes the province of the economy once the principle of social atomism and the system of need come to dominate. The result of this economic domination is that genesis and the (politically) normative apparently are united. Yet this is only an appearance. Division is not eliminated. Each of the spheres of economic society weighs-in as qualitatively identical to the others. The "politics" that results is the adjustment of a mechanical force-field toward quantitative equilibrium. The "politics" of each actor or group consists in behaving in a manner that increases its particular force so that its quantitative value carries greater weight than the others in determining the final equilibrium. The famous Marxian thesis, that the state is the "executive committee of the ruling class," makes perfect sense in this picture-frame. Similarly, the apparently opposed theses—that the role of politics has increased, or that it has decreased—can both be accepted. The role of politics has increased insofar as the extension of economic considerations to all aspects of life has given each and all of our activities a weight within the quantitative force-field. The role of politics has decreased insofar as individual economic calculation has replaced political decisions by the group as that which decides for us our collective way of life.

This domination of (economic) civil society over all aspects of life is New. It institutes a new vision of history. It would be an anachronism to follow the ideologues in rationalizing the advent of this social formation with notions that its origins lie in our nature as laboring animals, possessive individualists, or an instinct to truck and barter. One may explain its advent variously—with Weber's Calvinists, Marx's primitive accumulation and class struggle, the scientific and/or technological discoveries beginning in the sixteenth century, demographic shifts and a longue durée, etc., etc. Something New arose, whether the explanation of its origins is in politics or society, science, philosophy, or religion. A conception of the human being, of nature and our relation to nature, of time and history, spread through the interstices of social relations. The results were most evident in the sphere of the economy understood as the production and distribution of scarce goods; but they were felt throughout the society.

The dominance of the economic was the *result* of a revolution. Economic society cannot explain either the revolution which brought about its own domination or the one which would end its hegemony. All societies produce and reproduce the means of social self-maintenance. The manner in which they do it, the way in which this production and reproduction is integrated into their social being, differs. This difference in the way societies relate to production and reproduction can be understood from the perspective of genesis and validity. Economic relations are genetic social forces, whose validation depends on the political norms that unite the society. Only with the birth of capitalism does a theory of "political economy" make sense. Politics can explain the revolution that gave the economy pride of place; but economics cannot, in turn, explain either those politics which gave birth to it or those which will end its reign.

The triumph of political economy has been epitomized recently in Marcuse's concept of "one dimensionality." It appears that nothing New is possible any longer, that the economy can absorb any and every mode; that it has made change into its immanent principle. The rebel is no longer an oppositional figure. The affirmation of individuality only affirms the principle of social atomism which holds the system together. The outsiders, from whom Marcuse once thought change could come, are easily brought into the merry-go-round. There is no need to pursue this too familiar theme here. If there is no longer an outside, no distinction between genesis and validity, the temptation is to turn to the contradictory structure of the economy itself as the key to its transformation.

E. Crisis and Political Possibility

Hegel and Marx are not the only analysts to recognize the tendency to disequilibrium in an unrestrained individualistic capitalism. From the daily press to the economics textbooks to the classical founders, the problem of economic crisis is present constantly. Two polar types of analyses are usually offered. In the first instance, the crises are neutralized psychologically by attributing them to "natural" cyclical causes whose benign effect is to achieve an equilibrium in the system by raising or lowering wages/profits, production or savings, investment and interest rates, and even population growth. Or, from the side of the Marxists, crises are seen as leading to a continual linear growth of class organization and consciousness on the part of the workers who will ultimately be able to inaugurate the great socialist revolution. To these apparently polar explanations, governments have added variants of a third, which sees crises as the product of human choices which state action must counterbalance through different forms of "fine tuning." This, too, will pass as the pendulum moves.

Common to the explanations of crises is that each solves the problem by rendering it metaphysical, thereby avoiding it or making it merely epiphenomenal. In the first case, the resort to nature is explicit. Crises are the appearance of something deeper, a natural tendency toward equilibrium. They are a necessary purge, a sign of healing like the heightening of fever which immediately precedes the cure. Crises restore a natural, healthy competitive complexion to free enterprise; or they give rise to inventions or adjustments which increase the welfare of all. From the other side, the Marxist replaces the metaphysics of nature with a metaphysics of the historical process. Crises are again an appearance of something deeper, a necessary manifestation like the training of an athlete that will render the new healthy body immune from the old germs and capable at last of innovating freely and consciously. The state's explanation fares no better. When it is not reduced to tinkering with forces which it can adjust but cannot control, the state's action is legitimated by virtue of a rationalist metaphysics whose hubris is to assume that there is nothing which is not within the power of technical reason.

When crises are thus explained by being explained away, there is no room for a politics of change or for the question that is the advent of the New. Whether they are taken as natural, historical, or rational, their necessity produces a metaphysical result which is unquestioned and unquestionable; it makes no difference. This should not be surprising, since capitalist civil society is structured to reduce all otherness and difference to qualitative identity. It is not even clear when the term "crisis" is applicable in these conditions. Is the crisis measured in terms of unemployment, inflation, amounts or rates of profit, investment . . . ? One might envision statistics in any of these domains which would imply the existence of immense human misery and suffering. But there is no reason to expect that economic collapse in any or all of these domains will inaugurate the New Society. There is no reason to expect that any kind of *economic* misery will lead to radical political change.[11]

The persistence of capitalist crisis has to be understood as a *question*, not as the source of an answer. Capitalist civil society is not a homogeneous self-reproducing unity of individual atoms. It is a divided civil society. Capitalist civil division differs from past forms of social differentiation, which were qualitative distinctions that defined individuals in relation to a politically articulated whole. Under capitalism, Estates give way to classes, whose difference is primarily quantitative or economic, and only secondarily qualitative. The notion of class interest suggests a generalizability of the social divisions calling for political intervention. Whether the political intervention (or crisis-management) is performed by "the executive committee of the ruling class" or by a neutral administrative agency, the significant point is that it implies that something more and other than the economic is sought (even if it is only sought for the solution to economic problems). However perverted or distorted, the political sphere is still present. Its presence suggests that the reconciliation of genesis and validity is not achieved in fact by the reduction to capitalist civil society.

Looking backward from today, when the state's intervention into economic and social relations is obvious and accepted, one sees that our own conditions differ at most quantitatively from those in which capitalism was born. Lord Robbins's treatment of the attitude of the classical economists to the question of social welfare shows their awareness of the artificiality of the capitalist society that they were in the process of creating through governmental intervention.[12] They were aware too of the human costs of their project, however much they were convinced that its results, in the long run, would benefit the social whole. Polanyi's *The Great Transformation* stresses graphically and more critically the same points, to which other testimony could be added. What emerges from these arguments is that capitalist civil society is an essentially *political* creation. Like politics generally, this intervention is aimed at eliminating the conditions which called it forth, and so at eliminating the need for politics; that class rules best whose rule is seen least! The persistence of crises suggests that the venture cannot succeed, that the spheres cannot be collapsed, and that politics cannot be eliminated. This does not, however, mean that "revolutionary politics" is generated by, or legitimated through the economic form in which the crises appear.

F. The Agent of Revolution

Capitalisim is the first inherently dynamic society for which growth and change are essential to its social preservation. Capitalism's uniqueness cannot be stressed too strongly. Social historians have described vividly the radical transformation in behavior and attitude which capitalism demanded. Max Weber's *Protestant Ethic* begins from the wonder that Benjamin Franklin's common-sensical observations on daily life—"time is money" and the like—would have inspired in anyone not already accepting a capitalist *Weltanschauung*. Weber suggests that only the most profound personal transformation, a religious conversion, could account for a shift of such dimensions. Other historians have shown that, whatever the case in the realm of individual conscience, calculated force, usually with the assistance of the state, was necessary for capitalism's implantation. Once it was created, capitalism began to deliver the goods. Its material successes seemed to outweigh the miseries it cost; these material successes were its political legitimation. Only when material growth temporarily ceased, with the recurring of cyclical crises, was this political legitimization put into question.

Pre-capitalist societies were organized to prevent change; their social reproduction was oriented around constant repetition. The capitalist revolution did not take place in one blow, at one moment, through one discovery. (In this sense, the comparison, used above, with scientific revolutions is illegitimate. The source of the belief in a unique original act is a myth born with the French Revolution.) It can be asserted that the capitalist revolution has not been completed today, or—with equal justification—capitalism's origins can be traced back to the Renaissance and High Middle Ages in phenomena like the invention of double-entry bookkeeping or the development of perspectival painting! The capitalist process is a constant and continuing leveling or reduction of all spheres of meaning. Its precondition, therefore, is the existence of non-capitalist spheres which encourage and maintain its dynamism. The nature of these necessary non-capitalist spheres would give the guidelines for a sociological periodization of capitalism's internal development. Classical capitalism would be defined by the dynamic of national productive growth; its national success would then give rise to colonial capitalism, imperial capitalism, and today to a welfare-state capitalism. To these macro-levels, more microscopic details could be added. The salient theoretical point is that capitalism needs an Other to insure its dynamism.

Because it needs an Other to insure its dynamics of growth and leveling, capitalism is always threatened. Revolution, in the most commonplace sense of the term, is an immanent possibility which capitalism reproduces necessarily. The Other is *at once* the agent of potential overthrow as well as life-giving necessity for capitalism. (From this point of view, it was not wrong to think that colonial, or anti-imperialist, or client-outsider revolt was a threat to the capitalist system.) This Other is capitalism's conceptual "proletariat." The necessity of the proletariat to capitalism means that capitalism is the first social system which must put revolution necessarily on its agenda. The paradox is only apparent.

The necessary presence of this Other, the proletariat or agent of revolution, explains why capitalism is crisis-prone. It explains why politics cannot be eliminated in the self-reproducing capitalist civil society. It suggests that the unity of genesis and validity that would be created by a capitalism which "delivers the goods" is not possible. Marx's use of Hegel's logical concept of essence as a necessarily relational unity expresses this mutual dependence. Economic imperatives alone cannot explain the (political) structure of capitalist society because these imperatives depend on the non-economic spheres which they must confront and reproduce necessarily and continually. Capitalist crisis-management is always also crisis-production. If the recalcitrance of the proletarian Other is too great, the goods cannot be delivered and one has a "crisis of underproduction"; if the proletarian Other is integrated too fully, one has a "crisis of overproduction," which also halts the dynamics.

It has been necessary to speak in conceptual terms of a "proletarian Other" here in order to avoid a crucial error. Capitalism always creates an agent of revolution, and always puts revolution on the agenda. But the essential structure of capitalism means that this proletarian Other is *not real*. By "not real," I do not mean to imply that there are not real actors involved, struggling, suffering, making do. The point is that these actors are dependent on capitalism for their existence and possibilities, just as it is dependent on them for its own reproduction. Their relation is a structure of essence/appearance, where neither pole is independent or able to stand alone. Change in one necessarily changes the other. This is why capitalism is a uniquely historical society.

Marx's dialectical critique theory was built on the notion that the proletariat was the *real* agent of revolution. In it, genesis and validity were united. It *incarnated* the principle of a new society. In a relation of essence, each of the sides can play respectively the part of genesis or validity; but neither can unite the two in an independent (revolutionary) unity which would end their mutual dependence. The relative success of capitalism is due to its ability to unite genesis and validity in a process which is only temporarily disjoined in times of crisis. Capitalist politics can be only crisis-management (and crisis-production) because its task is defined by the need to preserve this unstable unity. Anti-capitalist revolutionary politics would have to break asunder this unity and create a new one, abolishing the dependent proletarian Other. In that case, however, this politics cannot be simply the expression of the *real* needs and actions of the actual proletariat at a given moment.

The theoretical notions of genesis and validity were introduced here by a comparison of the reformist and the revolutionary Marxist tactics identified with Bernstein and Lenin. Both options had to fail. Luxemburg's incorporation of both was unable to translate her political *question* into an institutional form. Had she lived, it is doubtful that she could have posed an alternative to the equally unsatisfactory Second and Third Internationals. The reason for this, in theoretical terms, is that her position, like the other two, took the proletariat as the *real* subject of revolution. The revolutionary party took the stance of normativity, from which it attempted to generate social conditions to match its unfalsifiable verities. The reformist party took the side of genesis, adapting its norms opportunistically to the needs of the moment. These were the only two options possible once the assumption of a real unity which would end the tension between the two poles had been made. Luxemburg's powerful critique and her insistent practical questioning still did not represent the kernal of an alternative approach.

The difficulties of assuming Marx's legacy are not accidental. They have theoretical roots. The necessity of a *real* agent of revolution is capitalism's need; the proletarian Other was seen to be immanent to the logic of capitalism. Capitalism's logic is inherently apolitical or reductive. It seeks continually to solve the questions it cannot help but pose. At the same time, however, this makes capitalism inherently unstable. Its immanently historical and crisis-prone character pose questions which it can solve only by dissolving them into its own reproductive movement. The political task today as yesterday is to find a way to fix those questions *as questions*, as political *problems which cannot be eliminated* by transformed productive relations. The logic of capitalism's social relations creates Marxism; revolution will be radical only when it goes beyond this logic.

Marx remains the starting point for any revolutionary political theory. His errors are as telling as his insights are provocative. The attempt to unify genesis and validity in a critique theory whose agent is the *real* proletariat founded a new style of theorizing. There are, in fact, "two Marxes," as many have come to recognize. There is the Marx for whom capitalism is the "really real" which generates a theory whose task is normative interrogation and criticism. This Marx is the heir of classical philosophy, whose thematic destruction (or "deconstruction") begins with Heidegger's transformation of Husserl's radical insights. But there is also the Marx for whom capitalism is a *problem*, a *question* which theory articulates and brings to consciousness. This is the Marx who thematizes class struggle as the constitutive tension of the capitalist social formation, and who makes possible a *political* theory which could escape the classical dilemmas. Whether this Marx can move beyond the theoretical to the practical problems posed by the author of the "Critique of Political Economy" is the question with which I leave the reader. As author, in quest of a "politics of critique," I suggest that there are more fertile fields to cultivate.

7

The Origin and Limits of Philosophical Politics

Post-war French philosophy is often seen as having been dominated by the omnipresence of political concerns. In fact, this political pre-occupation typifies more the philosophers than their philosophies, at least until the mid-1960s. The new direction inaugurated by structuralism began a shift whose final result (or deconstruction) was the replacement of philosophy by (a certain kind of) politics. The nature of this shift can be charted by a glance at the philosophers' attempt to understand the problem of totalitarianism which put into question their linear progressive model of historical development which implicitly or explicitly denied the autonomy of the political. The unmediated politicization of philosophy that emerged from the philosophical critique of totalitarianism in the 1970s gave place to a reaction that took the form of a fascination with a moralist liberalism which stresses individual freedom over the quest for social equality that was supposedly at the roots of the totalitarian misadventure. The wheel had turned its full cycle. The new liberalism is no more capable than was Marxism of articulating the proper place of the political. Yet this *philosophical* problem is the key to the formulation of any practical politics which can claim to be adequate to the demands of *modern* society. The precondition for its analysis is the recognition that totalitarianism is not simply the problem of Stalinism, nor is it reducible to a rhetorical weapon in a Cold War. The analysis of totalitarianism provides the key to understanding the dilemmas of politics within a modern democracy.

Luc Ferry's three volumes of *Philosophie politique*[1] are an attempt to right the balance by returning to the classical concerns of philosophy in order to rethink the conditions of the possibility of politics. This French attempt to produce a politics by (German, Kantian-Fichtean) philosophical means concludes, however, with a formalism, founded on the concept of the political republic, which leaves no place for concrete political action. The strength of its philosophical demonstration of the place of the political can be supplemented by Jürgen Habermas's recent attempts to formulate a critical theory capable of confronting the ''dialectic of enlightenment'' which encapsulates the paradoxes of modernity. Habermas accepts the French deconstruction of the notion of a constitutive subject while rejecting its nihilistic and cynical political conclusions. But his critique of the subject, and his attempt to replace it by a politics of the life-world, ultimately denies the autonomy of the political. A combination of the two approaches suggests the *methodological* determination of the place of the political and its relation to the concerns of philosophy. Ferry and Habermas delineate clearly the space within which a democratic politics can take root. Curiously, however, neither sees the *political* nature of such a theory.[2]

A. The Importance of Totalitarianism

The belated discovery of totalitarianism by French philosophers coincides with their tardy turn to political philosophy. These overpoliticized individuals were unable to translate their 'existential' engagement into what might be called philosophical praxis. The archetype is of course Sartre, whose attempt finally to come to grips with political philosophy in the *Critique of Dialectical Reason* (1960) was not—and has not been—taken seriously.[3] One difficulty lay in the treatment of Stalin, of whom Sartre's theory leads him to say that he ''is'' the party and the state, and that ''the very idea of the dictatorship of the proletariat is absurd.'' Sartre was not the first important French philosopher to criticize the Stalinism that he, and they, had defended in the Manichean mode of the Cold War. Merleau-Ponty's *Adventures of the Dialectic* (1955) had pointed to the snares awaiting any dialectical attempt to imprint in reality the conceptual unity of subject and object in a transparent vision. Nearly half of Merleau-Ponty's book was devoted to a critique of ''Sartre and ultra-Bolshevism.'' Despite the Russian invasion of Hungary the next year, which led many to leave the Communist Party, the theoretical lesson remained to be drawn.[4]

Totalitarianism seemed easy to explain away, to rationalize if not to justify. At the most elementary level, the Marxist could follow Trotsky (without necessarily acknowledging the source) in suggesting that the economic infrastructure is the crucial variable to which the political forms will gradually become adequate. Stalinism thus would be only a temporary, superstructural aberration. In the context of the Cold War, this suggested that the critique of totalitarianism plays into the hands of the enemies of socialism; the critique is said to treat the political variable as if it were the determining factor that permits condemnation of the real and presumably continuing social achievements of the Soviet Union. This political variant of the argument leads to a second version of the theoretical explanation. Totalitarianism is interpreted socio-culturally; it is said to be produced in regimes dominated by scarcity which, for historical reasons having to do with Western colonization and imperial domination, have been unable to develop the practice of active citizenship. Once again, the political form is treated as the dependent variable. The practical, Cold War, translation of this variant of the theory takes the form of support for anti-colonial and anti-imperialist struggles as the key to overcoming totalitarianism as well as for their own sake. As in the previous political translation of the theory, there is again no room, and no need, for a properly *political* theory of totalitarianism. The autonomy of the political is denied.

By the mid-1960s, with the end of the Algerian War and the completion of de-colonization, French philosophy was swept away by a new theoretical wave called structuralism. Louis Althusser attempted to formulate its political implications. The preface to *For Marx* criticizes "the philosophers without works . . . [who] made all works political" by means of a simple division between bourgeois and proletarian science (p. 12). The reason for this lack of an autonomous political philosophy is explained by Althusser as a result of the sociological fact that the French bourgeoisie had been revolutionary, drawing to its banner the most advanced thought of the time. Opposition to bourgeois social domination had to take the instinctively anti-intellectual form of *ouvrièrisme*. Althusser laments that this meant that his generation of Marxists "spent the majority of their time as militants when we should have also defended our right and our duty to know, simply to study in order to produce" (ibid., p. 13). Althusser claims that, thanks to Stalin—more precisely, "to his death, and to the XXth Congress"—the situation changed. Marxism can now be seen to be "not only a political doctrine, a 'method' of analysis and action, but also and above all, the *theoretical domain of a fundamental investigation*, necessary for the development not only of social science and the various 'human sciences' but also for natural science and philosophy" (ibid., p. 16). There is no need to expatiate here on the decade-long structuralist mode that swept at least the "various human sciences" on its way to becoming almost a self-parody.[5]

Making Marxism a science—indeed, *the* science—did not, however, make it a philosophy, or a political philosophy. Althusser's own acrobatic theory of "state ideological apparatuses" became so plastic that it led him finally to admit, in 1978, that "we can say it: there is *truly* no Marxist theory of the state." His social-scientific echo, Nicos Poulantzas, came to a similar conclusion even while distancing himself from Althusser: "One must come to grips with this truth: there is no Marxist theory of the nation."[6] The source of the difficulty is not only Marx.[7] Indeed, the supposed compatibility of structuralism as a general philosophy with political Marxism is open to doubt. The one characteristic shared by the various manifestations of the structuralist mode is the denial of the reality of the referent, be it the praxical subject or the given material object. As such, any claim to practical political relevance by any of these structuralisms—under the name of deconstruction, archaeology, libidinal economy, schizo-analysis . . . —depends on a further claim about the the nature of contemporary reality. It is here that structuralism is transformed into "post-structuralism" in the form of "postmodernism."[8] If capitalism's commodity logic has *really* penetrated the world, then not only has the project of industrial and cultural modernization come to an end, then too opposition or otherness (or "alterity," if you will) is no longer contained *within* the logic of capitalism. But then, the nature and place of politics also has to be reconceptualized.

A brief look at the attempt by the Derridean deconstructionists to apply their theoretical insights to political questions illustrates the difficulties that must be confronted when realized Marxism is seen as simply the logical conclusion of the capitalist project and capitalist reality is itself considered merely a "soft totalitarianism."[9] Derrida is generally considered "a man of the left," although he has never dealt either theoretically or practically with political theory. The ten-day long meeting at Cérisy-la-Salle devoted to Derrida's work confronted this issue in two quite different papers.[10] Gayatri Spivak drew from Derrida's critique of Western logocentrism the implication that the return of the excluded Other—women, the non-western world, the victims generally of capitalism—puts into question the domination imposed by Western rationality and its economic structures. Deconstruction's aim would be to open up thought to this excluded element whose admission to presence will then overthrow the inherited domination which was based on, and consisted in, its exclusion. Jacob Rogozinski proposed a more radical deconstruction: that of the notion of revolution itself. Revolution, with its supposition of an *arché* and a *telos*, is taken as a form of political metaphysics; Marx's attempt to overcome such differences as that of state and civil society by the creation of a wholly unified and transparent society is nothing but the destructive completion of metaphysics. One needs either a radically different politics, or a politics whose function is to preserve the differences that make thought—and freedom—possible. Inclusion of Spivak's excluded Other is thus condemned by Rogozinski's position as still containing a metaphysical remnant. Derrida himself, in the discussion, approved Rogozinski's argument but worried about its "anti-Marxist" implications for ongoing politics—thus returning again to that mode of philosophical behavior criticized by Althusser.

The inconclusive discussion at Cérisy was followed by the creation of a "Center for the Philosophical Study of the Political." The substantive formulation, "the" political, is not accidental. The Center's directors, Jean-Luc Nancy and Philippe Lacoue-Labarthe, explain in their opening statement[11] that since philosophy and politics were born together, the completion of Western philosophy in the domination of the political parallels the (Heideggerian notion of the) domination of modern technology as the completion of metaphysics. Thus, "in speaking of *the* political (*le politique*), we do not in the least intend to talk about *politics* (*la politique*). On the contrary, the questioning of the political, or of the essence of the political, forces us to return to the very political presupposition of philosophy (or, if you like: of metaphysics). The realization of the Marxian project appears from this point of view to be the necessary and literal achievement of the *telos* of Western philosophy as metaphysics. Although that was not his intention, Sartre's claim that Marxism is "the insurpassable horizon of our time" is thus said to be valid. Deconstruction has to show not only the futility of this project, nor simply its participation in the metaphysical tradition whose implicit *telos* it makes explicit. More important, although not itself a politics, deconstruction shows negatively the presuppositions to be avoided—e.g., the notion of a pre-existing individual subject who only *then* enters the political domain; or the notion of a pre-political society which somehow gives itself political structures. But the question of the positive content of deconstructive politics remains open. Despite the Center's various attempts, it seems only consequent that such openness remain; anything else would have to be, by definition, metaphysics!

The "Center for the Philosophical Study of the Political" was dissolved after less than two years. The reason for its dissolution recalls the old dilemmas against which Althusser had warned: apparently discussions at the Center had come to identify totalitarianism as a danger only in Marxist-type regimes. It treated Marxism as simply a nineteenth-century ideology to whose stress on equality was opposed an eighteenth-century emphasis on liberty and morality. The substantive formulation of the political permitted the substitution of ethical, aesthetic, and even religious argument in the place of practical distinctions. As a result, the Center was felt to have capitulated to the neo-liberalism and political conformism then sweeping France. Fraser points out the paradoxes of this position: Nancy and Lacoue-Labarthe wanted at one and the same time to reject their opponents' political positions and to assert the autonomy of "the transcendental pact . . . the interrogation of the essence of the political." Stress on the one excludes concentration on the other. For all of their talk about a "soft totalitarianism" produced by the metaphysical domination of the political that finds its expression in Lyotard's "postmodern condition," and which differs from the more concretely political analyses of totalitarianism offered by Claude Lefort, Nancy and Lacoue-Labarthe could propose only a vague notion of the need to renew with the transcendent dimension which the metaphysical political project seeks to incorporate into its self-transparent web of wholly political relations. They remained bound to the very philosophy which their deconstruction sought to overcome. The encounter with totalitarianism did not permit them to make a new departure.

The movement of French thought that begins with the inability to conceptualize the problem of totalitarianism concludes with the total domination of the concept, to the exclusion of the political *philosophy* which, for a moment, it appeared to make necessary. This paradoxical result was not necessary. The domination of the political leaves no place for politics, which then becomes precisely that radical Otherness that Spivak, in her way, tried to identify. But either the Otherness is defined negatively, by its exclusion from the system on which it therefore depends, or, if the Otherness is identified independently of the system, it becomes a positivist or an irrationalist moment about which nothing more can be said—unless, of course, the accusation of voluntarism is raised. The other option, a restored transcendence or a reasserted difference, falls prey to the accusation of quietism. Two recent proposals have sought to integrate the lessons of the contemporary French path to the political in the attempt to elaborate a political theory that is not incompatible with a practical politics. The first is that of Luc Ferry, the second comes from Jürgen Habermas.

B. A Kantian Proposal Inspired by Fichte

The first of Luc Ferry's three volumes of *Philosophie politique* refers, in its subtitle, to "The new Quarrel of the Ancients and the Moderns." Like the older dispute, this quarrel is neither strictly intraphilosophical nor bound to the aesthetic; its upshot and its foundation are both philosophical and political. The radicalized French critique of totalitarianism by the so-called new philosophers became a critique of reason *tout court*. The addition of French Heideggerianism to a Frankfurt-like "dialectic of enlightenment" threatened to lead to an abandonment of reason altogether. Heidegger can of course be read as a critic of totalitarianism, including its "one-dimensional" or "liberal" variant, as was seen in Nancy and Lacoue-Labarthe's proposals. From this point of view, modern domination is "metaphysical"; it is based on the Cartesian subject as "master and possessor of nature" armed with a "principle of reason"which it imposes on beings in the form of technology. In this process the concept of truth is destroyed by its definition as "certainty in representation." Since there are no external standards to which to appeal, the principle of reason treats the world as if it were, at least in principle, inherently rational and thus knowable by a subject whose cognitive task thus becomes simply calculation. Such an empty subject, in turn, becomes a will on which no constraint can be imposed legitimately; it becomes a pure "will to power" to which no goal is adequate and for which reason is simply an instrumental means. Heidegger's solution is the return to the ontological difference between Being and beings. His ontology emerges negatively from a reconstruction of the history of thought as a story of decline and forgetting. Practically, this means that Heidegger can argue that concrete political forms—liberal individualism or collectivism—are differences that make no difference. The concrete implication of this position, says Ferry, is drawn by Heidegger's student, Hannah Arendt, who, for example, in "Understanding and Politics," builds her argument on the impossibility of a rational understanding of the historically new. Ferry rejects the irrationalism of this project, which he labels pejoratively as "phenomenological."

Ferry suggests that the positive political consequences of the Heideggerian critique are drawn more effectively by Leo Strauss's proposal to return to the classical natural-law tradition, which at least guarantees the existence of some standard to oppose to the valueless and voluntarist willing of modern subjectivity.[12] But such a literal return to the order of nature as a pregiven, external, and transcendental standard would exclude such modern acquisitions as the principle of reason, autonomous subjectivity, and universality. Ferry wants to hold on to these, while still accepting the deconstructive critique of idealism and historicism as resulting from a subject-centered metaphysics imposing its principle of reason on a nature it seeks to dominate. Both are right; both are wrong. The

Straussian return to classical natural law abandons liberal democracy and the rights of man. The Heideggerian deconstruction abandons reason in favor of an onto-theology, and gives up moral action in favor of a rootedness in being. This acceptance of the critique accompanied by a rejection of its one-sided consequences recalls the Kantian strategy in the Transcendental Dialectic. But Kant did not stress the *positive* role of the Transcendental Dialectic; indeed, one sometimes has the impression that the *Critiques* as such are merely methodological or heuristic in their function. Different conclusions follow if one sees in Fichte's reading of Kant's Transcendental Dialectic the first philosophical deconstruction.[13] On this basis, Ferry proposes an argument that accepts Strauss's critique of the moderns without the anti-democratic drawbacks of his return to classical natural-law theory. The key to Ferry's construction is his positive interpretation of the antinomic structures of Kant's Dialectic which, so to speak, makes a virtue out of necessity. Strauss's critique can be accepted without sacrificing the freedom of the modern ethical subject. The intersection and co-presence of the two moments defines generally the place of the political.

After Ferry has demonstrated the necessity for and place of political philosophy, his second volume makes explicit some implications of the argument. Strauss objected to the subjectivism with which modern natural law replaces the classical duties by empty universal rights. Because these rights have no foundation outside the subject, morality is replaced by history which, in turn, becomes relativist historicism. This produces the contradictory result that the subjectivity "achieved" by modernity is replaced *de facto* by the objective logic of a factual world. Hegel called this the "Cunning of Reason." Its result is that both morality and politics are destroyed since neither has any place of its own. At best, modern morality would be a self-related freedom whose empty autonomy can become the generalization of subjective or private interest. Its political translation can become the foundation for the Terror in the French Revolution or the egotism of unchained capitalism. Indeed, one result of the dilemmas of modernity would be a caricatural Hegelianism—or Marxism!—which identifies freedom with necessity while reducing politics to history. Yet, as Ferry insists, Hegel did not reject the gains of modernity in favor of a return to the wholeness of Greek *Sittlichkeit*. A philosophy of history, which is intermediate between politics and pure philosophy, will have to provide the foundation on which a political theory can be built. Ferry's construction of what he calls in the subtitle to volume two "The System of Philosophies of History" builds from the Kantian Transcendental Dialectic. This permits him to accept criticism from what he calls the "phenomenological" orientation,[14] which rejects the idea of a wholly knowable history accessible to a subject applying the principle of reason, without having to adopt an irrationalism which, in one or another guise, abandons the achievements of modernity.

Beginning with a general argument about the nature and tasks of philosophy, Ferry sketches the structures which delimit any possible philosophy of history. The two most general poles are (1) the theoretical ontology typified by an "Hegelian" extension of the principle of reason to the real; and (2) the practical-ethical ontology exemplified by a "Fichtean" desire to transform the real in the name of a universal end given by the free subject. The combination of these poles of objective and subjective idealism results in (3) the "revolutionary science" of Marxism's portrait of an intelligible and controllable history. Their juxtaposition results in (4) the deconstruction of both of their ontological claims in the form of a Heideggerian phenomenology with its mysteries, miracles of being, and emergent novelty. Ferry's goal, obviously, is to present a unifying fifth possibility built on the necessary and yet antinomic structures of the four one-sided approaches, each of which is necessary to thought, but each of which is incomplete when treated alone and as absolute. Only in this manner can the autonomous space of the political be assured theoretically, since each of the four structural possibilities either reduces that autonomy (1 & 3) or renders it subjectively voluntarist (2) or irrational and unknowable (4). At the same time, Ferry's proposed philosophy of history avoids the determinism of rationalist historicism and insures that the ethical foundation of political action by the individual subject does not return to the pre-modern doctrine of natural law which Strauss sees as the only alternative.

Ferry's "criticist" philosophy is systematic in what he calls the "etymological" sense: the antinomic possibilities must be thought together, each making necessary the other. He illustrates his argument by demonstrating first how the Hegelian alternative provides a "rationalist negation of the idea of praxis," and then how the Heideggerian phenomenology supplies an "irrationalist negation of the idea of praxis." Kant is then introduced as a "deconstruction" in the sense that each option becomes metaphysical by virtue of its one-sided insistence on its own adequacy and completeness. Ferry proposes to escape from this metaphysics by treating the poles as antinomic in the Kantian sense. But like the Third Antinomy in the Critique of Pure Reason, the solution shows only the possibility of morality, not yet its necessity. This first antinomy thus leads to a second: morality cannot become metaphysical in its turn. The freedom of the will does not exclude either the causal rationality of the world or the contingency of that world. Ferry's solution returns to Kant,[15] whose *Critique of Judgement* overcomes the antinomical structures inherent in theoretical ontology and practical philosophy by showing that they are based upon the subsumption of the (rational or contingent) reality under the pre-given universality of concepts. Ferry treats Kant's alternative notion of reflective judgment (which begins from the particular in order to seek the lawfulness to which it is adequate) as a methodological principle from which he then derives a third antinomy that opposes the contingency of the real to the necessity of thinking it universally, in terms either of objective rationalism or of subjective practical reason. The difficulty lies in the elaboration of this third antinomic structure as either method or politics.

The upshot of Ferry's "system" of the philosophies of history is the demonstration of the mutual necessity of the poles presented in his three antinomies. The necessary opposition of rationalism and irrationalism points to the place of the free ethical will. The necessary opposition of ethics and the (contingent or rational) world indicates the need for a methodological principle of the type presented by Kant's reflective judgment whose foundation is the recognition of the contingency of the given world. The necessary opposition of this contingency to the universalist rationality of theoretical and practical philosophy closes the circle by showing that the political philosophy which thinks the unity of these three antinomies need not sacrifice either its ethical or its rational-causal orientation. To stress the one pole to the exclusion of the other would be yet another fall back into metaphysics. The independent place and necessity of the political is thus established from the standpoint of the demands immanent to the philosophical project.

The proof of Ferry's systematic pudding is presented in the third volume of *Philosophie politique*, which outlines the development "From the Rights of Man to the Republican Idea."[16] The argument takes off once again from the contemporary French critique of totalitarianism: can the defense of the rights of man, which emerges as the simple opposite of the totalitarian temptation, be a politics? The answer, of course, depends first of all on what is meant by the rights of man. Ferry points to the obvious oppositions, which become for him antinomies. He opposes the liberal notion of rights as freedoms from (*droits-libertés*) to the socialist notion of rights that demand state intervention for their realization (*droits-créances*). The theoretical foundation of this distinction lies in the antinomy between a rationalist supposition that expects a Cunning of Reason to lead from individual action to rational social results, and an ethical-practical assumption whose realization demands intervention by the will (in the form of the state). Rousseau is the central figure. Ferry leaves the level of system to look at the difficulties that emerged in the practice of the French Revolution. Sieyès's concept of the nation attempted to escape Rousseau's insistence that the general will cannot be represented. However, the result only transforms Rousseau's notion into a Kantian Idea of Pure Reason whose realization in the Terror was denounced by Hegel. On the other hand, Constant's demonstration that "ancient" liberty as Rousseau presupposes it must deny modern private freedom neglects Rousseau's distinction between the general will and the will of all whose conflation would indeed destroy that modern freedom. Preservation of the difference of the political and the private, and recognition of the general will as a normative principle of legitimation, suggests that Rousseau's theory should serve to limit and to delimit the sphere of state action. The proposed "dialectical" and "systematic" unity of Sièyes and Constant produces a distinction between the sphere of the state and that of a modern civil society founded on subjective freedom. From this simple illustration, Ferry draws striking conclusions.

Ferry's synthetic philosophy of history suggests that there are three possible political theories of human rights corresponding to the three antinomies. The constitutional debates during the Revolution of 1848 serve to illustrate the theoretical argument. The anarchist Proudhon, and the socialist Marx, represent symmetric options within the paradigm that sees an opposition between state and civil society. The one wants to dissolve the state into society, the other takes the inverse tack. The danger of each one-sided position is seen in their attitude toward the Declarations of the Rights of Man. The antinomy of statist and private rights suggests of course the need to preserve both poles, at least in principle. Tocqueville's liberal arguments against inscribing the right to work into the constitution appear to Ferry to satisfy this demand. But when this liberalism is expressed in Guizot's cruder criticism of majoritarian politics it is simply apologetic. But Ferry does not criticize Guizot's bourgeois ideology from the standpoint of its political consequences. He remains the philosopher. Political apology like metaphysics depends on a one-sided interpretation of an antinomic structure. Hayek's presentation of the logic of liberalism has the merit of making this explicit. When its inability to guarantee social justice on the basis of private egoism becomes apparant, Hayek's liberalism justifies its obdurance by recourse to the rationality of the market. But as Hegel already knew, this presupposes the existence of a Cunning of Reason, i.e., the rationality of history. Liberalism thus shows its own antinomic logic; its private freedom depends on the existence of a public rationality which it takes for granted but cannot prove.

Because the twin antinomies that emerge from the consideration of anarchism, socialism, and liberalism, parallel the "criticist" synthesis in the philosophy of history, one expects that their proposed resolution will take a similar form. The third antinomy for the philosophy of history opposed the contingency of the world to the need for a political philosophy which unites the moments of theoretical and practical reason. Ferry again develops the argument in a historically suggestive manner. One might have expected a formulation of such a hybrid as "democratic socialism" in this context; and Ferry does take up the positions of Jaurès and Léon Blum. But Jaurès cannot avoid the historicism that makes Marx's treatment of human rights unacceptable, while Blum's distinction between the means of taking power and those for exercising it is lame. The notion of republicanism, whose origins go back to the French Revolution, and whose development passes through 1848 before coming to fruition in France with the establishment of the Third Republic in 1875, provides Ferry with an alternative. The Republic is said to be a Kantian Idea of Reason; its complete realization is never possible. In practice, the Idea functions along two axes, paralleling the antinomic structures that underlie any political theory of human rights. The freedom from (*droits-libertés*) that liberalism seeks to guarantee is the premise for the existence of a human community within which individuals can seek to realize those freedoms that do demand intervention for their realization (*droits-créances*).The full realization of these latter never can be assured because their degree of fulfillment depends on contingencies such as the real wealth of a given society at a given moment. yet the status of the republic as an Idea of Reason means that it is itself a universal value of a type which does not fall victim to the historicist assumptions correctly criticized by classical natural-law theorists such as Strauss, and by "phenomenologists" from the Heideggerian deconstructionist tradition.

The solution is almost too good to be true. The republican Idea claims to unite the virtues of liberalism and those of socialism in a reflective structure that permits both of them to coexist without lessening their opposition. The claim parallels Ferry's earlier arguments: antinomies are produced, their necessity is demonstrated, and their solution by means of the Kantian criticist philosophy is offered. Ferry has developed a powerful machinery by which conflicting philosophical, and political, claims can be evaluated. However, its own status as a politics, its ability to propose concrete measures, is uncertain. If Ferry's goal is only the philosophical one—suggested by Althusser two decades previously as the imperative task for French philosophy—that seeks to articulate the proper place of the political, his recourse to republicanism as an answer is too simple. Its status as a Kantian Idea of Reason means that it is an always-already-present demand in human behavior. But when and how is the implicit demand of Reason made explicit? It is not enough to give a philosophical reconstruction of historical events, as Habermas will argue with his specific and innovative concept of reconstruction; and Ferry's own criticism of Hayek's substantively correct fear of "constructivism" in political philosophy points to the same difficulty. Ferry's Kantianism stresses the Transcendental Dialectic more than it does that other Kantian contribution, the notion of a form of judgment that proceeds from the particular to the universal. That notion of reflective judgment, however, will be seen to be the crucial missing link for a political theory. In order to make more explicit its role, some parallels with the recent work of Jürgen Habermas will be useful. If "human rights" are to become a politics, we must understand not just the antinomic structures of these rights and their potential realization; we must also redefine our notion of politics.

C. Habermas's Attempt to Preserve the Gains of Modernity . . . and of Marxism

Habermas's recent work is guided by a recognition that modernity cannot be equated simply with capitalism.[17] In reply to the critical question from the *New Left Review* whether his shift away from the paradigm of production to that of communication is not the abandonment of materialism, Habermas insists that he always understood materialism as both the explanation and the criticism of the dependency of the superstructure on the infrastructure, of the life world on the imperatives of accumulation.[18] The communication paradigm is said to do away with the expressivist model of the alienation and reappropriation of humanity's essential powers which was typical of the production-aesthetics of Kant, Schiller, and Hegel. Although he rejects what he calls the postmodernist abandonment of politics thesis, which he identifies with Derrida and Foucault in an important essay on "The Crisis of the Welfare State and the Exhaustion of Utopian Energies," Habermas also rejects what he calls "a specific utopia, which in the past crystallized around the potential of productivist society (*Arbeitsgesellschaft*)."[19] He proposes an analysis of what he calls "the New Unintelligibility'' which emerges in a situation ''in which the program of a social state which still builds on the utopia of a productive society loses the ability to open up the future possibilities of a collectively better and less endangered life'' (ibid., p. 147). This New Unintelligibility may explain why, in the above-cited interview, Habermas can suggest that in American politics with its actor-president, ''one can only reply with the cynical antics of the deconstructionists'' (*NLR*, p. 83). Similarly, when replying to a question about the pessimism in even his earlier account of the *Changing Structure of the Public Sphere*, he suggests that the deconstructionists ''give the only appropriate answer to this really existing surrealism'' (ibid., p. 97). But this is not, of course, his last word on the matter. Habermas is not proposing that a philosophy whose foundations he criticizes can become the basis for a rational politics.

Habermas offers no account of totalitarianism as such. Detailing his own philosophical path for the *New Left Review*, he suggests that his concern with the ''American version of the philosophy of praxis'' was useful for ''compensating the weaknesses of Marxism with respect to democratic theory'' (*NLR*, p. 77). Later in the interview, he repeats the statement from his ''Reply to My Critics'' that ''Nothing makes me more nervous than the imputation that because the theory of communicative action focuses attention on the social facticity of recognized validity-claims, it proposes, or at least suggests, a rationalistic utopian society. I do not regard the fully transparent—let me add in this context: or indeed a homogenized and unified—society as an ideal, nor do I wish to suggest any other ideal—Marx was not the only one frightened by the vestiges of utopian socialism'' (ibid., p. 94). From the other side, however, Habermas's analyses of modern society do tend in the direction suggested by the deconstructionist critique of so-called soft-totalitarianism. He criticizes, for example, not just ''the monetarization of labour power, but also the bureaucratization of the life-world which is experienced by broad strata of the population as a danger'' (ibid., p. 99). But he also points out the manner in which neo-conservatives can use this resentment to shift problems from the state to the market: rather than a democratization this tactic is nothing but the uncoupling of state activity from the pressures of legitimation demands (ibid.). Indeed, in another interview, with *Aesthetik und Kommunikation*, he explains that he finally settled down to write his two-volume *Theory of Communicative Action* because of the rise of a neo-conservative political reaction in Germany toward the end of 1977.[20] Habermas's philosophical work is not, however, simply the translation of his practical concerns.

After his approving citation of the Americans' adoption of ''the cynical antics of the deconstructionists,'' Habermas points out that this gesture is nothing new. The end of systematic philosophy was recognized already by the Young Hegelians, whose contemporaries we in fact remain. The hue and cry around the pretended novelty of the anti-systematicists is superfluous and naïve. Indeed, Habermas's reconstruction of modern philosophy in *The Philosophic Discourse of Modernity* begins with two lectures on Hegel himself, who already saw the dilemmas. The next four presentations examine the left and right Hegelian responses, Nietzsche's crucial role in making explicit the demand to move beyond the aporias of modernity, Horkheimer and Adorno's attempt at a modern synthesis, and Heidegger's undermining of Western rationalism. The discussion of Heidegger opens out to a consideration of the French critique of the philosophy of the subject as expressed by Derrida, Bataille, and the two stages of Foucault's development (the first being the deconstruction of the human sciences, the second the development of a general theory of power). The volume concludes with Habermas's presentation of his own theory of communicative action which is to replace the subject-centered reason whose deconstruction he accepts. This theory is shown to be able to understand that "normative content of modernity" which he describes broadly and concretely—as opposed to Ferry's simple normative Idea of the Republic—as "the increasing reflexivity of the cultural tradition, the universalization of values and norms, the freeing of communicative action from tightly circumscribed normative contexts, the diffusion of models of socialization which promote processes of individuation and the forming of abstract ego-identities, and so on" (*NLR*, p. 90). Such socio-historical generalizations need to be related to the imperatives of political practice if they are not to be reified in turn.

Like Ferry, Habermas accepts the deconstructionist critique of metaphysics; but unlike Ferry, he does not attempt critically to save the subject who is at its center. Some other commonalities and distinctions are worth noting. Ferry's always-already-present Kantian Idea parallels Habermas's counterfactual assertion of the normative orientation toward mutual understanding that is contained in all communicative action. Habermas's communicative community and his notion of an "ideal speech situation" have the status of Kantian Ideas. They express normative claims whose dogmatic or one-sided assertion must "lead to error insofar as they suggest a concrete form of life." One must avoid "the confusion of a highly developed communicative infrastructure of *possible* life forms with a specific singular totality which claims to incarnate the good life" (*NU*, pp. 161, 162). This refusal—or inability—to draw practical political contents from a philosophical theory is shared by Habermas and Ferry. In Habermas's case, however, the notion of praxis is thematized, in the form of the quest for understanding among plural participants in a discourse.[21] Habermas concretizes this assertion for the *New Left Review*. A free society is not simply one where communication free from domination exists. In the rationalized and highly differentiated modern world, one encounters increasingly reflexive cultural traditions, forms of individuation and generalization of values. This gain also entails a loss; it means that there are more situations where the background consensus which the traditional life world offered has crumbled. Social interaction in modern societies depends upon consensus among the participants, not on ideologies or the mediation of the market or the bureaucracy. "I recall these sociological considerations . . . " continues Habermas, "in order to make clear that I am no transcendental philosopher. I would not speak of 'communicative rationalization' if, in the last two hundred years of European and American history, in the last forty years of the national liberation movements, and despite all the catastrophes, a piece of 'existing reason,' as Hegel would have put it, were not nevertheless also recognizable—in the bourgeois emancipation movements, no less than in the workers' movement, today in feminism, in cultural revolts, in ecological and pacifist forms of resistance, etc.'' (*NLR*, p. 102). But the ''etcetera'' does not explain what unites all of these disparate and pluralistic social movements. Ferry would have recourse to the political form of the Republic; Habermas proposes instead that ''the life world is the resource from which the participants in an interaction draw the arguments about which they seek consensus; it is the equivalent for what the philosophy of the subject attributed to the synthetic action of consciousness in general'' (*PDM*, p. 379). Yet it is this very life world which, as Habermas himself shows, is being undermined by the development of modernity.[22]

The systematic claims of Habermas and Ferry share a recognition of the limits of modern philosophy. Ferry's Republic presents an apparantly formal solution; Habermas's life world seems more material. One strategy by which Habermas might demonstrate the existence of something like that synthetic life world which modernity disorganizes would be to delimit a properly modern concept of the political sphere. He himself suggests just such a strategy when he uses (in scare quotes), the substantive form ''*das 'Politische'* '' (*PDM*, p. 420). *The* political has become for modern societies the source of system steering problems and no longer the means for their solution. A difference between steering problems and problems of mutual understanding (*Verständigung*) becomes apparent. ''In short, the result of this awareness is a new state of consciousness in which the welfare state project becomes, in a sense, reflexive; it orients itself to the taming not only of the capitalist economy but also of the state itself'' (ibid., p. 421). As the description continues, one has the sense that Habermas has in fact encountered the problem of totalitarianism. ''Self organized publics must develop the astute combinations of power and intelligent self-limitation that are necessary in order to sensibilize the self-steering mechanisms of state and economy when confronted with the goal-oriented results of radical democratic will formation'' (ibid., p. 423). This sounds like a description of the self-limiting revolution crushed by the *coup d'état* of December 13, 1981 in Poland! Habermas's final pages return to the new social movements in the West. The nation can no longer be treated as the bearer of universalistic value orientations. Perhaps, suggests Habermas, Europe will provide a counter-image? ''Modern Europe created the spiritual presuppositions and material foundations for a world in which this mentality [of economic competition, expansion for its own sake, etc.] has occupied the place of reason: that is the true kernel in the critique of reason since Nietzsche. Who other than Europe could, from its *own* traditions, create the insight, the energy and the courage of a vision—all that would be necessary in order to take away the power of a no longer metaphysical but metabiological premise of a blind constraint to the preservation and the augmentation of the system?'' (ibid.,

p. 425). One cannot help overhearing the echoes of Husserl's remedy to what he analyzed half a century ago as the ''Crisis of European Science.'' Surely Habermas is not so naïve; in all events, his view of the limitations of what philosophy can offer has to temper any idealistic élan that may seize him momentarily.

These conclusions to Habermas's analysis of and counterposition to the ''philosophical discourse of the moderns'' are presented, so to speak, by a *via negativa*. Habermas insists that he is not presenting a philsophy; his goal is now called ''reconstruction.'' In the *New Left Review* discussion, Habermas admits that he had been concerned more with theory construction than with historical explanation (*NLR*, p. 89). His interviewers refer to his earlier article, ''Does Philosophy Still have a Purpose?'' which insisted that ''great philosophy'' has come to an end; philosophy is simply a branch of research among others (ibid., p. 85).[23] When it comes to action, Habermas explains his own ''somewhat restricted understanding of the task of philosophical ethics,'' namely that ''the philosopher ought to explain the moral point of view, and—as far as possible—justify the claim to universality of this explanation, showing why it does not merely reflect the moral intuitions of the average, male, middle-class member of a modern Western society. Anything further than that is a matter for moral discourse between participants'' (ibid., p. 84). This abstinence has strong theoretical grounds, suggested first in the *Theory of Communicative Action* and reasserted in *The Philosophical Discourse of Modernity*. Clarification of Habermas's methodological self-limitation will serve also to lift some of the ambiguity in his notion of the life world which is the foundation for the replacement of a politics based on the constitutive, laboring subject of the *Arbeitsgesellschaft*.

Habermas's notion of philosophical ''reconstruction'' depends upon his critique of the philosophy of the subject. He criticizes Alfred Schütz's phenomenological attempt to understand the life world for its traditional transcendental premise; the totality of the life world does not and cannot present itself to the seeking gaze of the philosopher who somehow stands outside of it (*TkH*, II, p. 590). Although its own positive proposals were based on an unacceptable foundation in the individual consciousness of the actors, Horkheimer's criticisms of ''traditional theory'' for its lack of self-reflection on the conditions of its own possibility remain valid. Habermas's own positive philosophical argument builds from critical theory; he suggests that ''the theory of communicative action can be certain of the rational content of anthropologically deep-rooted structures through an *at first* reconstructive analysis, i.e., one that begins unhistorically. It describes the structures of action and of understanding which can be read off of the intuitive knowledge of competent members of modern societies. No path leads from it back to a theory of history which does not *a fortiori* distinguish between problems in the logic of development and those of the dynamics of development'' (ibid., pp. 561–62). The italicized limiting of reconstruction to an ''at first'' unhistorical analysis, and the distinction between the logic and the dynamics of development suggest that Habermas does want more than his modest claim. But how can he get it? Immediately following the critique of Schütz, Habermas adds a subjunctive clause, suggesting that the life world does present itself "when an *objective provocation (Herausforderung)* appears which makes *the life world as a whole problematic*" (ibid., p. 590). But how does such a provocation provoke? The last paragraph of Habermas's book, three pages later, suggests a reply:

> The theory of modernity which I have sketched in its broad lines permits us to assert at least the following. In modern societies, the room for contingency in the interactions that have been freed from their normative context expands so far that the proper nature (*Eigensinn*) of communicative action is "practically true" both in the de-institutionalized forms of behavior in the familial private sphere and in the public sphere that is determined by the mass media. At the same time, the imperatives of the autonomous subsystems penetrate the life world and use the paths of monetarizing and bureaucratizing to force communicative action to approximate formally organized activity even where the action-coordinating mechanism of understanding is functionally necessary. Perhaps this provocative threat, this challenge (*Herausforderung*) which puts into question the symbolic structures of the life world *as a whole* makes plausible the reason for which that life world has become accessible *for* us (ibid., p. 593).

With this, as Habermas promised, the theory of communicative action rejoin the intention that animated Marx and the critical theorists in his wake. But does the return of this "great philosophy" fall victim to the *hubris* of the philosophy of the subject, "master and dominator of nature"? Habermas's rejection of theory construction in favor of a *re*constructive orientation marks the shift.

Habermas returns to the problem in the penultimate lecture of his *Philosophical Discourse of Modernity*, titled "A Different Path out of the Philosophy of the Subject: Communicative vs. Subject-centered Reason." Communicative reason proposes the replacement of the paradigm of knowledge adequate to its objects by a model that describes processes of understanding between subjects capable of speech and action. The subject does not disappear; it is simply decentered. Metaphysics errs when it treats the subject as the center or source from which the order of things is to be understood, constructed, or constituted. Communicative reason is always-already in process; to understand it we simply take the stance of one, then another, then a third of the participants. In so doing, we can *reconstruct* the knowledge which is being applied in the performance. With this reconstruction, continues Habermas, the distinction between the transcendental and the empirical is dissolved, as Piaget's genetic structuralism or Kohlberg's moral theory demonstrates. This means that our knowledge of the life world is always *a tergo*. The life world as a totality is present for us only prereflexively. When we seek to know that life world, we can reconstruct only its formal pragmatic structures. We can speak only of "structures of the life world in general, not of specific life worlds in their concrete historical dimension." From this perspective, the individuals in the life world are products of that world, not its producers. ''The life world reproduces itself in the measure that these three functions, which go beyond the perspective of the actor, are fulfilled: the cultural tradition must be continued, norms and values must serve to integrate groups, and new generations must be socialized'' (*PDM*, p. 349). But if one wants to look at a particular life form, continues Habermas, one must give up the perspective of rational reconstruction and proceed historically, using narrative means for which the psychoanalytic dialogue of patient and analyst provide the model. With this distinction reappears, again, the distinction between a logic of development and the dynamic of that development on which Habermas had placed great weight. Instead of developing his argument here, Habermas turns aside to take up an ''exemplary'' postmodern, Foucault-inspired critique of Kant (ibid., pp. 352ff.). A comment along the way returns us to our starting point. The Nietzschean Kant reading ''must destroy the connection of the critique of pure and of practical reason with the critique of judgement'' (ibid., p. 356). Could one not, recalling Ferry, treat Habermas's recurring poles of rational reconstruction and provoked historical narrative as antinomic? Would their unity lie in a political theory—or rather, in a theory of the political? And is the *Critique of Judgement* the key?

The critique of the philosophy of the subject seems to make political theory impossible. Politics can be defined as the action, or the reflection, of society on itself. The decentered world of communicative rationality excludes the possibility of conceiving society as itself a subject—for itself, or for some outside actor. Habermas borrows from Luhmann's systems theoretical account according to which the political is simply one specialized subsystem whose job is to affect the social whole. Habermas's suggestion that true rationalization—as opposed to colonization—in the continuation of the cultural tradition, the integrative functioning of norms and values, and the socialization of new generations can take place only through processes of communicative understanding means that Luhmann's more mechanically functioning system will be unable to reproduce itself politically. This, it will be recalled, was what led the neo-conservatives to their critique of the welfare state, whose decoupling from the economy insulates it from potential critique since the citizens can now blame only their individual fate, governed by the impersonal laws of the market. But this same structure led Habermas to his optimistic projections about the new social movements, and perhaps even a common European consciousness as forces for the future. Such projections come from the stance of the rationally reconstructive philosophy. From the side of the ''provoked'' historical narrative, Habermas can offer little beyond sympathy. Thus, to return one last time to the *New Left Review* interview,[24] Habermas seems disappointed that the German Greens gave up their identity as a social movement to become a political party which must obey the imperatives of party logic. And to this bit of rational reconstruction of developmental rule systems he adds that it is the ''SPD, without which, if we are realistic about it, nothing can be moved'' (*NLR*, pp. 100–101).

My purpose is not to criticize Habermas's political choices. Their theoretical foundation seems to be the antinomy of reconstructive and narrative logics, which is in fact resolved to the favor of the former. Yet another possibility was sketched toward the end of *The Philosophical Discourse of Modernity*. Habermas notes that "modern, quite decentered societies maintain in their communicative everyday action a virtual center of self-understanding. . . . Granted, this center is also a projection, but it is an effective one" (*PDM*, p. 417). Could one see here a Kantian Idea? Habermas goes on to speak of the public sphere, which is itself composed of public spheres, each of which is open to other public spheres. "All partial public spheres point to a global public sphere, in which the society as a whole forms a knowledge of itself" (ibid., p. 418). This knowledge is "in fact temporary. But this reflective knowledge of the society as a whole *does exist* (*es gibt* . . .)" (ibid.). But this "given" or really existing knowledge cannot be shifted onto a steering mechanism, the state, in the manner proposed by systems theory. Indeed, Habermas suggests that there has been a shift in the very foundation of the enlightenment notion of a democratically legitimate state power. As the state began to intervene not simply to control the economy but also to regulate the communicative life processes of the citizenry, it tended to lose its legitimacy. This explains the general discrediting of the welfare state, with the left as with the right. Here, Foucault's analysis of the manner in which power relations are inscribed into the most minute capillary actions of social reproduction is on the mark. And here, Habermas makes his proposal for recognizing the birth of those self-organized and self-limiting public spheres of which, I suggested, the Polish *Solidarnosć* movement provides an example.

Habermas's critique of the philosophy of the subject provides also a critique of political theory, left and right, as it has been inherited from the enlightenment. The difficulty is precisely the all-encompassing nature of the argument, the fact that it holds for the left as well as the right. This is a dilemma shared with the critique of totalitarianism in its general form. Habermas took up his pen in 1977 because of his worry about the rising neo-conservative wave. Although his lectures on modernity could be said to have a political backdrop in the phenomenon of the new social movements, he doesn't ask whether these movements are not themselves two-sided in their implications, even though the last public meeting held at his Max-Planck Institut addressed precisely that theme.[25] Perhaps this is because Habermas believes that the "rational reconstruction" of the developmental logic of modern society permits him to distinguish progressive from regressive tendencies. Yet, one would like something more. Habermas speaks of the fact that "From the dark and polyphonic projections of totalities, there is also formed in modern societies a diffuse common consciousness" (*PDM*, p. 417). Would not its narration be useful in understanding the historically specific narratives of the new social movements? The notion of a "common consciousness" (*Gemeinbewusstsein*) recalls a key element in that *Critique of Judgement* which Ferry insisted was so important for understanding the relation between the science of the first *Critique* and the ethics proposed by the second *Critique*. Perhaps the missing element in Habermas's argument, as in Ferry's lies with Kant's third *Critique?*

D. A Sketch of a Method

Ferry's explicitly antinomical approach, and Habermas's implicit use of the same notions, are developed through a critical appropriation of the deconstruction of the philosophy of the subject as it has dominated modern metaphysics. Both seek to save the possibility of political praxis by giving it a rational foundation that avoids the postmodern cynical gesture. Ethics and science must not exclude each other, nor can one take the place of, or determine, the other. Ferry's republican solution need not be incompatible with Habermas's rejection of the modern welfare state. The republican political institutions do not pretend to steer the social totality; they claim only to create the public space in which Habermas's ''common consciousness'' and ''public spheres open to public spheres'' receive their explicit articulation. From this point of view, Ferry's concern with the institutionalization of the political can serve as an explicit form of Habermas's ''virtual center of self-understanding.'' In this way, it would provide for the actors themselves a measure for the developing dynamic narrative whose evolution Habermas can judge only by standing back to perform his rational reconstruction. On the other hand, Ferry's actors seem to be traditional pale cognitive figures whose involvement in ''new social movements'' is difficult to imagine.[26] Indeed, the qualification of the movement as ''new'' would appear to Ferry as smacking of that ''phenomenology'' which he decries for example in Hannah Arendt. Comparison of the two theories suggests the desirability of a perspective that can combine—without conflating—the theory of action proposed by Habermas with the political framework suggested by Ferry. One could, on the basis of Kant's *Critique of Judgement*, propose such a different orientation.

The antinomies confronted by political theory can be reformulated. Husserl's phenomenology oscillated frustratingly between a *genetic* reconstruction of the purified facts of consciousness and the attempt to account for the *normative validity* of these immediate presentations. The key to the unification of these two perspectives was to be located in the status of their data as ''phenomenologically reduced.'' The reduction was to guarantee the purity of the material available either to the genetic or to the normative approach. The problem, which Husserl never solved adequately, was to account for the motivation of the reduction itself. Why should ''natural consciousness'' undertake its self-purification? Habermas's solution in his critique of Husserl's follower, Schütz, had recourse to a ''provocation.'' That is, however, an appeal to a *deus ex machina*, or to await an accident, neither position being adequate to the demands of modern rationality. Could one not, with Ferry, make a virtue out of necessity? Recognition of the antinomy involves remaining within it. Remaining within it, however, does not mean abandoning one or the other option. To the contrary, recognition of the necessity of the antinomy is only possible through the constantly renewed attempt to transcend it. Insofar as a political theory should be able to account not only for permanence but for change, remaining within the necessary antinomy serves both functions.

The notions of genesis and validity can be applied to the systematic structure of the Kantian project in order to show the place of the political within its framework. The Transcendental Deduction of the Categories in the *Critique of Pure Reason* is formulated differently in each of the editions of that work. The first edition provides a genetic account of the manner in which the threefold synthesis brings together the categories of the understanding with the manifold of sensibility. The same demonstration is provided in the second edition by reference to the normative Transcendental Unity of Apperception, that "I think" which must accompany all of my representations. But the demonstration is not complete in either variant, and recourse to the temporalizing Schematism (which should not be necessary for the normative second edition, but which Kant preserves) does not help. The problem is that while Kant has shown how the manifold of sense is subsumed under the categories, he has done so only from the point of view of these categories. His demonstration is still normative, even in the guise of a genetic presentation.[27] Kant has to show also, from the side of the sensible manifold, why it should be *receptive* to the categories imposed. This, it may be suggested, is what the demonstration of the teleological structure of nature in the *Critique of Judgement* offers.[28] The predicative judgment which subsumes the particulars under the universal, thereby making genesis depend on normativity, and the reflective judgment which proceeds from the particular to the universal, making normativity depend on genesis, are both necessary to the Kantian system.

To speak of the critical philosophy as forming a system can lead to difficulties. One potential systematic interpretation of Kant suggests that the writings on history form a "fourth critique" which serves to unite the steps through which Kant's own efforts developed. From this point of view, the *Foundations of the Metaphysics of Morals* are said to be incomplete because they presuppose the fact of freedom, whose possibility but not whose necessity was demonstrated in the Third Antinomy in the first *Critique*. The *Critique of Practical Reason* is said to attempt to remedy this lack by its Postulates of Practical Reason. The existence of God, Immortality of the Soul, and Freedom are to guarantee that one will act morally since, under these conditions, one can know that action undertaken solely from a good will will indeed have results (eventually) in the phenomenal world. But the Postulates are not sufficient precisely because they are only postulates. The third *Critique* suggests a different account of the reasons for which the individual will be led to act morally. The ethical significance of the beautiful, and the experience of the sublime in nature provide subjective and objective grounds for this assumption. But since that judgment is only reflective and subjective, a further guarantee is needed. The philosophy of history, suggested in the "Idea of World History from a Cosmopolitan Point of View" can then be introduced. That attempt to demonstrate the compatibility of individual practice with the rational-moral development of world history is supplemented in the essay on "Theory and Practice," before being brought to completion in "Perpetual Peace."

This proposed demonstration of the role of the political in completing the Kantian system is based on two symmetrical moments which point to two desiderata for a political theory. The historical demonstration has recourse to a kind of Cunning of Reason in demonstrating the manner in which, behind the backs of the actors, their behavior constitutes a world which grows increasingly rational. This is clear in the famous passages about a stepmotherly nature wise enough to know that although we wish for harmony and concord, only conflict creates the conditions from which peace will emerge. The problem—which Ferry's Fichte saw only partially—is that this argument assumes the action of a *constitutive* subject. In this case, parallel to the contribution of the third *Critique* to the first, there must be a demonstration of the *receptivity* of the world to the actions of that subject. But one cannot assume either that the subject will act, or that these actions will in fact have the effect intended. That, after all, was the thrust of the distinction between the noumenal intention and the phenomenal result. To the demonstration of the receptivity must be added, therefore, a second argument which shows not only the possibility but the necessity of the subject's acting. If one reaches for the third *Critique* as a model, the problem can be formulated by asking which *particulars* make not only possible but necessary the reflective judgment. No more than I can call any randomly selected thing "beautiful" can I demand or expect political action to take place or to meet with success in any or every circumstance.

The systematic approach to Kant errs in arguing from the point of view of a theory of constitution. It is simply another form of the error criticized by the deconstruction of the philosophy of the subject. But the systematic approach does have the virtue of making clear two *methodological* criteria which any political theory must fulfill. Political theory must be able to identify those particulars which call for and make necessary political judgment (or action), and it must be able to explain why the world will be receptive to that action. These criteria are methodological, and they are interdependent, the first corresponding to the orientation toward genesis, the second to that of validity. Their analytic usefulness can be demonstrated by turning to the problems raised by Habermas and Ferry.

Adoption of the antinomical pair genesis and normativity as the principle axes for a political theory permits an account both of the historical events which interest Ferry and of the contemporary political scene surveyed by Habermas. The example of the French Revolution, as reconstructed by François Furet in his *Penser la révolution française* can serve as a first illustration. Furet brings together the Tocquevillian account of an *Ancien Régime* which has brought about the revolution structurally but is unable to recognize its own work, with the query of Augustin Cochin into the strange transformation that led Frenchmen so suddenly and unexpectedly to revolutionize their mode of behavior. Tocqueville is concerned with normativity; Cochin wants to explain genesis. Neither is wrong, but neither alone explains the Revolution. Explanation depends on the co-presence of the two poles. Furet's reply to the vexing question, When did the Revolution end?, can be reformulated in the new terms. The end is symbolized for Furet when the actors no longer appeal to "the" Revolution to legitimate their choices. When they have recourse to concrete goals sought, or to the constitutional or institutional results of earlier successes, the actors are opting for one or the other pole of the antinomy. "The" revolution is neither the action, nor the results; "the" revolution is itself its own genesis and its own normative standard. By extension, if the Republic is the realization of the French Revolution, this is because the Republican form makes necessary the co-presence of the genetic and the normative.

To reformulate Habermas's analysis of contemporary political life, some further conceptual machinery is necessary. Ferry's account was seen to suffer from its inability to account for particular action, in part owing to his stress on the Republic as a Kantian Idea at the expense of that other Kantian insight, the notion of reflective judgment. The republican framework did have the virtue, however, of being able to explain the receptivity to the political actions undertaken. Some such framework has to be presupposed by the Habermasian argument. Habermas needs to be able to explain when, and why, social movements are progressive. His general account of the decoupling of system and life world leads one to expect the emergence of societal reactions to which he himself at times applies the lable "pathological."[29] The application of the metaphor of "colonization" to the life world in the *Theory of Communicative Action* sharpens the problem suggestively since we know, for example and unfortunately, that anti-colonial political movements have not always produced positive results. Pathological symptoms are characterized for Habermas by their being withdrawn from the arena of action and argument oriented toward social understanding. Movements manifesting such pathologies may be generated by the problems of reproducing the life world; but this does not guarantee that such movements will be able on their own to give themselves institutional stability in a manner that permits healing the pathologies which gave rise to them. Such movements would be "particulars" which, because their form does not invite forms of reflective behavior, are not capable of universalization. They would lack the normative force that makes action truly historical. This is not to say that anti-colonial revolts are "wrong," nor that they are doomed. It suggests, rather, the need to understand them *politically*.

Habermas's twin political concerns are neo-conservatism on the one hand, and the new social movements on the other. Both are characterized by their rejection of the welfare state in its advanced form, although their solutions are substantively different. Neo-conservatives seek to de-democratize the public sphere by withdrawing responsibility to the private or the market spheres. Habermas tries to show the developmental logic that condemns their project, even while worrying about its immediate practical effects. Could the procedure not be inverted? When does the neo-conservative reaction become possible? What are the particulars to which it appeals in presenting its political project? Are these in fact receivable by the society? The project is based on the possibility of separating genesis (the market and its logic) from normativity (the rationally groundable values transmitted by the society). If the project has emerged, it is because this separation does in fact exist. Are, then, the new social movements a potentially successful reply? To justify that claim, the movements would have themselves to carry the antinomic unity of genesis and normativity. Insofar as they lean to one side or the other—stressing movement at the cost of institutions, letting fixed goals replace developmental learning, universalizing abusively their own particularity, or neglecting the concrete social anlayses that show why success reasonably can be expected—they themselves, like the neo-conservatives to whom they are a response, become part of the problem, not its solution.

The introduction of these four categories—particularity and receptivity, genesis and validity—is not simply a device permitting a reformulation of the approaches of Ferry and Habermas. The claim is stronger. Ferry had too encompassing a theory of the political; he had no way to describe particular political action. Habermas had too encompassing a theory of action; he had no way to explain the place of properly political action, and the reasons to expect its success (save perhaps by "rational reconstruction" after the fact). The ability to reformulate both theories suggests that their virtues can be combined in the new approach while their disadvantages can be overcome. That could appear to be simply a high-level ecclecticism. The analysis of totalitarianism, from which this discussion set out, provides the capstone on the demonstration. Althusser was right; a specific theory of the political must be formulated. But that theory cannot be so all-encompassing that everything becomes political. Totalitarianism cannot be equated with a particular historical regime; nor can it become, so to speak, the signature of the modern world. It is a political phenomenon, which arises in particular conditions, and which can not be successfully implanted at will. If it is to succeed, totalitarianism needs to present the real and material unity of the genetic and the normative claims—which is precisely what it cannot do without denying its own total nature. Uncovering the reasons for this inability depends upon the development of a theory of democracy that makes modern political philosophy necessary and possible.

The contemporary deconstruction of totalitarianism has remained at the level of the very philosophy it wants to surpass. Without a theory of democracy, it is condemned to remain bound to what it seeks to deny. The mediation between the two approaches can succeed only on the basis of a methodology which can explain both its own origins and its limits. Ferry and Habermas have provided the framework within which this method can claim its autonomy as a critique which is political precisely because it is conscious of these origins and limits. If neither thinker has seen fit to develop the theory of democracy that would realize this system, the reason lies in Ferry's insistence on a radical criticism of the Marxian legacy, and in Habermas's parallel intention to inherit the results of that legacy. In neither case, is the legacy treated as what it is: a *question* without which a modern political philosophy dissolves into either a foundationless politics or an abstract philosophy. Perhaps this explains, finally, the absence of the question of *revolution* within the philosophies that seek to inherit the critique of totalitarianism.

8

Rousseau and the Origin of Revolution

A. Origins and Revolution

''Origin'' implies the constantly threatened dialectical unity of genetic and normative grounds. The origin of revolution would explain how that phenomenon is generated at the same time that they justify its claim to normative validity. Genesis alone does not imply validity. Cases of unsuccessful, although materially understandable, revolt testify to this thesis, as do instances of successful seizure of power which, in Marx's words, simply reproduce ''the same old shit.''But normativity alone does not suffice either. Ought does not imply is, nor does correct theory entail successful practice. If the normative theory attempts to impose itself on practice, the result, as Hegel's *Phenomenology* already taught us, is the Terror, if not totalitarianism. Explanation which invokes genesis of validity alone reduces the *question* of revolution.

Origins are not empirically real. If the origin is taken as a real genetic force, it either becomes a linearly acting cause or an ontologically necessary essence engendering its transparently adequate appearance. As a source of real genesis, the origin then has the effect of reducing revolution to a mechanical or ontological necessity. The result of such a reduction is the loss of the difference between the previous state and the (normatively) better revolutionary result. Hence, one must be quite careful with metaphors of a society pregnant with its future as one must avoid the suppositions of a constant, linear progress of History, even when no *telos* is assumed. The loss of difference reduces revolution to reform.

But the normative alternative projection of a real origin fares no better—in fact, its results may be worse. If the normative claim is taken as the real origin, a party capturing power is perfectly justified in imposing its institutions on society. Insisting on materially realizing the norms, this revolutionary stance does not reflect on the fact that in so doing it too abolishes the difference which made it revolutionary. Where the real genetic position totalizes from the is, the real normative stance totalizes from the ought. The source of the error lies in the assumption of a real origin.

Origins are not simply ideal either. They are not transcendental conditions of the (real or normative) possibility of events or institutions. The ambiguous parenthesis which asks whether such transcendental origins are conditions of real or normative possibility/validity suggests that ideal origins reduce and abolish the differences of genesis and validity through a false totalization. The ideal interpretation of origins as a false totalization confusing the crucial distinction is illustrated by Michel Foucault's analysis (in *Les mots et les choses*) of the tabular form of representation. This mode of argument demonstrates the unitary presuppositions of apparently divergent theories, for example, of an economics stressing production and another stressing consumption. The tabular representation is a spatial image which permits a classification of apparently diverse phenomena by first reducing them to appearances in a homogeneous space. Genetic phenomena such as production or the evolution of species, and normative systems such as consumption or classificatory biological schemes, are brought together on the ideal *tableau* which abolishes their differences and permits comparison. Politically, the apparently divergent content of, for example, Locke's and Wolff's theories, is neutralized by their common tabular representation of natural law as an ideal origin.

Marx's theory of critique attempted to unite dialectically the standpoint of genesis and validity without destroying the independence of either. His criticism of the ''practical party'' and the ''theoretical party'' in the ''Introduction to a Critique of Hegel's *Philosophy of Right*'' demonstrates his awareness of the dangers of taking either stance in isolation. In the same essay, and on the basis of this critical proposal, Marx argues that the origin of the revolution lies in the proletariat, whose genetic claim as the product of capitalist development is coupled with a normative demand for universality because it is the ''nothing'' which can make no partial but only total claims on society and history. In this essay—as opposed to much of his and his followers' work—Marx does not take the proletariat as an empirically real source of genesis or validity, nor as an ideal representation against which to measure empirical phenomena. The proletariat as origin is both the subjective agent and the objective product of a temporal history whose smooth linear progress is put into question by the originary status of the proletariat. The theory of critique is not a positive or a normative theory; it is the expression of the immanent social question which the existence of the proletariat poses.

Marx and Marxism were not able to maintain the dialectical tension of a simultaneously genetic and normative interrogation. The proletariat was reduced, either to a factual force or to a future ideal; its unity was stressed over against its differential structure.[1] The basic fact of revolution—that it creates and makes possible the creation of the radically new—was thus lost. History was conceived as a necessary linear progression at whose end freedom was finally to manifest itself. From an open, *question* defined by the dialectic of genesis and validity, history was transformed into an answer to all questions. The basic uncertainty of a temporality in which revolutionary leaps are possible was reduced to a spatial morphology defined by the positivity of proletarian action. The opacity of the originary revolutionary question became the transparency of a tabular history, and Marxism became a "science."

Rousseau provides a fruitful source for the recapturing of the originary phenomenon of revolution. Rousseau confronts repeatedly the problem of origins, and with it the task of understanding the leap or revolution instituted by socially contracted civilization. He is aware of the need to maintain the paradoxical interrogation by avoiding the positivization or idealization of his social contract. Thus, for example, the social contract is originary in the specific sense that its presence cannot be presupposed and yet, once it comes into existence, it is the source of the legitimation of its own genesis. The successful social contract legitimates but does not explain away the risks and accidents which Rousseau describes in the process of its genesis; but at the same time, its particular genesis is not separate from its legitimacy. The social contract is in this sense a question and not an answer. What is more, Rousseau is aware—as Marx was not—of the need to institutionalize this interrogation without transforming it into a positive solution to the "riddle of history." Although we shall see that he did not succeed in this latter attempt, his grappling with the problem of republican institutions as a way of preserving the question of origins adds a dimension to revolutionary theory.

B. The Nature of Nature

To label Rousseau "revolutionary" is of course not to make him a proletarian (despite his plebian affectations), or to put him at the causal roots of the French Revolution; nor is it to classify him as the founder of a modern moral individualism, or to treat him as the father of Romanticism. Everyone has their own Rousseau. The *Social Contract* was his least read writing during his lifetime; yet it came to be invoked by both revolutionary and counter-revolutionary after 1789.[2] Although he admitted in the *Confessions* (Bk. IX) that he had come to realize that all facets of life were determined by politics, it was his moral, anti-political message, conveyed most powerfully in the *Nouvelle Héloise*, that captured his contemporaries. When the Revolution made him an honorary ancestor along with Voltaire and the philosophes, it was repairing posthumously a bitter quarrel which had divided them personally and politically—a quarrel whose stakes remain today. There can be no doubt of Rousseau's hatred of injustice in all its forms; but hatred and criticism do not constitute revolutionary thought, any more than the desire to do good will in fact have good results. If Rousseau is revolutionary, this will have to be shown in the basic structure of his thought. Isolated phrases, rhetorical flourish, or personal intervention no more make one a revolutionary than does the manner in which his contemporaries, or posterity, read his work.

Rousseau's "nature" breaks with the tabular representation typical of his times. Starobinski's brief study of Rousseau and Buffon demonstrates this point, although that is not the explicit aim of the essay.[3] Rousseau's *Discourse on the Origins of Inequality* relies frequently on Buffon's *Histoire naturelle*, even though Buffon sets the orders of nature and culture in parallel while Rousseau wants to oppose them: What seems to have struck Rousseau is Buffon's insistance that in fact we have no adequate philosophical anthropology; that European civilization should not be assumed the only or the best social form; and that perhaps the savage is in better circumstances than are we moderns. Buffon's method also appealed to Rousseau: one begins from an elementary form, which is described exhaustively in order to see better, *by contrast*, its differences from the more complex forms. Thus, the first part of the *Second Discourse* describes simple, natural man. This "man" has properties very similar to those which Buffon ascribed to the animal; he is, in a word, happy—and, adds Rousseau, free, although this latter qualification needs further explication. Starobinski cites Buffon to show the parallels. For example:

> Animals are not in the least subject to all these miseries; they do not seek pleasures where there can be none: guided by sentiment alone they never err in their choices; their desires are always proportioned to the possibility of pleasures; they sense as much as they are pleased, and are pleased as much as they sense. Man, on the contrary, in seeking to invent pleasures, has only ruined nature; in seeking to force his sentiment he only abuses his being and digs in his heart an emptiness which nothing afterwards is capable of filling.[4]

Rousseau of course argues that this "man" described by Buffon is already civilized man. His question is the historical one: how—by what *revolution?*—did "man" become this civilized creature haunted by false desires and blinded to satisfaction? Buffon cannot ask or understand this historical question; in his reply to Rousseau[5] he simply points to facts, to the sociability of man, the need for a family if the infant is to survive. But his, as Starobinski notes, is hardly a reply; at best, it points out just how radically new Rousseau's *question* was for the spatially classificatory thought of the enlightenment. The novelty of Rousseau begins with this question. Buffon had been willing to admit that one possible source of the coexistence of multiple species lies with man's cultivation of nature; but he immediately placed the new products of this activity in the classificatory space of the table, thereby eliminating their novelty. Rousseau's question is whether man cannot cultivate *himself*, transform *himself*; and if so, whether this does not imply a rupture of the space of history, the introduction of a temporal dimension.

At the beginning of the *Second Discourse*, Rousseau proposes, in a famous phrase: "Let us then begin by putting aside all the facts, for they have nothing to do with the question.'' Similarly, the first Book of the *Social Contract* begins: ''Man is born free and everywhere he is in chains. . . . How did this change come about? I do not know. What can make it legitimate? I think I can answer that question.'' Rousseau is adopting the normative standpoint of validity in order to lay clear the genetic underpinnings of the historical rupture by which natural man became civilized. This same normative approach will permit him to criticize the results of that social genesis without appeal to an external standard. This can be seen in Rousseau's reply to Voltaire's criticism: ''You call a writing in which I pleaded the cause of humanity against itself a trap . . . but I showed men how they made their own unhappiness by themselves, and consequently that they could avoid it.''[6] Rousseau's philosophical or methodological approach explains many of his differences with the ideological criticisms of the philosophes, and many of the reasons that, today, we find it difficult to recognize the revolutionary implications of his thought. For example, Colletti's Marxist reading notes that Rousseau was ignorant of economics—although, he adds, this did not prevent Rousseau from developing an important critique of modern civil society.[7] Yet,it is Rousseau's question, the question of origins, that is responsible for the continuing relevance of his work. It is this *question* which distinguishes him from the (superficially read) tradition of German Idealism inaugurated by Kant.

The standard of Rousseau's normative critique is natural man. This is not a primitivism, anti-intellectualism, or irrationalism contrasted favorably to the refined manners and culture of the enlightenment; Rousseau's aim is not, as Voltaire ironized, that we again walk on our four paws. It is first of all a criticism of the psychological presuppositions of the natural-law tradition which appeals to fact, as Buffon had done in his reply to Rousseau. Rousseau rejects the use by Grotius, Pufendorf, and the jurisconsultes of the presupposition of a natural sociability of mankind to refute Hobbes or utilitarianism; similarly, he rejects Locke's presuppositions of pre-stately property, just as he criticizes Hobbes's ''war of all against all'' for taking the effect of civilization for its cause. From such presuppositions, it is impossible to explain the *origin* of vice, or its overcoming. By assuming from the outset what they want to prove, these apparently different natural-law theorists deny the temporal reality of history; they construct a pre-fabricated spatial bridge when a temporal leap is necessary.

One cannot, Rousseau insists, establish historical right (or norms) by appeal to fact. In our language of originary revolution, Rousseau's demand breaks with the tabular spatial juxtaposition by introducing the possibility of a temporal rupture in the continuum; the origin of the present state of affairs is not really present, or reflected, or expressed by the existent society. If one does not make room for such a rupture in the classification, then the practical result is the reforming position of the philosophes, for whom, as Cassirer notes, the state becomes ''a mere welfare state.''[8] The position of the philosophes is one of ''political opportunism''[9] based on a eudaemonian or utilitarian ethics where security is more important then freedom. If Rousseau had accepted the radical distinction between morality and politics, private and public affairs, he would have been locked into an apolitical stance condemned, like the philosophes, to impotence in real politics because of this theoretical supposition. Not only did Rousseau have to reject the philosophical common sense of his times; he had to make clear to his reader the efficacy of his paradoxical premise, in the *Second Discourse* as in *The Social Contract*.

Rousseau's biography, and the works which made his contemporary reputation, complicate the task of interpretation. If we compare Rousseau with the Abbé St.-Pierre, whose writings on perpetual peace and polysynodie Rousseau edited, there might appear to be grounds for assuming that the distinction of politics and morality was his premise in political theory as in private life. Cobban describes St.-Pierre as a typical enlightenment reformer who introduced the term ''bienfaisance'' into the current discussion. He continues:

> Among his *projets* were those for perpetual peace, for a graduated land tax, for diminishing the number of lawsuits, for improving schools, for reforming spelling, for extirpating the Barbary corsairs, for rendering dukes and peers serviceable, for making honorific titles more useful to the State, for a system of annuities, for making the writing of bad books—romances, catechisms, sermons and the like—more honourable for their authors and more useful to posterity, for improving the system of government, for making roads passable in winter, for dealing with beggers, and many others, down to a project for a patent portable armchair.[10]

Rousseau's method permitted none of this polymorphous reformism. When he did come to treat the details of political arrangements in his projects for a Polish and a Corsican Constitution, he could conceive his task only from the position of the classical legislator, not from that of the practical everyday politician who has to deal with men and conditions as they have become and who therefore abandons the norm to work with what is given him by history. The practical Rousseau cannot be judged at this level; his ''practice'' depends on a specific kind of theory whose ''nature'' is defined by the originary structure.

If Rousseau's invocation of natural man were only the appeal to a static and external moral norm parading as a political standard, he would be interesting to us at best as a (quite subtle) critic of the social manners and follies of his times, as the Marxist Colletti tends to portray him. Rousseau from this point of view would be a kind of neo-stoic opposing the ataraxie of primitive man to the opinionated and frenetic social penchants of the modern. In fact, however, the normative critique which discloses natural man as origin does not treat the state of nature either as a pre-existing and unqualifiedly good condition or as a real origin whose presence throughout the subsequent history of its effects provides the basis for a (moral) critique of historical development. Rousseau's position does not depend on the real existence of the state of nature, or on the possibility of the desirability of a return to it. Man's primitive condition is described as that of ''un animal stupide et borné.'' This animal is said to be ''free,'' and it does indeed immediately satisfy its passions. But there is no use for its freedom in the isolated conditions of the state of nature; and the passions are correspondingly limited. The normative function of Rousseau's "nature" puts into question its descriptive and historical status. The critique of the sociological presuppositions shared by the different natural-law theorists takes on a new sense. The "state of nature" exists only for already socialized men. This paradoxical assertion accentuates the originary structure of "nature" for Rousseau.

Rousseau does not, and admits that he cannot, give either a historical description or a causal argument for the move from nature to society. He invokes accident, fortuitous circumstances, the calamaties of nature and geography to account for the coming together of groups of naturally isolated men.[11] Whatever the reason invoked for their assembly, it is important that Rousseau does not explain it by a psychology of real natural sociability or material human need. Indeed, the stress on accident as opposed to a logical or a causal explanation is not, so to speak, accidental or illogical. Rousseau wants to make clear that the state of nature is not a real origin of civilized society; between the two stages of history there is a gap, a rupture, the birth of a new time. Physical and immediate need satisfaction does not draw men together; on the contrary, it disperses them. Only when that isolated pleasure is not possible do men come together. They do so for their own ends and purposes, and in this act they create social institutions which attempt to preserve their previous state at the new level, denying in this way the radical novelty of their own act, reducing the temporally new to a figure within the space of the *tableau*. Similarly, in accounting for the origin of language Rousseau rejects the then current hypothesis which attempts to account for that most civilized product in terms of the reality of human needs which drive primitives to utter sounds which gradually are refined into articulate linguistic codes which can then represent or imitate mimetically a real infrastructure of human needs or relations. The many discussions in Rousseau of the immediacy of the passions, their virtues and those of the simple life, cannot be interpreted either as the immediate opposition of morality to politics or as the representation of real nature or natural man as a standard external to and critical of established social relations. It is not simply to the opposition of nature and culture that Rousseau appeals.

C. The Origin of Natural History

Starobinski's suggestive study of Rousseau—*La transparence et l'obstacle*—suggests an interpretation of the state of nature as origin. The state of nature represents a transparency for which Rousseau continually strives in his life as in his art; but the ambiguity of this transparent origin emerges at every moment that its realization becomes plausible; the real thickness of nature, its independence, throws up an obstacle, whose overcoming becomes the task of art or politics. Once the state of nature has been lost, it can never be recaptured in its immediacy because temporality has replaced spatial co-existence; yet the quest for a return of the originary state is that which motivates human development in history. This motivation only arises with society, with the loss of the state of nature which institutes the notion of natural law as temporal origin (not as spatially present reality). It is only apparently paradoxical to assert that the ''state of nature'' arises only once it is in fact left behind; the state of nature and natural law are social and thereby historical products. They cannot be conceived as the pre-given potentiality of humankind, a kind of natural sociability; that assumption denies the leap that introduces history. Only when the obstacle is recognized does the transparency of the origin become a goal. Only in society does natural law exist; but its existence is that of an origin, not that of a real thing. Only in a politically constituted society are questions of morality posed to the individual. Natural law and morality are, therefore, both genetic and normative: they are originary. Rousseau's normative question does not uncover an originary fact; it discovers the genesis of the normative question itself. For this specific reason. Rousseau's theory becomes understandable as a revolutionary or critique theory.

The political arrangements proposed by Rousseau can be understood without contradiction once his theoretical approach is seen as a critique. However, for whatever reasons and in the interests of whomever, the social contract comes about. If the contract is assumed to be normative or valid, it is by definition a reciprocal contract. Rousseau is unsparing in his criticisms of any asymmetry in the contract, whether it be the individual contract of slavery (which, following the Romans, some natural-law theorists could justify as freely undertaken; and which Rousseau condemns as both asymmetrical and as dealing with an inalienable possession: freedom) or the social contract of subordination to a sovereign (whether in Hobbes's version, or as modified by Pufendorf's ''stipulation''). The symmetry or reciprocity entailed in the normative social contract implies that in joining the community each individual follows his own self-interest. The famous passages in which Rousseau describes the contract as an ''alienation'' of natural liberty must be read with caution. The society or sovereign to which freedom is alienated must be structured so as to return that natural freedom—which never really existed!—as socially guaranteed. This guarantee must be both normative and genetic. What is more, since the natural freedom of self-satisfaction in nature which led to dispersion of self-satisfying atoms was useless and only instinctual, the new social freedom achieved by the contract entails more than just the immediate happiness of natural man; it carries with it the introduction of reason, of virtue, and of justice, which did not previously exist. There is apparently a temporal, dialectical process moving from the freedom of the state of nature, through the creation of history in which the development of reason and civilization at once potentially can enrich humanity and yet render it vicious and immoral, to a return to a greater and positively defined freedom among other human beings in a society where obedience to the sovereign is in fact only the obedience which virtue owes to itself. It is this dialectic which gives natural freedom the definition that it was lacking in the state of nature. To its abstract theoretical formulation in the political writings corresponds its popular literary expression in the *Nouvelle Héloise*.[12]

The social contract explains the genesis of society, and stands at the same time as the normative criterion of its legitimacy. The problem is how it can generate the society which, only then, gives validity to the natural law which is its precondition. The natural-law tradition had explained the genesis of society and its political sovereign contractually. But its theorists were not only divided on the logic of this contract; more important, they could not agree on the normative criteria in terms of which to judge the form of social sovereignty that resulted. One set of problems that emerged turned around the question of the ''last instance'': in the case of dispute, are the contracting people or the sovereign institutions to decide? This entailed the question whether there are limits on sovereignty, and if so, which? Was there a natural-law limitation, as the Thomist theory and dynastic states had it; or a limit imposed by the aim for which individuals freely contracted, as in the liberal tradition; or were there fundamental written constitutional laws which limited sovereign action as the Protestant theorists thought? None of the solutions proposed proved sufficient. To natural law was opposed the imprescriptible right of conscience; to the aims of society was posed the question of who is to interpret them and suspicion of the casuistry of ''tacit consent''; while the constitutional solution had the problem of limiting sovereignty and inviting civil war since a sovereignty which is divided, or which the people do not in fact exercise, is merely rhetorical. The source of the problem in each case was that sovereignty was conceived as a *real thing*, modeled after the contract which supposedly gave rise to private property. Rousseau's insight was that sovereignty is not a thing; the sovereign is the (collective) social will, the ''volonté générale,'' which like individual will and freedom is by definition inalienable. And, as Derathé insists, while the idea that in principle the people are sovereign was not new, the stress in the nonsubstantial, on the will which is inalienable, was new. Obedience to the sovereign is therefore not obedience to a real and singular person; it is obedience to the general will in the institutions of a republic. Rousseau's position is epitomized when he cites Pliny's remark to Trajan: ''if we have a prince it is to preserve us from having a master.''[13] To make sense of Rousseau's argument, the relation of the individual will to the general will must be shown to be both genetic and normative. This demands a theory of political institutions.

D. The Institutions of Social History

Interpretors have struggled with the apparent paradox that the contracting individual wills produce a general will which, in turn, stands as sovereign and norm over them. Despite Rousseau's repeated criticisms of all forms of despotism—including the ''enlightened'' physiocratic ''legal despot''—many have interpreted the General Will as a kind of Hobbesian fiction justifying the suppression of the individual freedom Rousseau wanted to protect. Rousseau cannot escape the reproach by arguing that the contract which creates the General Will is a rational one based on reasoned comparison of the alternatives, since his natural man is defined as immediate, as not exercising that comparative form of rationality which emerges only in society where natural *amour de soi* becomes social *amour propre*. It might be said that Rousseau had in mind an image of the Greek polis whose ethical customary life molded the individual will such that, instinctively, it chooses the general good. Or, his educational theory of the production of private virtue could be added to his discussion of civil religion as belated recognitions of the paradox, and attempts to overcome it. But such an option for either type of education would also violate the immediate freedom which Rousseau attributes to the original contractors.[14] Hume had confronted this paradox, and generalized it to any contract theory. The validity of the contract presupposes a contract in terms of which the promise made in the contract is valid and enforceable; and the second earlier contract in turn has a similar presupposition, such that an infinite regress ensues, from which Hume can escape only by adducing utility as the justifying factor in a contract. Rousseau does not disagree about the role of utility; but he knows full well that what is "useful" in the eyes of one may not have the same value for another. He saw also that this argument was in fact that of the French monarch. He therefore added to the utility criterion the primacy of freedom, for otherwise despotism remains possible for whoever defines social utility. But "freedom" here cannot refer to a real, empirical fact; Rousseau's concern is to retain the freedom of origins.

The General Will does not exist in the isolated state of nature before the contract constitutes it; yet the validity of the constitutive contract is judged by its conformity to the General Will. One might make the same apparently paradoxical claim for any social convention; for example, private property is only instituted and recognized once the constitution of the modern sovereign state destroys the particularism of feudal traditions. But a conventional right like private property cannot be universal or normative, as indicated by Rousseau's critique of Locke for presupposing as natural a psychology which is in fact that of civilized man.[15] A right granted by convention is a particular and alienable right; the individual or society could persist without it. Rousseau's "buffonian" method of focusing on natural man for purposes of comparison suggests that there are also inalienable rights, without which man would not be man. Freedom is such an inalienable right, and the social contract is instituted to protect it. To think of freedom as a property which I could alienate—for example in a contract of slavery, which would at least assure me bed and board, or save my threatened life—is to deny what is the origin of my humanity. Freedom does not have the kind of "reality" of a thing about which conventions can be established, and which can be alienated in a contract; freedom is not (a) property; freedom is the originary basis of any valid contract, the source of its genesis and the criterion of its validity. If "natural circumstances" or accident drive men to institute a social contract with one another, this contract will be not only valid, but useful if and only if it institutes and preserves freedom. The freedom which the contract institutes and preserves is at once individual self-good and the good of all; freedom depends on institutional arrangements which articulate the notion of the General Will and permit the natural instinct of self-conservation to be maintained and dialectically enriched in the originary interplay whereby normativity calls forth genesis and vice-versa.

By holding to the standpoints of both genesis and validity, the critique method permits an understanding of the institutional preservation of the individual and the general. Rousseau did not explicitly articulate the method of critique; but he was aware of its implications. Describing his approach to D'Alembert, he asserts that "the subjects and the sovereign are but the same men considered in different relations." Derathé generalizes this methodological approach in his clarification of Rousseau's originality:

> If Rousseau's theory has been interpreted differently, this is because it has not been seen that he uses successively two different points of view, such that the error is to confuse questions of origins with problems of value."[16]

As opposed to the natural-law theories which were developing the notion of the sovereign state while adapting to the empirical conditions of their times by basing sovereignty in the people but then arguing that an implicit contract alienated its exercise to governmental institutions of one or another kind, Rousseau's originality is his insistence on the inalienable nature of sovereignty. The General Will is sovereign; its nature as will entails its freedom, which cannot be alienated. But the General Will, like the state of nature, is only constituted in the social contract itself; it is not the external genetic source from which the state is constituted as its social representation; it is rather the grounds of the validity of any state form, at the same time that it generates the lawful relations among individual wills which are the General Will. A state form which violates the General Will is illegitimate, however much it may contribute to the individual quest for utility or security. State institutions must preserve the freedom of the contracting individuals; yet these institutions must also be independently sovereign. This double demand explains why Rousseau is not a simple democrat or a precursor of "totalitarianism." He does not want simply the preservation of particularity in opposition to the state, any more than he approves the submersion of individuality by the state. For the same reason, Rousseau could admit to the accusations of the Geneva procurer Tronchin, that the *Social Contract* justified the frequent total transformation of governmental institutions if the people were to so will. Rousseau's politics do not fit the standard categories.[17]

Many commentators have seen a contradiction between the theory of the sovereign General Will and the moral conscience on which Rousseau usually puts so much stress, while omitting it in the *Social Contract*. The two approaches might be reconciled through the assumption that individual conscience takes back its rights in those areas of particularity where the General Will, because of its generality, is not competent. Rousseau's arguments for the right of opinion, and for freedom of religion, are based on the fact that these do not affect the community as a whole. But the problem with this approach is that, in the last analysis, it is the sovereign who decides what affects the community just as it is the sovereign who decides what is useful to the community. Rousseau's theory avoids this problem insofar as his definition of sovereignty as the General Will avoids making it into a *thing*, into the personal or executive exercise of authority which society would have to limit, control, or divide. The social contract has both a genetic and a normative aspect which are unified in the contractual act but separated in their presentation. What is alienated in the contractual act is simultaneously given back by the General Will which the pact institutes. The pact is not a Hobbesian contract among individuals for the benefit of a third, like an insurance policy protecting the security of another. The social contract institutes a republican form of government under law, guaranteeing freedom through the reciprocity of duty and right which its generality assures. The contracting individual does not enter into a monolithic whole in which particularity is destroyed. The difference of points of view, of genesis and validity, means that the same individual is at once particular, at once general. The normative General Will is only valid if it generates individuality; the individual, in turn, is validated as individual by participation in the general. Republican freedom under law guarantees equality and reciprocity; it is a protection and, indeed, the producer of individuality, not its suppression in the name of a real, concrete institution claiming factual sovereign universality.

E. Republican Politics as Morality

The interplay of the genetic and normative approaches permits Rousseau to formulate a political theory which is moralist and a moral theory which is political. Living alone, natural man was happy, immediately satisfied, and free. Social man must be virtuous, just, and also free. Social man does not sacrifice or alienate his original capacities; these are maintained through the dialectical enrichment. Rousseau takes care to present his political institutions without appeal to ideal, religious, or moral factors external to social life. The transformation of immediate passion into more rewarding virtue is portrayed vividly in his literary work, particularly in the *Nouvelle Héloise*. But even if the demonstrations of art are rejected, and if the illustration which he tried to give in living his own life is not convincing, his legal republicanism provides a further conceptual argument. Derathé notes in passing that Rousseau cannot be considered a socialist despite his stress on equality and community.[18] The reason for this is that Rousseau was concerned with a justice and freedom which are moral virtues that can only be instituted politically; he was not concerned with a real physical equality, which was not even the starting point in the state of nature. While it is true that Rousseau saw the dangers of the accumulation of private property (in his *Encyclopedia* article on "Political Economy," and later in his proposed constitution for Corsica), his political institutions did not aim at the kind of tabular spatial organization of social interdependence illustrated by Quesnay's *Tableau*. He observes in his proposed constitution for Poland that those states which have many laws need them because of an inherent corruption of the citizens. His opposition to direct democracy was directed against its tendency to the formation of "partial societies" based on particular interest. It was not so much that such particular interest distorted the social fabric, but that the pursuit of particularity led to corruption. It was better, he thought, to have all participate in decisions, even if they might err, rather than to run the risk of corruption, which is the worst political evil because it destroys freedom. If political unanimity in a state is not possible, he concluded, this indicates that a moral decline has set in, and that political failure will follow.

It is ultimately Rousseau's theory of republican law which, as Derathé insists and Rousseau recognized, ties together the genetic and normative aspects of his political thought. Sheldon Wolin's history of Western political thought, *Politics and Vision*,[19] stresses that the political theory which accompanies the rise of the sovereign national state is characterized by a reaction against the forms of personal domination experienced in the feudal tradition. Rousseau fits well into Wolin's generalization. In his personal life and in his theory, nothing haunted him more than the thought of personal dependence. But Wolin's concern to show the parallel of the decline of properly political thinking and the rise of capitalist civil society leads him to underestimate the political logic of Rousseau's legal theory. Because of the historical leap from isolated, immediate natural man to the potentially virtuous social individual that the contract institutes, the law comes into being as *doubly universal*: normatively universal in its object, and genetically universal in its source. The legislative will is thus strengthened and simultaneously limited. In Derathé's concise formulation, "If the sovereign makes the laws, it can make only laws."[20] The sovereign is and remains the people, who cannot alienate their will. A government or executive which enforces this will is of course necessary, but it is only the executor of the legislative will from which it remains separate. The legislature is will; the executive represents force; and force cannot legitimately dominate over will. This is the reason that Rousseau is opposed to representative government, observing for example that the English are free only at the moment of the vote, by which very gesture they abdicate their freedom to the representatives. If, in a large territory such as Poland, representation is absolutely necessary, Rousseau insists that the representatives elected must be given the imperative mandate, and must report frequently and directly to their constituents. Whatever one may think of Derathé's attempt to explain away this opposition to representative government as due to the political experiences with which Rousseau was familiar, the most important aspect of the argument is that in rejecting representation Rousseau is breaking with the tabular classificatory method; he is rejecting the notion of a real sovereign whose will can be expressed in the form of a table of legal decisions declared by the executive sovereign.[21] The law is not simply the impersonal statement of a conventional code of social relations, nor is it the reflection in legal form of nature's own laws. The law is political. Its normative demands for universality generate specific constraints on the particular participants who must give up the immediacy of individual satisfaction in order to gain the virtue and justice of general satisfaction in which the natural passions are preserved at a higher social level. Republican politics is a morality; and morality can be realized only in a republic.

Reference has already been made to the use and abuse of Rousseau during the French Revolution, and to this effect on the sensibility of his contemporaries. But Rousseau was also, in important ways, a classical author, many of whose ideas were in the air of the times. While his legal republic explicitly permitted frequent institutional changes, his model was still the classical Greek polis whose few institutions were anchored in the habitual intercourse of the citizens which enjoyed a permanence such that few political actions were in fact necessary.[22] Rousseau is able to paint a picture of the decline of this civilization as calculating—comparing reason comes to dominate the simpler passions and virtues. But while he puts great stress on the qualitative gap that separates natural from social man, and while he can describe in general terms the reconciliation which the legal republic would bring by restoring the natural balance as he promised at the outset of the *Social Contract*, he is not able to think the leap between the civilization whose abuses he condemns and the one which he sees as normatively necessary. He can depict it in the lives of individuals, and try to live it in his own life; and he can imagine external legislative modes (as in the Corsican and Polish Constitutional projects) for its introduction. He can criticize the utilitarianism and opportunism of the philosophes in their efforts at amelioration. But, in the last resort, his radical normative approach falls short. Perhaps this is an inherent limit, owing to Rousseau's recognition that to describe the bridge between the two phases would entail the kind of illicit presuppositions about human nature which he criticized so acutely in the work of the natural-law theorists. Or, perhaps it is a temperamental quality of Rousseau himself, as Starobinski tends to depict it. In fact, the problem lies in Rousseau's not having sufficiently radicalized his break with the presuppositions of the tableau. The genetic moment is sacrificed; the moral is separated form the political.

As will, the General Will can always take back and remodel its own decisions. This means that the will is, from the outset, unchanging and unchangeable. Despite Rousseau's criticisms of the ill effects of reason in the growth of civilization, the will somehow remains separate from these. If one were to make the best case for him, Rousseau's argument would be that the primacy of the politics of the General Will serves, through the mediation of the universality and reciprocity guaranteed by the nature of republican law, to protect the individual and leave him free to grow in nonpolitical areas. Thus, the isolated individual whom nature's satisfactions permit to live happily in isolation from others is preserved in a social setting where the enrichment of interdependence is added. Rousseau would then fall into that Western tradition which Hannah Arendt decries for its separation of the personal and the political, and its assumption that freedom begins on the other side of politics. But Rousseau wanted politics to be more than just an appendage to or a guarantee of private satisfaction. Despite the influence of the Greek model of long-term institutions and few political choices, his theory of sovereignty demands participation. One would expect, therefore, an analysis of the process of the growth of the will; and the connection between politics and morality established by the critique theory should lead in the same direction. The author of *Emile* does not offer a political theory of the growth of the will because, in the last resort, the political institutions that he presents still are articulated in tabular form, as a kind of institutional classification whose arrangement would permit relations of transparency. He avoids the danger of the representation of a real sovereign will; but at the same time he does not articulate the difference of genesis and validity into a structure which would preserve both of these stances as independent. The legal republic ultimately collapses genesis and validity into a seamless spatial unity from which the dimension of temporality whose introduction made possible the whole process is excluded. *The General Will has no history*.

F. The Temporality of the Political

Rousseau's unification of the moral and the political in a republican theory is vitiated by the attempt to achieve a dialectical *synthesis* of the genetic and the normative moments. The roots of this error lie in the equation of history and temporality. The paradoxical structure of the "state of nature" which exists only and always after society has obliterated its illusory reality defines the *temporal* structure of all human action; but it is only apparently *historical*. Starobinski's picture of a movement defined by the constant quest for transparency in the face of an always reappearing obstacle constituted by the action seeking to realize the transparent relation of the subject to the world conflates the two modes in which humans act within the social world. Full transparency can, by definition, never be achieved; but, also by definition, humans can never cease to seek it. This structure defines the leap which is temporality. It cannot, however, be equated with human history, as if there were a gradual and ascending process through which humanity (or the individual) approached ever more closely to the ideal of full rationality. Such a picture of the development of the General Will through historical phases is precisely what Hegel's *Philosophy of Right* draws from Rousseau.

This criticism of the temptation toward dialectical synthesis rules out the obvious corrective to Rousseau's theory. An ahistorical General Will which exists in the institutional form of the republic has replaced the properly genetic moment by a normative theory which claims to be able to account for genetic action. Normative republican law is said to induce the citizens to generate the particular laws which satisfy the imperative of a sovereign "who makes only laws." Particularity is to be avoided; laws are to be few and simple; if unanimity is not present, moral decline must have already begun. Hannah Arendt describes the difficulty that emerges from this portrait:

> The citizen's moral obligation to obey the laws has traditionally been derived from the assumption that he either consented to them or actually was his own legislator; that under the rule of law men are not subject to an alien will but obey only themselves—with the result, of course, that every person is at the same time his own master and his own slave, and that what is seen as the original conflict between the citizen, concerned with the public good, and the self, pursuing his private happiness, is internalized. This is in essence the Rousseauian-Kantian solution to the problem of obligation, and its defect, from my point of view, is that it turns again on conscience—on the relation between me and myself.[23]

The attempted dialectical synthesis of the genetic and the normative poles in the form of the moral and the political short-circuits the authentically temporal originary position presented in *The Social Contract*. Rousseau's static republican institutions cannot be given life by the addition of a dose of morality. That would mean the elimination of the properly political moment which introduced the originary theory.

Rousseau's political theory becomes apolitical and tabular because *it excludes nature*. Rousseau broke through the classificatory image of nature as an immediately real presence; the originary state of nature arises only once society is already constituted. The state of nature that results from this explicitly accidental process of sociation is at once normative and genetic. This structure is presented by the General Will as sovereign. When this General Will is portrayed in the institutions of the republic, and when its action is described in the form of republican laws, the normative is equated with the universal. The quest for universality—which is simply one form of the attempt to attain transparency—is taken to be sufficient to explain particular actions by individuals or by the sovereign. The cost of this unification of the political and the moral is correctly criticized by Arendt. More important, the political and the moral are identified insofar as both types of action work by a process of subsuming the particularity of *real* nature under their universal lawfulness. This, however, was precisely what the classificatory tabular treatment of nature as fully present had also intended.

The "nature" excluded by the dialectical synthesis of the political and the moral is not simply the 'other' of thought, the particular that stands opposed to the universal, the resistance that opposes and calls for action. The point is not to integrate a history into the General Will, promising to complete its quest for dialectical synthesis or transparency. Rousseau's fundamental insight makes evident the originary leap which institutes temporality. This leap, for which no logic or causality can account, institutes at the same time the state of nature. This nature is not a fiction, a hypothesis, or an ideal condition existing outside of time any more than it is the tabular nature on which historical progress attempts to inscribe itself. Its originary structure does not define it as a generality incapable of particularization. To the contrary, it is always particular and always historical precisely to the extent that it must be constantly instituted as originary at the same time that its originary structure can never be made permanent. This defines its temporal structure. In this sense, Rousseau formulates a theory of revolution. The political reflection which institutes nature as temporal is not susceptible to reduction to a theory of history. Revolution is the rupture with history, the advent of the new, which can never be predicted but only made.

III
The Working Critic

9

The Politics of Modernism: From Marx to Kant

A. Avant-Gardes and Vanguards

The torch of avant-garde art passed to America at the beginning of the 1950s, at the very moment when political repression and massified pluralist conformism were at their height. By the end of the decade, the relation was inverted. The avant-garde was materially integrated into the expanding university; its product entered the curriculum of the "liberal imagination" or joined the market for what Harold Rosenberg labeled "The Tradition of the New." Lionel Trilling rejected the "adversary culture," while repentant drummers like Leslie Fiedler set out in search of a "real" America which an elitist "alienation" from mass life supposedly denied. But then again, the "end of ideology" and the "lonely crowd" gave way to a political renewal with the sit-ins in the South, the emergence of Fidel and Che—and the Goldwater "crusaders from the barbeque pits" (I. Howe).

The 1960s seem to have been the decade of the vanguard, while the avant-garde modernism was bent on demonstrating the action-prophecy of Tinguely's self-destroying machine sculpture at the Museum of Modern Art. Pop glorification and serialization of the banal had as its "materialist" counterpoint the stress on the immediate materiality of the art-object, its reduction in status to Greenberg's "decorative" or Rosenberg's "anxious object." The symmetry at the end of this decade is not so clear as its beginning. The vanguardism that remained when the "new left" acquired a third-world tinted Marxist orthodoxy had become nothing but an avant-garde object of contemplation. The avant-garde, on the other hand, in its search for the New, had in a sense introjected the political painting of the vanguard-art '30s, creating a variety of new "realisms" as it returned toward representation.

Avant-gardes and vanguards claim to be representatives of *something*; they are the delegates or forerunners of a mighty mass, of History itself. Although their lives bear a charm, their hour on stage must be a short and fretful one. Their History is neither the cyclical natural revolution of the seasons, nor the eschatological leap to the City of God. It is a History which, precisely because of its dogged and dogmatic secular character, becomes in its own eyes the only Holy left on the calendar. The politically-minded historians tell us that this History came into its own when capitalism finally effaced the remnants of the traditionalist cultures toward the end of the nineteenth century. When this History passes, so too will its avant-gardes and vanguards. Indeed, their task is precisely to bring about their own demise—a paradox which bears reflection, since an exploited proletariat may define its goal as its own elimination as exploited, alienated class, but this ''Hegelian'' figure of thought is harder to conceive in the case of the art object or artist. This paradox is also the basis of various theories of intellectuals as a new dominating class, articulated from the Left (Gouldner) or the Right (neo-conservatives). That, however, is another issue.

An always present danger is that avant-gardes become *ersatz* vanguards, and *vice-versa*. Whatever the relation of art and politics, we know that the two are not identical. One can see, however, why the substitution might take place in specific conditions. Once it became impossible to deny that the proletariat was not playing its designated role in transforming the Russian into a World Revolution, or when the deformed and deforming character of the society instituted in the name of that proletariat could not be ignored, then those who placed their bets on History could turn to culture and art as the new midwife and spiritual guide. If the cultural revolution is said only to prepare the ground for the political one, this transfer may not be too dangerous. The more frequent case, however, finds the one serving rather as a substitute gratification driving the other from the stage.

Two souls, alas, seem to dwell in the breast of modern History. Were we premoderns, we would try to unify them into one Subject, transcending the tension between art and politics. As secular moderns, we have to remain earthbound to History. The Frankfurt School, and in the context just sketched, Herbert Marcuse, illustrate some of the structures of the modernist project. Marcuse knew that Marx's proletariat is not the agent of History (although the Great Refusal and the Outsiders of *One-Dimensional Man* implicitly use the same philosophical apparatus on which Marx based his nineteenth-century claim). He knew too that Soviet Marxism is deformed and deforming (although in his 1958 treatment of this theme Marcuse was cautiously optimistic that a rational political negation of this negation might yet be possible). What Marcuse never abandoned was the negative power of art sketched already in his brilliant essay of 1937 criticizing ''Affirmative Culture'' and returning as the theme of his last published book whose German title is *The Permanence of Art*.[1]

The premoderns are not the only ones to attempt to reduce the two souls to one—one dimension, we might well say here. A few illustrations from Marcuse will show the parallel reductions of Soviet and advanced Western society. For example, in *Soviet Marxism*, Marcuse talks about the repetition of linguistic ''rituals'':

The value of these statements is pragmatic rather than logical, as is clearly suggested by their syntactical structure. They are unqualified, inflexible, formulas calling for an unqualified, inflexible response. In endless repetition, the same noun is always accompanied by the same adjectives and participles; the noun 'governs' them immediately and directly so that whenever it occurs they follow 'automatically' in their proper place. The same verb always 'moves' the proposition in the same direction, and those addressed by the proposition are supposed to move in the same way. These statements do not attribute a predicate to a subject (in the sense of formal or of dialectical logic); they do not develop the subject in its specific relations.[2]

The Soviet situation turns out, on Marcuse's account, to have family resemblances to our own social relations in the capitalist West. For example, *One-Dimensional Man* criticizes the pragmatic insistence on speech as designation, finding it to be magical, authoritarian, the ritual denial of mediation. There is an "[a]bridgement of the concept in fixed images; arrested development in self-validating, hypnotic formulas; immunity against contradiction, identification of the thing (and of the person) with its function."[3] In each case one finds the rejection of transcendence, of development or change, of contradiction or negation. It is not that art is reduced to politics, or *vice-versa*; rather Marcuse sees a general leveling in all spheres of life to the common denominator of production for its own sake.

The productivist reductionism does, however, affect the soul, and thence politics and art. In *One-Dimensional Man*, as earlier in *Eros and Civilization*, Marcuse presents an incisive criticism of the "therapeutic" goals of contemporary social science, psychology, and philosophy. Each specialty, for apparently humane and even socially critical reasons, seeks a cure for an "unhappy consciousness" which, like the Hegelian model from which Marcuse takes this concept, cannot be so easily trivialized. The same problem is addressed in *Soviet Marxism*, with some of the same examples:

If Tristan and Isolde, Romeo, and Juliet, and their like are unimaginable as healthy married couples engaged in productive work, it is because their (socially-conditioned) 'unproductiveness' is the essential quality of what they stand for and die for—values that can be realized only in an existence outside and against the repressive social group and its rule.[4]

The problem is not merely artistic or cultural; it is also political. For example, in the context of the Russian Revolution:

Kollontai, who is considered as the representative spokesman of revolutionary sexual morality, sees in childbearing and child raising a mode of 'productive labor', and brands the prostitute as a 'deserter from the ranks of productive labor.'[5]

Soviet and modern Western society appear to Marcuse to share this productivism and its logic, although his 1958 analysis of Russia envisages the possibility of a (dialectical) revolt from within the logic of the system whereas the Great Refusal of *One-Dimensional Man* is explicitly the product of the outsider, and is non-dialectical.

When he turns to the place and role of art in *Soviet Marxism*, the optimistic dialectical logic gives way to a description that is interestingly close to that of *One-Dimensional Man*.

> But art as a political force is art only insofar as it preserves the images of liberation; in a society which is in its totality the negation of these images, art can preserve them only by total refusal, that is, by not succumbing to the standards of the unfree reality, either in style, or in form, or in substance. The more totalitarian these standards become, the more reality controls all language and all communication, the more irrealistic and surrealistic will art tend to be, the more will it be driven from the concrete to the abstract, from harmony to dissonance, from content to form.[6]

These terms—irrealistic and surrealistic, abstract, dissonant, formalist—which characterize the "total refusal" of the administered Soviet society could also describe the succession of avant-gardes which have arisen within the capitalist Historical order. Both social forms would seem to be equivalent in Marcuse's eyes, and only art would in fact criticize them validly. The implication would be that art replaces politics, so that the avant-garde becomes the *ersatz*-vanguard. The politicization of avant-garde art, in turn, would explain the various forms of "anti-art" which arose during the '60s as well as a certain "aestheticization of politics" in the West. But especially this latter development recalls images like Marinetti's description of the battlefield as art, or the notion of Hitler's Nuremberg Rallies as a "communication system." Marcuse had to draw back. The negation carried non-dialectically by art had not been legitimated immanently. Its external criticism permitted the avant-garde to claim to be the vanguard of History.

Marcuse's last two books defend the "performance" of art as art while at the same time they confront its relation to politics. *Counter-Revolution and Revolt* emphatically rejects modernist anti-art claims to replace politics:

> The abolition of the aesthetic form, the notion that art could become a component part of the revolutionary (and pre-revolutionary) *praxis*, until under fully developed socialism, it would be adequately translated into reality (or absorbed by 'science')—this notion is false and oppressive: it would mean the end of art.[7]

Similarly, in *The Permanence of Art*, he insists that "the discourse of the end of art belongs today (differently than with Hegel) to the ideological arsenal and to the possibilities of *counterrevolution*."[8]

Marcuse sympathizes with the instinctive anti-elitism and the activist pragmatism that wants to democratize creativity by putting an end to the split of art and life. Yet he is insistent on art as art: ''To interpret this irredeemable alienation of art as a mark of bourgeois (or any other) class society is nonsense.''[9] Indeed, he is willing to admit that ''Revolutionary art can very well become the *enemy of the people*.''[10]

Marcuse's political argument for the permanence of art is that anti-art makes the artist unnecessary without thereby making creativity something general. To declare or decree that daily life is art is not to change daily life. Not only is this anti-art naïve; it is potentially dangerous. ''The truth of art,'' Marcuse insists, ''lies in breaking through the monopoly on reality as it is exercised in the existing society.''[11] By denying itself as art, by becoming reality, art opens itself to co-optation and to control. The dialectical Marcuse of the Frankfurt School returns. The denial of form and creativity as something elitist is only an ''abstract negation''[12] of domination. As part of reality and no longer its critical transcendence, art is no more a protest against but rather a part of the established order. The avant-garde that takes itself for a vanguard becomes simply a commodity, part of the society of the spectacle.

Marcuse's arguments are nearly convincing. The shadow of doubt is cast by the immanence of secular modernist History which poses the problem of vanguards and avant-gardes. The most wiley and reflective participant-commentator on modern art, Harold Rosenberg, has criticized Marcuse as ''an instance of the intrinsic conservation (sic: should be conservatism) of the contemporary Marxist outlook on art. In the name of a future new society, it rejects the changing imaginative substance of the present.''[13] More specifically, Rosenberg notes that ''Marcuse is committed to the art object; modernist notions of art as action, event, process, communication seem to him distortions of the inherent nature of art.''[14] This criticism predates Marcuse's last books which clarify his position on the latter point. Before accepting his defense, however, the first charge needs amplification. Rosenberg's article is titled ''Set out for Clayton!'' Clayton is the fictional town described in Kafka's *Amerika* where everyone is an actor in a ''nature theater.'' Karl Rossmann's rather good-natured escapades on our shores move toward the happy end of departure toward Clayton when Kafka's manuscript breaks off. Marcuse would no doubt condemn this naturalism as destroying the possibility of negation, of integrating the revolt (of Karl, and the unemployed and exploited) into a seamless web of sameness. But the significant point about Clayton (and perhaps about Kafka's relentless modernism, his world without transcendence or appeal) is that there are no spectators in Clayton's ''nature theater,'' and hence no spectacle. Modern art, it seems, is more complicated than its vanguardist translators will admit.

Marcuse's disposition of the territorial claims of art and politics, like the debates of the avant-garde with the vanguard, is not sufficiently radical. It accepts the terms in which the claimants pose their demands, forgetting that these are the inherited traditional titles from the Old Regime. Rosenberg's criticisms stand scrutiny. The "permanence" of the modern—not that of art or the art-object—should be the focus. Because the modern explicitly rejects external and traditional norms and values it can only be studied on its own terms, with its own tools. Framing the issue in terms of avant-gardes and vanguards at first suggests Marxism as the source of critical evaluation. In fact, the adequate tools of analysis will turn out to be those of Kant, as another great protagonist of American modernism, Clement Greenberg, has suggested. Since "the essence of Modernism lies . . . in the use of the characteristic methods of a discipline to criticize the discipline itself," the beginnings of this immanently self-critical tendency are found "with the philosopher Kant."[15] This assertion of the priority of the Kantian philosophical critique over marxist politics shocks both the philosopher and the historian of modernism who were brought up with a distant admiration for a Kant whose stature as a classic stripped him of any but antiquarian or schoolboy interest. To justify the central place of Kant, a self-criticism of our representation of modernism will follow an arc from Marx to Kant.

B. Revolution and Revolutionaries

Harold Rosenberg drew the modernist implications of Marx's theorizing over thirty years ago. "The resurrected Romans"[16] begins from Marx's famous depiction of the revolutionaries of 1789 who, blinded by the immensity of their undertaking and incapable of conceiving that their action was creating a world-historical *novum*, costumed themselves as the Roman heroes their literature and painting had taught them to venerate. Marx applies what is in effect an Aristotelian dramatic theory to these bourgeois-as-Romans: through their action and its results they, like the tragic hero, will come to learn who they are and what their disguised passions have made of them. The actors of 1789 could not consciously undertake the project of creating a capitalist order; they had neither the knowledge nor the courage to look such a task in the eye. Masking themselves in the dramatic personae of antiquity kept their passions kindled until finally—in the tragic defeat of the revolution they *thought* they were making—they could recognize themselves for what their everyday reality in fact had made of them: a bourgeoisie reproducing itself and its society. Such, broadly speaking, is the Marxist political critique. The Marxian philosophy, however, puts into question this political schema.

The self-deceiving bourgeois travestied in Roman robes is not the modernist revolutionary. Marx thought of himself, and of his revolutionary proletariat, as the great debunker, the clear-eyed realist whose broad shoulders could support the weight of history, come what may. But when the author of *Capital* came to describe revolutionary practice, his approach shifted. The *18th Brumaire* describes the *theater* of bourgeois revolutions which "storm swiftly from success to success; their dramatic effects outdo each other; men and things seem set in sparkling brilliants; ecstasy is the everyday spirit."[17] In contrast, proletarian revolutions

> criticize themselves constantly, interrupt themselves continually in their own course, come back to the apparently accomplished in order to begin it afresh . . . recoil ever and anon from the indefinite prodigiousness of their own aims, until a situation has been created which makes all turning back impossible, and the conditions themselves cry out: *Hic Rhodus, hic salta!*

This contrast is consistent but troubling. For the proletariat to act, it is the ''situation'' that ''makes all turning back impossible,'' and the ''conditions'' that ''cry out'' for action. On the other hand, although it had to disguise the fact from itself, the bourgeoisie actually creates a historical *novum*, breaks the historical continuum, ruptures time, transforms conditions and situations. The clear-eyed and realistic proletariat only brings to fruition what history already placed in the cards. This recalls the caricature of Hegel for whom freedom would be the recognition of necessity. It calls to mind the resigned preface to his *Philosophy of Right* which argues for the rationality of the actual while insisting on the impotence of theory which can only paint its (modernist?) ''grey on grey'' after the fact. Or, at the practical level, one thinks of Hegel's World Historical individuals whose short-run conscious action makes them the unconscious tools of History's Plan.

Marx's modernist revolutionary returns thematically in a lecture Rosenberg delivered at the height of the political/aesthetic confusion of vanguards and avant-gardes at the end of the 1960s.[18] He begins from the famous repetition, again in the *18th Brumaire*, of events in history, first as tragedy then as farce. Marx had shown how each class on the French stage is impotent, so that the field is left free to the ''theatrics of revolutionary revivals'' by Louis Bonaparte the Nephew. The farce occurs because the motor of history, class struggle, has been stilled. The farce is a farce because it is played on a stage somehow above or apart from the ongoing rush of historical progress. One could say—as Engels did later, and as our contemporaries groping vainly for some sort of ''marxist'' theory of state and politics try to maintain—that this proves *a contrario* that class struggle is the real motor of history, since precisely its absence permits such a farce. But that is category-juggling in the minor tradition of negative theology. The situation described by Marx in fact depicts the limits of the Marxist theory of history; or, at best, it shows the limits of what Marx means when he talks about ''history.'' The conclusion to the *18th Brumaire* supports this assertion. The pamphlet predicts that the fall of the imperial mantle from the shoulders of the Nephew will also demolish the stature of the Uncle at the Place Vendôme. The meaning seems to be that the farce of the Nephew's lumpen regime will debunk the myth of the Uncle which prevented the French proletariat from examining lucidly its own ''situation'' and courageously acting as material ''conditions'' demand. Then, the demystification accomplished, the historical drama will progress as its vanguard completes its assigned role.

Modernist avant-gardes and vanguards act at the service of History, yet the very nature of modernism demands rejection of any transcendent or external justification, including justification by appeal to History. Rosenberg's conclusion is rather pessimistic. Granted, the first time may be tragedy and the second farce; what about the third, the fourth, the fifth . . . ? How long until that "situation," those material "conditions" bring the *Hic Rhodus, hic salta?*

Marshall Berman's more recent reading of the problem provides a counterpoint to Rosenberg.[19] He summarizes his results:

> I have tried to read Marx as a modernist writer, to bring out the vividness and richness of his language, the depth and complexity of his imagery—clothes and nakedness, veils, halos, heat, cold, etc.—and to show how brilliantly he develops the themes by which modernism will later define itself: the glory of modern energy and dynamism, the ravages of modern disintegration and nihilism, the strange intimacy between them; the sense of being caught in a vortex in which all facts and values are whirled, exploded, decomposed, recombined; a basic uncertainty about what is basic, what is valuable, what is meaningful, even what is real; a flaring up of the most radical hopes in the midst of their radical negations.

Berman's theoretical premise is that "modernism [is] the realism of our time." But his political conclusion is based on a forced and self-contradictory syncretism. On the one hand, he sees Marx's "great gift" as "not a way out of the contradictions of modern life, but a surer and deeper way into these contradictions." On the other hand, these contradictions are such that "people's lives are going to keep falling apart" until "radical social and economic changes come about." And that, he adds, "could be a while." The difficulty is that Berman's "radical social and economic changes" don't come about from the "surer and deeper way into these contradictions" of his modernism. The changes, the solution, are to come from a different sphere—the social-economic—than the modernism which poses the problem in the first place.

That Marx wrote a book called *Capital* instead of a compendium under the heading *Socialism* testifies to the modernism of his self-understanding. That he also wrote a *Communist Manifesto* indicates that he is caught in the dilemma of the avant-gardes and vanguards. *Capital* portrays a radical uprooting of traditions and transcendences; it shows the constitution of a new temporal rhythm, a new History. No more natural cycles or transcendent values hinder the M-C-M', the money exchanged for (materially indifferent) commodities whose processing brings the cycle to a qualitatively identical but quantitatively increased close. Capitalism's M-C-M' is continual expansion, dynamism, and change of expanded reproduction of the Same. It is value begetting new value, self-referential, immanent (pseudo-) creation. Once established, capital tends to leave nothing outside its systemic self-reproduction and expansion; everything and anything become food for its voracious process. Opposition or criticism must therefore be immanent to this structural reproduction of the Same. Vanguards and avant-gardes are caught in the cycle however much they may wish or even imagine themselves apart from it. The *Communist Manifesto*'s description of capitalism's "stripping the halo" from professionals and intellectuals through the commodification process that profanes "all that is holy" shows Marx aware of their problematic position. Yet the *Manifesto* does appeal to History; like Berman, it mixes its media syncretically. It does this most tellingly in its central argument: the definition of the Communist.

By realizing History's immanent goal, the avant-garde or vanguard servant of History paradoxically eliminates the preconditions of his or her own existence. The consequences of this paradox can be seen in the theoretical definition and the practical behavior of Marx's Communist. The Communist is defined in the *Manifesto* as having "the theoretical advantage over the rest of the proletariat of an insight into the conditions, the path and the general results of the proletarian movement." The *hubris* expressed here is stunning. Theoretically, it flies in the face of Marx's own account of the modernist temporality of capitalism. It supposes that the Communist is both inside and outside, both participant and transcendent observer in capitalism's reproduction of the Same. The practical consequences are seen in assertions such as this one, from *Class Struggles in France*, that the revolution could not possibly have been socialist because "the state of economic development on the continent at that time was not ripe enough for the elimination of capitalist production." The same stance justifies the warning, in the *Neue Rheinische Zeitung*, that one must beware of "moving ahead of the revolutionary process of development, pushing it artificially to a crisis, pulling a revolution out of one's pocket without making the conditions for that revolution." In a word, this caricature of the Hegelian secretary to the World Spirit can become the Secretary General of the Party. The foreknowledge of the vanguard impels it to impose itself as the "selfless servant"[20] of Truth whose *conservator* it is.

Part of the *hubris* of the Communist is an apparent modesty and selflessness, a parental or pedagogical concern for those still caught in History's wheel, and even what at first glance might be confused with a democratic faith. This behavior by the Communist vanguard, shared with the artistic avant-garde, fits the immanence of modernism and modernity. The revolutionary is not guided by ideas, utopias, classical models. His or her critique is nothing but the self-critique of capitalism; revolution is inexorable; no force can dam its flow since—as in the case for capitalism's self-reproduction—nothing can maintain itself outside of it. Revolution is the actualization of an essential truth, a pre-given potential brought to actuality by the catalyst of the revolutionary. The revolutionary doesn't debate in order to convince; he or she only presents the "facts" as revealed by revolutionary science; as with Plato, to know the good is to do the good. There is an appearance of democracy here, as Plato had already seen, since the Truth is that one good which we can all share without its possession implying monopoly. But it is a democracy whose results are pregiven, like the democracy of the community of scientists whose methods and problems are predefined, and whose apparently free action in fact ensues with algorithmic necessity. The parental or pedagogical revolutionary will be the Socratic midwife bringing the slave to actualize the innate Idea. It is not for nothing that Marx's writings abound in midwife imagery, womb-and-birth metaphors, seeds and germinations.

The *hubris* and modesty are simply two sides of the same coin. Choose your passage from Marx. Either side can be more than amply illustrated. *The German Ideology* appears modest in asserting that "Communism for us is not a *state* (*Zustand*) which must be established, an *Ideal* according to which reality must be formed. We call communism the *actual* movement which eliminates the present state of affairs." Here the revolutionary would be but the modest "speaking part," as Rosa Luxemburg put it in her polemic with Lenin's views on the role of the party.[21] A year later, in *The Poverty of Philosophy*, the revolutionary gets more latitude: "The economic relations first of all change the mass of people into workers. The domination of capital has created for this mass a common situation, common interests. Thus this mass is already a class over against capital, but not yet for itself." The revolutionary now has to bring to actuality (to its self-consciousness or "for itselfness") what is only implicit in the class situation. This, of course, was the theoretical justification of Leninism and its later Stalinist form. Yet, speaking of an actual movement which he came to see as a model, Marx wrote of the Paris Commune that "the working class has no fixed and pre-given utopias to introduce through popular referendum. . . . It has no ideals to realize; it has only to free the elements that have already developed in the womb of the collapsing bourgeois society." The only consolation this paradoxical back-and-forth can offer is that anything and everything can find textual justification. The proletariat, in Castoriadis's image, is the constitutional Monarch of History: taking credit when all goes well, blaming its ministers for deviations from the true path!

The coin whose symmetrical sides are *hubris* and modesty is drawn from the treasures of capitalism. The revolutionary is the agent of the proletariat which, according to Marx, incarnates the "solution to the riddle of history." But this is the "riddle" of capitalism, not that of all human history. Capitalism creates the proletariat, and capitalism's continual process defines its tasks at any given moment. Its self-actualization or "for-itselfness" is therefore only the realization of the immanent logic of capitalism. This is not the creation of radically New social relations in the way that capitalism's temporality was said to introduce modernity in the place of feudalism. Marx's revolution, and his revolutionary, are caught in the paradoxes immanent to the dilemmas of modernism and modernity. While the modest or "reformist" Marxist fought it out with the *hubris* of the "revolutionary" within the Second International, capitalism careened toward the first modern, World War. The reformist argued, with Bernstein, that "the movement" is more important than prescriptive goals assigned by theory. His or her opponent, especially Lenin's Bolshevik, insisted on the final goal which the Party must bring from without to a class preoccupied by mere economic demands. After the terrible few years' hiatus of War, they renewed their opposition.

The paradoxes confronted by the revolutionary vanguard have the same structure as those faced by the modernist avant-garde. The philosophical categories, genesis and validity (or normativity) permit a clearer formulation. In the case of the vanguard, the reformist is suggesting that genesis—"the movement"—determines the eventual success of the result. The revolutionary, on the other hand, is opting for normativity because only a knowledge of the ends permits a correct choice of the means. Similarly for the avant-garde, a genetic approach stresses the act-aspect of the creative process while the normative orientation moves from the end sought to the means for its achievement. The case of the art-work implies an intuitive move toward a reformulation. The successful modernist creation preserves the tension of genesis and normativity whereas the work becomes stilted, either pedantic or childish, when one or the other side dominates. Think of Pollock on the one hand, Rothko on the other! If the act, the genetic, were dominant, or if the normative pictorial suppressed the painter altogether, the canvas would fail as its constitutive tension collapses. A similar structure prevails in modern capitalism.

C. Genesis and Validity: The Problem of Ideology

The tension between an approach built on genesis and a construction premised on normativity is a modern (although not specifically capitalist) phenomenon. Classical ontology and its worldview took for granted that what was first in the order of Being (as Norm) also had precedence in the world of Becoming (as genetic source). The classics of course knew the dualisms of Becoming/Being, Is/Ought, Real/Rational, Particular/Universal, and so on. But these dualisms were embedded in a single rational cosmos. The classical world was inclusive: a both/and, not an either/or. The shifts called the Renaissance, Reformation, and birth of Modern Science introduce a tension which necessitates a choice; the dualism becomes exclusive when the external guarantee that held together the world as coherent cosmos is no longer self-evident. This tension reaches theoretical explicitness in Kant, where the two versions of the "Transcendental Deduction" in the *Critique of Pure Reason* stand sharply as the option for genesis or the orientation to normativity. The remainder of Kant's work is an attempt to hold this tension without fusing it. In politics the same structure peaks in the French Revolution with the conflict between the Jacobin appeal to "le peuple" as genetic source of further action as opposed to the Thermidorian claim to "une légitimité révolutionnaire" as normative ground for setting limits on action.

Marx's analysis of ideology makes implicit use of the problematic tension between genesis and validity. As Claude Lefort points out,[22] Marx did not simply *apply* the criticism of ideology to the various social representations and individual attitudes in order to refute them by reduction. It was the Enlightenment that specialized in such reductive debunking, and it was Feuerbach who summed it up in the epigram, "Man is what he eats" (*Man ist was er Isst*). Marx's notion of ideology was significantly different. He did not criticize from a position outside or above the object criticized. Marx *discovered* ideology as the fundamental or immanent structural characteristic of a particular historical form: capitalism. This means that, for the Marxist, religion is *not* ideology. Ideology is not simply false-consciousness of whatever kind. That is too general an assertion to be useful. Ideology is only possible when the traditional external, transcendent legitimations give way to capitalism's recklessly self-expanding immanent value-logic. *The German Ideology* is misleading; one does better to take as a model the famous first chapter of *Capital*. But even here, the paradox of vanguardism leads to caution and further nuance.

Capitalism's modernism is a reply to the tension that emerged as the classical synthesis began to break down. Capitalism's self-reproduction in the cycle of M-C-M' continually creates the possibility of qualitative difference, a New which must be reduced to quantitative Sameness. Capital continually expands, invades new worlds, and creates new needs; yet it can preserve itself only by making certain that what it produces remains immanent to its fundamental logic of Sameness. Ideology is that process by which normativity (embodied, for example, in the contractual logic of equivalence exchange) or genesis (embodied, for example, in the new needs and possibilities created by expanded reproduction) serves to legitimate the system of capitalist domination by reducing difference to Sameness. The traditional society faced no such problems because its appeal to external justification makes all things appear part of a hierarchical organism. Capitalism no longer has this luxury; it produces difference continually and explicitly, and it must always reduce that difference to identity, by appeal either to normativity or to genesis. Ideology is thus a process structurally homologous to capitalism's M-C-M'; or, to put the point more strongly: *capitalism is ideology!*

This brief formulation of the process of ideology helps to explain the dual option confronting the vanguard revolutionary. The proletariat is the agent of revolution, the "solution of the riddle" of capitalism. Marx formulates the logic of its position in Hegelian language: it is the "nothing that can become everything" because it has "no particular but only general" griefs. Marx also suggests a formulation closer to the terms employed here—namely that the proletariat is, or is supposed to be, the *real* unity of genesis and normativity. The proletariat is the product of capitalism and the producer of capitalism. It is, in Lukács's phrase, the subject-object of history. The norms of which it is the bearer are generated by the very capitalist system which it is destined to overthrow. Marx's critique theory unites at one and the same time a genetic theory which explains how capitalism comes into being and reproduces itself, and a normative theory of the revolution that will overthrow it. Genesis and normativity are incarnate in the proletariat. The problem for the revolutionary is to avoid opting for one side to the exclusion of the other; to avoid reformist trade unionism as privileging genesis, and to avoid revolutionist Leninism as overstressing normativity.

This structure of revolution as the successful unification of genesis and validity is the solution to capitalism's *own* riddle. If capitalism's ideological process integrates difference and avoids the threat of a New which it nonetheless continually produces, it would seem that we face a situation as frustratingly paradoxical and repetitious as modernism's continual devouring of its avant-gardes! The syncretism for which Berman's "realism of our time" was criticized a moment ago comes back to front-stage.

D. The Ideology of Real Origins

Marx's claim is that the proletariat is the *real* unity of genesis and normativity. The proletariat would then be the real *origin* of revolution, the immanent source of the genetic impulse toward transformation and the immanent justification of the validity of the change itself. But this claim puts Marx in the situation whose logical contradictions structured the interaction between vanguards and avant-gardes. The typical modernist refusal of any transcendent, supra-historical justification is coupled with an implicit reliance on History as being precisely that justification. Explicating the grounds of this paradox will permit avoidance of some of the distortions in the results of revolutions made in Marx's name.

Contemporary philosophers, in the wake of Freud and Heidegger, have devoted much effort to exorcising the myth of *real* origin. Logically, an origin cannot be real, or realized. If the origin is a real presence generating a series of events as its result, then it is either itself caused by something, or it is a "first cause." In the former case, one confronts the problem of a regression; in the latter, the events following the origin are accidents or "appearances" with no independence or reality of their own. No real event or thing can exhaust or satisfy the origin; each measure is a partial realization and determination of it; but were it fulfilled it would be a cause, not an origin. The origin, rather, must be absent. But if the origin is taken as a (real) absence—i.e., the "nothing that can become everything," the proletariat which is not yet "for itself"—then it can never be realized because any satisfaction would be a delimitation of the radicality of the origin. Its realization would be its destruction, and thus the elimination of its originary function. In a word: either the origin manifests or realizes itself, in which case it is no longer originary; or it remains an originary but undefined source and goal, in which case there is nothing more that can be said of it. Yet, if not "real," the origin still has its effect; it is, Hegel would say, *wirklich*, actual. "*Es wirkt*," i.e., it has its effects, but it's "work" cannot be conceived in terms of the (Marxist) model of productive labor.

Freud comes to the aid of the philosopher insofar as the logical notion of origin can be specified for the individual as the psychological phenomenon of identity. The progress of Freud's discoveries shows the actuality, the effective work, of the origin while eliminating its reality. In his early clinical accounts, Freud believed his hysterical patients who explained the source of their troubles in a real event, usually of a sexual nature (or in a real lack or need, again sexual). Gradually, he came to realize that this "event" was more often than not a fantasy, or at least the fantasmatic embroidering that reveals *and* conceals "something" that gives the patient the fundamental set of meanings or the identity in terms of which life is lived (genesis) and events interpreted (normativity). The identity of the individual, the origin of *this* particular individuality, is thus imaginary. But this imaginary origin is of course very real in the life of the individual, generating a series of otherwise inexplicable actions, and serving to give meaning or validity to events which, to the observer not privy to the imaginary identity, appear random. Thus, the paranoiac's "discourse of identity" generates modes of behavior which become self-validating, and it justifies this mode of behavior in a narrative which, once the premise is shared, makes perfect sense. "Cure" for Freud, like philosophy for the Heideggerian, consists neither in eliminating the problem of origins or identity nor in realizing these origins; the key, rather, is to destroy the illusion of their reality.

The French Revolution provides a useful illustration of the implications of this notion of origin. The claim made earlier was that it presents a radical choice between the option of genesis (the Jacobin appeal to "le peuple") and that for normativity (the Thermidorian "légitimité révolutionnaire"). The usual interpretation suggests that it is a "bourgeois" revolution and hence the origin of modern capitalism. A simplified "Marxism" suggests that the bourgeoisie overthrew a feudal order which was constraining its growing productive capacities; indeed there are passages in Marx which would justify such a straightforward causal explanation. But that interpretation neglects the "resurrected Romans" while its definition of capitalism reduces a system of social relations to a merely economic structure for material production and reproduction. The discussion of capitalism-as-ideology suggested another angle of vision which integrates but also goes beyond the causal account of origins. The philosopher and the psychoanalyst posed the problem of origins when the breakdown of the classical ontological framework no longer assures identity in time and homogeneity in space. The quest for origins and the search for identity go hand-in-hand. The same is true, *mutatis mutandis*, in the drama of modern history.

The significant question concerning the French Revolution is not "why" it came about but "what?" was/is it? This question of identity was posed by the Revolution itself, as it proceeded through phases, temporary halts, debates and self-doubts, coups and restorations. When did "it" really begin? With the calling of the Estates-General? the refusal of the Third Estate to leave the hall? the Bastille? Or did it begin, as Tocqueville provocatively suggests, already in 1787? When did it end? With Thermidor? the Directory? the defeat of Babeuf? the Consulate? the Empire? Or, ought one not observe, with François Furet, that

> The history of the French 19th century in its entirety can be considered as the history of a struggle between the Revolution and the Restoration across episodes dated 1815, 1830, 1848, 1851, 1870, the Commune, the 16th of May, 1877. Only the victory of the republicans over the monarchists at the beginning of the Third Republic marks the definitive victory of the Revolution in the depths of the country: the lay teacher of Jules Ferry,

> that missionary of the values of 89, is the symbol more than the instrument of that long victorious battle.[23]

In its own process, and then again in its effects through the next century, the Revolution acts exactly as did Marx's revolutionary proletariat described in the *18th Brumaire*: self-critical, interrupting itself in its course, returning to the apparently accomplished to begin it again, recoiling from the prodigiousness of its own aims. . . . Missing only is the *Hic Rhodus, hic salta!*

Furet presents two strands of analysis which need to be integrated in order to understand the Revolution. On the one hand, there is Tocqueville's account of a long revolution whose sources predate 1789 or even 1787. This revolution is rooted in the administrative centralization and territorial unification sought by the politics of the so-called Enlightened Despots. These structural changes alone could not *make* a revolution. To them was added a new mode of political action, analyzed particularly by Augustin Cochin in the functioning of the revolutionary "societies" Jacobins. This revolution carried by the message of the Enlightenment and institutionalized in the *Sociétés de pensée* was the necessary complement to the "long" structural revolution. The Tocquevillean analysis concentrates on the question of normativity; that of Cochin centers on the genesis of action. The French Revolution is the simultaneous presence of these two strands. It should not, therefore, be surprising that the Revolution is continually preoccupied with the question of its own identity; that the Revolution sees itself as originary; and that the the posterity of the Revolution continually turn back to it in the search for self-understanding. This is why the French Revolution can be called the first modern Revolution, and why it is the model for all the others. And it is in *this* sense that the French Revolution is a "capitalist" revolution.

The advent of modern capitalism in France also marks the end of the French Revolution in a very specific sense. Capitalism's ideological structure means that the question of origins, the relation of the genetic and the normative legitimation, is eliminated as a problem. Ideology "solves" the question of origin by stressing one or the other pole. In this sense, capitalism as an economic system is an *answer* or solution to a question whose roots are social and whose primary form is political. But at the same time that capitalism's advent marks the end of the Revolution of 1789 it also preserves the question of revolution itself. Capitalism-as-ideology not only covers up the question of origins by its option for one or the other pole; capitalism also continually reposes that question because its own internal process is also continual creation. This is why there appears a structural isomorphy between the French Revolution and the proletariat of the *18th Brumaire*.

The similarity between revolution in modern capitalism and the French Revolution should not, however, veil their radical difference. The French Revolution poses a political problem to which modern capitalism gives a temporary response which is unstable because it is ideological. Marx's proletarian revolution, in its turn, promises to overcome capitalism's instability. But that Marxian revolution takes the proletariat as the *real*—if not yet "for-itself"—incarnate unity of the genetic and the normative aspects of the capitalist process. It makes the proletariat a real origin, in terms of which it elaborates a "discourse of identity" which is a form of false consciousness no different from that of the "resurrected roman" bourgeoisie or the Freudian neurotic. This is the theoretical reason that neither capitalism nor the actually existing socialisms have been able successfully to create democratic republics which satisfy at once the demands of society and those of the polity. The French Revolution from this point of view presents the problem haunting our own politics in its most radical form: the normative question of the republican polity arises simultaneously with the genetic question of social (not simply economic) justice. Capitalism occluded this questioning, as did the Marxian proletarian revolution. It is returning in practice today, yet we lack the self-critical tools necessary to understand it.

E. From Marx to Kant

The return to Kant appears peculiar, even on the theoretical grounds set out here, since Kant is usually accused of having presupposed a radical disjunction between genesis and validity—the sensible world and the categories that seek to grasp its conditions of possibility, or more radically, the difference of phenomena and noumena—in the first *Critique*. This radical disjunction is said to have been widened in Kant's ethics, whose result is a formal and abstract *Rechtsstaat* at the social or political plane. What is more, Kant's separation of genesis and validity is based on a transcendental argument which explicitly avoids the question of origins by presupposing the giveness of that synthetic *a priori* knowledge or that ethical action whose "conditions of possibility" it then sets out to deduce. And, of course, Kant's taste in art is surely not that of the avant-garde, nor was his life that of the vanguard militant.

Kant's writings on history, which have been called a "fourth *Critique*,"[24] suggest a somewhat different approach. The fundamental dualism of the first *Critique* is expressed most sharply by the Third Antinomy which shows the necessity of thinking that everything which occurs has a lawful natural cause, as well as the necessity of thinking a causality expressed in free human actions. Without the latter, morality is impossible. Yet Kant's theory in the first *Critique* gives no way of grounding a causality of freedom. The second *Critique*, and the *Foundation of the Metaphysics of Morals* attempt to resolve this problem in terms of a "primacy of the practical." Unsatisfied by that too formal solution, Kant's *Critique of Judgement* is then interpreted as a return to the problem, this time invoking implicitly the problematic of genesis/validity and the question of origins. But the solutions he apparently offered—the notion of "genius" and the natural "happy chance"—are unsatisfactory precisely because they postulate a *real* origin. Consequently, the historical writings are read as Kant's attempt once again to resolve the dualism of nature/freedom from which his critical enterprise had begun.

Kant's theory of history is also a political theory of a type which at first appears familiar although in fact it will put into question the vanguardist approach. Kant formulates his approach to history in terms that the Marxist should appreciate: those of the relation of theory to praxis. This is the orientation of the 1784 essay on "Cosmopolitan History," and it returns in Kant's last published work, the 1798 "Conflict of the Faculties." In the latter, Kant replies to his own question "How is history *a priori* possible?" with the assertion that "it is possible if the prophet himself occasions and produces the events he predicts."[25] But Kant's prophet and Marx's revolutionary predict and act on quite different theoretical grounds.

The theory of history offered in the 1784 essay on "Cosmopolitan History" makes implicit use of categories which Kant fully thematized six years later, in the *Critique of Judgement*. Within the context of Kant's own struggle with his dualist presuppositions, and in the broader context of modernism that has concerned us, the advances of this third *Critique* are astonishing. The first two *Critiques* were troubled by the ambiguous genitive in their title: a critique "of" pure or practical reason could be a critique from without, in terms of externally given standards; or it could be the self-critique, operating with immanent measures given by pure or practical reason itself. The difference between the two interpretations of the genitive is that between the classical and the modern approaches that have led us back to Kant. The *Critique of Judgement* goes beyond this alternative; it is an explicit self-criticism of "the means of criticism." The crucial distinction between a predicative or determinative judgment and a reflective judgment, as well as the notion of a teleological causality present in our judgment of the organisms of nature, permit Kant to go beyond the constraints of his initial dualism. At the same time, although this was not his intention, Kant can be read as formulating a theory of the modern.

Kant's theory of history becomes a political theory because of a particular twist he gives to the familiar introduction of organic analogies and teleological concepts into political and historical explanations. The immanent, self-critical project suggests that an object has a teleological structure when it is self-caused; when it becomes what it is by realizing its own plan; when consideration of the particular always leads to and demands understanding of the whole or universal. Such a teleological structure is that of the organism which fascinated scientists as well as political theorists in Kant's time. Its implications emerge once Kant asks the critical question: what kind of judgment permits the scientist or the citizen to make this teleological claim? Kant distinguishes determinant or predicative from reflective judgment. The former asserts, in the manner of causal science, that a real predicate is attached to a real subject. It makes this assertion monologically, claiming it to be valid for any particular subject in the same experimental situation. The reflective judgment, on the other hand, does not concern a real object; it is the action of a subject on itself by means of a consideration of the world outside itself. Leaving aside the application of reflective judgment in the science of nature and its extension to the "cosmopolitan" theory of history that Kant had presented in 1784, the crucial problem for the political ''prophet'' is the shift from a monological, abstract, and formal individual subject to a public actor capable of producing the growth or change that is history. The form of judgment of the ''prophet'' making history *a priori* will not be that of either the vanguard or the avant-garde.

Consideration of the aesthetic judgment of beauty, and of the aesthetic experience of sublimity, explains what makes the application of teleological judgment to history both theoretically valid *and* political. The experience of the sublime is an awareness of the overpowering greatness of an object; sublimity is something for which I can hope but which I can never really reach. The result of the experience of sublimity is a feeling of incompleteness, of respect for the object and dissatisfaction with myself. From this experience emerges a new awareness of the Ethical task, a new recognition of the humanity in my own person. The subject here is capable of growth, of *Bildung*, of interaction with others. The monological or transcendental subjectivity that make Kant's first two *Critiques* formal and abstract is thus surpassed. The judgment of beauty, which is Kant's major concern, brings more than just this advance beyond the formal growth or *Bildung*. My judgment of beauty must be able to claim universal assent. That means that it must go beyond the particularity of its object and that of its subject; it must be lawlike and it must be public. The beautiful is neither the natural nor the willfull, since those antinomic categories from the first two *Critiques* are redefined by the immanent self-reflection of the third *Critique*. The beautiful is the experience of the immanence of nature and will; it is a ''purposeless purposefulness.'' This means that the object is judged to be beautiful because of properties whose lawful relation cannot be proven by causal science because there is not room for purpose in nature. The reflective judgment of beauty presents, rather, a ''lawfulness without law.'' Proof of such a judgment cannot follow the model of the first critique with its transcendental, abstract ''I think'' as subject asserting a predicate of a real object; proof, rather, must be achieved through a public and intersubjective process of reflection whereby agreement comes into being. This kind of ''lawfulness'' implies the step to politics.

Kant insists that the only philosophically adequate form of political sovereignty is the Republic. He rejects the democratic form of sovereignty (although not the democratic Republic) because it conflates the conditions of genesis with those of validity by making the assumption that ''le peuple'' (or their hedonistic or utilitarian desires) are a real origin. Although Kant's Republic appears superficially to be merely the formal and abstract *Rechtsstaat*, the self-reflective categories from the third *Critique* suggest a modern reading. Republican law is not like the causal laws of nature; it is structured like the judgment of beauty's ''lawfulness without law'' which is justified through a public process of interaction. That is why Kant continually repeats the injunction from the 1784 essay ''What is Enlightenment?'' which insists on the ''freedom to make public use of one's reason at every point,'' and rejects ''any contract made to shut off all further enlightenment.'' Enlightenment is not a one-shot unmediated experience; freedom is not simply formal or self-referential autonomy. The experience of the sublime is not yet political; indeed, in its modernist avant-garde forms, it may become anti-political, the foundation of a vanguardist politics. On the other hand, the judgment that this object is beautiful does not mean that *only* this object can be beautiful; beauty is plural; it is not given once-and-for-all but can be created, anew and differently. The Republic preserves without conflating particularity and universality as does the aesthetic judgment.

Interestingly, Kant's rejection of the democratic form of sovereignty makes clear why his republican argument is not merely formal. The goal cannot be to exclude popular participation since that would exclude the public validation necessary to reflective judgment. "The touchstone of everything that can be concluded as a law for a people," asserts Kant, "lies in the question of whether the people could have imposed such a law on itself." Kant will not accept the Enlightened Despot's "realist" argument that people are too stupid to govern themselves, noting that " 'as they are' ought to read 'as we have *made* them by unjust coercion, by treacherous designs.' " His point turns on the rejection of any assertion of a *real* origin, a real and permanent solution to the political riddle of history. Kant's concern is with the growth of freedom, the creation of the new. He warns against "a contract made to shut off all further enlightenment from the human race," which "is absolutely null and void even if confirmed by the supreme power, by parliaments, and by the most ceremonious of peace treaties." The Republic is to be an institutional form guaranteeing that the public political forum remains always open. Like the French Revolution, the Republic preserves the tension of genesis and normativity which defines an origin.

Although Kant's "prophet" functions well once the Republic exists, he is unable to explain the origin of this originary republican form. In one of the *Löse Blätter* found after his death, reflecting no doubt on the French Revolution, Kant had written:

> In order to institute a Republic from a *pactum sociale* there must already be present a Republic. Hence, the Republic cannot be instituted save by *force* (*Gewalt*), *not* through *agreement*.

This recourse to providential nature to justify a political path that Kant thinks both prudent and right could be said to entail a leap of faith which is wholly unmodern. But the organic teleology Kant has in view is clearly *not* an appeal to an external, traditional form of justification. The precondition for this teleological assertion is the originary tension of the genetic and the normative entailed in the reflective judgment. Since reflective judgment of just this type is characteristic of a republican public, the implication is that the task of Kant's "prophet" is to bring to the public agenda precisely this originary question. That is why, in "Perpetual Peace," he asserts that "All maxims which stand in need of publicity in order not to fail [to achieve] their end agree with politics and right combined." Marx's revolutionary who supplies answers based on the dictates of scientific necessity is to be replaced by the Kantian "prophet" who poses the questions that thematize the origins of a modernity which is not simply the product of causal, mechanical, or technical necessity.

The republican solution is usually criticized for its neglect of the problems of social—usually meaning economic—justice. This objection, however, presupposes the logic of capitalism (and Marxism) based on a division between the domain of civil (or economic) society and that of the political state. Enough has been said about the dead-ends of vanguardist logic to put the objection into doubt. Moreover, the analysis of capitalism-as-ideology suggests that opting for either the political state or the civil society is just the kind of false resolution immanent to the logic of domination in modern society. Social or economic justice is obviously a political problem, not something that the predicative logic of natural science can solve. The same is true for the problems of politics: they cannot be addressed without consideration of social justice.

The danger is the separation and privileging of the one or the other pole—a danger which is the omnipresent structural pull of capitalism itself, and to which the reformist or revolutionary Marxist positions correspond. The Kantian "prophet," who recognizes the "permanence of the modern" and avoids the temptation *really* to solve the "riddle" of history by ending history, is forced, as a republican, to deal with social (and economic) justice. But because of the type of reflective and, therefore, public judgment that such a "prophet" applies to material as well as to aesthetic problems, his or her "solution" is itself continually put into question, opens up rather than closes off the public stage of history. Setting off for Clayton, the "prophet" lives in a republic without spectators!

10

The Origins of Revolution

A. The Place of Philosophy

Marx saw himself as the first modern revolutionary. His contempt for utopians, humanitarians of varying stripes and dreams was matched only by his disdain for those whose arguments lacked the rigor of science. The preface to *Towards a Critique of Political Economy* (1859) provides an autobiographical description of how Marx came to his revolutionary stance. Marx mentions a manuscript which he and Engels composed in 1845 which was "left to the gnawing criticism of the mice." This manuscript was published in the twentieth century as *The German Ideology*. Marx says that it was not published at the time because its authors had achieved their goal, self-understanding. The implication appears to be that the "ideology" against which Marx and Engels defined their own position was the philosophical tradition culminating in Hegel and his followers. The further implication—over which much polemical and political ink has been spilled—was that the work preceding, or perhaps also including, *The German Ideology* is somehow "non-marxist" because too philosophical. One then opposes a "humanist" youth throwing about concepts like "alienation" or "radical needs" to a "scientific" grey-bearded revolutionary. And, depending on one's temperament, one can use the humanist-philosopher to criticize the results of so-called socialism; or the results to criticize the philosopher's inaction.

As revolutionary, the scientific and the humanist Marx in fact have a common problem. Revolution is distinguished from revolt; it is not an accident, an irrational product or mysterious gift. Modern revolution claims to be necessary—either rationally (logically) necessary or materially necessary. Thus, in Marx's case, there is first a kind of logical (or ontological) argument in terms of the structures of alienated labor which works in terms of the negation and the negation-of-the-negation; and there is then a kind of materialist demonstration offered in the theory of necessary capitalist crisis. Between these two extremes, one finds, for example, in the first part of *The German Ideology* a kind of world-historical panorama portraying the necessary progress of humanity as it continually creates and satisfies new needs. Each of these arguments for the necessity of revolution is a *theory*. Each leaves open the question of the relation of theory to the actual *practice* of the revolutionary.

The theory/practice problem is specific to modern revolution. When Kant addressed himself to ''The Old Saying: It May be True in Theory but it doesn't work In Practice'' (1793) he broke new ground. Marx himself had confronted the problem in its classical form in his doctoral dissertation on Greek philosophy. In one of his working notes for the dissertation, Marx speaks of the task of ''making the world philosophical and making philosophy worldly.'' Again, the quest expressed here is not new with the modern revolutionary; the dualism of Is and Ought, the Real and the Ideal, Genesis and Validity has stood at the origin of Western philosophy. What is new, however, is the solution which Marx offered only a few years later, in 1843. The ''riddle of history'' is to be solved by the really existent *proletariat* produced (''artificially'') by a specific social formation whose negation it incarnates. The proletariat is an object which can become a subject, a product which is its own producer, a reality whose demands are the idea. It expresses the riddle *and* the solution! If philosophy is understood as the grappling with the classical dualisms, then the proletariat is the elimination of philosophy, its overcoming, the destruction of all metaphysical speculation.

Even when he first proposed the proletarian solution, Marx knew that it contained an ambiguity. He knew that the proletariat was not the same as those poor who, the Bible tells us, will always be with us. The proletariat was produced by capitalism which, in the Germany of the 1840s, had only begun to gain a foothold. Hence, Marx anticipates the ''formation'' of this proletariat which is produced ''artificially.'' One can understand Marx's turn to the study of political economy as a way of demonstrating the economic logic by which such a proletariat will be formed. But there is a further aspect to Marx's argument. The proletariat which will be formed is only an object, a product; it must be brought to consciousness, to subjectivity. In 1843, the only image Marx could find for this process was that of the ''lightning of thought'' which would have to strike this ''naïve soil of the people.'' From this point of view, the analyses of alienation, of the formation of radical new needs, or even the specificity of Marx's critique-theory are the necessary elaboration of his first insight. In a word, the proletariat contains within its own definition the dualism which it seeks to eliminate. This dualism will plague it and its theories.

The ''specter haunting Europe'' with which the *Communist Manifesto* begins is a curiously chosen image which expresses the ambiguity of Marx's solution. Obviously, the materialist who felt that he had overcome philosophy-as-ideology considered this specter to be something quite real. But what? The proletariat, one would think; or at least the proletariat-as-in-formation. Yet the next phrases of the *Manifesto* explain that every opposition party in Europe finds itself labeled and branded as "Communistic," and that this means first that they acknowledge communism as "a Power," so that, second, the present *Manifesto* should be published so as to demystify this specter by explaining or describing what communism really is. These two aspects of the specter are then discussed theoretically in the first two sections of the *Manifesto*. What emerges there is simply an elaboration of the ambiguous dualism that constitutes the proletariat: the first section shows how the bourgeoisie produces "its own grave-diggers" while the second section talks about the communists who know "the line of march, the conditions, and the ultimate general results" of the movement, and whose task is the "formation of the proletariat into a class."

Although he rejected philosophy and its dualisms, Marx nonetheless elaborated a specific style of theorizing. Nearly everything he wrote was titled or subtitled "a critique." The critique style of theory explains the at first glance surprising praise that Marx bestows throughout his life on the "civilizing process" of capitalism. It also explains why his life's work was a book called *Capital*—subtitled "A Critique of Political Economy"—and not a volume called *Socialism*. Writing to Lassalle, Marx explained that the goal of *Capital* was to be "a presentation, and through the presentation a critique of what is presented." Critique, in other words, is the *self*-critique of the object it describes. Theory is not applied from without; it is not an abstractly universal criterion applied to a particular social system. Critique is immanent; revolution is inexorable; the bourgeoisie produces "its own grave-diggers" in an economic system which carries the socialist future "in its womb." This style of theory fits perfectly the ambiguity of the proletariat. It presents spectrally, as in a revealing mirror, the true essence, the facts, of a social system which seeks to veil itself in ideology. The demystification of the critique will then correspond to the real experience of real proletarians; the lightning of thought will strike.

This theory as immanent critique is the key to the optimism of the modern revolutionary. Possessing—or better, possessed by—this self-critique of capitalism, *he* becomes the real, incarnate bearer of the ideal, the unity of the traditional dualism. He does not have to argue, convince, or judge; all he does is speak the facts, the very capitalist facts by which capitalism condemns itself. The revolutionary can thus be apparently quite modest, even democratic and tolerant. The *Manifesto* insists that the communists are not separate from other working-class parties, nor are they the representatives of any interests but those of the proletariat as a whole. They can represent the whole, Marx thinks, because of their theory which gives "understanding [of] the line of march, the conditions and the ultimate general results of the proletarian movement." But this apparent modesty, this empirical, democratic tolerance is in fact the greatest *hubris!* No philosopher would make the claim to be the real expression or the voice of the social totality; that is usually reserved for the caricature of Hegel imagining himself as secretary of the World Spirit. The *Manifesto* transforms this Hegelian philosophical secretary into the Secretary-General of the Party.

My claim is not, or not simply, that a certain kind of immanent critique theory *had* to have certain political consequences; people are not consistent with theories when it comes to action. Further, the essential ambiguity of Marx's critique or proletarian theory meant that it was open to various interpretations, only one of which has been alluded to thus far. Because the proletariat was supposed to become the real unity of the philosophical dualisms it was only *potentially* the "solution to the riddle of history." Philosophical considerations thus remain relevant.

B. Philosophy and Historical Action

The ambiguity of the proletariat stems from the fact that it is on the one hand the product of capitalism and therefore an object; and on the other hand, it is (at least potentially) a subject capable of understanding and transforming its alienated and/or exploited world. Depending on which of these two aspects of proletarian politics is stressed, one can become either a "reformist" or a "revolutionary." If the necessary character of capitalism's self-critique is the center of one's preoccupations, then political action consists in working with the current of history without rocking the boat. One then attacks the "voluntarism" of those who want to go too far too fast—while risking, on the other hand, the danger that one's own gradualism in fact works to temper the decline and to put off the final victory. The situation is the inverse if one tries to be a "revolutionary."

The history of the Second International, of its demise with the outbreak of World War, and of the creation of the Third International (and re-creation of the Second) after 1917 could be traced in terms of these two options. That, however, would not be of great interest here; and, moreover, would of course lead to multiple scholastic nuances since each party was of course building from a common source: the ambiguity of Marx's own theory.

Lenin's theory of the revolutionary party in *What is to be Done?* is consistent with the interpretation I drew in the preceding discussions from the *Communist Manifesto*. Lenin suggests that although the proletariat is quite aware of its exploitation (*not* of its alienation or new needs, as in the young Marx), its immediate reaction to this is only defensive. The everyday experience of capitalism leads only to "trade union consciousness," the attempt to make the best of a bad lot within the confines of established social relations. Therefore the task of the revolutionary party is to intervene, politically, from outside, with the aid of its theory which permits it to teach—more precisely: to lead—the proletariat to transcend its immediate interests toward a "political class consciousness" which recognizes the necessity of total social transformation. And, one could say, that is precisely what the Bolsheviks did in 1917. The agent of the Russian Revolution was not so much the proletariat as the Leninist party. (Whether this party in fact articulated the true aspirations of what proletariat there was in Russia at the time is not important here. Nor are the "circumstances" which are claimed to have prevented it from realizing those aspirations. Important is only Lenin's going beyond economic immediacy and its immanent logic to introduce the *political* dimension of revolution.)

Although Lenin's theory of the Party is prefigured in the *Manifesto*, another of his formulations is significantly pre-Marxist. His 1904 pamphlet, *One Step Forward, Two Steps Backward*, continued the Russian debate to which *What is to Be Done?* was a contribution by adding the historical specification that the revolutionary is a "Jacobin indissolubly connected to the interests of the proletariat." The need to refer to history for justification is interesting. It implies a break with the immanent logic of the critique theory. It could be used naïvely (or meanly), as when one looks to history for edifying examples[1] that explain present choices. This is how Stalin used it, for example, to justify his alliance with Zinoviev and Kamenev against the leader of the Red Army, Trotsky, who was pictured as a new Bonaparte. This was how Trotsky in his turn used it from exile a few years later when he called the advent of Stalin a repetition of Thermidor. But there is more to be said about historical action, and its interpretation.

Marx's own writing of history was (usually) less naïve and edifying than his successors'. It was he who criticized the French revolutionaries for dressing up in the garments of the past in order to hide from themselves the radical consequences of their own actions. It was Marx who criticized nineteenth-century revolutions for cloaking themselves in the garb of the French Revolution. And it is to Marx that we owe the recognition of the past as weighing "like a nightmare on the brain of the living." What Marx-the-historian saw was the essential ambiguity of action, its open-endedness and multiplicity of meaning. Historical actions in this sense do not have a cause; they have an *origin* which I shall try to show is structured by the tension of the dualism that constituted classical philosophy and which the proletariat is supposed to overcome.

C. Action and Origins

What do the modern revolutionary whose justification is the self-critique of the facts themselves and the revolutionary who returns to an often mythologized but nonetheless real event share with each other? Why are these two attitudes often combined in one and the same person? From the standpoint of history as edification, the French Revolution is originary in that it proves that the historical continuum can in fact be broken, that *new* beginnings are possible. Before 1789 a theory of immanent self-critique could not have been revolutionary. Before 1789 the most audacious *critic* could not present an immanent *critique*.

On a theoretical plane, 1789 points to problems for the immanent critique theory. Can one take the transition from feudalism to capitalism as the model for a leap beyond capitalism? Was the French Revolution "bourgeois" because its principal actors and their goals were bourgeois; or were the (unintended?) consequences of the Revolution the emergence of a bourgeois society? Further, what is one to make of the fact that bourgeois societies grew in other countries without the aid of a revolutionary midwife?

The problem for the immanent critique theory is that if the revolution is a leap then it can*not* be caused by pregiven material fact or the immanent logic of social conditions. If it were explained by such a reduction to the facts, then it would not be a revolution and the origin of a *new* history. On the other hand, revolution can't come from nowhere, from voluntarism and will-power. There must be some material bases for its advent. We are caught, once again, in the Marxian version of the philosophical dualism. One sees how the Marxist can take either side when he confronts the French events. The analysis may point to the way in which political transformations of the superstructures—the end of feudal privilege and development of contract law, for example—create conditions for the emergence of a capitalist economy. But the other side of the coin quickly presents itself. The revolution is said to have been "merely political" because it does not destroy but only transforms the mode of exploitation of the population. The debate can continue . . . but its point is lost!

The modern revolutionary who looks to science and critique and the edifying revolutionary who turns to history for examples share the belief that actions have causes, or *real* origins. One finds vivid expressions of this in Marx, for example when he insists that "it doesn't matter what this or that individual proletarian thinks or does but what the class is and *must* do." What is being stressed here is the idea of origin as generating action, as the genesis of practice. The other side of the coin stresses the normative model of origins, assuming human rationality and the need for legitimation of actions to be taken. Normative legitimation is then provided by the representation of the historical event as real: the impact of David's *Oath of the Horatii*, or of republican history in general, on the French revolutionaries could serve as an illustration.

Both explanations are symmetrically incomplete because they make the same mistake: taking the origin as real. Before explaining the nature of this mistake, and why it is a mistake, we need to make an excursus into the historiography of the French Revolution. Lenin's invocation of those events is just one example of the manner in which "the" French Revolution—however one chooses to define its nature and scope—has colored the way in which we think about time and history. The French Revolution meant that the leap, the rupture, was possible; it meant that new problems, crises, and possibilities could be recognized for the first time. The revolution is a constant presence, for the revolutionary or the conservative or the reactionary who conjure it up or away.

D. The French Revolution as Origin

The originary character of the French revolution is seen in the fact that its promise has remained *necessarily* unfulfilled. The promise is not simply an object of contemplation or a mirror for one's self-legitimation; nor is it an external, utopian standard permitting judgment on the present; nor is it the "positive ideology" of liberty-equality-fraternity as human values. All these were roles which the Greeks or Romans could and traditionally did play prior to 1789, since no one dreamed of an *actual* return to the Golden Age, however and wherever they pictured it. The French Revolution, on the other hand, has had a different kind of presence ever since its earliest historian, Burke, and his conservative German followers. It was present as an *immanent* threat or hope whose metaphorics and historiography were also a political statement. It was present, in a word, just like the *specter* invoked by the *Manifesto*.

The Revolution had no single concrete result that could have marked its success and thereby justified a halt in the process. Freeing "man" from the bonds of feudal and corporate traditionalism, the Revolution sought to create the world anew. It invented its own calendar, created a new system of weights and measures, initiated new feast days and holidays, sought to found a new religion. Real motives and interests of course existed, but they could only be expressed in the new revolutionary language, as can be seen in any of the great debates of the times. Only the cold shower of the Terror, and the appearance of Bonaparte with the promise of Empire, could bring the festival of continual creation to a halt—and even then the debate about the phases, duration, and results of the Revolution continue among the historians and politicians. Thus, the most reflective of recent French historians, François Furet, asserts:

> The history of the French 19th century in its entirety can be considered as the history of a struggle between the Revolution and the Restoration across episodes dated 1815, 1830, 1848, 1851, 1870, the Commune, the 16th May 1877. Only the victory of the republicans over the monarchists at the beginning of the Third Republic marks the definitive victory of the Revolution in the depths of the country: the lay teacher of Jules Ferry, that missionary of the values of 89, is the symbol more than the instrument of that long victorious battle. The integration of the villages and peasantry of France into the republican nation through the principles of 89 would thus have taken at least a century. . . . The victory of a republican Jacobinism which was so long tied to the dictatorship of Paris, is only gained when it is supported by the majority vote of rural France, at the end of the 19th century.[2]

But, Furet continues, even the victory of the republic has not exhausted the originary character of the revolution, which lives on in the twentieth century as the ideal of "the" revolution which is necessary because the realization of the nineteenth century's Republic has not satisfied the (undefined and undefinable) expectations placed in it.

The manner in which the nineteenth century conceptualized the Revolution as the demand for the real instantiation of the Republic suggests that one function of the originary event is to create a real *rupture* in the historical continuum of experience. The result of the rupture is not only chronological; it is also social. Nothing can be taken for granted in a society riven by the self-questioning that its broken historical self-image entails. Social hierarchy that had been accepted unquestioningly and envisaged as an integrated *spatial* order of groups co-existing next to one another becomes social division and competition for dominance. In this sense the Revolution as a real event posits or creates a *revolutionary temporality*, setting forth the New not as an essence or structure already existing potentially and ready to be capitalized but as a problem or question. This is why, when the republican formulation of the origin is realized by the end of the nineteenth century, the question does not simply fade away; history does not end in normalcy; the origin remains as a problem, formulated now as the question of "the" revolution. The implication is that the notion of the French Revolution as a *real* origin is deceptive insofar as its reality can never be pinned down anatomically to a fixed set of events or demands which could be realized in the way, for example, that the physical properties of a newly discovered entity can be exhaustively analyzed and its uses fully elaborated, or a building constructed from a blue-print. Thus, in the case of the French Revolution, Furet points to problems of chronology: did it begin, as Tocqueville suggests, as early as 1787, when the bankruptcy of monarchical politics was evident; or was it the call for free election of the Estates General, or the transformation of the Estates General from a traditional tripartite body deliberating separately to a unitary body; or was it the storming of the Bastille that was crucial? When did it end? With Thermidor, the Consulate, the Empire, the Restoration . . . ? Was the end symbolized by the abandonment of the new Revolutionary Calendar? Or, could one read the entire nineteenth century as the prolongation of the Revolution (as the demand for the Republic)? Or, does it continue into the twentieth century (as the search for "the" Revolution)? The historian's question poses the theoretical problem of origins.

When the French Revolution is taken as a real origin of the present and its problems and questions, the event serves as the basis of what Furet calls a "discourse of identity," or what I called an "edifying" view of history. Every historical period, and even the different social strata within a period, can situate itself and identify its functions by relating to the originary event. Ethnography too illustrates this edifying discourse of identity. The functioning of the originary myths of a society at once explain the *genesis* of its social order while giving *normative* justification to those social structures. Usually, the identification proceeds smoothly as a glorification of the continuity of past and present which orders the different social functions within the group according to a *spatial* coexistence. At other times, such as the Renaissance, the quest for identity entails a rupture which puts into question the adequacy of the present to the normative image of the past as superior to the present. In this case, the critical power of the fact cannot simply be integrated into the spatially ordered functional whole. The new fact introduces discontinuity between genesis and validity, and thereby poses the temporal question of the possibility of a new arrangement. In this sense,it poses the question of origins.

The edifying discourse of identity which looks to the French Revolution as real origin is fundamentally different from the smooth integration offered by the myth *and* from the kind of discontinuity illustrated by the Renaissance image of the classical age. In both of those cases, the origin is fixed, identified, static. The origin there is external, not immanent as in the modern claim. The immanence of origins—from the city of God to the history of man—is the source of our modern notion of history as well. The French Revolution is an origin which self-consciously reflects on itself as origin, which questions itself continually, debates with itself as it progresses, takes each accomplishment as a temporary phase in a total rupture with all fixation on the past.[3] This mode of action as a continual process of creation (and destruction of the past) is isomorphic to the specific historicity of capitalism whose rapacious and iconoclastic character prevents the fixation of origin as unique and permanent. Capitalist society is the continual overcoming of the present in the form of expanded reproduction. This is why Marx praises it, sees it as immanently revolutionary as opposed to the structure of traditional societies. Thus, in reply to the above question of the way in which the revolution inaugurates, or consecrates, the capitalist mode of production, the answer must not be the reductive thesis of a 'materialism', as if the Revolution somehow permitted the breakthrough of material forces which had been lying dormant in the womb of an anachronistic superstructure, *nor* that the Revolution created superstructures which somehow permitted the growth of these material forces. The assertion must be that capitalism and the French Revolution have what Weber called an "elective affinity" because of their shared ideological form of temporality.

The edifying discourse of identity supposes a real origin which can be fixed and identified as either a genetic source of the present or a normative standard of judgment on the present. The ideological structure of capitalism which both denies and affirms the continual production of novelty accounts for the continual effectiveness of the revolutionary invocation of the French Revolution in the nineteenth and twentieth centuries. The failed revolutions try to relive the originary event as their real model, as Marx continually observes. But even the successful ones are only temporary halts whose institutionalization and fixation in terms of the balance of real social interests shows itself inadequate to the temporality of the originary thrust. No more than the capitalist can copy previously successful modes can the revolutionary copy previous revolutions. If the transition to socialism is the move to a new form of social relations, it cannot follow the model of the French Revolution as real origin. Revolution against capitalism entails a different temporality, and a different relation to origins.

E. Philosophy and Revolutionary Origins

Contemporary philosophers, in the wake of Heidegger and Freud (as well as the modernist movements in the arts), have devoted much effort to exorcising the myth of real origin. Logically, an origin cannot be real, or realized. If the origin is a real presence, generating a series of events as its result, then it is either itself caused by something, or if it is a "first cause" the events that follow it are merely (Spinozistic) accidents with no independence or reality of their own; they cannot be taken as the realization of the origin. No event or thing can exhaust or satisfy the origin; each measure is a partial realization and determination of it; but were it fulfilled it would be a cause not an origin. *The origin must be absent*. But if the origin is taken as a (real) absence, then it can never be realized because any satisfaction would be a delimitation of the radicality of the origin; its realization would be its destruction, and thus the elimination of its originary function. The situation is similar to the concept of essence of Hegel. Either the origin manifests and realizes itself, in which case it loses its power as originary; or it remains an originary but undefined source and goal, in which case there is nothing more that can be said of it. Yet, if not "real," the origin has still its effect. What is its mode of existence?

Freud comes to the aid of the philosopher. Just as Furet showed the social function of the notion of origin in the "discourse of identity," so too can we see origin's function for the individual in the psychological phenomenon of identity. The progress of Freud's discoveries maintains the notion of origin while progressively questioning its reality. Early on, Freud believed the accounts of his hysterical patients who explained the source of their troubles in a real event, usually of a sexual nature (or in a real lack or need, again sexual). Gradually, he came to realize that this "event" was more often than not a fantasy, or a fantasmatic embroidering revealing *and* concealing something which gave the patient a fundamental set of meanings or an identity in terms of which life is lived and events interpreted. The identity of the individual, the origin of *this* particular individuality, is thus *imaginary*. But this imaginary origin is of course very real in the life of the individual, generating a series of otherwise inexplicable actions, and serving to give meaning or validity for the individual to a congeries of events which, to the outside observer not privy to the imaginary identity, appear random. Thus, the paranoiac's self-identity generates modes of behavior which become self-validating, and justifies these behaviors in a narration which, once the premise is shared, makes perfect sense. "Cure" for Freud, like philosophy for Heidegger, consists not in eliminating the problem of origins or identity but in destroying the illusion of their reality. It is not thought on the reductionist midwife model, nor that of causal science; a specific mode of judgment is involved, to which I can only point here.[4]

An origin is the dynamic interplay of presence-absence, a revealing which must also conceal. If the origin were fully present, there would be nothing for it to originate; there would be a plenitude which "was, is, and will be," and the question of origins would never be posed. If the origin were fully absent, the situation would be structurally identical. If I were the individual who I was, am, and will be, then I would have no history; just as I have no history if I am no one, simply a product of my circumstances. The same holds true for the historical event: the French Revolution is neither wholly determined and complete, nor is it simply the product of forces existent outside of it. The revealing-concealing nature of the origin has the same structure in both cases. I am, and the Revolution is, what is done in the material world; but consideration of these behavioral traits does not exhaust the significance of either me or it. For the psychoanalyst, the same action performed by several individuals can have a variety of different psychodynamic explanations; actions are overdetermined, not reducible to a linear model of cause and effect. The same over-determination holds true for the historian's account of action. The presence-absence dualism to which the philosopher points is simply his version of the tension of genesis and normativity to which I have frequently called attention. And the conclusion is the same: neither side can be privileged, the tension must be maintained.

The specificity of the French Revolution as origin, and the source of its elective affinity with capitalism, lies in its nature as an action which is its own origin. There is nothing outside the Revolution, nothing which does not get its meaning from this source. The Revolution generates actions from its own momentum; and these actions are in turn legitimized by their revolutionary origin. The part is infused with the sense of the whole, which can tolerate nothing outside itself. The Revolution must continually seek after closure and totalization in order to maintain its identity; anything outside of it threatens its very existence. Thus, with Furet, one might date the "end" of the Revolution at the moment when, after Thermidor, with the advent of the Directory, legitimacy was no longer earned by direct appeal to "le peuple" as immanent origin and norm but now referred only to a constitutional legality established by actions now safely in the past and external to the present. With the appeal to constitutional legality the question of origins lost its radical, threatening character. The nineteenth-century attempt to realize the promise of the Republic, and the twentieth century's quest after "the" Revolution are, from this point of view, simply the completion of the system, not its overthrow. The nineteenth-century demands took the Revolution as an origin in the genetic sense, whereas the twentieth century took it as an origin giving normative validity and hence different demands. In either case, however, what must be stressed is the elective affinity not only of capitalism and the French Revolution, but also of both with the revolutionary proletariat of Karl Marx when it is taken as real origin in either the genetic or the normative sense.

The philosophical (and psychoanalytical) notion of origin permits both the identification of the error that takes the origin as real and, more important, it suggests a rather different research agenda for those interested in political change. I say "research agenda" quite explicitly, for the first and most important lesson from the foregoing is the danger of taking one's theory as an Archimedean point from which to move the world. To say that there is no real origin is to say that there is no revolutionary subject, no bearer of the future of humanity, no Savior. Learning to act in the immanence of the present, learning to think within the paradoxical constraints of modernity's continual questioning of principles and its quest for origins, are the first steps.

F. The Origin of the Political

If the elective affinity or structural isomorphy among the French Revolution, the advent of capitalism, and the Marxian revolutionary proletariat is accepted, the first conseqnece is that each of them has to be re-evaluated. More particularly, the usual picture of a capitalist economic system taking root and form in an archaic-society which it then transforms and dominates is misleading on several accounts. I would claim, rather, that one can trace the emergence of a series of new *political* problems in the late eighteenth century as the different national variants of the modern state take form. These political problems can be conceptualized through the work of the philosophers in the tradition inaugurated by Kant (and closed by Hegel-Marx); they can be recognized in the legal and constitutional issues which were summarized at the time under the banner of republicanism; and they can be traced in the growing administrative centralization and complexification that passed under the banner of Enlightened Despotism. In each of these instances, the solution which vanquishes its opponents is the creation of an independent ("capitalist") economic sphere. Capitalism thus emerges as the solution (or pretended solution) to a series of *political* problems. These political problems lose their distinctiveness once capitalism becomes the reigning center of life, the "real origin" which both generates actions and gives normative legitimacy or meaning to these same actions. The political does not, however, simply disappear.[5]

The political questions which the advent of capitalism (as well as, in their own ways, the French Revolution and the Marxian revolutionary project) covered over must be rediscovered, reactivated. The rediscovery passes along the path taken by Marx himself: the tradition from Kant to Hegel. However one may criticize Marx, his work encapsulates the wealth of the tradition of German Idealism; the contradictions and difficulties of Marx are not due to some subjective failing on his part which we late-comers could somehow correct with hindsight. Retracing the path of German Idealism should not be—as it usually is, especially since Lukács's masterful "reification essay" in *History and Class Consciousness*—the demonstration that the "telos" of that movement, its unity and totality, is summed up in Marx. On the contrary, the path of the movement must be "From Marx to Kant" if one is to rediscover those political questions which, with Marx, are occluded by the dominance of the capitalist economy. By the same token, the reactivation of these rediscovered questions demands the same movement "From Marx to Kant." The modern revolutionary, from whose claims these reflections began, cannot serve as role model. His assumptions are, in fact, part-and-parcel of the economic logic that destroys the independence of politics. Insofar as one assumes that Lenin's Bolsheviks are true to this model, their success at modernizing economically the backward Russian territory shows them to have been simply more efficient (or ruthless!) than run-of-the-mill capitalists.

By using the category "modernity" to describe what is usually simply called capitalism, I want to suggest a broader definition and field than the merely economic. Modernity is that form of social relations (and relations to nature) which emerges when all tradition, external origins of legitimation are destroyed and when the genesis of events is no longer explicable by a causal logic. Modernity is defined by the immanence of origins; it is a social formation which continually questions itself and its identity. Social relations, defined by the immanence of the question of origins are by their very nature political. Modern politics is the manner in which a society reflects—and acts—upon the immanence of its own origin—on the fact that the members of society *must* define continually, in word and deed, the kind of society they are and want to be. The old hierarchies and distinctions among individuals which were legitimized by gods or nature or reason—by an external origin—can no longer be accepted. Above all else, this means that modern politics must be democratic and public (or what the eighteenth century called "republican"). The principle of immanence means, further, that modern politics can never come to some final solution or arrangement where participation and debate are no longer necessary. That would mean fixing a point or principle as a *real* origin, a cause which *nolens volens* becomes external to the system over which it exerts its perhaps enlightened but surely despotic power. Decisions of social justice or questions of economic interest must therefore be formulated and resolved as political in this modern sense—and the inverse mode must be avoided, i.e., the political must not be reduced simply to the economic.

The danger for modern politics is to act as if its origins were real; that is, to stress either the genetic or the normative at the expense of the other. A constitution, Bill of Rights, and other normative mechanisms cannot replace the genetic processes (including the economic) of civil society, any more than the genetic can determine the normative. Political liberalism and economic liberalism must not exclude each other. Put in a different manner, the danger is the dominance of the social reformers, but it is equally the victory of the animadversions of the neoconservatives. The usually proposed "third way" *via* bureaucracy or technocracy is equally to be excluded. The logic of origins shows the impossibility of the assumption that modern society can be dealt with quantitatively if only the proper common denominator can be found. Although it tends toward unification at one pole, modernity refuses a politics which, in the guise of science and technology, destroys its own preconditions.

Finally, there is a positive conclusion. If we can show that modernity is structured by the tension of genesis and normativity which poses the question of immanent origins which defines the parameters of democratic politics, it follows that the task of the "revolutionary" is to discover and to create ways to preserve this originary questioning. Not that we take the world in our hands; not that we form a new party; but rather, to paraphrase the young Marx of 1843, that we look at what people are already in fact doing, and show them through our critical questions and actions the *originality* of their own action.[6] The attempt to reduce social movements to the logic of cause/effect, the definition of social questions as concerned with either (economic) genesis or (political-legal) normativity, are moves that the established powers encourage precisely because they reduce the radical question of democracy and origins to the solvable and the familiar. In the context of modernity, "revolutionary politics" is revolutionary because it is political.

11

Reading U.S. History as Revolutionary

A. The Philosopher, the Historian, and the Revolution

Historians correctly warn their political-scientist friends against the danger of a sheerly present-centered reading of the stakes of politics. Thus for example, French politics must be understood as overdetermined by the attempt to complete or to conclude the movement inaugurated in 1789. German politics has to be understood similarly as overdetermined by the early legal codification by Friedrich, and by the failure to complete the 1848 Revolution. American political history, on the other hand, has forgotten, if not repressed, its revolutionary origin. Americans act as if their revolution had been somehow preordained, the logical outcome of the principles of freedom developing freely on a virgin continent. However they interpret their origins, Americans do not consider their roots as *political*; their country is assumed to have been "born liberal." This should give the political historian pause; what *was* it, really, that American Revolution? Its antipolitical results seem to invalidate the usual distinction between the social character of the French and the self-limiting political thrust of the American Revolution. And yet that argument correctly underlines the properly political *origin* of the American Revolution. The historian has to turn to the philosopher; how could the history that followed the American revolution deny its own origin? The philosopher has to reread the originary movement in order to discover its operative presence within the historical path it originates.

The path of the American Revolution can be divided into three distinct moments of which the participants were fully conscious. There was first of all the slow ripening which began at the end of the Seven Years' War, known in those English colonies as the "French and Indian War." The situation was simple: the French had been defeated; the colonies no longer needed the protecting power of England, whereas the mother country, now master of an empire, had to take measures to govern its new possessions while repaying the debt occasioned by the war. It was quite logical to attempt to make the colonies pay; the war had brought them benefits, and now peace would bring new profits. At the same time, it was quite traditional to govern the empire by mercantilist politics. But the colonials were headstrong provincials; they wanted above all to be left alone. They resisted the new measures, basing their protests on what they called "the rights of an Englishman." Although they were also driven by economic interests which they could not admit (perhaps not even to themselves), the colonists were forced during the years that followed 1763 to make clear what they meant by the "rights" of an Englishman. Their first political formulation of these rights was presented by the Declaration of Independence in 1776. But the principles that underlie that Declaration can only be understood if the theoretical sedimentations that accumulated during thirteen years of debates and struggles are taken into account.

The revolution could not stop simply with the conquest of sovereignty. Once independence was declared, it had to be realized concretely—which meant first of all that the War of Independence had to be won. Hearts and minds had been transformed by the long debate concerning their rights; now the experience of the war gave a new sense to the autonomy that the Declaration affirmed. The colonies were Thirteen, and proud of their differences; the majority of them took their autonomy so seriously that they felt it necessary to include the Declaration of Independence in their state constitutions. But the War of Independence was the struggle of an entire nation. The national constitution—which was not ratified until shortly before the end of the War—instituted a confederation of autonomous States. Such a political form could not guarantee the collective future. Once the war had concluded, centrifugal tendencies came to the fore. The loose confederal form had to be rethought. The key concept was representation, a notion whose problematic application to the relations with the mother country had given a foretaste of the difficulties it entailed. Now the concept had to be used to conceive the relations between the sovereign nation and the sovereign States *and* those between the free citizens and the political institutions which were supposed to incarnate or at least guarantee that freedom. The relation between the representation of political sovereignty and the representation of social freedom had to discover a new articulation.

The debate concerning representation brought together the lessons of the first and the second periods of the Revolution. The Constitution of 1787 can be read as their synthesis. That Constitution is often interpreted in terms of its liberal and capitalist results. Such a reading evades both practical and theoretical problems. For example, the Constitution makes no provision for the existence of political parties, much less for the two-party system which is supposed to explain the remarkable stability of American politics. The Constitution does not explicitly provide for the process of judicial review which permits the dis-ideologization of politics by the mediation of the judiciary. These two institutions emerged in the wake of what contemporaries called the "Revolution of 1800" which brought the

Jeffersonians to power. But the image of a republic divided into political parties, as well as the idea that laws voted by the representatives of the people could be overruled by a nonelected branch of government, would have shocked those Americans who had learned to fight for their rights and for their autonomy during the Revolution. Indeed, those who affirm that these inventions are compatible with the Constitution are often criticized by the "progressive" historians who see the Constitution as a conservative coup d'état, a kind of American "Thermidor." But the politics that underlies the "progressive" critique avoids the problems that led the historian to philosophy, and the philosopher to history. The "progressives" insist on the need to return to the principles of the Revolution as incarnated in the Declaration of Independence. They thus suppose that the Revolution could be defined simply, immediately, and conceptually. This permits them to avoid the challenge of *reading* the Revolution. They can then confine themselves to "demystifying" the deviations of two hundred years of political history.

B. Principles for Reading

Rather than interpret it in terms of its realization, the reality of the American Revolution needs to be read from the standpoint of its self-theorization. That theory was constantly reformulated during and by the revolutionary experience. Its structure was doubly reflexive. At a first level, it articulates the three periods through which the Revolution developed; these can be defined respectively as the *lived experience* (*le vécu*) of the struggle for sovereignty, the *conceptualized* form (*le conçu*) of that autonomy, and the political *reflection* (*le réfléchi*) of these first two moments. The lived experience corresponds to immediate or prepolitical existence; the conceptualized form expresses the social relations instituted by that lived experience; what is reflected as the unity of these two moments makes explicit their political implications. This articulation is then repeated within each of the three revolutionary periods. For example, the lived experience of the first period corresponds to the brute givens of colonization, including two crucial absences: the existence of an open frontier and the nonexistence of social orders. The colonials conceptualize their particular experience only when the English intervene in what had been until then a self-regulating society. The reflection of that autonomous society occurred when the question of political independence is posed explicitly. But that reflection is not a kind of Hegelian or idealist consummation.[1]

This doubly reflexive structure explains how each period takes up anew and develops the theoretical conclusions of the preceding one. The moment of the political in which one period culminates institutes the lived experience of its successor. An example will clarify the institutional functioning of this logic (*logique instituante*). The Declaration of Independence did not conclude the revolutionary experience; that declared independence had to be given adequate institutional form. The members of the Continental Congress left Philadelphia to return home; more important than the national struggle was the attempt to invent constitutions adequate to the particular *society* of their home states. That the thirteen sovereign states should create different institutions from one another does not contradict the political unity realized by the Declaration of Independence. The social diversity becomes a contradiction only when it is necessary to *reflect* the national sovereignty in a confederal Constitution. That Constitution had to incarnate unity while conserving diversity in the same way that the social experience of the struggle against England was reflected in the Declaration of Independence that unified a diversified country. But that *political* unification of social diversity could only be unstable, in the first as in the second case; the reflective status of the political had not yet been defined; the revolution had to continue. The unstable political unity of the Confederation thus presents the *lived experience* of the third period.[2]

Before turning to the articulation of the third period, the paradox from which we began must be underlined: the American Revolution was through and through a political movement, and yet it was incapable of understanding itself politically. The progressive critics who want to return to its supposed political principles forget that a Civil War broke out in 1861, opposing those who based themselves on the princples of the Declaration, those who defended the autonomy of the confederated states, and those for whom the Union was the supreme value. This suggests the need for a different reading of the political foundations of American history. Our categories of lived experience, its conceptualized form, and its reflected moment are useful insofar as they avoid the temptation to analyze effects in order to seek their causes. These categories cannot be imposed from without on a completed history; they are in principle open, like the American democracy originated by the Revolution. Their foundation lies in a theory lived first of all at the pre-political level, then conceived at the level of the social, and finally reflected in a Constitution which can only be understood within the context of a revolution of, and by, the political. This is the sense in which the American Revolution is exemplary.

C. Reading American Theory Historically

The theoretical lived experience of the colonials was a mélange whose first expression was the demand for the "rights of an Englishman." That concept had the advantage of being at once historically rooted while remaining open, if not vague. This "right" was expounded in terms of concepts drawn from natural or contractual law, from Greek, Roman, or English history, and of course from the Bible. When the English interventions forced them to conceptualize this "right," the colonists had recourse to what is called whig thought. Whig theory begins from the premise that the existence of society depends on the presence of a Power whose essence is to seek always to expand at the cost of Freedom, which must constantly defend itself. This theory could be interpreted historically in an optimistic or a pessimistic vein. The optimistic view sees Freedom reconquering its rights after the Norman conquest, first with the *Magna Carta*, then with the

Declaration of Rights, and finally in the Glorious Revolution which gave birth to a stable society organized around the new, limited, and balanced Power called "the King in Parliament." The pessimists, on the other hand, argued that conquering Freedom is not inevitably bound to be successful; the excesses in both directions that followed the Revolution of 1640 could be cited to warn against naïve optimism. These pessimists, appealing as well to a stern Protestant authority, could become critics of the established order; as such, they acquired the name "Old Whigs."

When Old Whig theory is turned against the established Power, its biblical roots lead it to encounter classical political theory. If Power can expand, the reason must be that Freedom has been "corrupted"; Freedom lacks the virtue necessary for good politics, which must be founded on the distinction between the common good and private interest. Thus, the Old Whigs acquired the name "Commonwealthmen." This version of whig thought dominated in the colonial struggle once the Americans were forced to define what they meant by the "rights of an Englishman."[3] From this starting point, the colonial opposition could conceptualize its claims at the social level; resistance was justified by a critique of the "corruption" of the prosperous English society and by the appeal to colonial virtue. That virtue was no abstraction; it was affirmed through tactics of popular resistance whose result was forms of social self-government. This movement, initiated by the merchants, quickly passed to the direction of popular committees called Sons of Liberty. The social struggle became political once the question of sovereignty was posed. This passage to the political took time; it originated in the Old Whig political theory, which had to be led to reflect on the contradiction between the primacy of Old Whig Freedom and the equally Old Whig affirmation of its republican institutional form in the Commonwealth. That contradiction was hidden by the Declaration of Independence; it was conceptualized only in the second period, and reflected finally in the third.

The first Continental Congress met in 1774. This Congress had no legitimate political status. It could only propose resistance, suggest compromises to a Parliament which refused to grant it any political status, and finally dissolve itself to return to the states. That is to say, the first Congress depended on social conditions (including the social and economic interests of the English merchants to whom their compromises were in fact addressed). A second Congress met in 1775. Its delegates considered themselves still to be ambassadors from their states. But this time, after some inconclusive debate, it opted for independence (and although it made a final conciliatory gesture, it was directed this time to the King, because social pressure had not affected the attitude of Parliament). On the basis of what "right" did the delegates found their political claims? The Declaration of Independence incorporates two arguments: the proclamation of certain "self-evident truths" is followed by a historical recapitulation of the misdeeds accumulated since 1763. That second and longer part of the Declaration clearly draws the implications of Old Whig logic: it shows that England had been "corrupted" and that American freedom must separate itself from the Old World in order to protect its self-evident rights. This suggests that these rights define political sovereignty. But the Declaration did not propose any political institutions capable of guaranteeing those rights against their eventual corruption or the degeneration toward that anarchy that had followed the Revolution of 1640. This makes clear the contradiction in Old Whig thought; its resolution depends on a political reflection of the status of the Congress which issued the Declaration, whose sovereignty was founded neither on self-evident rights or truths, nor on the particularity of social conditions.

The now free colonists adopted the Republic as the reflected form of their new institutions. This catch-all concept hid an issue that had been present during the first period and which could now emerge as the lived experience of independence in the second period. This crucial problem was defined as the question of *representation*. England had sought to legitimate its mercantile policies by means of the concept of "virtual representation." A good power is one that represents the common good of society; the "King in Parliament" is supposed to guarantee that representation by the immediate co-presence of the three Estates of the Kingdom in the elaboration of law. This implied that the colonies had no more need to be represented than did the English citizens of Manchester. But self-government had defined the lived experience of the colonists; they had invented theoretical refinements—for example, the distinction between internal and external taxes—in order to justify their resistance. Now free, their republican representation had to take a form different from the English model. The representation of social orders could not be adopted in a country which had no orders; but the positive mode by which sovereignty, freedom, or self-evident rights could be represented was not clear. What, in fact, was to be represented? The constitutions adopted by the independent states sought a social form adequate to the lived political experience of the first phase as it was now reflected by the question of representation.

The contrast between the constitution of Pennsylvania and those of the other states illustrates the difficulty that confronted the newly independent Americans. The colonial political leaders of Pennsylvania had sought to slow the movement toward independence whereas these same leaders, in the other colonies, had taken the direction of the movement. The new men who created Pennsylvania's free constitution were aware of the fact that their society was based on a relative equality of conditions. They adopted a unicameral legislature accompanied by a weak executive and an elected and revocable judiciary. All laws had to be made public and debated before being adopted a year later by the legislature. A Council of Censors was to be popularly elected every ten years to function like a sort of classical Senate permitting the people directly to repeal unjust or unpopular laws. These democratic measures were to assure a direct and continuous representation of society. They contrasted with the attempts made by the other states who sought to filter representation in order to make sure that it had an explicitly political status.[4] Thus, all of them instituted bi-cameralism, some made either the executive or the judiciary more independent, and none created a Council of Censors. These latter constitutions express a consistent whiggism. They conceptualize representation as a technique for protecting social Freedom by means of a system of checks and balances. But without the existence of social estates whose essential freedom is defined by their political function as social orders, bi-cameralism or the executive or judicial veto could not be justified. The question of representation was not resolved, in Pennsylvania or elsewhere.

The problem of representation became explicitly political; when the creation of a national Constitution became necessary. The states had been particularist even though the presence of a common enemy in war had unified them externally. The Continental Congress had no real power; George Washington's army appealed vainly to it for help. The Confederal Constitution proposed in 1777 was not ratified until 1781, shortly before the decisive battle of Yorktown. A country which had insisted so strongly on its rights made war without any legitimate political authority. There was never a proposal, as during the French Revolution, to mobilize the nation through the appeal to ''*la patrie en danger*.'' Once independence had been won, the Confederal Congress remained without power. Its members were representatives of the states bound by an imperative mandate; they were incapable of creating a national politics. This weakness posed the political question which became the lived experience of the third period. The impotence of the nation put into question at once the direct democracy of Pennsylvania and the traditional whiggism of the other states. This third period thus reflects at one and the same time the pre-political lived experience of self-evident rights and their representative conceptualization in autonomous societies of the states. The Old Whig primacy of Freedom and the republican insistence on the realization of the Commonwealth had to be unified in a Constitution which makes explicit the political status assumed by the Declaration of Independence and put into practice by the Confederal Congress.

The new Constitution was called ''federal'' in order to convince the states that it would not rob them of their social freedoms. The debate concerning its ratifications makes explicit the theory underlying the process of the Revolution as a whole. The opponents of the Constitution who criticized especially the lack of a Declaration of Rights based their arguments on the whig theory which sees the political as a threat to freedom. But the political cannot be conceptualized as the guarantor of pre-political freedoms any more than the reflection of politics is the mere representation of pre-existing social rights; those freedoms and those rights are born with the political whose concrete realization they instantiate. That is why the proponants of the new Constitution had no difficulty, after ratification, in directing the constitutional adoption of a Bill of Rights, which consists in the first ten Amendments to the Constitution rather than being inscribed as the preamble or premise of that fundamental law. The Constitution reflects a different lived experience of freedom and another conceptualization of a society in which that freedom is manifested. The Constitution is concerned with a freedom and rights which are directed to a future in which they can take on new forms. In a society without estates or orders, freedom takes the form of equal and shared *political* rights; the Constitution founds only *the right to have rights*. The theoretical status of this foundation will permit us to explain the birth of political parties and the justification of judicial review.

D. Reading the Framers' Reading

The reading of American history in terms of the theory of its revolution can be developed further if we consider the reflection on that revolutionary experience produced by the authors of *The Federalist Papers*. That volume of essays, written during the debate on the ratification of the Constitution, sought to reassure those who saw the new Constitution as a threat to the freedom of the individual or to the social rights of the states. But the analysis has implications that remain actual. For example, Hamilton (in Nr. 9) and Madison (in Nr. 10) sought to reassure the classical whigs who feared that an ''extended republic'' must necessarily fail. The danger they feared was the emergence of ''factions'' which would proliferate necessarily because of the sociological diversity of a large territory. The multiplication of these factions was taken to be the prelude to the anarchy which, classically, is the prelude to tyranny. *The Federalist* accepts the sociological diagnosis but rejects its political implications. Factions are to freedom what air is to fire. Rather than seek to suppress them in the name of a wholly unified society, the authors of *The Federalist* see in them the guarantor of freedom because, in an extended republic, they will each be the counterweight to the others. This argument was taken up again by the pragmatic pluralism of liberal sociology in the 1950s. It could be used, *a contrario*, by the progressive critics who sought to explain the apolitical nature of a society whose political parties are condemned to be only coalitions of interests reduced to their common denominator. But these contemporary sociological explications neglect the constitutional structure; they reduce it—as did the constitutions of the thirteen states—to a simple technique invented by a political science which is in fact simply a one-dimensional sociology.

A second analysis in *The Federalist* has contemporary relevance which illustrates the difficulty. This time, the authors attempt to explain the system of checks and balances set up within the Constitution itself. If the three branches of government were only articulated to block each other reciprocally in order to permit *society* to function according to its own rules, government would be blocked, politics would be impotent, and the citizen would be left to the mercies of the law of the strongest. The contemporary right criticizes the checks and balances as the root of the impotence, the inconsistency and the incapacity of the government to decide in the national interest; the contemporary left sees in this same structure a social pluralism crowning the weakness of the political level which thereby assures the domination of capital. *The Federalist* takes up the problem in Number 51. ''In framing a government which is to be administered by men over men, the great difficulty lies in this: you must first enable the government to control the governed; and in the next place oblige it to control itself.'' The sociological analysis of factions within an extended republic is not sufficient in this explicitly political context. Thus, the same Number 51 adds that, "whilst there being thus less danger to a minor from the will of a major party, there must be less pretext, also, to provide for the security of the former, by introducing into the government a will not dependent on the latter, or in other words, a will independent of the society itself." But how can this argument against the separation of politics from society be brought into harmony with the defense of a bi-cameral legislature whose Senate has precisely the function of checking the impetuous will of the majority?

The crucial argument is found in *The Federalist's* explicitly *political* theory of representation. Number 63 explains that the Senate stands as the federal instance since the Senators are named by the states. The three branches of government are of course all republican, hence all representative. *What* they represent, each in its own way, is the sovereign people. But this representation is not conceptualized in terms of the imperative mandate given by society to politics any more than it is reflected in terms of the idea of virtual representation. After showing that the Ancients already made use of the principle of representation, *The Federalist* underlines the fact that "the true distinction between these and the American governments, lies *in the total exclusion of the people, in their collective capacity*." This apparently paradoxical assertion, underlined by its author, seems to confirm the "progressive" denunciation of a constitutional coup d'état. But a different reading shows it to be in fact the foundation of *political* democracy. The sovereign people is *everywhere and nowhere*: everywhere, freedom always will find its champion; nowhere, none of the institutions of government can claim to *be* the totality of the people, to speak the truth of the people, to incarnate the reality of that political "will independent of the nation itself" which was criticized in Number 51. It is in this sense that the American federal republic institutes a democracy.

This theory of representation can only be understood in terms of the lesson learned in the course of the Revolution. The question of sovereignty debated with England had been determined by the dilemma of the *imperium in imperio*; the relation between the parts and the general interest of the empire had to be brought to explicitness. Whig theory did not lend itself to a federal solution; hence, the colonists fell back on the Old Whig primacy of freedom. That justified independence, but its limits became apparent during the elaboration of the state constitutions. Shays's rebellion, which finally brought the issue to a head in 1787, was not a *jacquerie* but rather the ultimate recourse of society against the state. It posed again the question of political power.[5] The Continental Congress represented the nation without being able concretely to incarnate it. Society functioned, but without political foundation; left to itself, it ran the risk of foundering into anarchy before becoming tyranny. The Framers of the Constitution had to find a political foundation capable of protecting society against its own worst instincts. That foundation, incarnated by the Constitution, was nothing but the sovereignty which had been affirmed already in the Declaration of Independence and practiced by the Continental Congress; but this time it was thematized explicitly as political. The sovereign people, everywhere and nowhere, exists in the mode of the *symbolic*; it is that instance which permits society to act upon itself. The political medium established by the Constitution is neither the economy nor individual interest; democratic politics concerns rights, whose first and foundational right is the right to have rights.

E. The Institutions of Democracy

This reading of the theoretical foundation of the American Revolution permits an explanation of the birth of two phenomena which today determine American political life. A republican politics is founded classically on virtue, that ability of the citizen to (be able to) abstract from his private interests in order to consecrate himself to the common public good. The Puritans of New England as well as the Cavaliers of the South were not shy in invoking that virtue which they defended against the corruption of English society. They proved their virtue during the first period of the Revolution when their social self-organization taught them their ability to govern themselves as a sovereign people. Once independence had been won, and prosperity had returned, they began to doubt themselves. The existence of new fortunes won by sometimes doubtful or speculative practices contrasted with a stern poverty which broke out in revolt with Shays, or made democratic Pennsylvania nearly ungovernable. Although all of the state constitutions contained provisions for protecting, even for creating, virtue, neither the Constitution of 1787 nor *The Federalist* makes it primary. That absence explains the place that the political parties came to occupy. Their roots in a still pre-modern schema of political thought explain why there could be only two parties. Each of them must be able to claim to incarnate that virtue which no longer has a place in the modern democratic constitution; and they can only make such a claim by denouncing their competition as—in a contemporary if not modern phrase—the representatives of the Evil Empire.

The birth of political parties is often explained by the opposition between the proto-capitalist commercial and fiscal policies of Hamilton and the agrarian democracy of which Jefferson dreamed. But this sociologizes relations which are in fact political (and it forgets that the much-praised farmer of Jefferson was a small agrarian capitalist). Both parties had supported the new national Constitution; the agreed-upon task now was to give it a content that could endure. It would be a retrospective reading to reduce their propositions to their social implications. The French Revolution brought their divergences to a head. Jefferson's supporters saw in it the successor to their own struggles and hopes; Hamilton's allies feared that its anarchical course would contaminate their own republican experience. The Hamiltonians made fun of the generous and naïve optimism which prevented the Jeffersonians from understanding the hard requirements of governing a sinful and easily corrupted humanity; they admired the stable institutions of England, which they hoped would come into being gradually at home. The Jeffersonians could only see these attitudes as "aristocratic," as "monarchist,'' or as the preaching of ''anti-republicans'' who had no confidence in a public opinion which they sought to control rather than obey. After a first period during which opinion deferred, as it had always deferred, to its established leaders who thus had no reason to act as partisan politicians, the Hamiltonians had to seek to identify themselves with a ''national interest'' said to exist above and beyond everyday politics. Their party could base its appeal on the denunciation of the Jeffersonians as meddlesome factional politicians, anti-republican because they placed partisan interests above the national interest.

The two parties that emerged from the founding period changed their names during the course of American history; yet that history has always been the scene of a struggle between two parties each claiming to incarnate a politics based on republican virtue. Treated as a system, this bi-partite structure is essentially modern and democratic despite its pre-modern foundation.[6] To accept the fact that society is fundamentally divided and yet still one is to go beyond the classical conception of a republic founded on the *reality* of a *res publica*. It would be a simplification to reduce the birth of political parties to a socio-economic analysis; *The Federalist* already suggested that approach in Numbers 9 and 10 before moving to a properly political account. Nor should one follow the functionalist political scientists who see in the party system simply the reply by the political system to challenges posed by its environment. It is true that parties fulfill functions, for example by binding the executive and legislative branches or by mediating relations between the citizens and the government, the states and the nation, or by leveling regional differences in the process of agglomerating diverse interests. But to limit oneself to these approaches is to avoid the essential philosophical question: how did it come about that society could be conceived as at once unified and divided: How could democratic practice be instituted and opposition be recognized as legitimate? Political modernity cannot be reduced to the criteria of a pseudo-Weberian rationalization process.

The modern nature of the system of political parties can be explained when we recall the way in which the Constitution articulates the *symbolic* nature of the political. Political parties exist in the same modality as do the branches of the federal government; none can claim to incarnate once and for all power, knowledge of the common good, or of the law. This symbolic existence of the sovereign power was the foundation of the peaceful transfer of powers during the ''Revolution of 1800.'' This same symbolic nature of power explains how the Americans came to accept *judicial review* by a nonelected branch of government. That practice was born in the wake of the ''Revolution of 1800.'' Only a society whose essence is to be divided can understand that there will always be a confrontation between two rights which claim to represent the common good at the same time that each knows that in the long run the political system can only refute them. The birth of the party system and the practice of judicial review are thus bound together by the heritage of the Revolution. American judicial practice did not remain long within the path traced by the *political* logic of the Constitution; contemporary American law seems rather to lend itself to sociological or political scientific analyses. Nonetheless, if one seeks to understand the properly political history of the country, one cannot ignore constitutional law and its foundation: the future-oriented right to have rights.

At the conclusion of this reading of American political history in terms of its Revolution, we can return to our categories of lived experience, its conceptualization, and its reflection. According to that schema, the lived experience of American history is the Constitution. The three phases of the Revolution, and their specific articulations, constitute the contents of that lived experience—contents capable of being reactivated and rearticulated. The conceptualized form of that American political life is the party system. Its developments can be understood in terms of the sedimentations of the lived political experience in the society. But the politics of the parties is in turn dependent on the reflected instance, which is the process of judicial review. Its foundation is not the individual as portrayed by the whig vision of the small owner—although that interpretation could dominate judicial practice during long periods like the one that culminated in civil war. The foundation of constitutional law is not society; constitutional law is the foundation of society—as one saw, for example, during the Civil Rights Movement when judicial decisions catalyzed political action. That contemporary illustration makes it clear that the reflected form of the political is not the conclusion or the goal of political action. One cannot stress sufficiently the fact that the constitutional decisions concerning civil rights were founded by *Amendments* to the Constitutions—indeed, by amendments voted after the Civil War—added to the amendments that constitute the ''Bill of Rights.'' This means that the great transformation of contemporary American life can itself be understood only in terms of that first and primary political right which is the right to have rights. American politics is constantly confronted, as it has been since the Declaration of Independence, by the question of those rights which are taken to be ''self-evident truths.'' In the last resort, these rights are evident only in light of political practice, which itself is founded on that first and primary right to have rights.

We have to listen one last time to the political scientists who introduce a *caveat*. The appearance of what has been called the ''Imperial Presidency'' seems to show that American political life has come to be defined by the Presidency. This deformation of the system of checks and balances is explained today by the near-disappearance of the political parties whose legitimacy was founded by reference to that pre-modern notion of virtue; the modern Presidency seeks to present itself as the incarnation of the national interest. Hamilton seems finally to win. The confirmation of this new direction today would be the fantastic abuses of foreign policy-making power in the ''Irangate'' affair. But that label recalls that before this latest scandal, there was ''Watergate,'' and that the reflected form of the political cannot be neglected. But one should not be an idealist either. American political life since the end of the War has passed through periods during which it was first the judiciary, then the executive, and then the legislative branch which claimed to be the incarnation of that sovereignty which the Constitution institutes as symbolic, *everywhere and nowhere*. Although a usurpation cannot be excluded *a priori*, and although the established order cannot be treated as sacred, one has to admit that the Constitution furnishes the bases that permit a modern democracy to reaffirm itself. Beyond as well as prior to a politics based on interest, the American Revolution, by instituting democracy, founded politics as a struggle for right and for rights.

Notes

Notes

Preface

1. This point is made first of all negatively, in Chapter 1, "Kant's Political Theory: The Virtue of His Vices." Its positive implications are drawn in Chapter 5, "Kant's System and (Its) Politics." The systematic argument is more fully developed in *From Marx to Kant* (Albany: State University of New York Press, 1985). I should note here that I have made stylistic modifications in all of the previously published chapters, changed their conceptual language in some cases, rewritten their introductory or concluding parts in others. It was not possible, however, to eliminate all repetitions, although I have tried to avoid them when I could do so without cutting into the flow of each chapter.

2. The reasons for Marx's temptation to reductionism are explained in Chapter 2, "On the Transformation of Critique into Dialectic: Marx's Dilemma." An attempt to provide a more satisfactory Marxism is found in Chapter 6, "Restoring Politics to Political Economy." Once again, I have made stylistic changes in these chapters, but was not able to eliminate all repetitions.

3. This "going beyond" did not of course imply that the Heidelberg theory was politically more "progressive." Indeed, the Heidelbergers were generally quite nationalistic, at times in a nostalgic mode typified by Dilthey's historical essays on Prussia and on Friedrich the Great, at times in the form of a *Realpolitik* of which Weber was the chief advocate. This is not the place for an extended discussion of a problem which has not been seriously addressed in the history of ideas. Thomas E. Willey's *Back to Kant. The Revival of Kantianism in German Social and Historical Thought. 1860–1914* (Detroit: Wayne State University Press, 1978) is perhaps a descriptive beginning, but only that.

4. Luc Ferry (with Alain Renaut) has proposed a biting, if not always justified, critique of the French post-modernists as political thinkers from the philosophical standpoint which I discuss in Chapter 7, "The Origins and Limits of Philosophical Politics." C.f., *La pensée 68* (Paris: Gallimard, 1986). Jürgen Habermas, whom I discuss in the same chapter, has also entered into the debate with the French in *Der philosophische Diskurs der Moderne* (Frankfurt: Suhrkamp Verlag, 1985).

5. This point is made in greater detail in *Defining the Political.*

6. First published in 1977, that book was republished with a substantial afterword reflecting on the logic immanent to my arguments in 1987 (London: Macmillan, and Minneapolis: University of Minnesota Press). Although the arguments presented in that afterword are not repeated here, the preparation of the present volume was in my mind while writing it.

7. (Albany: State University of New York Press, 1985.)

8. (London: Macmillan and Minneapolis: University of Minnesota Press, 1988.)

9. My study of *La naissance de la pensée politique américaine* (Paris: Ramsay, 1987) was a preliminary part of that larger project, as the reader of Chapter 11, which sets it in context, will see. The untitled larger study will follow the inverse structure developed in *From Marx to Kant*. To the three philosophical chapters will correspond three historical chapters, whose dilemmas parallel those presented to the philosopher. The two ''methodological mediations'' demanded by philosophy take the political form of the birth of political parties and the development of constitutionalism. The philosophical conclusion of the historiographical study parallels the single political conclusion to *From Marx to Kant*.

Introduction: The Politics of Critique

1. The relation betwen the originary intuition developed in the following chapters and the systematic philosophical edifice in which they were finally housed in 1985, under the lapidary title *From Marx to Kant*, is not simply that of the implicit to the explicit, the tentative to the elaborated, the experiment to the lawful formulas explaining its results. I will make use of the positive conceptual program proposed there in the elaboration of the simple intuition as originary in the second section of this introduction. The present volume forms a pair with the essays published under the title *Defining the Political*. The complement to *From Marx to Kant* will take the form promised in that volume, namely a study of the Prussian, American, and French paths to a modern political system. The importance of that investigation for the definition of the political nature of the ''politics of critique'' is stressed in the third section of this introduction. An aspect of that larger analysis was published as *La naissance de la pensée politique américaine*.

2. This is not the place for a discussion of the New Left and its devolution from movement to mode to Marxism . . . or of the return of something like the New Left, in all its ambiguity, in the ''new social movements.'' These issues are raised in *Defining the Political*.

3. One might say that just this process has taken place in the contemporary totalitarian experiences, whether those that can claim some ancestry in the Marxist movement, like the Bolshevik or ''Russian'' Revolution, or those that are quite pure illustrations of the aberration sketched theoretically here, such as the Pol Pot experience in Cambodia. The problem is more complicated than this sketch—which uses Marxism only as an illustration of a more general problem that affects any venture in critique and not only its political form—can convey. Within the frame of Marxism, see my ''afterword'' to the new edition of *The Marxian Legacy* (London: Macmillan, Minneapolis: University of Minnesota Press, 1987).

4. The passage is from a letter from Marx to Ruge, dated September, 1843, and published in the unique issue of the *Deutsch-Franzözische Jahrbücher*. I should mention in the present context that I used this citation as a motto to my edition of the *Selected Political Writings of Rosa Luxemburg* (New York: Monthly Review Press, 1971), and to the first edition of *The Marxian Legacy*. The development of simple intuitions is not linear; false paths, strategies of avoidance, are not to be condemned as ''errors,'' as if political philosophy were a problem for social engineers.

5. Marx's immanent dialectical theory of the relation of philosophy and radical politics has not stood well the test of time. The equation of the 'really real' with the essential; the identification of both with the human; the reduction of all aspects of human life to a common denominator; and the conception of human history as once and for all reaching its (predetermined) ultimate destination—have been denounced as naïve, mythological, even dangerous. More surprising perhaps than this political critique is the contemporary philosophical shift; instead of a two-tiered universe of essences and appearances, Being and beings, or even causes and effects, a new pluralism claims to inherit the radical mantle under the philosophical name of 'deconstruction' and on the basis of the political program of 'democracy.' No longer is the present viewed as the product of a past pregnant with a future waiting to be liberated by radical philosopher-midwives; it is the present which is to be liberated both from the chains of the past and the claims of the future. The right of difference becomes the foundation of all other rights; identity or universality is rejected in favor of particularity or otherness which are said to instantiate the claim to be radical. To be radical for the deconstructive democrat is to refuse the idea that there could be common roots and a universal foundation shared by humanity.

Marx is replaced by Nietzsche, politics by anti-politics, critique and criticism by affirmation. The refusal is so radical that its own position presents inversely identical strategies of avoidance to those analyzed here. The attempt to integrate Marxism and deconstruction has been made particularly by Chantal Mouffe and Ernesto Laclau in *Hegemony and Socialist Theory* (London: New Left Books, 1986); for a critical and political evaluation, see ''Another Resurrection of Marxism,'' in *Defining the Political.*

6. A further aspect of this problem will emerge in a moment. The dialectical theory assumes that the mediation is something real—either empirically or rationally—in which both polar moments participate really. The notion of the symbolic or the originary nature of the political will be seen to provide a different type of mediation. For the moment, it suffices to see how the search for a mediation functions as a strategy of avoidance. This is not the only such strategy; for contemporary politics, however, it will be seen to emerge gradually as the principal one.

7. A critical analysis of attempts to inherit that ''legacy'' within the context of modern democratic societies is presented in *The Marxian Legacy.* The afterword to the new edition provides supplementary arguments to the presentation of ''critical theory'' offered here in Chapter 3, and to the discussion of Habermas's recent work in Chapter 7.

8. As indicated in the Acknowledgments, Terry Cochran called my attention to the work of de Man, which I read with profit and excitement. De Man did not stop with the pattern of *Blindness and Insight*; he went on to analyze *The Resistance to Theory*, and at the end of his life was working on issues centering around the interrelations of power, critique, and history. I am unsure whether de Man's notion of ''reading'' should be identified with my originary intuition; nor am I certain that my strategies of avoidance are identical to his ''resistance'' to theory. There is a shared concern with the nature, necessity, and status of critical activity but an important difference insofar as de Man turns toward politics from a concern with history and its rhetoric whereas my path inverts the priorities. But perhaps the difference of approach is simply another instance of possible strategies of avoidance? (The finished essays from de Man's last period will be published by the University of Minnesota Press, which also published—with useful introductions by Wlad Godzich—the two earlier volumes.)

9. This dilemma was formulated most explicitly by Horkheimer and Adorno in their 1947 book of the same title. Although the problem appeared within the Marxian legacy, Horkheimer and Adorno's analysis is sometimes closer to that of Rousseau, which makes the problem co-eval with human sociation as such. But the kind of political resolution that is drawn from Rousseau in Chapter 5 would be foreign to the Frankfurt philosophers. A mediation between the two approaches is suggested by Habermas's reformulation of the problem in terms of his *Theory of Communicative Action.* For the intermediary steps, *The Marxian Legacy*, is more complete than the sketch offered here in Chapter 7.

10. This reading of Kant goes against the idealist or materialist versions of Kroner or of Lukacs, which see Kant seeking and failing to mediate between the poles, as in the further development of German Idealism. Idealist or materialist, the quest for mediation and the claim to dialectical immanence become strategies of avoidance. Critique is replaced by systematic philosophy in order to avoid the arbitrariness of criticism. It is worth noting that Kroner and Lukacs published their studies at the same historical moment. Cf., Richard Kroner, *Von Kant bis Hegel* (Tübingen: J. C. B. Mohr [Paul Siebeck], 1921, 1924) and Georg Lukacs, *Geschichte und Klassenbewusstsein* (Neuwied: Luchterhand Verlag, 1968, originally, 1923). Neither the materialist nor the idealist saw the relevance of Kant's republican political theory, on which I put great weight, to the actual politics of the young Weimar Republic.

11. The reader will find an apparent inconsistency in my use of the concepts ''reflective'' and ''reflexive'' in the chapters that follow. The usages differ even though their referent is always the act of critical judgment. In the first case, the ''reflective'' judgment begins from a particular to seek its lawful correlate in a process which the *Critique of Judgement* defines in opposition to the ''subsumptive'' judgment of science and morality. This judgment is crucial in ''unmaking a case.'' It permits the critique to affirm its autonomy and dignity. The ''reflexive judgment,'' on the other hand, while placing a similar structural accent on the particularity of critical judgment, acquires its motivation or legitimacy from the systematic imperatives that rule out the (materialist or idealist) dialec-

tical mediation that eliminates the place of critique. This formulation suggests that it is more useful when the concern is with "making a case." I have tried to be consistent in *this* usage even while leaving the two spellings to designate what is structurally an identical mode of argument.

12. Kant did not write a "Critique of History" in the manner in which a dialectical ontology like that of Hegel or a dialectical humanism like that of Marx would propose. Nor does Kant's approach to history lend itself to the "game" through which Hegel makes the (self-)critique of history encompass also the history of critique, i.e., of philosophy. Kant's historical writings are not the attempt to discover *in reality* the mediations missing among his theoretical and practical *Critiques*. That would be simply another strategy of avoidance, which the two early historical essays of 1783 sketch before the new, republican theory is fully developed in "Perpetual Peace." The fact that this late essay integrates the entire critical system into an open political project explains why Chapter 5 stands out in this volume as the only extended textual commentary.

13. An example of the first type is suggested by the reading of Kant in Chapter 1, where I could only point toward the kind of political institutions that the critique would require while spending most of my time undoing strategies of avoidance. The return to Kant in Chapter 5 illustrates the second type of analysis. Kant's conclusion—that only a politics which *must* present itself publicly to the judgment of a critical citizenry agrees with morality and with justice—makes explicit the generative function of political institutions which, in the earlier account, served a normative function. But the symbolic nature of the medium uniting and differentiating the critique from the institutions of politics remains implicit in the central notion of "hospitality" as that which makes the entire account work. Kant's argument could still be read realistically, along the lines of his earlier theory of "cosmopolitan history" whose evasive strategies were unmasked in Chapter 1. My point, however, is not philological; it is philosophical.

14. The error is not hard to make—as I inadvertently demonstrated when I wrote (p. 55) that normativity "constitutues" the class. That assertion neglects the manner in which the symbolic is effective, *wirklich*. A better account of this functioning is found in Chapter 10's presentation of "the" revolution as functioning as a genetic origin for nineteenth-century republicans and as a normative origin for twentieth-century radicals.

15. As with the other, technical categories invoked in this section, the notion of, and necessity for, a specific originary method is developed in *From Marx to Kant*. There is, however, a significant difference between the presentation here and that earlier argument. The methodological moment was introduced there in order to avoid what I called the "constitutive error," i.e., the tendency to treat the origin as a cause, the symbolic as real, theory as practice. The equivalent to the presentation of the constitutive error in the present context is the discussion of "strategies of avoidance." It should be added that what was called "philosophy" in relation to "the political" is here defined as "critique."

16. It must be stressed, once again, that this argument concerns the symbolic domain which defines the *sense*, not the reality, of the objects to which it refers. As noted a moment ago, the place of a distinct originary method was introduced in *From Marx to Kant* to avoid the "constitutive error" which ignores this crucial distinction. On the other hand, it is legitimate to speak of "practical" in this connection insofar as the unmasking of strategies of avoidance forces the critique to assume its autonomy. To speak of method as practical, however, is not yet to say that it is political.

17. The symbolic character of the originary structure explains why the "crisis" is felt as a *legitimation crisis* and not as an economic, social, or even a political crisis.

18. Once again, the discussion of modernity here concerns the symbolic, the sense of a historical moment, not its empirical reality. Paul de Man expresses nicely the pattern of avoidance that leads historians to mistake the place of the symbolic. He talks of a "reconciliation of memory with action [which] is the dream of all historians." This is achieved by treating modernity as the product of history "in a common genetic process [that] is highly satisfying, because it allows one to be both the origin and the offspring at the same time." The son understands the father, takes further the work of the father, and becomes himself a future father of new offspring. (In *Blindness and Insight*, p. 183.)

19. The crucial analyses of totalitarianism and its relation to democracy are furnished by Cornelius Castoriadis and Claude Lefort. A lengthy discussion of these issues, and of the difference between their analyses, is found in the new edition of *The Marxian Legacy*.

20. These final remarks are perhaps more lapidary than they should be. I have refrained from going into greater detail since many of the arguments are developed in the essays published as *Defining the Political*. Insofar as that volume is the complement to this one, I have tried to avoid repetition as much as possible. The elaboration of the nature of that originary modern state which defines the politics of the ''politics of critique'' will be presented in the volume which complements *From Marx to Kant*.

Chapter 1. Kant's Political Theory: The Virtue of His Vices

1. For biographical details, cf. Karl Vorländer, ''Kants Stellung zur franzözischen Revolution,'' in *Philosophische Abhandlungen Hermann Cohen gewidmet* (Berlin: Verlag Bruno Cassirer, 1912).

2. This reduction tends to characterize contemporary political thinking in general, as Sheldon Wolin argues convincingly in his *Politics and Vision* (Boston: Little, Brown, 1960).

3. Vorländer makes this argument in his *Kant und Marx*, in 1911, as German imperial politics was heating up the world scene. His argument could be instructively compared with the debate among the Social Democrats, begun already in 1898. See, for example, the discussion by Rosa Luxemburg, ''Militia and Militarism,'' in *Selected Political Writings*, Dick Howard, ed. (New York: Monthly Review Press, 1971).

4. Franz Mehring, ''Die Neo-Kantianer,'' (1900), reprinted in Hans J. Sandkühler and Rafael de la Vega, *Marxismus und Ethik* (Frankfurt am Main: Suhrkamp Verlag, 1970). This volume contains a useful selection from the debates which I have been considering.

5. Dick Howard, *The Marxian Legacy* (London: Macmillan, 1977; New York: Urizen Press, 1978). Second edition, revised with a new afterword, (Macmillan: London, and Minneapolis: University of Minnesota Press, 1987).

6. ''Perpetual Peace,'' cited from Hans Reiss, ed., *Kant's Political Writings* (Cambridge: Cambridge University Press, 1970), pp. 118–19. I will give the German references to the *Akademie Ausgabe* when necessary, under the abbreviation *AKA*, followed by the volume and page number. Here, *AKA* 8: 373.

7. *Lose Blätter*, ed. R. Reicke, *Altpreuss. Monatsschrift*, 31, 589, cited by Vorländer, in Sandkuhler and De la Vega, p. 285.

8. *AKA* 6: 188. My translation.

9. *Kritik der Urteilskraft*, Dr. Otto Buek, ed. (Berlin: Verlag Bruno Cassirer, 1914), p. 210n. My translation.

10. Leonard Krieger, *The German Idea of Freedom* (Chicago: University of Chicago Press, 1957), p. 125.

11. ''Conflict of the Faculties,'' in Reiss, p. 184.

12. ''On the Common Saying: 'This may be True in Theory, but it does not Apply in Practice','' in Reiss, p. 90.

13. Cf. *AKA*, 5: 185.

14. ''Conflict of the Faculties,'' in Reiss, pp. 187–88.

15. *Fragmente aus dem Nachlass*, cited in Norman Kemp Smith, *A Commentary of Kant's 'Critique of Pure Reason'* (New York: Humanities Press, 1962), p. viii.

16. Hans Saner, *Kants Weg vom Krieg zum Frieden* (Munich: R. Piper & Co., 1967).

17. *Fragmente*, 8: 622, cited by Max Adler, in Sandkühler and De la Vega, p. 188.

18. *Critique of Pure Reason*, A751f, B779f, in N. K. Smith translation, pp. 601–2.

19. Lewis White Beck, *Studies in the Philosophy of Kant* (Indianapolis: Bobbs-Merrill, 1965), p. 38, and *passim*.

20. Ibid., p. 30.

21. *Critique of Judgment*, *AKA* 5: 195; translation modified from Bernard, p. 32.

22. Cf. the final long passage from the *Metaphysics of Morals* which I cite at the conclusion of this discussion (n. 51), where Kant's argument returns in a more explicit political context. Compare, too, in this context, the passage on Plato's Republic as a ''utopia'' in the first *Critique* (B 372) with the following passage of the 1798 ''Conflict of the Faculties'': ''All forms of state are based on the

idea of a constitution which is comparable with the natural rights of man, so that those who obey the law should also act as a unified body of legislators. And if we accordingly think of the commonwealth in terms of concepts of pure reason, it may be called a Platonic *ideal* (*respublica noumena*) which is not an empty figment of the imagination, but the eternal norm for all civil constitutions whatsoever, and a means of ending all wars'' (in Reiss, p. 187).

23. On the context of the essay, see Gerard Raulet, ''Us et abus des Lumières, Mendelsohn jugé par Kant,'' *Les Etudes philosophiques* (1978): 297–313.

24. It would be worth a separate study to show how *practically* influential Kant's arguments came to be. Here, the mention of some of the leading ''Kantian'' reforming bureaucrats will have to suffice, beginning with von Zedlitz, the Minister of Education to whom the first *Critique* is dedicated, and whose reactionary replacement, Wöllner, is perhaps best known for having censored Kant. The list would include: Humboldt, von Schön, von Schrötter, Klein, Altenstein, and to some extent even Stein and Hardenberg. Hans Rosenberg's *Bureaucracy, Aristocracy and Autocracy. The Prussian Experience, 1660–1815* (Boston: Beacon Press, 1966) sums up the situation as follows:

> Before 1800, the doctrines of German Idealism acquired political significance only in the Prussian bureaucracy. Not only did the administrative apparatus of the state provide an institutional setting for constructive action; the rigor, rudeness, intolerance and soullessness of Frederick's rulership affected the bureaucrats directly and stiffened their will to resist royal oppression with the aid of liberal principles . . . [They accepted Kant's assertion concerning ''self-incurred tutelage.''] . . . To the bureaucratic disciples of Kant, individual freedom to think was the gateway to professional happiness, to self-disciplined discretionary action, to their own political liberation, and to the replacement of erratic dynastic autocracy by a more magnanimous and more efficient form of despotic government, by humanized bureaucratic absolutism ''which will find it more advantageous to itself to treat man who thence-forth is more than a machine, in accord with his dignity'' [Kant] (p. 189).

One could add many further passages from other historians of the Prussian experience, but this will suffice here. Cf., my discussion of Enlightened Despotism in *Defining the Political*. As noted, I am preparing a comparative study of the Prussian, French, and American paths to modern politics which will form the political counterpart to the theory of my *From Marx to Kant*.

25. At the outset, I should note that ''civil society'' does not have the meaning it has had since Hegel-Marx, as Manfred Riedel shows nicely in *Bürgerliche Gesellschaft und Staat bei Hegel* (Neuwied: Luchterhand, 1970). But, see n. 33, below.

26. ''Conflict . . . ,'' in Reiss, p. 178.

27. Kant is not so naïve about the effects of ''le doux commerce'' as were Montesquieu and his generation. He is often critical of it, to the point that the ''Third Definitive Article'' of ''Perpetual Peace'' stresses the ''Conditions of Universal Hospitality'' as a way of avoiding the unequal exchange and domination of colonial ventures, as several Marxist and non-Marxist (e.g., Karl Jaspers) commentators have noted.

28. See my account in *The Development of the Marxian Dialectic* (Carbondale: Southern Illinois University Press, 1972). This is, of course, the ''immanent critique'' whose dilemmas are discussed above in the introduction.

29. *AKA* 7: 331.

30. ''Conflict . . . ,'' in Reiss, p. 183.

31. See para. 29, as well as paras. 59 and 86.

32. ''Introduction to the Theory of Law,'' in Reiss, pp. 133–34.

33. It is worth noting here, since the Marxists make such a central point of it, that one can find in Garve's ''Essay über die Moden'' of 1792 a description of a nearly modern form of civil society, as Reinhart Koselleck has noted in his *Preussen zwischen Reform under Revolution* (Stuttgart: Ernst Klett Verlag, 1967), pp. 121ff.

34. ''Theory and Practice,'' in Reiss, p. 67 n.

35. *AKA* 4:412, 414.

36. Reiss, pp. 66, 67 n.

37. ''Perpetual Peace,'' in Kant, *On History*, ed. Lewis White Beck (Indianapolis: Bobbs-Merrill, 1963), p. 112.

38. See Albert Hirschman, *The Passion and the Interests* (Princeton: Princeton University Press, 1977). Also, Seldon S. Wolin, *Politics and Vision* (Boston: Little, Brown and Company, 1960). And, Patrick Riley, ''On Kant as the Most Adequate of the Social Contract Theorists,'' in *Political Theory* 1 (November 1973).

39. ''Perpetual Peace,'' in Beck, pp. 126–27.

40. H. Lübbe, ''Dezisionismus in der Moraltheorie Kants,'' in Lübbe, *Theorie und Entscheidung* (Freiburg: Verlag Rombach, 1971), Lübbe's argument seems to me rather far-fetched.

41. ''Theory and Practice,'' in Reiss, p. 79.

42. ''Perpetual Peace,'' in Beck, p. 134.

43. ''Theory and Practice,'' in Reiss, p. 78 n.

44. ''Metaphysics of Morals,'' in Reiss, p. 163. (Kant's italics.)

45. Riley shows rather nicely how the same position by Rousseau demands as its corrective the idealization of a polis and its Sittlichkeit in ''A Possible Explanation of Rousseau's General Will,'' *American Political Science Review* 64 (March 1970). On this, see the discussion of Rousseau in Chapter 8, below.

46. ''Theory and Practice,'' in Reiss, pp. 82–83.

47. Ibid., p. 74.

48. Karl Vorländer, ''Kants Stellung zur Franzözischen Revolution,'' in *Philosophische Abhandlungen Hermann Cohen gewidmet* (Berlin: Verlag Bruno Cassirer, 1912), p. 225.

49. *AKA* 5: 375.

50. ''Conflict of the Faculties,'' in Reiss, p. 177.

51. ''Metaphysics of Morals,'' in Reiss, pp. 173–74.

52. Karl Jaspers, *Die grossen Philosophen* (München: R. Piper & Co., 1957), pp. 554–55.

Chapter 2. On the Transformation of Critique into Dialectic: Marx's Dilemma

1. The literature of these confusions is not systematic, since the distinction is of minor importance for non-Marxists, and unquestioned for the Marxists (most of whom never mention individual ''right'' Hegelians, sticking to group characterizations). The most useful starting point in English is still L. Krieger, *The German Idea of Freedom* (Chicago: University of Chicago Press, 1973). The anthology, *Die Rechtshegelianer*, edited by H. Lübbe, as well as Lübbe's chapters in *Politische Philosophie in Deutschland*, are useful despite the author's own political biases.

2. I have dealt with this material in more detail in *The Development of the Marxian Dialectic*. The literature has grown enormously, of course. I mention my own early work here only because, pursuing the goal of understanding how and why Marx moved from philosophy to political economy as the key to revolution, I tended to accept the claims for dialectical synthesis, on the same basis for which I now put it into question. *Caveat emptor!*

3. Citations from Marx, or from Marx and Engels, will not be given independent footnotes when their source is clearly given in the text, and when that source is widely available, as for example the present case where the ''Introduction to a Critique . . . '' is easily found in anthologies, and the essay is relatively short. (Often the translation will be my own, or modifications of the usual English ones.)

4. The citation is taken from Iring Fetscher, *Der Marxismus. Seine Geschichte in Dokumenten* (München: Piper, 1962, 1964, 1965), 3 vols. which has many important sources conveniently collected. On Guizot's originality as the theorist of a rising bourgeoisie that emerged from the French Revolution, see Pierre Rosanvallon, *Le Moment Guizot* (Paris: Gallimard, 1984).

5. Selections are found in Fetscher, Vol. 1, pp. 157–58 and Vol. 3, pp. 144–45.

6. See Hans-Josef Steinberg, *Sozialismus und deutsche Sozialdemokratie* (Hannover: Verlag für Literatur und Zeitgeschehen, 1967).

7. See Jürgen Habermas, *Knowledge and Human Interests* (Boston: Beacon Press, 1971), pp. 1–65. A brief commentary is found in *The Marxian Legacy*.

8. There is a crucial problem, to which we shall return, for Marx as well on this score. If capitalism is ideological, then the revolution should bring about the end of ideology. If ideology is defined by the split of subject and object, then its end should entail their unification. Thus, the young Marx talked in the *1844 Manuscripts* about there being only "one science," and about the science of man as a science of nature, and the science of nature as the science of man. The temptation is to see this unity as achieved by the proletariat, either pre- or post-revolution. This view, however, hypostatizes the proletariat, either as the revolutionary object produced by capitalism and destined to eliminate it, or as the revolutionary subject incarnating true human values. It leads directly to—or at least legitimates—Soviet totalitarianism.

The point here, however, is that ideology is not only the split of subject and object but *also* the claim to legitimate the unity of the division by privileging one or the other pole. This unity-in-difference cannot be overcome by eliminating difference unless one choses a totalitarian solution. The task, rather, is to preserve the difference, enriching it while avoiding a false closure. This is the task of a reovlutionary *politics*.

9. Within the "Marxist" tradition, the particularist structure of capitalism and the ideological attitude of vulgar economics have also made their appearance. Two examples will illustrate the point. Eduard Bernstein, the father of "revisionism," attempted to demonstrate that Marx's predictions of increasing proletarianization of the "middle classes" was erroneous by citing statistics of stock ownership on the one hand, and on the other, by pointing to the increasing numbers of small businesses which spring up after every economic crisis. Some years later, the exiled oppositional leader Leon Trotsky attempted to distinguish his opposition to Stalinism from that of bourgeois capitalism's opposition to the Soviet regime by insisting that the Stalinist system was "a degenerated workers' state" which, even though "degenerated," was still socialist because the means of production were owned by the state. Common to both of these approaches is the standpoint of vulgar economics. Both set out from the relations of the individual to the means of production; both operate in terms of property ownership. Thus both remain on the level of ideology insofar as they take the immediate appearances for the fundamental social relations constituting the system. In fact, however, what is central is the nature of the total system as defined by relations of alienation and domination. The forms of ownership are but appearance.

10. A somewhat different account of the same phenomena is given in Sartre's *Critique of Dialectical Reason* under the rubric of the "practico-inert" and the action of "seriality." For a summary and criticism see *The Marxian Legacy*.

11. The relevant passages referred to here are found in Fetscher, Vol. 1, *passim*.

12. Ralph Miliband, *The State in Capitalist Society* (New York: Basic Books, 1969).

13. This "nightwatchman" function is in fact hardly minimal, as Karl Polanyi demonstrates in *The Great Transformation* (Boston: Beacon Press, 1957). The creation of "frameworks" is a difficult and long-term task, wrenching society from its traditional social relations while creating new ones that must be preserved against popular pressures. As Claude Lefort, to whom this analysis of ideology is deeply indebted, points out, Marx tended to see history as passing from feudalism to capitalism without taking into consideration the intervening stage of absolutism. This explains not only Marx's neglect of the properly political; Lefort shows too why it leads Marx to underestimate and to misunderstand the advent of the rights of man. On Lefort, see *The Marxian Legacy*, especially the new afterword to the second edition.

14. The latter view is developed in Jean-Paul Sartre, *Critique de la raison dialectique* (Paris: Gallimard, 1960). Its inadequacy and implicit rationalism are criticized in *The Marxian Legacy*.

15. It might be objected that I am reducing the rich ambiguity of Marx's own thought, as well as doing away with the modifications that he introduced as a result of historical experience or polemical necessity. There is no doubt that a "better" Marx could be constructed if one were to bring to bear his historical writings, his correspondence, and his development. In the next section, I will give specific examples of his more open theorizing. The interpretation given in this section is justified not only by the argument that this theorization has been the dominant one among political movements which call themselves Marxist; equally important is the need to take seriously Marx's own theoretical self-understanding in order to see what it is that makes his theory a coherent, consistent whole.

16. This linearization of social development posed a thorny problem in the case of Russia. Marx put aside his work on *Capital* to study the question whether the communal "socialism" of the peasant "mir" could be the basis of a socialist transformation. Lenin's first book, *The Development of Capitalism in Russia*, argued for the linear view. Trotsky's theory of "combined and uneven development" attempted to show how Russia could skip a stage. After 1917, the theory of the "weakest link" was elaborated. Then came the theory of "Socialism in One Country." This was followed by the dilemma faced by the newly liberated ex-colonies of the 1960s. And here we stand.

17. Published later as Nikolai Bukharin, *Historical Materialism: A System of Sociology* (New York: International Publishers, 1933).

18. See the relevant passages in Fetscher, Vol. 1, *passim*.

19. These passages come from Max Horkheimer's brilliant but disillusioned essay "Authoritarian State." For the context, see *The Marxian Legacy*.

20. Oskar Negt, "Marxismus als Legitimationswissenschaft, Zur Genese der stalinistischen Philosophie," in *Deborin/Bucharin: Kontroversen über dialektischen und mechanistischen Materialismus* (Frankfurt am Main: Suhrkamp, 1969).

21. This description is based on the analysis by Claude Lefort in his 1964–65 Sorbonne Lectures. For the context, see *The Marxian Legacy*.

22. Once again, I am heavily endebted to Lefort for the following discussion, although here I do not develop fully the symbolic and imaginary dimensions of history that he stressed. Those aspects of his theory are treated in the afterword to the second edition of *The Marxian Legacy*.

23. The shock of Louis Bonaparte's coup can be measured by its effect on another great theorist of capitalism, de Tocqueville. François Furet has shown how Tocqueville modified his *social* theory of democracy, which he had first thought he could apply as well to the "Ancien Régime" and the Revolution. The coup directed his attention to the properly political sphere, which he, in his own way, had tended to reduce to the social as Marx had tended to reduce it to the economic. Cf. F. Furet, *Penser la révolution française* (Paris: Gallimard, 1978).

24. Karl Marx, *Friedrich Engels Werke* (Berlin: Dietz, 1956–68), Vol. 32, p. 570.

25. Ibid., Vol. 17, p. 655.

26. *Socialist Appeal* (January 17, 1939); cited in Heinz Abosch, *Trotzki Chronik* (München: Carl Hanser, 1973), p. 141.

Chapter 3. Hermeneutics and Critical Theory

1. Hans-Georg Gadamer to Richard Bernstein, 1 July 1982, trans. James Bohman, appendix to *Beyond Objectivism and Relativism: Science, Hermeneutics and Praxis*, by Richard Bernstein (Philadelphia: University of Pennsylvania Press, 1983), p. 262.

2. Ibid., p. 264.

3. Bernstein, *Beyond Objectivism and Relativism*, p. 231.

4. Hans-Georg Gadamer, *Wahrheit und Methode*, Vierte Auflage (Tübingen: J. C. B. Mohr, Paul Siebeck, 1975), pp. 258, 259.

5. Ibid., p. 283.

6. The modern hermeneutics that sets itself off from the "philosophy of consciousness" typical of historicism, Dilthyian *Einfühlungsphilosophie*, or methodological *Verstehen*, makes a virtue of necessity—it literally ontologizes its own embarrassment. It explains that we cannot pose the question of foundations because these foundations found our very being-as-questioning. We cannot pose the question of beginning because we have always already begun. Whether the hermeneutic circle is conceived ontologically, as with Gadamer, or linguistically, as with Apel, the dilemma remains. Philosophy cannot rule out the question of foundations without risking the accusation of irrationalism. But a modern philosophy cannot invoke foundations whose normative character it cannot justify immanently.

7. Hegel argues, for example, that "peoples without a state may have passed a long life before arriving at this their destination. And during these periods, they may have attained considerable development in some dimensions." He continues more explicitly, "It is the state which first presents

subject matter that is not only adapted to the prose of history, but involves the production of such history in its very being. Instead of government issuing merely subjective mandates sufficing for the needs of the moment, a community that is acquiring a stable existence as a state requires formal commands and laws, comprehensive and universally binding prescriptions. It thus produces a record as well as an interest in understandable, definite transactions and occurrences which have results that are lasting.'' G. W. F. Hegel, *Werke*, vol. 12: *Vorlesungen über die Philosophie der Geschichte*, ed. Eva Moldenhauer und Karl Markus Michel (Frankfurt am Main: Suhrkamp Verlag, 1970), p. 83.

8. This is argued explicitly by Hegel in the resigned tones of his preface to the *Philosophy of Right* trans. T. M. Knox (Oxford: Oxford University Press, 1967), for which philosophy can only ''Paint its grey on grey'' after the fact, when ''the owl of Minerva'' has taken flight. For a theoretical argument making this point from the perspective of Critical Theory, see Jürgen Habermas, ''Hegel's Critique of the French Revolution,'' in *Theory and Practice*, trans. John Viertel (Boston: Beacon Press, 1973), pp. 121–42.

9. Max Horkheimer, *Sozialphilosophische Studien*, ed. W. von Brede (Frankfurt am Main: Fischer, 1972), pp. 33–46.

The research proposed for the Institute asks why the working class has not fulfilled its designated function. The changed economic, psychological, cultural, legal, and religious conditions of modern capitalism are to be examined empirically and integrated theoretically by the renewal of that ''social philosophy'' whose inadequate foundation in German Idealism will be completed by the equivalent of a modern Marxism. Nowhere does the lecture put into question the adequacy of the Marxist manner of posing the questions. It questions only the nineteenth-century solutions offered by orthodox Marxism.

10. Max Horkheimer, ''Traditionelle und Kritische Theorie,'' *Zeitschrift für Sozialforschung* 6 (1937): 245–92; Max Horkheimer and Herbert Marcuse, ''Philosophie und Kritische Theorie,'' *Zeitschrift für Sozialforschung* 6 (1937) 624–31 (Horkheimer), 631–47 (Marcuse). Marcuse's contribution to the discussion is translated as ''Philosophy and Critical Theory,'' in *Negations*, trans. Jeremy J. Shapiro (Boston: Beacon Press, 1968), pp. 135ff.

11. Horkheimer, ''Traditionelle und Kritische Theory,'' p. 630.

12. Marcuse's interpretation of Descartes, like Marx's presentation of Epicurus in his *Dissertation*, sees a different implication in this subjectivism. Horkheimer's argument is concerned with the methodology of the social sciences whereas Marcuse's concern is to ground a philosophically Critical Theory which can no longer appeal to the proletariat. See Marcuse, ''The Concept of Essence,'' in *Negation*, p. 50.

13. Marcuse, ''Philosophy and Critical Theory,'' pp. 135–36. (I have changed Shapiro's translation of the penultimate sentence to stress that both *must* (soll) be brought together, i.e., that this imperative is an active task.)

14. Cf. the brilliant argument of George Schrader, ''The Status of Teleological Judgment in the Critical Philosophy,'' *Kantstudien* 45 (1953–1954): 204–35. I have developed this argument in a broader context in my *From Marx to Kant*, whose entire fifth chapter is devoted to ''The Logic of Receptivity.''

15. Jean-Paul Sartre, *Critique de la raison dialectique* (Paris: Gallimard, 1960), *passim*.

16. Jürgen Habermas has pointed to the major problems of this proposal. See the concluding chapter to his *The Theory of Communicative Action*, vol. 1: *Reason and the Rationalization of Society*, trans. Thomas McCarthy (Boston: Beacon Press, 1984), pp. 339–403. To summarize Habermas's point, it is not possible to reduce a social totality to one form of reason. Communicative (and emancipatory) reason must always function alongside instrumental reason if the society is not to be pulled apart by the centrifugal weight of the individual atoms seeking self-preservation at the cost of destroying the mechanisms of social reproduction.

17. Paul Piccone has argued this position in numerous essays in the journal *Telos* of which he is the editor. Its political consequences can be quite problematic because their reductionism excludes any *political questioning*, as for example in the assertion that the feminist movement is simply necessary for the expanded reproduction of a blocked capitalist society. As if things were so simple, or society so rational in its irrationality!

Two other positions are possible within the framework of the political goals of Critical Theory. Along the lines of Walter Benjamin or Theodor Adorno, one could attempt to recover an intimation of the suppressed totality through the lightning of a mimetically based critique founded either in art or in the structures of the everyday. Or, along the lines of Ernst Bloch, one could propose a kind of ''anticipatory hermeneutics'' which develops the immanent futurity that traditional hermeneutics covers over through its classical orientation. On the former see Habermas, *The Theory of Communicative Action*, 1:339–403; on the latter, see Burghardt Schmidt, *Ernst Bloch* (Stuttgart: G. B. Metzler Verlag, 1985).

18. Theodor W. Adorno, *Negative Dialektik* (Frankfurt am Main: Suhrkamp Verlag, 1966), p. 13. Habermas's reconstruction of Marx's philosophical debt to German idealism expresses this difficulty by speaking of the need for a ''Fichtean moment'': since ego is itself only in the act of relating to the world, there must be a moment of intersubjectivity which transcends the subject philosophy of the Kantian ''I think'' and unifies and makes my representations mine. This Fichtean moment is translated by Habermas as the phenomenon of class consciousness in Marx's reconstruction of the capitalist civil society.

19. This is most explicitly stated in Kant's theses on ''The Idea of History from a Cosmopolitan Point of View.'' For an interpretation of Kant from the perspective to which I can only allude here, see Chapter 5, ''Kant's System and (Its) Politics,'' and *From Marx to Kant*.

20. See my essay, ''Enlightened Despotism and Modern Democracy,'' in *Defining the Political*.

21. See the afterword to the second edition of *The Marxian Legacy* for a detailed presentation of this problem.

Chapter 4. Why Return to the American Revolution?

1. For example, a colleague who teaches sociology regularly asks his students at the beginning of each semester to classify themselves. Without fail, he finds neither men nor women, rich nor poor, students nor workers . . . but only psychological classifications. I'm generous, kind, critical, depressive . . . in short, 'the social' is empty. It doesn't make sense anymore.

2. The ''logical'' consequences of this ''dialectic of enlightenment'' can be illustrated by Peter Sloterdijk's hugely successful popular essay *Kritik der zynischen Vernunft* (Frankfort am Main: Suhrkampf, 1983), or better yet by certain ''deconstructive'' analyses inspired by philosophers such as Lyotard, Deleuze, Guattari, or Baudrillard.

3. This is the argument suggested in ''L'Ouverture'' by Jean-Luc Nancy and Philippe Lacoue-Labarthe in *Rejouer le politique* (Paris: Galillée, 1981). That talk marked the opening of a short-lived ''Center for the Philosophical Study of the Political'' in Paris. See Chapter 7, part A below.

4. Lefort's evolution and his recent work are discussed in my *The Marxian Legecy*, and also in the afterword to its 1987 second edition.

5. In ''Natural Law and Revolution,'' English translation, Jürgen Habermas, *Theory and Practice*, trans. John Viertel (Boston: Beacon Press, 1973).

6. See the famous Trilateral Commission report on a ''crisis of ungovernability'' in democracies that would necessitate limiting democracy in order to preserve it! See Crozier, Huntington, and Watanuki, *The Crisis of Democracy: A Report on the Governability of Democracies*.

7. See Dick Howard, ''La Déclaration d'Indépendance,'' in *Dictionnaire des oeuvres politiques* (Paris: PUF, 1987).

8. See Dick Howard, *La naissance de la pensée politique amèricaine* (Paris: Ramsay, 1987).

9. Derridean-Heideggerian critics Nancy and Lacoue-Labarthe speak of this situation as a ''soft totalitarianism.'' This designation adds nothing to the analysis. It would be better to speak of social or political forms of totalitarianism.

10. As I have demonstrated elsewhere, the analysis of the particular depends on the political, whereas the analysis of receptivity belongs to philosophical theory (or, in this case, to social theory). Cf. *From Marx to Kant*.

11. The best overall analysis of that social activity which leads to the political is found in Pauline Maier's *From Resistance to Revolution* (New York: Vintage Books, 1972). There are many specific

studies of the social activity that became a political revolution; the first of these was published by Carl L. Becker, *The History of Political Parties in the Province of New York, 1760–1776* (Madison: University of Wisconsin, 1909).

Chapter 5. Kant's System and (Its) Politics

1. These distinctions are elaborated in greater detail in my *From Marx to Kant*. My claim here is not philological. I am not asserting that Kant *intended* to develop the implications that I will draw here. The approach seems to me to be useful in attempting to make sense not only of Kant's theory but of the tasks of a theory of modernity in general. That, however, is another issue. The claim here is more limited and modest.

2. Hannah Arendt claims that Kant is guilty of this same error which is even more patent in Hegel and in Marx. She asserts that "in Kant, in contrast to Hegel, the motive of the modern escape from politics into history is still quite clear. It is the escape into the 'whole,' and the escape is prompted by the meaninglessness of the particular." ("On History," p. 83) There are certainly grounds for this assertion, and not only in the 1784 essay. In Kant's last published work, the *Conflict of the Faculties*, he asks himself "How is history a priori possible?" His reply recalls the earlier position. "The answer is that it is possible if the prophet himself occasions and produces the events he predicts." (Cited in Reiss's translation, *Kant's Political Writings*, Cambridge: Cambridge University Press, 1970, p. 177. In the following text, I will be citing from L. W. Beck's translation which flows somewhat more smoothly. As the sections are short, and the context is clear, I have not footnoted all citations. Reference is to Kant, *On History* (Indianapolis: Bobbs-Merrill, 1963).) Once again, my claim here is not philological. The point is that, like any great thinker, Kant is often contradictory. The sense of his work emerges only from another perspective than his own.

3. Such a syncretism is presented by a variety of authors, of whom I shall mention here only my own earlier attempt, "Kant's Political Theory: The Virtue of his Vices," reprinted here as Chapter 1. *Caveat emptor!*

4. The basis of the argument is moral, but it becomes central to the later political theory. In the remarks introducing the Definitive Articles, Kant asserts that "all men who can reciprocally influence each other must stand under some civil constitution." What needs to be shown is the justification for this duty which, itself, is the precondition for any and all other duties.

5. This is clearly directed at Frederick the Great, to whom Kant later makes an an apparently fawning reference. Meinecke's *Die Idee der Staatsräson* (München: R. Oldeburg, 1976) gives a lengthy list of instances to which Kant may be alluding in the chapter devoted to Frederick. The Political Testament of 1752 explicitly breaks with the moralism of the young Prince's "Anti-Machiavelli." Sixteen years later, at the end of the Seven Years War, Frederick writes: "Let it be deeply impressed in your mind that there are not great Princes who do not have the idea in their head of expanding their kingdom (*Herrschaft*)," pp. 357–58.

6.These arguments have troubled commentators, beginning with the reviews of Kant's essay by Fichte and Schlegel. Fichte's review presents more Fichte than Kant, in fact, and does not bear reading today. He is too concerned to find himself in Kant, and therefore pays little attention to the inner problems of Kant's text. Fichte's *Werke* VII, pp. 427–36 (Berlin: Walter de Gruyter & Co., 1971). Schlegel's review is more ambitious. Titled a "Versuch über den Begriff des Republikanismus, veranlasst durch die Kantische Schrift zum ewigen Frieden," it is found in the *Kritische Friedrich-Schlegel-Ausgabe*, Bd. 7,erste Abteilung, (Schoningh, 1966), pp. 11–25. Although influenced by Fichte, Schlegel makes several significant points in attempting to give a democrataic component to Kant's republicanism. He rejects Kant's use of the "mechanism of nature" to rule man, arguing in its stead for a "Greek" practical science. He also argues against Kant's rejection of democracy on the grounds that what Kant is talking about is in fact a ochlocracy. His major insight, however—which is also present in his excellent review of Condorcet's "Esquisse d'un tableau historique des progrès de l'esprit humain" (in ibid., pp. 3–9)—is that Kant does not make explicit the task of understanding the "inner development of humanity"although he does glimpse the possibility at one point. The one point where he grasps it, says Schlegel, is the discussion we are about to follow. By opting for the mechanical art, Kant is forced, says Schlegel, to add the appendix on the moral politican which avoids the necessary turn to politics an active form of ''political education'' (*politische Bildung*).

7. This ''should'' is based on systematic, not philological considerations. The fact that the ''Secret Article'' was added to the second edition, and that Kant may have wanted to keep a symmetry in his text, could explain its place. I cannot give any better explanation, any more than I can explain the difference Kant intended by the distinction between the Supplements (*Zusätz*) and the appendices (*Anhänge*). Hence, I refer to both as ''supplementary materials.''

8. This point is presented in luxurious detail in Hans Saner's well-documented but theoretically uninteresting *Kants Weg vom Krieg zum Frieden* (München: R. Piper Verlag, 1967).

9. In the discussion of the Definite Articles, the difficulties of this domain will appear to be much greater than Kant pretends here. If my argument were only philological, this sentence's contradiction to the interpretation I will give of international law would be a refutation.

10. The nineteenth-century French Republican translator of Kant, J. Barni, notes that this should also have led Kant to oppose a hereditary monarchy! (''Kant et la révolution française,'' *Revue de Paris*, 15 mars, 1856, pp. 481–508).

11. My discussion in Chapter 8 of ''Rousseau and the Origin of Revolution'' does not deal with the difficulty that guides the following presentation. The reasons for Rousseau's inability to articulate a theory of representation would need to be brought into that text, as a supplement more than as a correction.

12. One must pay homage to Kant's historical sense. He does not discuss the question of empire theoretically in this Article, where he limits himself to more polemical remarks, comparing savages to the European states (where the difference is that the savages eat their victims while the Europeans use them to increase the number of their subjects, and the quantity of their instruments, in preparation for new wars). He returns briefly to the theoretical issue in the first Supplement (p. 113 of the Beck edition), where he notes that such an Empire would quickly become a ''soulless despotism,'' its laws would lose their vigor, anarchy would gradually emerge.

The empirical justification of Kant's theoretical-historical argumentation was presented more than a century after he wrote. The German historian Otto Hintze posed the question of the origins of the representative constitution in an essay by that title. Hintze's comparativist history demonstrates that Western Europe was the only place where such a political form developed precisely because of the rise and role of international diplomacy which meant that a *de facto* federation of independent states existed and would persist in spite of any attempt to subsume them under an empire. This is, unfortunately, not the place for a lengthy excursus; fortunately, Hintze's essay has been translated recently into English in Felix Gilbert, ed., *The Historical Essays of Otto Hintze* (New York: Oxford University Press, 1975). Practical implications for today are drawn in my *Defining the Political*, Chapter 14, ''The Republic and the International Order.''

13. This suggestion permits a plausible interpretation of the difference between the types of Articles and their order. The immediately applicable articles refer to measures to be taken by the Republic itself in relation to other states. These correspond to the ''doctrinal'' orientation. The permissive Articles describe situations over which the Republic has no control directly. These correspond to the ''critical'' framework. The first immediately applicable article forbids the ''tacit reservation.'' It is the precondition for publicity. The next permissive Articles deal with the framework conditions which must be resolved before the Republican internal politics re-enter the discussion.

14. See Chapter 9, ''The Politics of Modernism: From Marx to Kant.''

Chapter 6. Restoring Politics to Political Economy

1. Cited in R. Rosdolsky, *Zur Entstehungsgeschichte des Marxschen ''Kapitals''*. Band 1. (Frankfurt am Main: Europscsche Verlagsanstalt, 1968, p. 18, n. 21).

2. When citing Marx, I will usually refer to the source in the text itself. Since nearly everything Marx wrote is available in many editions in English, I shall not burden the text with explicit page references unless the source is difficult to find.

3. All citations in this paragraph come from my essay, ''Theory, the Theorist and Revolutionary Practice: Rosa Luxemburg'' in *The Marxian Legacy*. Translations are from my *Selected Political Writings of Rosa Luxemburg* (New York: Monthly Review Press, 1972).

4. This would explain why Vol. I begins with the long and abstract discussion of the commodity and ends with the apparently concrete and historical account of ''primitive accumulation.'' It would also insist on the fact that Vol. I treats only production, while Vol. III looks at the process as a whole. The integral place of Vol. IV, the ''theories of surplus value,'' would also be explained in this context. The literature on the ''logic'' of *Capital* began to swell, especially in the German political left, during the late 1960s. The study by Roman Rosdolsky, referred to in n. 1, is one of the most important. From the standpoint of a ''bourgeois'' Hegelian, one must be able to confront the arguments posed by Klaus Hartmann's *Die Marxsche Theorie* (Berlin: de Gruyter, 1970). The anti-Hegelianism inspired by Louis Althusser's *Pour Marx* and *Lire le Capital* (both Paris: Maspero, 1966) is unconvincing on both philological and philosophical grounds.

5. Leo Baeck's account of the Pauline religion and its relation to Judaic traditions bears rereading in this context. The present assertion is found in the essays translated and introduced by Walter Kaufmann, *Judaism and Christianity* (Cleveland and New York: Meridian Books, 1961), in the essay on ''Romantic Religion'', p. 260. It is adumbrated in ''The Faith of Paul,'' pp. 146ff.

6. I have expanded these arguments concerning the French Revolution in chapter 10, ''The Origin of Revolution'' and in another context, in chapter 9, ''The Politics of Modernism: From Marx to Kant.''

7. On the general theoretical difficulty here, as presented in the Marxian theory of ''class'' and its variants, see the exceptional study by Jean Cohen, *Class and Civil Society: The Limits of Marxian Critical Theory* (Amherst: University of Massachusetts Press, 1983). The political implications (as a critique of unavowed Leninism) are drawn in Cohen and Howard, ''Why Class?'' in *Between Labor and Capital*, ed. Pat Walker, (Boston: South End Press, 1978), pp. 67–96.

8. See Sheldon Wolin's *Politics and Vision* (Boston: Little, Brown, 1961), which is still the best introduction to political theory I know.

9. The myth of the reactionary Prussian is dealt with in most recent books on Hegel's political thought. For example, S. Avineri, *Hegel's Theory of the Modern State* (Cambridge, 1972), C. Taylor, *Hegel* (Cambridge, 1975), or W. Kaufman, *Hegel's Political Philosophy* (New York, 1970).

10. The worst, and best, example of this style is Lukacs's *Der Junge Hegel*, whose thesis, in a nutshell, is that where Hegel was right he anticipates Marx: where he was wrong; the fault lies in the historical conditions of underdeveloped Germany.

11. This point is argued in detail by C. Castoriadis throughout his work over the past fifteen years. For details, see *The Marxian Legacy*. The insistence on the radicality of the New is another of Castoriadis's central themes.

12. Lord Robbins, *The Theory of Economic Policy in English Classical Political Economy*, Second Edition, (London: Macmillan, 1978).

Chapter 7. The Origin and Limits of Philosophical Politics

1. Luc Ferry, *Philosophie politique*, 1: Le droit: la nouvelle querelle des anciens et des modernes; 2: Le système des philosophies de l'histoire; 3 (with Alain Renaut): Des droits de l'homme à l'idée républicaine. (All Paris: Presses Universitaires de France, vols. 1 and 2, 1984, vol. 3, 1985.)

2. The juxtaposition of Ferry and Habermas is suggested by Habermas himself in his reply to questions posed by *Le Monde* to a number of philosophers during the summer of 1984. Habermas tries to nuance his often repeated and at times disdainful or frustrated criticisms of contempoary French philosophy by pointing to the important contributions that during the last 20 years have come from ''Bourdieu, Castoriadis, Foucault, Ricoeur and Touraine,'' but the tone of his article is scolding. Nonetheless, at its conclusion, he notes that '' . . . the example of the political philosophy of Luc Ferry shows that the productivity of the younger generation is not exhausted—and that it has freed itself from the new philosophers' fear of coming into contact with the teutonic master-thinkers.''

Reprinted in Habermas, *Die Neue Unübersichtlichkeit* (Frankfurt am Main: Suhrkamp Verlag, 1985), p. 137. The "methodological" arguments proposed here are developed in *From Marx to Kant*.

3. It was not taken seriously by Sartre himself, who never completed the promised second volume. In his "Autoportrait à 70 ans: entretiens receuillis par Michel Contat" (*Nouvel Observateur*, juillet, 1975) Sartre took back his assertion in the *Critique* regarding Marxism as "the philosophy of our time: one cannot go beyond it because the conditions which engendered it are still present" (p. 29). Sartre doesn't explain which conditions have changed, or whether it was his own philosophical position that had changed; before his death,he found himself in the company of his old enemy, Raymond Aron, along with the "new philosopher" famed for his denunciation of the "master-thinkers," André Glucksmann, at the Elysée palace appealing to President Giscard to come to the aid of the Vietnamese boat people. I have tried to show the systematic reasons that underlie Sartre's political incompetence in *The Marxian Legacy* and in "Politics before Praxis," in *Defining the Political*. The following quotation from *Critique de la raison dialectique* (Paris: Gallimard, 1960) is found on p. 630.

4. One might say that this lesson was drummed finally to the attention of the public by the "new philosophers" in the wake of the "Soljenitsyn shock" of the late 1970s. But the "new philosophers" were no more philosophers than they were new. Where philosophy is concerned with problems, they looked for solutions—in their case, in a moralist absolutism useful for rhetorical purposes but hardly helpful as an analytic tool. If they borrowed their critique of totalitarianism from Merleau-Ponty—and from Lefort and Castoriadis—they did not learn from their masters how to *think* about their results.

5. One might have thought that May '68 at home, or August '68 in Czechoslovakia, would have dampened the enthusiasm for the new science. On the contrary, as Pierre Grémion's *Paris-Prague, 1968–1978* (Paris: Julliard, 1985) shows in convincing detail. May was interpreted as making the need for science even more imperative in order to avoid the spontaneity and "humanism" that distorted the movement. August, and the "normalization" that followed the Russian invasion, could be read along the lines that "the infrastructures are OK, the superstructures need to be transformed" (p. 119). Condemnation and approbation could be combined in the hope that took the political form of "euro-communism." The other option, which will be discussed in a moment came to be called "poststructuralism," for reasons which, if not simply chronological, are not clear to me. They may have to do with the identification of structuralist political theory with Althusserian Marxism.

6. The Althusser passage is found in "Enfin la crise du marxism," in *Il Manifesto, Pourvoir et opposition dans les sociétés post-révolutionnaires* (Paris: le Seuil, 1978), pp. 242–43. The Poulantzas citation is from *L'Etat, le pouvoir, le socialisme* (Paris: Presses Universitaires de France, 1978), p. 230. Both citations are taken from Grémion, *Paris-Prague*, p. 321.

7. Nonetheless, it is also Marx's fault, as I tried to show in *The Marxian Legacy*.

8. The terms get complicated here, the more so as their manifestations in French, American, and German intellectual contexts show significant differences in the "referents." For a useful summary, see Andreas Huyssen, "Mapping the Postmodern," in *New German Critique*, 33 (Fall, 1984). Huyssen's argument is that "poststructuralism is primarily a discourse of and about modernism, and that if we are to locate the postmodern in poststructuralism it will have to be found in the ways various forms of poststructuralism have opened up new problematics in modernism and have reinscribed modernism into the discourse formations of our own time" (pp. 38–39). For Huyssen, the association of modernism and avant-garde art with social and industrial modernization is no longer valid. Modernity is not something to be traversed, however trying and difficult the crossing. Poststructuralist analysis reveals that modernist culture itself is in crisis. Huyssen sees a "growing sense that we are not bound to *complete* the project of modernity [Habermas's phrase] and still do not necessarily have to lapse into irrationality or into apocalyptic frenzy" (pp. 48–49).

From the standpoint of an explicit Marxism, I find unconvincing Fredric Jameson's attempt to elaborate postmodernism as a necessary stage in a developmental logic of capitalism to which the structuralist analyses of Althusser and Lacan, among others, would be adequate. See his "Postmodernism, or The Cultural Logic of Late Capitalism," *New Left Review*, 146 (July-August, 1984).

9. Nancy Fraser's "The French Derrideans: Politicizing Deconstruction or Deconstructing the Political," *New German Critique*, 33 (Fall, 1984) provides a useful summary of the debates. She is, however, more optimistic than I about the possibilities in this direction when she answers her own question, whether deconstruction is a "temporary way station on the exodus from Marxism now being traveled by the French intelligentsia. It is not and cannot be a permanent resting place," she concludes (p. 143).

10. See *Les fins de l'homme: à partir du travail de Jacques Derrida* (Paris: Galillée, 1981).

11. Reprinted in *Rejouer le politique* (Paris: Galillée, 1981). The volume also contains papers presented by each director, as well as presentations by Etienne Balibar, Luc Ferry, and Jean-François Lyotard. (A presentation by Paul Thibaud made during the year was not printed.) The citations in this paragraph are found on pages 15 and 16.

12. It may be worth noting that Ferry's presentation of Strauss takes him with the seriousness he deserves. M. F. Burnyeat's demolition of Strauss's philosophical technique in the *New York Review of Books* (May 30, 1985), and his attack on Strauss's influence as teacher and expositor for "gentlemen" and "puppies" is a vigorous ideology-critique. Ferry's treatment of Strauss as a *philosopher* in the tradition of Heidegger is more satisfying. Interestingly, however, the angry replies to Burnyeat by the Straussians do not resurrect the philosopher.

13. Ferry's treatment of Fichte would take us too far from the present concern. His technical analysis, which is lucidly presented, acknowledges profusely his debt to the various works of Alexis Philolenko. Suffice it that Fichte is not reduced to the "subjective idealist" who develops the subjective potentiality of the Kantian breakthrough only to be flanked on the objective side by Schelling before both of them are *aufgehoben* by Hegel. The puzzling structure of the *Wissenschaftslehre* is explained by Ferry as owing to Fichte's desire to first deconstruct the errors of metaphysics before proceeding to elaborate his own philosophical system.

14. The usefulness of this descriptive category is not always clear; Ferry seems to cast his net too wide. Thus in the polemic written with Alain Renaut, *La pensée 68. Essai sur l'anti-humanisme contemporain* (Paris: Gallimard, 1985), Ferry finds himself criticizing brutally and without nuance the Nietzo-Heideggerian influences on French thought which resulted in a relativistic individualism that refuses to acknowledge the notions of truth, value, humanism, etc. etc. Often pertinent in themselves, the critiques of Foucault, Derrida, Bourdieu, and Lacan are not tied adequately to the book's apparent subject: the *political* import of May '68. A bit more "phenomenology" would have been helpful! For a critique, by one of those who come under attack, see Jean-François Lyotard and Jacob Rogozinski, "La police de la pensée," in *L'autre journal*, Nr. 10, décembre, 1985, pp. 27–34.

15. The return passes through two fascinating chapters presenting Fichte's overcoming of Kant's implicitly rationalist philosophy of history and Rousseau's alternative built from a romantic presupposition concerning the state of nature. Although Fichte is crucial to Ferry's argument as a whole, it is not clear to me whether this is only because Fichte draws to explicitness what is implicit in Kant, or for more substantive reasons.

16. This study was co-authored with Alain Renaut. A fourth volume has been promised, treating "Historicism and the Social Sciences."

17. Not even with its "late" form which he described in *Legitimation Problems*. Habermas never fully defined "late" capitalism in that book. He does offer a definition in his *Theory of Communicative Action*, but there he no longer works from a direct sociological account. His suggestion is that rationalization processes take hold first in the sphere of the economy, then in that of political administration; their final object is to penetrate—to colonize, as he puts it nicely—the "life world" or what he sometimes calls the expressive sphere. Capitalism reaches its "late" phase when this last project is its object.

18. "A Philosophico-Political Profile," in *New Left Review*, 151 (May–June, 1985). Page references in text with abbreviation *NLR*. The present citation is found on p. 96.

19. Jürgen Habermas, *Die Neue Unübersichlichkeit* (Frankfurt am Main: Edition Suhrkamp, 1985). Page references in text, with abbreviation *NU*. The present citation is from p. 145.

20. The interview is reprinted in *Die Neue Unübersichtlichkeit*; the cited remarks are on pp. 180–81. The first draft of the theory of communicative action had been presented in 1971 at the

Christian Gauss lectures at Princeton. It is now published in *Vorstudien und Ergänzungen zur Theorie des kommunikativen Handelns* (Frankfurt am Main: Suhrkamp Verlag, 1984). One might suggest, on the basis of the discussion at the end of the recently published *Der Philosophische Diskurs der Moderne* (*POM*) (Frankfurt am Main: Suhrkamp Verlag, 1985) that Habermas's concern with the nature and implications of the ''new social movements''—feminism, ecology, peace movement—led him to write the new study (to which I refer as *TkH*, followed by a volume number and page).

21. Habermas speaks of the ''mediation that Marx and western Marxism expected from social praxis . . . [in which] historically situated, physically embodied reason which is confronted by nature is mediated with its other'' (*PDM*, p. 368). But this Marxian perspective still bases itself in a philosophy of the (producing) subject; ''a wholly different perspective emerges when we translate the concept of praxis from labor to communicative action. We then recognize interdependences between language systems which disclose the world and inner-worldly processes of learning . . . learning processes are no longer only canalized through processes of social labor and ultimately through the cognitive-instrumental relation to nature. As soon as we give up the paradigm of production, we can assert an internal relation of sense and validity for the entire contents of the reservoir of meaning—and not only for the segment of meaning limited to linguistic expressions that take the form of assertions and intentional propositions'' (ibid., 373). The consequence is drawn somewhat later: ''Once we give up the praxis-philosophical understanding of society, as a self-referentially macro-subject which is introjected into the individual subjects, then the corresponding models for the diagnosis and the overcoming of the crisis—division and revolution—are no longer useful'' (402–3).

22. The situation is in fact more technical and complex. The *Theory of Communicative Action* develops the notion of the life world in the context of a theory of social rationalization which tried to explain the separation of the processes of system and social reproduction. Increasing complexity and increasing rationality go hand in hand. At a point, however, a kind of ''dialectic of enlightenment'' intervenes; what was a gain becomes a loss, or at least a threat. At this point, there arises the ''*empirical* question, when does the growth of the monetary-bureaucratic complex touch domains of action which cannot be reformulated as system integrative mechanisms without pathological side-effects. The analysis of Parsons's theory of media has led me to the assumption that this limit is reached when systematic imperatives intervene in the region of cultural reproduction, social integration, and socialization of the individual'' (*TkH*, II, p. 548). At this point, Habermas continues, a critical theory of society becomes possible.

The difficulty concerns the status of Habermas's ''empirical'' assumption. For example, he asserts that ''the probabilities for conflict-free reproduction processes do not in the least grow with the degree of rationalization of a life world—what happens is that the level on which the conflicts can appear simply shifts'' (*PDM*, p. 403). On the other hand, in pre-modern societies certainly, and in some domains of modern society, rationalization of the life world is integrative at the systematic level; that was the thrust of Habermas's reinterpretation of Weber. Further, Habermas in another context seems to accept Arato's notion that the life world in totalitarian societies can successfully oppose an ''instrumentalization by the imperatives either of an economy operating with constraint or an autonomous bureaucracy'' (''Replik auf Einwände,'' in *Vorstudien und Ergänzungen zur Theorie des kommunikativen Handelns*, pp. 569–70).

There are systematic reasons for this apparent multivalence in the utilization of the concept, as we shall see. A convenient presentation of the difficulties can be found by comparing pages 186 and 189 in the *Aesthetik und Kommunikation* interview. Cf. for a more detailed presentation of the difficulties sketched here in the context suggested by Ferry, the afterword to the new edition of *The Marxian Legacy*, where Habermas's theory is analyzed in the context determined by Marxism.

23. See also the answer in the *Aesthetik und Kommunikation* interview: ''The thinker as a form of life, as vision, as expressive self-presentation is no longer possible. I am no producer of *Weltanschauungen*; I would in fact like to produce a few small truths, not the one great truth'' (p. 207).

24. The slight overtone of guilt implied here is due to the fact that Habermas frequently expresses his frustration at the inability of critics to distinguish between what he says as philosopher, as individual, as political actor, and so on. On the other hand, Habermas did, after all, republish these mate-

rials, indicating that he does take them seriously. He does not, of course, reprint every interview he gives, publish personal diary materials or what-have-you.

25. The presentations have been published in Wolf Schäfer, ed., *Neue Soziale Bewegungen: Konservativer Aufbruch im bunten Gewand?* (Frankfurt: S. Fischer Verlag, 1983).

26. This was written before I had the unhappy experience of reading *La pensée 68*. It is based on the inadequacy of the explicitly political and quasi-historical account of the antinomic ''politics'' of human rights presented in the third volume of *Philosophie politique*. The results are, to put it simply, frustrating.

27. The normative can function genetically, and the genetic can play a normative role. The dogmatic forms of rationalism and empiricism can serve as simple illustrations here.

28. See George Schrader, ''The Status of Teleological Judgement in the Critical Philosophy,'' *Kantstudien* 45 (1953–54):204–55.

29. For example, in the *Aesthetik und Kommunikation* interview, p. 195.

Chapter 8. Rousseau and the Origin of Revolution

1. Cf., for an analysis of some of the most subtle attempts which retain the originary analysis, *The Marxian Legacy*, especially the afterword to the 2nd edition.

2. Iring Fetscher discusses in some detail the use and abuse of Rousseau by both sides during the Revolution, following and supplementing Joan McDonald's *Rousseau and the French Revolution*, 1789–91. (Iring Fetscher, *Rousseaus politische Philosophie*, (Neuwied: Luchterhand Verlag, 1968) Yet, as François Furet still argues:

> Between 1789 and the 9th of Thermidor, 1794, revolutionary France makes of the paradox of democracy explored by Rousseau the unique source of power. It integrates society and State by the discourse of the people's will; and the ultimate figures of that obsession with legitimacy are the Terror and war which are finally inscribed in the competition of the different groups for the appropriation of the democratic principle. The Terror recomposes in the revolutionary mode a kind of divine right of public authority. (Furet, *Penser la révolution française*, Paris: Gallimard, 1979, p. 108).

Furet's point is not, of course, that this ''Rousseauism'' was explicit; his concern is to show the presence of a more general, a philosophical problem, underlying the lived experience of the times. For an even larger historical framing, cf. Jacques Julliard, *Le faute à Rousseau* (Paris: Editions du Seuil, 1985).—On the other hand the counter-revolutionary invocation of Rousseau is curiously literal and unimaginative. For example, it tried to show that he was in fact a supporter of tradition who opposed radical and violent revolution; it also used Rousseau to criticize National Assembly's representational function which overstepped the bounds of its mandate and substituted its will as majority for that of the general will; and later it criticized the revolutionary unification of legislative and executive powers, against which Rousseau had inveighed. This contrast should be born in mind as Rousseau's paradoxical argument is opened up in the following discussion.

3. In *La transparence et l'obstacle* (Paris: Gallimard, 1971).

4. Ibid., p. 389.

5. Cited in ibid., pp. 391–92.

6. Cited in Georg Gurwitsch, ''Kant und Fichte als Rousseau-Interpreten,'' in *Kant-Studien*, Vol. XXVII, 1922, p. 145. This article, by the man who would become the famous French sociologist, Georges Gurwitsch, is a model of theoretical acumen. Its author was then a Privatdozent at Saint-Petersburg. Cf., also Cassirer's reading of this in terms of the theodicy problem on which he confronts the stances of Voltaire and Rousseau, in *The Question of Jean-Jacques Rousseau*, Peter Gay, trans. (Bloomington: University of Indiana Press, 1963), p. 76.

7. Lucio Colletti, *From Rousseau to Lenin* (New York: Monthly Review Press, 1972, p. 157). Colletti, however, goes a bit far when (pp. 184–85) he moves from Rousseau's critique to Marx's essay *On the Jewish Question* and the elimination of political alienation (or what Rousseau calls representation) through the ''withering away of the state'' thesis.

8. Cassirer, p. 60.

9. Ibid., p. 68.

10. Alfred Cobban, *In Search of Humanity. The Role of the Enlightenment in Modern History* (New York: George Braziller, 1960), pp. 127–28.

11. A similar problem in accounting for the birth of society is found in Kant, for example in the "Conjectural Beginning of History."

12. The problem with this "dialectical synthesis" is suggested by the fact that the "society" depicted in *Le Nouvelle Héloise* corresponds to what the Greeks called the *oikos*, the domestic *space* of unfreedom.

13. Robert Derathé, *Jean-Jacques Rousseau et la science politique de son temps* (Paris: P.U.F., 1950), p. 106. The implication of this point will return when we discuss republican law in a moment.

14. It would pose too that Marxian question: who educates the educators? Riley's essay, "A Possible Explanation of Rousseau's General Will" (in *American Political Science Review*, vol. LXIV, March 1976) poses this problem quite clearly in counterdistinction to Sklahr's more psychological reading. Instead of confronting the problem of the relation of the genetic and normative approaches, Riley's proposal is to point to the classical Greek influence that makes Rousseau's solution different from those of Locke or Kant. A too easy conclusion to an otherwise well-posed analysis!

15. A more detailed criticism of such suppositions is found in MacPherson's well-known study, *The Political Theory of Possessive Individualism* (Oxford: Oxford University Press, 1962).

16. Derathé, p. 165; the citation to D'Alembert is in Derathé, p. 252. Of course, where Derathé speaks here of "origins" and "value," I would use the terms genesis and validity.

17. The importance of Derathé's study, which stands out in the literature, lies in his stress on the newness of Rousseau's theory. The only objection that might be raised from this point of view concerns Derathé's attempt to render Rousseau's position adequate to our own times—but that is another matter.

18. Derathé, p. 361 n. 4.

19. Boston: Little, Brown, 1960.

20. Derathé, p. 356.

21. This position of the natural-law theorists, and especially Pufendorf, surely marked an advance in the development of western liberty. It remains the foundation of much of our own political freedom today. Rousseau's criticism is therefore all the more pertinent.

22. One sees this influence too in the ideal community of the *Nouvelle Héloise*, particularly in the relation of the little harmonious community to its servants and to the production of the necessities of life. The problem, however, is that this community is founded not on the model of the *polis* but on that of the *oikos*. The "happy" relation of masters and servants described by Rousseau is hardly a sufficient model for a free polity. Cf. also Riley's essay, cited in n. 14.

23. Hannah Arendt, "Civil Disobedience," in *Crises of the Republic* (New York: Harcourt Brace Jovanovich, 1972), p. 84.

Chapter 9. The Politics of Modernism: From Marx to Kant

1. Herbert Marcuse, *Die Permenez der Kunst. Wider eine bestimmte marxistische Aesthetik. Ein Essay* (München: Carl Hanser Verlag, 1977), p. 37. The subtitle of Marcuse's essay should be stressed. It is also interesting to note that Marcuse wrote this volume in German, after years of publishing in English. (Henceforth, *PK*) The following discussion of Marcuse relies on a paper that I presented at the New York Marxist School to commemorate Marcuse's death. That previously unpublished text is reprinted as delivered in *Defining the Political*.

2. *Herbert Marcuse, Soviet Marxism* (New York: Vintage Books, 1961), pp. 71–72. (Henceforth *SM*) I will return to the last aspect of this argument later, since the development (*Bildung*) of the subject is crucial to my thesis. See also the discussion of Rousseau in chapter 8, above.

3. Herbert Marcuse, *One-Dimensional Man* (Boston: Beacon Press, 1964), pp. 96–97. (Henceforth *ODM*)

4. *SM*, p. 229.

5. Ibid., p. 233.

6. Ibid., pp. 117–18.

7. Herbert Marcuse, *Counter-Revolution and Revolt* (Boston: Beacon Press, 1972), p. 107. (Henceforth *CRR*)

8. *PK*, p. 37.

9. *CRR*, p. 108.

10. *PK*, p. 43.

11. Ibid., concluding chapter, and p. 18.

12. *CRR*, p. 93.

13. Harold Rosenberg, *The De-Definition of Art* (New York: Horizon Press, 1972), p. 249.

14. Ibid., p. 248.

15. Clement Greenberg, ''Modernist Painting,'' in *The New Art: A Critical Anthology*, Gregory Battock, ed. (New York, 1966), p. 101. Cited in Donald B. Kuspit, *Clement Greenberg, Art Critic* (Madison, University of Wisconsin Press, 1979), p. 136. Marcellin Playnet cites Greenberg as saying (in my translation): ''Because he was the first to criticize the very means of criticism, I call this philosopher the first true modernist.'' *Paris-New York* catalog, p. 122.

16. Reprinted in Harold Rosenberg, *The Tradition of the New* (New York: McGraw-Hill, 1965).

17. As I am citing the well-known passages from Marx, and indicating their source in the text, I have not pinpointed any of the passages from Marx to one or another of the editions or translations of his work.

18. Harold Rosenberg, ''Politics of Illusion,'' reprinted in *Discovering The Present* (Chicago: University of Chicago Press, 1973)

19. Marshall Berman, ''All That Is Solid Melts Into Air,'' reprinted in I. Howe, comp., *25 Years of Dissent* (New York: Methuen, 1979).

20. The term is from S. Wolin, *Politics and Vision*. It is first used with reference to Plato, whose political theory is structured by the same paradox to which I have pointed: it is a politics whose goal is the elimination of the political. The ''selfless servant'' politician reappears frequently; his most recent avatar is the technocrat (liberal, conservative, or Marxist) in power.

21. Rosa Luxemburg, ''Organisational Questions of Russian Social Democracy,'' in Dick Howard, ed., *Selected Political Writings* (New York: Monthly Review Press, 1971).

22. See ''Marx: d'une vision de l'histoire à l'autre,'' and ''Esquisse d'une genèse de l'idéologie dans les sociétés modernes,'' reprinted in Lefort, *Les Formes de l'histoire* (Paris: Gallimard, 1978).

23. François Furet, *Penser la révolution française* (Paris: Gallimard, 1978), pp. 16–17.

24. The editor of Kant's writings *On History* (Indianapolis: Bobbs-Merrill, 1963), Lewis White Beck, notes that this suggestion was made by Renato Composto in *La quarta critica kantiana* (Palermo, 1954), p. xviii, no. 14.

25. As with citations from Marx, I have not specified the edition or page (and the translations are usually my own). The source is clearly given in the text, and can be found either in the above Beck edition, or in Reiss's edition, *Kant's Political Writings* (Cambridge: Cambridge University Press, 1970).

Chapter 10. The Origins of Revolution

1. I will shortly be using François Furet's term ''discourse of identity'' to adumbrate or replace this term. However, ''edifying'' history is of course a well-known genre and the butt of many a critic, though it has never, to my knowledge, been dealt with as here.

2. François Furet, *Penser la révolution française* (Paris: Gallimard, 1978), pp. 16–17.

3. Compare the following passages from *The 18th Brumaire* in which Marx describes the revolutionary proletariat. They provide material for conclusions to be drawn shortly.

> Proletarian revolutions . . . criticize themselves constantly, interrupt themsleves continually; in their own course, come back to the apparently accomplished in order to begin it afresh . . . recoil ever and anon from the indefinite prodigiousness of their own aims, until . . .

''Until,'' Marx continues, ''a situation has been created which makes all turning back impossible, and the conditions themselves cry out: *Hic Rhodus, hic salta!*

I separated the conclusion to the passage because it seems to me that the reference to ''the conditions themselves'' marks a dangerous shift in the structure of the argument, as should be clear from my criticisms in the text.

4. Cf., the above discussion of Kant both in ''Kant's Political Theory,'' and ''Kant's System and (Its) Politics.'' The theory of judgment is developed more specifically in *From Marx to Kant.*

5. See the discussion of Enlightened Despotism in *Defining the Political.*

6. From this point of view, cf. the brief work by Cornelius Castoriadis, ''Ce qui est important,'' written in 1959 for a small ultra-left journal and reprinted in *L'expérience du mouvement ouvrier*, 2 (Paris: UGE, 1974). This short piece sums up, in an important sense, an elaborate theoretical edifice to which I owe a great deal.

Chapter 11. Reading U.S. History as Revolutionary

1. It should be stressed that I have inverted the Hegelian ordering which portrays the concept as integrating the moments of the immediate (being) and its reflexive mediation (essence). The reason for this inversion is that Hegel's system is not capable of thinking the autonomy of the political, as I tried to show in *From Marx to Kant.* For Hegel, the social poses the question of the political whereas it is the inverse relation which defines the true problem of modern societies, as we shall see in the case of the American Revolution.

2. It would be tempting to add to this double structure a third moment which would make explicit to themselves each of the first two moments. Such a third moment would present directly the institutional functioning of the political logic (*logique politique instituante*). The claim then would be that the autonomy won in the first period is explicity conceived at the level of the individual lived experience during the second period; and that the particularity of the states is reflected explicitly at the social level during the third period. The result would be that the entire two hundred years' history of the republic would be considered as making clear the properly political logic which determines the elaboration of the Constitution of 1787. Thus, the lived experience of a socially fragmented Confederation would have become untenable once popular revolts broke out in the states. Shays Rebellion would have catalyzed the energies of those who met at Philadelphia to create the new Constitution. That Convention represented diverse interests which refused to sacrifice their own particularity. The compromise proposed to popular ratification claimed, in the oft-cited phrase of Solon, not to offer the best constitution but only the best that the citizens could accept. The result of this compromise would be the depoliticization of American life in a society where capitalism and the common interest are considered as identical. But this is precisely the thesis that I want to invert by reading reality in terms of its theory! Once again, a Hegelian dialectics cannot account for the political. The third moment is reflective, not reflexive.

3. It would of course be wrong to neglect the religious aspect of colonial thought. I do not emphasize it here insofar as it is the political form of the lived religious experience, particularly in the case of New England, which influenced the development of the Revolution as such. If the religious element is treated as if it were simply and integrally transferred to the political level, the result can only be abusive simplifications of the type which claim, for example, that the easy acceptance of political parties flows from the lack of an Established Church and from the plurality of religious sects in the colonies . More important is the fact that the religious reading of the political theory underlying the revolution would neglect the social aspect of English ''corruption'' and the ''virtue'' the colonists sought to oppose to it. The revolution would then acquire a Manichean or ahistorical character.

4. This does not contradict the earlier assertion that the constitutions of the states intended to represent *society*. The explicitly political form of representation incorporated in these state constitutions was assumed to be necessary in order to guarantee that the essence of society, its common good, would be correctly recognized. In this sense, the constitution of Pennsylvania and those of the other states do not differ; each assumes that there *exists* something called the common good, although they

differ about the political institutions necessary for its discovery. We shall see that the federal Constitution of 1787 works in terms of a different, a properly political, logic.

5. Shays and his men were endebted small farmers who risked losing their land because of the lack of hard currency which prevented them from paying their taxes.

6. A demonstration *a contrario* can be found in Martin Van Buren's *Inquiry into the Origin and Course of Political Parties in the United States* (New York: Augustus M. Kelley, 1967 reprint of the 1867 edition). Van Buren was the first professional politician to reach the presidency. Although his own practice was wholly pragmatic, and although he insisted that party loyalty is the most important of all political principles, his *Inquiry* is founded on the opposition of Good and Evil that is typical of pre-modern politics. (The only exception to this is his justification of the controversial Veto of the Bank Bill by Andrew Jackson. The constitutional theory which Van Buren applies to justify his president's choice is precisely the one presented here.)

One should note here that historians and political scientists distinguish between a first and a second party system. The first is said to be founded on political principle, the second on men and the positions they seek to occupy. The first party system is said to end with the presidency of James Monroe, called the "Era of Good Feelings." The election of 1824, which brought John Quincy Adams to power on the basis of the "Corrupt Bargain," sealed the fate of the old system. The presidency of Andrew Jackson, with Van Buren as his vice-president, marks the new stage. The parties are routinized, rationalized, made into electoral machines which function to mediate between the elector and the government as well as being mediators between the executive and the legislative branches. These sociological distinctions would need to be reconsidered in the light of the *political* interpretation of the Constitution offered here. I will suggest such an orientation at the conclusion of this chapter.

Name Index

Subject Index

Dick Howard is professor of philosophy at the State University of New York at Stony Brook and senior fellow at the Research Institute on International Change at Columbia University. He has been a visiting professor in political science at Columbia University and in the critical theory program at the New School for Social Research as well as at the Ecole des Hautes Etudes en Sciences Sociales and the Collège International de Philosophie in Paris. He has contributed to *Revue Française de Science Politique, Telos, Praxis International, Dissent, Esprit, Philosophy and Social Theory, Review of Metaphysics, La Lettre internationale, Merkur, Les Tempes Modernes, Etudes Polémologiques, Aesthetik und Kommunikation, Man & World*, and *New Political Science*. He was editor and co-translator of *Selected Political Writings of Rosa Luxemburg* (1973) and *Serge Mallet's Essays on the New Working Class* (1975). Howard's most recent books are *From Marx to Kant* (1985), *La naissance de la pensée politique américaine* (1987), *Defining the Political* (Minnesota, 1988), and *The Marxian Legacy* (second edition, Minnesota, 1988).